Out to Eat

Paris 2001

Lonely Planet Publications
Melbourne • London • Paris • Oakland

Lonely Planet *Out to Eat – Paris*

1st edition – May 2001

Published by Lonely Planet Publications

Lonely Planet Offices
Australia Locked Bag 1, Footscray, VIC 3011
USA 150 Linden St, Oakland, CA 94607
UK 10a Spring Place, London NW5 3BH
France 1 rue du Dahomey, 75011 Paris

Photographs Simon Bracken

Publishing managers: Adrienne Costanzo & Katie Cody
Series Editor: Donna Wheeler
Layout & series design: Wendy Wright
Mapping: Lachlan Ross
Cover design: Simon Bracken
Coordinating editor: Katharine Day

ISBN 1 74059 081 3

text & maps © Lonely Planet 2001
photos © Lonely Planet Images 2001

Printed by The Bookmaker International Ltd
Printed in China

One cannot think well,
love well,
sleep well,
if one has not dined well.

Virginia Woolf

Out to Eat – The People

This book was written by Parisians living in Paris who are accustomed to travelling (for the most part) and are curious about discovering new flavours (for you). They visited the restaurants,

cafes and bars on a strictly anonymous basis and tested all the places mentioned.

The coordinating authors were Julien Fouin, Oliver Bauer, Thomas Hofnung and Jean-Bernard Carillet. The team of reviewers consisted of Jérôme Bauer, Socrate Georgiadès, Sylvie Bouche, Louise Ranck, Régis Couturier, Yann Champion, Mathilde Puech, Sophie Courade, Rose-Hélène Lempereur, Pauline Pothion, Franck Médioni, David Kanner, Éric Delon, Jean-NoëlDoan, Sandrine Dupain, Leslie Lepers, Zahia Hafs, Didier Férat, Cécile Bertolissio, Valérie Police, Didier Buroc, Caroline Sahanouk and Olivier Cirendini.

The bar and cafe features were written by Frédérique Odasso and Bénédicte Houdré, Arno Lebonnois and Jean-Jacques Le Gall, Géraldine

Paqueron, Claire Sniehotta and Julien Templier. Other features were written by Julien Fouin, Claude Albert, Didier Férat, Christine Coste, Thomas Hofnung and Isabelle Le Thiec.

From the publisher

This English edition was translated by James Cannon and Chris Andrews, and Adrienne Costanzo liaised with Lonely Planet Paris. The book was coordinated by Katharine Day, edited and proofed by Yvonne Byron, Katie Cody, Katharine Day, Joanne Newell, Hilary Rogers and Donna Wheeler. Wendy Wright was responsible for layout and design with assistance from Vicki Beale. Lachlan Ross was responsible for the maps with assistance from Paul Clifton, Alison Lyall and Natasha Velleley. Thanks to Bibiana Jaramillo for her technical support and thanks to the Paris office themselves, in particular Caroline Guilleminot and Sophie Le Mao-Hofnung.

Viaduc Café (p 193)

Out to Eat – The Book

A large section of every Lonely Planet travel guide is devoted to local food and the best places to eat it. Then we thought, why should only travellers have access to such information? The Out to Eat guides are for all those who love eating out – locals as well as visitors.

Instead of a comprehensive listing, this *Out to Eat – Paris* offers a judicious selection of restaurants, cafes and bars, highlighting the attractions and individual character of each one to help readers narrow down the options.

We visited numerous establishments before settling on the 500 included in this guide. Each is recommended not only for the quality of its food, but for its atmosphere, service, décor and value for money. For our authors, the decisive criteria for including a restaurant was the wish to go back there themselves and to recommend it to others. Clear symbols indicate whether a place is noisy, offers an appropriate setting for business meals, caters for vegetarians, or has a terrace.

Every restaurant, cafe and bar in this guide was visited by a Lonely Planet author, who ate or drank there in complete anonymity before duly paying the bill.

Finally, this guidebook is free from restaurant advertising, which means that its authors' opinions are uncompromised.

This book draws on the vast resources of local knowledge at Lonely Planet's Paris Office. The authors, all of whom are Parisian, are seasoned travellers familiar with the authentic cuisines of countries throughout the world.

Guide to the Guide

Organisation
Out to Eat – Paris contains a restaurant section broken up into chapters by arrondissement and then listed in alphabetical order, and a series of cafe/bar features (including everything from local bars and *cafés-concerts* to tea rooms) grouped together within the chapters.

Best
These are our personal favourites from each arrondissement, usually restaurants with a unique character. Three restaurants are nominated at the start of each chapter.

The Listings
Each establishment has been visited one or more times by at least one person. The opinions expressed in this guide are highly subjective and are the responsibility of the author in question. Dishes are seasonal, prices change and staff – including chefs – move on. Each establishment has been recommended for the quality of its food, but also because it offers at least one other attraction: décor, ambience, service or location. We visited many other establishments but didn't include them in the guide because they lacked that little something extra that, for us, makes all the difference.

Cuisine
For the most part, the terms used in the guide are self-explanatory. The term 'international' is occasionally used to describe cuisine with diverse dishes.

Opening hours
The opening hours listed in the guide refer to hours when orders are taken. Customers can obviously finish their meal in peace once they've ordered.

Reservations
This details whether the business accepts reservations and, if so, when they are necessary.

Maps
The map for each arrondissement indicates the precise location of the restaurants, cafes and bars. In each review, the map reference is indicated in the margin next to the name of the establishment.

Metro
Both the closest Metro and RER stations are indicated.

Price Fields
Price fields show the complete range of prices on each restaurant's menu, for example 'starter: 50FF-75FF' where 50FF is the price of the least expensive starter on the menu and 75FF is the most expensive. Prices were correct at the time of research.

Set menu/Plat du jour prices
These indicate the set menus and plat du jour dishes that are available, usually without prior arrangement.

Credit cards
The following abbreviations are used: AE (American Express), CB (Carte Bleue), DC (Diners Club), EC (Eurocard), V (Visa), MC (Mastercard) and we indicate which businesses accept euros (€) as well as French francs.

Smoking
Smoking is still the norm in Paris restaurants and we have indicated which places have nonsmoking tables. We cannot though guarantee the availability of them and we recommend that you check with the restaurant first.

Wheelchair access
Only restaurants equipped with a toilet that has been purpose-built or adapted for wheelchair access are listed in the index as having wheel-chair access. Access suggests that wheelchairs will also easily get into the restaurant and have ease of movement once inside. Unfortunately we can't guarantee this, and we urge you to telephone ahead to confirm facilities.

Dress code
Very few of the restaurants listed here apply an official dress code. The ones that do have been indicated. Please check with the restaurant for details.

Entertainment
This provides details of a restaurant's in-house entertainment (dancing, live music, performances).

Indexes
Restaurants are grouped in the following indexes – index by cuisine, index by suburb and index by special features (including whether the restaurant is open late, has outdoor seating, a private room, caters for children, or has wheelchair access), helping you to find the right place for every occasion.

Write to us

Things change – prices go up, opening hours change, good places go bad and bad places go bankrupt – nothing stays the same. So, if you find things better or worse, recently opened or recently closed, please tell us and help make the next edition even more accurate and useful.

Every morsel of information you send will be read and acknowledged by the appropriate author, editor or publisher. The best contributions will be rewarded with a free Lonely Planet book, and excerpts may appear in future editions of *Out to Eat – Paris*, so please let us know if you don't want your letter published or your name acknowledged.

Write to us:
Lonely Planet Out to Eat
Locked Bag 1, Footscray VIC 3011 Australia
☎ 61 3 8379 8000 fax 61 3 8379 8111
email: out2eat@lonelyplanet.co u.au

Symbols

 Totally smoke-free.

 Smoking Text accompanying this symbol explains whether there are smoking restrictions, separate smoke-free dining or smoking throughout.

Vegetarian Options
Each restaurant has been rated for the quality and range of vegetarian dishes (those that contain no meat, including fish and seafood) on offer on the regular menu. 'Carrot' icons indicate the rating. Bear in mind that menus do change so if you have any special dietary requirements it may be best to contact the restaurant in advance.

 Various and/or interesting vegetarian options.

 All-vegetarian menu or excellent vegetarian options.

 Quiet Noticeably quiet, even when busy.

 Medium noise Not noticeably quiet, and you can generally hear conversation at your own table without straining.

 Noisy Can be very noisy when busy (either due to music or the acoustics of the space). You may have to raise your voice considerably to be heard in conversation.

 Outdoors Outdoor dining options for fine days or nights.

 Business Exercise the expense account. This place is suitable for business occasions. Expect professional table service, compatible clientele, adequate table spacing and comfortable noise levels.

1er Arrondissement

Tuileries

Palais Royal

Les Halles

Châtelet

1er Arrondissement

It takes time to savour the play of shadows and light created by the perfect lines of this fascinating, complex arrondissement. Sculptures merge with trees, grassy lawns, flowers, pools and fountains while casual strollers lose themselves in the lovely promenade stretching from the gardens of the Tuileries to the square courtyard of the Louvre. A few metres away, under the arcades of the rue de Rivoli, the pace quickens with bustling shops and chaotic traffic. Parallel to rue de Rivoli, rue Saint-Honoré runs from place Vendôme to the Halles, leaving in its wake the Comédie-Française, the colonnes de Buren and the gardens of the Palais-Royal. Opulent, affected, but anxious to please, this street combines classic style with new trends, tasteful colours and pure lines with a quiet atmosphere. The Forum des Halles and rue Saint-Denis seem miles away but are already visible, soliciting unwary passers-by with bright lights and jostling crowds. There are those who frown upon its wild side, but the first arrondissement remains a place where history and culture embrace on the banks of the Seine.

L'Absinthe
French

☎ **01 49 26 90 04**
24, place du Marché Saint-Honoré, Pyramides, Tuileries

Map: 1 D4

Métro: Tuileries, Pyramides

 Smoking throughout

 Pavement tables in summer

L'Absinthe is in the heart of the financial district and close to the Opéra, so during the day it's frequented by suits, while at night it's evening dress on show. A young and energetic team runs this classy restaurant and bistrot. For starters, the velouté de châtaignes (chestnut) is remarkably smooth and creamy. You can either choose from the menu, which changes every two months, or from the daily specials. The serves are always generous and presented with flair – a sprinkle of cumin on the edge of your plate to give it a lift, or fresh thyme ... A red wine sauce is poured over the souris d'agneau et son chou blanc braisé (lamb with braised white cabbage) and it is fabulous! The atmosphere is warm and relaxed, especially if you choose the very drinkable Crozes-hermitage from the extensive list of quality wines.

Open: Mon-Fri noon-2.15pm, Mon-Sat 7.30pm-11pm; reservations advisable

Set menu: 158FF (two courses), 198FF (three courses)

AE CB EC MC V; €

Androuët sur le pouce
French (cheesemaker)

☎ **01 42 97 57 39**
49, rue Saint-Roch, Pyramides

Map: 1 D5

Métro: Pyramides

 Smoking throughout

 Pavement tables

This place pays tribute to the two great French passions: wine and cheese. Lovers of the latter can enjoy an assortment of cheeses, or savour the stuff in hot or cold tartines made with toasted Poilâne bread, served with a seasonal salad and a glass of wine. The restaurant's wine waiter has carefully selected vintages that bring out the full flavour of the tartines which sport evocative names such as tartine de la mer Egée, tartine du Berger basque, tartine de l'Isula or tartine des Jours de Fêtes. A platter of fifteen cheeses offers the ultimate initiation rite, a trail of flavours which allows you to discover or rediscover classic as well as underrated cheeses, from the mildest to the strongest. Androuët sur le pouce is ideal both for a quick, enjoyable lunch and a languid evening of pleasure.

Open: Mon-Fri 11.30am-2.30pm, 7pm-9.45pm; reservations advisable for dinner, not accepted for lunch

starter: 32FF-39FF
main: 49FF-180FF
dessert: 32FF-39FF
Plat du jour: 65FF

MC V; €

L'Auberge de l'Hautil (Jean-Pierre)
French

☎ 42 61 40 83
33, rue Saint-Roch,
Pyramides

Map: 1 D4

Métro: Tuileries, Pyramides

Entertainment: Magician performs evenings

Smoking throughout

At his tiny inn, adorned with wall coverings from another age, Jean-Pierre summons aperitifs and yesterday's heroes (Edith Piaf, Serge Lama) to help recreate an old-fashioned, picturesque, slightly madcap setting. Tourists looking for a bit of local colour are ecstatic while natives savour the owner's larger-than-life welcome and the incredible journey back in time. The menu offers great classics such as escargots de Bourgogne (Burgundy snails), museau en salade (salad with brawn), côte d'agneau aux herbes (lamb chops with herbs) and aiguillettes de canard (duck) sauce vigneronne. While meat dishes have pride of place, there are also some gorgeous seafood offerings. The presentation of the soupe de poissons avec rouille et croûtons (fish soup) is a spectacular ritual. A great wine list and generous digestifs make customers feel totally at home and are among the many highlights of this trip down memory lane.

starter: 60FF
main: 95FF
dessert: 25FF
Set menu: 145FF (three courses)
Plat du jour: 95FF

EC MC V

Open: Mon-Sat 7.30pm-10.30pm; reservations advisable

Aux Caves Sélections
French

☎ 01 42 36 46 56
7, rue de Montorgueil,
Les Halles

Map: 1 E8

Métro: Les Halles, Étienne Marcel

Entertainment: Wine tastings from 140FF

Smoking throughout

Unless you're in the know, it's easy to miss the tiny secret staircase winding up beside the entrance to a cellar, where some 400 carefully selected wines await their hour. Upstairs, you'll receive a warm welcome in the small room, dominated by a bar at the far end. Once you've chosen a tasty dish of oysters, charcuteries, cheeses or a cassoulet from Castelnaudary, you can move on to the serious business of wine. The list of elixirs is changed every month, and buffs will be able to make some eminently drinkable discoveries, like the marvellous organic Bergerac or the Côtes du Ventoux with its charming scent of currants. Organise a group of at least eight friends and book yourself in for an evening of wine tasting. The proprietor prepares dishes specially to complement the wines and it's superb.

starter: 24FF-60FF
main: 24FF-60FF
dessert: 25FF-40FF

CB, EC, MC, V

Open: Mon-Sun noon-2pm, 5pm-10pm; reservations advisable

1er ARRONDISSEMENT

La Bettola
Italian (Sicilian)

☎ 01 42 60 06 71
31, rue de Richelieu, Palais Royal

Map: 1 D6

Métro: Palais Royal, Pyramides

 Nonsmoking tables available

For over twenty years, people have been gathering at Mr Rosario's restaurant, between the fontaine Molière and the Comédie-Française, to enjoy sophisticated Sicilian dining. All the dishes are made to order and you won't find any pizza on the menu at this bettola (tavern). The octopus salad with olive oil and lemon is one of the best you'll find in Paris, and the roasted peppers are a pleasure to enjoy more often. If you are lucky enough to be here on a Friday, order the pasta con le sarde: a delight that combines various kinds of fish and fresh fennel. The involtini (exquisite beef olives) show that meat eaters haven't been forgotten either. There's no doubt about it, La Bettola, the only Sicilian restaurant in Paris, is worth going out of your way for.

Open: noon-2pm, 7.30pm-11pm; reservations essential

starter: 65FF-75FF
main: 55FF-148FF
dessert: 38FF-45FF
Set menu: 98FF (lunch)

AE CB EC MC V

Les Boucholeurs
French (seafood)

☎ 01 42 96 06 86
34, rue de Richelieu, Palais Royal

Map: 1 D6

Métro: Palais Royal, Pyramides

 Smoking throughout

Pleasant surprises are waiting for you at this seafood bistro opposite the statue of Molière and a short stroll from the gardens of the Palais-Royal. Exposed beams are livened up by a collection of black and white fishing photos on the walls. You get the picture: this is the place to eat your fill of mussels all year round (there are 15 or so different mussel dishes), not to mention oysters, scallops and fish. Try coques au basilic (cockles with basil), moules au curry (curried mussels), haddock poché or soupière de boulots cuits en pot-au-feu (a tureen of stewed whelk), all fresh from the sea. The owners are from the Poitou-Charentes region, and their enthusiasm for its produce is infectious. Another nice touch – the menu gives the daily tide levels.

Open: Mon-Fri noon-2pm, Mon-Sat 7.30pm-10pm; reservations advisable

starter: 41FF-64FF
main: 77FF-110FF
dessert: 40FF
Set menu: 119FF
Plat du jour: 90FF

CB MC V

Bars & Cafes – 1er, 2e & 9e

L'académie de billard 84, rue de Clichy, Paris 9e, Place de Clichy ☎ 01 48 78 32 85 Métro: Place de Clichy (Map: 9 B2)

A magnificent place with high ceilings, huge Art Deco mirrors, moleskin banquettes and a central glass ceiling. This former turn-of-the-century brasserie (converted into stables during the war) has the charm of a decrepit Argentine tango hall. Soak up the timeless atmosphere of this other-worldly setting.

Open: daily 10am-6am; By the glass: beer 17FF, champagne 30FF; coffee 8FF; Billiard championship in May; dress code applies, cash only

A Priori Thé 35-37, galerie Vivienne, Paris 2e, Palais-Royal ☎ 01 42 97 48 75 Métro: Bourse, Palais-Royal (Map: 2 E6)

This salon de thé with its cosy, *belle époque* décor is in an ideal spot. Along with your cappuccino, fresh fruit juice or tea, you can sample one of the desserts of the month – tarte au chocolat, crumble aux pommes et fruits rouges or gâteau au fromage blanc. Weekend brunches, with scones and eggs, are resolutely British.

Open: Mon-Fri 9am-11.30am, noon-6pm, Sat 9am-11.30am, Sat & Sun noon-6.30 pm; Coffee 15FF, cappuccino 20FF; snacks available; credit cards accepted

Bushwacker's 10, rue de Caumartin, Paris 9e, Havre-Caumartin ☎ 01 44 94 05 64, Métro: Havre Caumartin, Opéra (Map 9: J2)

A new Aussie bar in the finance district with wallabies and didgeridoos are as much a part of the décor as bushrangers. The owners still need to work on the atmosphere, but the circular bar – with a wide range of Australian and English beers – encourages interaction with other customers.

Open: daily noon-2am; By the glass: beer 19FF, champagne 40FF; coffee 10FF; meals available; entertainment: concerts Fri nights; credit cards accepted

Café Véry/Dame Tartine parc des Tuileries, Paris 1er, Tuileries ☎ 01 47 03 94 84 Métro: Tuileries (Map: 1 E3)

This modern glasshouse was designed by Stinco and is supported by a wood and aluminium structure. In winter, the calm, light-filled interior is a delight and in summer, you can cool off in the shade of the trees near Étienne Martin's statues of embracing lovers. The gardens stay open late so you can dine under the stars.

Open: Oct-March: daily noon-11pm, April-Sept: daily 9.30am-midnight; By the glass: beer 19FF, méthode champenoise 28FF; coffee 12FF; meals and snacks available; credit cards accepted

Comptoir Paris-Marrakech 37, rue Berger, Paris 1er, Châtelet Les Halles ☎ 01 40 26 26 66 Métro: Châtelet Les Halles (Map: 1 F7)

Right in the heart of the frantic Halles, Comptoir Paris-Marrakech is an ode to languor. Soft lighting, thick velvet curtains and cosy couches blot out the noisy activity outside. During the day you can sip organic herbal tea or cinnamon milk. In the evening, join the beautiful people over a pastis with liquorice – the latest craze.

Open: Sun-Thurs noon-2am, Fri & Sat noon-3am By the glass: beer 25FF, champagne 55FF; coffee 15FF, snacks available from 3pm to 7pm, CB EC MC V

La Jungle 56, rue d'Argout, Paris 2e, Place des Victoires ☎ 01 40 41 03 45 Métro: Sentier, Les Halles (Map: 2 G6)

A small corner of Africa in the big jungle of Paris. Masks and animal skins have even tropicalised the rococo mouldings, straight out of a 19th-century brothel. The festive atmosphere attracts all manner of cats, who sip their dépanneur (rum with ginger), listen to the griot (storyteller) or sway to the rhythms of African beat music.

Open: Mon-Fri 10am-2am, Sat & Sun 4pm-2am; By the glass: beer 12FF; coffee 8FF; meals and snacks available, live entertainment Wed, Thurs and Sun; CB V

Kata Bar 37, rue Fontaine, Paris 9e, Pigalle ☎ 01 40 16 12 13 Métro: Blanche (Map: 9 B4)

You barely notice the Kata Bar among the neon lights of Pigalle. Its long, narrow room with minimalist décor features a curious distillery over the bar, high-perched iron tables and stools and frequent exhibitions. A discreet meeting place.

Open: daily 5pm-2am; By the glass: beer 15FF-25FF; coffee 12FF; exhibitions of paintings, photographs & calligraphy; credit cards accepted

Le Next 17, rue Tiquetonne, Paris 2e, Montorgueil ☎ 01 42 36 18 93 Métro: Etienne Marcel (Map: 2 H7)

This place used to be called the Baraguoin before it was taken over and revamped by the owners of the Steps, just nearby. It's a good spot for night owls in search of a cosy atmosphere: a main room with character and exposed rafters, a little salon with wooden benches, as well as a billiard table and games.

Open: Tues-Sun 6pm-2am; By the glass: beer 15FF (after 9pm 20FF), champagne 40FF (after 9pm 45FF); snacks available, Wed open DJ (bring your own vinyl); Thurs DJ (soul); Fri & Sat French touch house, CB EC MC V

Normandy Hôtel 7, rue de l'Échelle, Paris 1er, Palais-Royal, Musée du Louvre ☎ 01 42 60 30 21 Métro: Palais Royal, Musée du Louvre (Map: 1 E5)

This magnificent bar in the luxurious Normandy Hôtel is open to the public. A watering-hole for journos from the Canard enchaîné, it's still suitable for a discreet meeting, provided the agenda isn't political. The open fireplace, leather armchairs and soft lighting guarantee a peaceful, relaxing time.

Open: Mon-Fri 11am-midnight, Sat & Sun 11am-1pm, 6pm-midnight; By the glass: beer 35FF, champagne 60FF; coffee 25FF; snacks available; credit cards accepted

Papou Lounge 74, rue Jean-Jacques Rousseau, Paris 1er, Les Halles ☎ 01 44 76 00 03 Métro: Châtelet-Les Halles, Etienne Marcel (Map: 1 F7)

This bar-restaurant is off the beaten track and has an authentic feel, perhaps because the two brothers who own the place share a fascination for the Papuans. It's perfect for a drink after a movie at the Halles. Behind the bar, Sean and Kean will account their round-the-world adventures, backed up by souvenirs on the wall.

Open: Mon-Fri 10am-2am, Sat 11am-2am, Sun 5pm-midnight; By the glass: beer 20FF, champagne 50FF; coffee 12FF, meals and snacks available; basement room with DJs for parties; credit cards accepted

Salsa Loco 70, rue Condorcet, Paris 9e, Pigalle ☎ 01 40 82 91 56 Métro: Pigalle, Notre-Dame de Lorette (Map: 9 D7)

Crazy about salsa and all things Latin American, Fred decided to call his bar Salsa Loco. The warm rhythms of Afro-Cuban music can be heard here well into the small hours. His range of rums (white, golden or aged for seven years) and excellent ti-punch or mojito will keep you awake for hours.

Open: Tues-Sun 7pm-4am (Tues-Sat in winter), By the glass: beer 10FF, champagne 40FF, credit cards accepted

Le Tambour 41, rue Montmartre, Paris 2e, Les Halles ☎ 01 42 33 06 90 Métro: Châtelet-Les Halles, Sentier (Map: 2 G7)

'This isn't a luxury hotel' shouts the waiter as he wipes a table with the back of his apron. The service is brisk, the crowd mixed and often rowdy. Enjoy the recycled street furniture, the straightforward cuisine and the cocky staff.

Open: daily 24 hours (restaurant noon-3pm, 7pm-2am, Fri & Sat until 4am); By the glass: beer 11FF-16FF, champagne 35FF; coffee 6FF-8FF; meals and snacks available, AE V

1er rrondi

Map: 1 E7
Métro: Bourse, Louvre-
Rivoli, Les Halles,
Palais-Royal

Entre Ciel et Terre ☎ 01 45 08 49 84
Vegetarian
**5, rue Hérold,
Bourse du Commerce, Les Halles**

Entre Ciel et Terre is near the Place des Victoires and not far from the Louvre. It has an
appealing, light-filled interior with stone and
half-timbered walls displaying works of art.
Strictly for the benefit of vegetarians, and
nonsmoking ones at that, the chef has come
up with a menu that's highly original in presentation and content. Fans of organic food will be
delighted by this healthy and balanced cuisine,
including corn crêpes with cheese, wholemeal
galettes, and lentils with coconut. Gourmets
will appreciate the fantaisie des crudités et des
légumes (a combination of raw and cooked
vegetables flavoured with thyme or cumin).
There's plenty to munch away on while happily
sipping a 'pétillant' (sparkling) or still wine
(organic of course). The homemade pastries
flaunt themselves temptingly, including the
tarte aux pommes gratinées (apple tart) or the
gâteau à l'orange nappé de chocolat.

starter: 23FF-53FF
main: 56FF-71FF
dessert: 21FF-43FF
Set menu: 69FF-87FF
(lunch), 107FF (dinner)
Plat du jour: 59FF

AE CB MC V

Open: Mon-Fri noon-3pm, 7pm-10pm; salon de thé 3pm-
6.30pm; reservations advisable

Map: 1 E9
Métro: Les Halles, (exit
Rambuteau)

Smoking throughout

Pavement tables in
summer

L'Épicerie ☎ 01 40 28 49 78
French
**30, rue Montorgueil,
Les Halles, Etienne Marcel**

In the rue Montorgueil you can still find some
of the old wholesalers from the time when Les
Halles was a functioning food market: butchers,
fishmongers, grocers specialising in fresh fruit
and vegetables. That's where L'Épicerie gets its
produce, and that's how it manages to go on
serving quality food at a reasonable price. The
ochre décor is simple, but livened up by old
spice tins. About 10 traditional regional dishes
form the basis of the menu, which varies according to the season. The velouté de potiron
(pumpkin soup) served in a rustic bowl is
flavoursome and wonderfully creamy. You can't
go past the speciality of the house: confit de
canard with pommes sarladaises (baked sliced
potatoes). The skin on the duck has just the
right amount of crunch and the tender meat
melts in your mouth. Sauces range from juniper
berries, coriander, ginger or cinnamon). Among
the desserts, the soufflé, with its chocolate
sauce inside, is irresistible.

starter: 35FF-45FF
main: 60FF-95FF
dessert: 30FF-35FF
Plat du jour: 60FF

CB EC MC V; €

Open: Mon-Sat noon-3pm, Mon-Sun 7.30pm-midnight; reservations advisable (especially in the evening)

CHOCOLAT FONDANT
KOHLER

L'Épicerie

L'Estaminet de Gaya
French

☎ **01 42 60 43 03**
**17, rue Duphot,
Madeleine**

Map: 1 C2

Métro: Madeleine

Dress code applies

   Smoking throughout

L'Estaminet de Gaya occupies the premises of an old turn-of-the-century Portuguese bar, hence the attractive blue tile decor. Apricot and prune-coloured walls, a fountain surrounded by flowers, bunches of hazelnuts and lavender, and mirrors and paintings all give the room on the ground floor an intimate charm. The upstairs room isn't as cosy, but suits the local businessmen who get together around its well-spaced tables. The chef, Pascal Bataille, does a 'marché du jour' (daily market special), which provides a choice of three entrées, and three mains, two of which are invariably fish. As the name suggests, the menu changes every day. You have to try the bouillabaisse; it's a pageant of splendid flavours. Skilful distillations of seasonings and spices characterise the sophisticated cuisine of the Estaminet, right down to the pleasantly unusual desserts. Taste, prices and service are all equally good.

Open: Mon-Fri noon-2.30pm, 7pm-11pm; reservations advisable

starter: 68FF-125FF
main: 140FF-188FF
dessert: 60FF
Set menu: 172FF

AE CB EC MC V

1er ARRONDISSEMENT

Map: 1 C2
Métro: Concorde
Nonsmoking throughout

Le Foyer Concorde
Polish

☎ 01 42 60 43 33
263 bis, rue Saint-Honoré, Concorde

This secluded Polish restaurant in rue Saint-Honoré is tucked away in the crypt of the église Notre-Dame-de-l'Assomption, which was handed over to the Polish community of Paris in 1850. Le Foyer Concorde is run by a Catholic association (and is normally open to members only), but a small contribution of 10FF is all that's needed for the warmest of welcomes. Raviolis à la viande (meat ravioli), bigos (sauerkraut ragout), goulach de chasseur ('hunter's goulash') served with potatoes and salted gherkins, or roulade de bœuf farcie et son gruau de sarrazin (beef roulade stuffed with hulled buckwheat) are among the authentic dishes on offer. This hearty fare shows its rural origins, but is extraordinarily flavoursome and inexpensive. Poland doesn't produce wine, but the menu includes French vintages, and the typically Polish beer goes perfectly with the bigos and sauerkraut.

starter: 25FF-45FF
main: 35FF-75FF
dessert: 19FF-28FF
Set menu: 59FF, 82FF, 95FF
Plat du jour: 45FF

cash only

Open: Tues-Sat noon-3pm, 7pm-10pm, Sun noon-10pm; reservations advisable

---

Map: 1 F9
Métro: Les Halles

Smoking throughout

Pavement tables

La Fresque
French/international

☎ 01 42 33 17 56
100, rue Rambuteau, Les Halles

The Les Halles neighbourhood lost its character a fair while ago, but this spacious inn with its constant buzz reminds you that the food markets were once nearby. The crowd is on for a chat and out for a good time, which suits the waiters, who like to stop and have a laugh. The cuisine takes some surprising turns but is perfectly assured. From the classic (but rare) tartiflette (baked potatoes, cheese and bacon) to the more exotic filet d'autruche (ostrich fillet) or poulet tandoori sauce yaourt (tandoori chicken with yoghurt), it's clear your tastebuds are in for a journey. To whet your appetite, try the assiette de la Fresque, which combines tapenade, doubitchou (ricotta, pesto and garlic) and aubergine tonique (stewed eggplant and tomatoes with coriander, garam masala and yoghurt). If there's still a little room, the tiramisù and the apple crumble will overcome the firmest resolutions.

starter: 36FF-45FF
main: 50FF-78FF
dessert: 32FF
Plat du jour: 66FF

CB V

Open: Mon-Sat noon-2pm, daily 7pm-midnight; reservations advisable

1er ARRONDISSEMENT

Fusion
Chinese

☎ **01 47 03 98 28**
9, rue Moliére,
Palais Royal

Map: 1 E5

Métro: Pyramides

 Nonsmoking tables available

You'll make all sort of discoveries in this tranquil restaurant that specialises in excellent modern Chinese cuisine presented in a French style. Among the entrées, which come in small or large serves according to your appetite, the pork balls coated with rice are a special treat. If you want to be trendy, choose a dish that's been fashionable in Peking since Gengis Khan: Mongolian fondue. Fond of duck? The magret de canard is exquisite (the plum and vegetable sauce is simmered for more than three hours). For dessert, make sure you save space for a caramelised pear with ginger. Another plus is the friendly proprietor, Henri, who will help you to choose from 33 different Chinese teas, including the surprising blue 'Buddha's skull' tea, which is very good for the heart. Fusion offers a unique excursion for your taste buds, eyes and spirit.

starter: 22FF-55FF
main: 45FF-65FF
dessert: 10FF-20FF
Set menu: 68FF (lunch only)

V; €

Open: Mon-Fri noon-3pm, 7pm-11.30pm, Sat 7pm-11.30pm; reservations advisable (evening)

L'Incroyable
French

☎ **01 42 96 24 64**
26, rue de Richelieu,
Palais Royal

Map: 1 E5

Métro: Bourse, Palais Royal

 Smoking throughout

 Courtyard tables

'The real gourmet takes as much delight in a slice of bread and butter as in a grilled lobster, provided the butter is top quality and the bread well-kneaded.' Colette's aphorism is reflected in the menus at this hundred-year-old cafeteria, located on the ground floor of a 1643 mansion. L'Incroyable resembles an inn from a light opera, with old engravings, mirrors and plates on the walls. Colette offers simple, flavoursome cuisine in the form of three set menus, featuring œufs mollets au vin rouge (medium-soft eggs poached in red wine), terrine de foie (liver terrine), tarte aux poireaux des sauvages (leek tart), confit de canard et sa compote d'oignons (confit of duck with onion compote), truite fuseau de lard (trout with bacon) and, for dessert, compote d'abricots au miel (stewed apricots with honey). You can see why tourists flock to L'Incroyable: nicknamed the 'Palais-Royal Cafeteria', this restaurant's high-quality, inexpensive cuisine evokes the Paris of yesteryear.

Set menu: 85FF, 115FF, 140FF

AE CB V

Open: Mon-Fri 11am-2am; reservations advisable

Map: 1 E9

Métro: Étienne Marcel

Nonsmoking tables available

Pavement tables

Joe Allen
American

☎ 01 42 36 70 13
30, rue Pierre Lescot,
Les Halles

If you're looking for a little bit of New York in Paris, Joe Allen is the place to find it. Photos of movie stars on the walls, a television perched over the superb bar, music to match the decor: it's all there, authentic and warm, like the welcome. As for the food, it's simple but finely done. The marinated sardine fillets served on toast are a speciality and they're delicious too. The chef makes the best hamburgers in town, but he also does grilled tuna with pesto sauce, or spinach sautéed in olive oil, topped with fresh tomatoes and basil. The home-made purée is a must-try item. When it came to dessert, we were very tempted by the apple crumble, but finally surrendered to the pecan pie with bourbon. Celebrate the next American public holiday here.

starter: 36FF-55FF
main: 80FF-140FF
dessert: 40FF
Set menu: 112FF
and 140FF
Plat du jour: 80FF

CB, EC, MC V

Open: daily noon-2am; reservations advisable

Joe Allen

La Mousson
Cambodian

☎ 01 42 60 59 46
9, rue Thérèse,
Palais Royal

Map: 1 D5
Métro: Palais Royal,
  Pyramides

 Smoking throughout

In a neighbourhood that's known for its rather cold beauty, La Mousson warms the heart and the palate. A peaceful, almost family atmosphere prevails, and Lucie, the proprietor, pirouettes among the tables, dispensing smiles and good humour, accompanying each dish with a joke or one of her inimitable observations. The food she serves is a delight: if you're familiar with the traditional bo bun, you'll find it completely transformed by a mixture of spices, herbs and flavours. The wonderfully tender chicken with basil is another good choice. However, it would be almost sacreligious to neglect the speciality of the house: the nun bachok curry. It's worth making the trip to the Mousson just to taste this delicious cocktail of rice vermicelli, chicken and crab, marinated in a rich, thick, slightly sweet curry sauce.

starter: 32FF-44FF
main: 54FF-65FF
dessert: 14FF-16FF
Set menu: 69FF (lunch),
  99FF (dinner)
CB EC MC V

Open: daily noon-2.30pm, 7.30pm-10.30pm; reservations essential

---

Le Paquebot (en la botella)
Spanish

☎ 01 42 21 19 00
14, rue Sauval,
Les Halles, Le Louvre

Map: 1 F7
Métro: Louvre

 Nonsmoking tables
  available

From the deck of an elegant *paquebot* (steamship), choose your port of call as you sail upon the ocean of Iberian cuisine (tapas, cassolettes, paellas ...). Savour the comyluichanthe (stuffed piquillos with mushrooms, quail délices with chocolate), the black rice or the rice *en croûte* (baked in the oven with lamb, mushrooms and vegetables). The chef's creativity is also reflected in the sweet tapas: ravioli de grenade (pomegranate ravioli), cava sorbet and caramelised nèfles (medlars). You can also indulge in a short hot chocolate, pain perdu (French toast) and ice cream, natilla (custard) or mandarin sorbet. Exhibitions of contemporary Spanish art complement the aesthetic presentation of the food. Among the large range of wines, the Pedro Ximenez, made from raisins, is a perfect way to end this gourmet cruise.

starter: 40FF
main: 80FF-110FF
dessert: 40FF
Set menu: 80FF, 100FF,
  130FF, 160FF
Plat du jour: 60FF-75FF)
CB V

Open: Tues-Sat noon-2.30pm, 7.30pm-11.30pm; reservations not accepted

The trippiest toilets in town

A trip to the loo at some of Paris' bars and restaurants goes beyond the merely utilitarian. Check out the unusual conveniences at La Chaise au Plafond (4e arrondissement) – you'll enjoy the Norman cow theme – or the restrooms at Lèche vin (11e arrondissement), which, after the pious imagery at the bar, plunge you into a riot of pornography. The owner of Pèse-personne (14e arrondissement) decorates his toilets with bounced cheques. At L'Autre Café (11e arrondissement), men and women meet at a back-to-back wash basin, and are excused for momentarily thinking they've been reincarnated as the opposite sex. The high-tech men's at Café de la Musique (19e arrondissement) operates by infrared. If it's ambience you're after, try the pistachio- and purple-coloured bower at De La Ville Café (10e arrondissement), the stone urinal at Buddha Bar (8e arrondissement) – which flushes in the wink of an (electric) eye – and the Eastern décor of the patio (with a running fountain in the middle) below deck at La Barge (12e arrondissement). Don't miss the mimetic toilets at Taka (18e arrondissement, see p.266), partitioned off by a Japanese screen, or the outback atmosphere of the dunnies at Café OZ (5e arrondissement, see p.80). For Indian kitsch straight out of Bollywood, Lal Quila (15e arrondissement, see p.228) is a must! At Khun Akorn (11e arrondissement, see p.169), a sophisticated Asian setting transports you to the other side of the world, while the Lilliputian urinals at Dar Zap (20e arrondissement, see p.286) will pique your uriosity. The painted chapel at Café Bourdelle (15e arrondissement) inspires a moment of reverent contemplation. There are also vast, beautiful spaces reminiscent of a time when the upper classes spared no expense to fit out their bathrooms: at China Club (12e arrondissement, see p. 145), everything is made of wood, marble and terry towelling.

Map: 1 E9

Métro: Étienne Marcel

Smoking throughout

Pavement tables

Pattaya

Thai

☎ 01 42 33 98 09
29, rue Étienne Marcel, Montorgueil

Jacques and his charming Thai wife opened this restaurant together in 1980. The authentic style of this old market bistrot – housed in a deep, narrow room – has been maintained. Among the entrées, don't miss the traditional spicy beef salad and the prawn salad flavoured with lemongrass, mint and coriander. One mouthful of the scallop curry with coconut milk and scented rice and you'll be off in another world. The garlic and pepper prawns are renowned throughout the neighbourhood. Don't leave without having shared a dessert of bananas with coconut. This classic Thai cuisine might not be ground-breaking but it offers a finely controlled burst of flavours. You can see why bookings are highly recommended.

starter: 37FF-60FF
main: 50FF-68FF
dessert: 25FF-35FF

V; €

Open: Mon-Sat noon-2.30pm, 7pm-11pm, Sun 7pm-11pm; reservations advisable

Le Relais chablisien
French (Burgundy)

☎ 01 45 08 53 73
4, rue Bertin-Poirée, Châtelet

Map: 1 H8

Métro: Châtelet

 Nonsmoking tables available

 Pavement tables

(VOL)

Claudine, the owner, is from the Chablis region in Burgundy and is proud of it. In this 17th-century tavern, with its exposed beams, cooking is done in the traditional Chablis way – with lots of sauces. But, amazingly, the food isn't heavy. The vegetables, which are steamed to keep them firm and flavoursome, are the secret. Start with terrine maison aux foies de volailles avec ses oignons confits (homemade chicken-liver terrine with preserved onions) or fricassée d'escargots (snail fricassée). Continue with the generous pavé de charolais (thick beef steak) or the coq fermier au vin d'Irangy (free-range rooster with Irangy wine), which is especially good. The owner sometimes branches out with fish from 'foreign' parts such as salmon, but rest assured, the sauce is 100% Chablis. It's not surprising that this restaurant is patronised by inveterate foodies and clients keen to try authentic regional cuisine, including the students from the Japanese school of design next door.

Open: Mon-Fri noon-9.30pm; reservations advisable

starter: 48FF-65FF
main: 99FF-110FF
dessert: 41FF
Plat du jour: 99FF

CB EC MC V

Map: 1 D6

Métro: Palais Royal, Bourse

Nonsmoking tables available

Terrace tables

Restaurant du Palais Royal

French

☎ 01 40 20 00 27
Jardin du Palais Royal, 110,
Galerie de Valois,
Palais Royal

As surroundings go, you can't do much better than the arcades, refined gardens and 17th-century architecture of the Palais Royal. Dining on the terrace in summer is a rare and unforgettable luxury. Red and apple green velvet, a lovely high ceiling and indoor plants create a sober, quiet atmosphere inside. The salade de poivrades d'artichaut aux pamplemousses (artichoke and grapefruit salad), exquisitely fresh, is enhanced by delightfully crunchy carrots and green beans. Taste and presentation are equally important: try the bass, delicately flavoured with a bay leaf and accompanied by an ethereal purée. The volaille fermière marinée aux épices (marinated free-range fowl with spices) and the rognon de veau grillé entier (whole grilled veal kidney) are both delicious. Upstairs, a mischievous look from Colette on a lithograph by Cocteau recalls another love affair with beautiful cuisine.

starter: 56FF-98FF
main: 98FF-198FF
dessert: 52FF-68FF

AE CB DC EC MC V; €

Open: Mon-Fri noon-2.30pm, 7pm-10.30pm (terrace orders taken until 10pm in summer); reservations advisable in winter, essential in summer

2ᵉ Arrondissement

Opéra

Bourse

Bibliothèque Richelieu

Place des Victoires

2ᵉ Arrondissement

The Bourse (Stock Exchange) is this arrondissement's financial heart, the Sentier its rag-trade outlet, the Opéra its ode to music and dance. From rue de la Paix, where famous jewellers strut their stuff, to blvds Poissonnière and Bonne-Nouvelle, where stalls and fast-food outlets advertise their existence with garish neon signs, the second arrondissement is a real hotch-potch of styles. Near the palais Brongniart and Agence France-Presse, banks and insurance agencies have set up their head offices in solid, elegant 19th-century buildings. Business and finance types in smart suits and dresses abound. A sense of moderation is de rigueur. At the table or the counter, discretion and restraint rule this hyperactive world. The décor and atmosphere change as soon as you hit rue d'Aboukir or rue du Sentier. Retail and wholesale outlets as well as clothing work-shops buzz with the sound of haggling. This arrondissement is a busy place during the week. And its neighbourhoods are divided by a thin line. You only need cross the street to find yourself in an area characterised by a completely different look, feel and rhythm. On weekends, most of the hustle and bustle is concentrated on the Grands Boulevards or towards the Étienne-Marcel district.

Au sans souci
French

☎ **01 42 36 09 39**
183, rue Saint-Denis,
Étienne Marcel

Map: 2 J6

Métro: Réumur Sébastopol,
Étienne Marcel

Entertainment: Football
matches on big screen

 Smoking throughout

 Pavement tables in
summer

A Stendhalian figure in his own way, owner Michel Godon has written on a wall: 'J'ai cherché par le rouge et le vert à traduire les grandes passions humaines' ('I've sought to portray the great human passions with red and green'). This inscription captures the spirit of this colourful bistro, whose regulars include local tradespeople. The salade auvergnate or the salade de chèvre chaud (warm goat's cheese salad) set the tone for simple but high-quality cuisine. Top marks go to the meat dishes, including the tender bavette à l'échalote (flank steak with shallots) and the mouthwatering rumsteak au poivre (rump steak with pepper sauce), which you can wash down with the 'vin du jour'. The owner personally buys the wines from small producers and has a marked preference for burgundies and beaujolais. Play 421 (a dice game), exchange jokes, have coffee or just a quick bite: Au sans souci has something for everyone.

Open: Mon-Sat 7.30am-late; reservations not accepted

starter: 25FF-55FF
main: 50FF-65FF
dessert: 28FF-30FF
Set menu: 69FF

CB V

Le Grapillon
French

☎ **01 40 28 96 04**
32, rue Tiquetonne,
Montorgueil

Map: 2 H7

Métro: Étienne Marcel

 Smoking throughout

The Grapillon looks small and dark from the outside, but over the past few years this restaurant, with its simple décor and friendly atmosphere, has enjoyed a well-deserved success. It's the ideal spot for quiet dinner with friends or a romantic evening. For starters, try the wonderfully flavoursome home-made foie gras, or the croustillon de chévre aux pommes (goat's cheese with potatoes), and continue with the onglet de veau servi avec sa sauce aux pleurotes (flank of veal served with a pleurote mushroom sauce) or the gourmand de volailles farci au foie gras (chicken with foie gras stuffing). For dessert, you could succumb to the fondant au chocolat or plunge into a crème brûlée. The quality cuisine is complemented by faultless service. And the wide range of prices will allow everyone to find something they like without breaking the bank. Don't miss this delightful gastronomic experience.

Open: Mon-Sat 9.30am-2.30pm, 6pm-11pm; reservations advisable

starter: 38FF-65FF
main: 78FF-85FF
dessert: 30FF
Set menu: 70FF (lunch)
Plat du jour: 49FF

CB

2ᵉ arrondi

Map: 2 G6

Métro: Sentier

Smoking throughout

Pavement tables

starter: 55FF-60FF
main: 69FF-72FF
dessert: 38FF-42FF

MC V; €

Il Buco
Italian

☎ 01 45 08 50 10
**18, rue Léopold Bellan,
Montorgueil**

Chef Aldo speaks with pride (and a charming accent) of his background in Modena, a gastronomic centre in the Italian region of Emilia. An original menu at this new restaurant changes daily depending on what's available at the Montorgueil market. Bring on the antipasti: bruschetta au chèvre et aux lamelles de courgettes (bruschetta with goat's cheese and zucchini strips), aubergines aux pignons de pin caramélisés servies sur un lit de roquette (eggplant with caramelised pine nuts served on a bed of rocket) and mozzarella millefeuille. Viva la pasta: torchiette del paradiso (sausage, tomato and broccoli) and tortiglioni del cacciatore (freshly picked cep mushrooms, cream and pesto). Gigot d'agneau à la menthe (roast lamb with mint) was the only meat dish on offer when we visited. For dessert, the panna cotta is a real surprise. Il vero gusto.

Open: Mon-Fri noon-2.30pm, 8pm-11pm, Sat 8pm-11pm; reservations advisable

---

Map: 2 H6

Métro: Étienne Marcel,
Sentier

Smoking throughout

Pavement tables

starter: 56FF-72FF
main: 54FF-118FF
dessert: 30FF-35FF
Plat du jour: 78FF-118FF

AE CB DC EC JCB MC V

Little Italy Caffé
Italian

☎ 01 42 36 36 25
**92, rue Montorgueil,
Les Halles, Étienne Marcel**

This pasta place is happily reminiscent of a Milanese trattoria. The long, narrow room (with wooden bar, large bench seats and crowded tables), good-natured service, background music and a constant buzz of conversation all contribute to the ebullience and joie de vivre. The menu features a great selection of antipasti while the salads, such as the carpaccio di melanzane (grilled eggplant on a bed of lettuce with black olives, anchovy fillets, tomatos and oregano), are simple, delicious and generous. Pastawise (more than 20 different types), it's impossible to choose between the tagliatelles boscaïola (cèpe, chanterelle and button mushrooms with crème fraîche) and the ravioli della casa avec ricotta et basilic (homemade ravioli with ricotta and basil). No room left for cheese or dessert ... oh well, just a caffè illy (a cappuccino) and the bill!

Open: Mon-Sat 10am-3pm, 7pm-midnight; reservations not accepted

Sushi passion

Five centimetres in diameter, 2.5cm high and a few quickly dispatched grams...
There's not much to them, yet sushi have taken the capital by storm. These
small mouthfuls of raw fish and rice, delicately flavoured with vinegar, are sold
today at more than 200 outlets throughout Paris, each offering its own varia-
tion, each attracting a different clientele (a hip crowd on the Champs-Elysées,
fashion freaks on the fifth floor of the Galeries Lafayette, students around the
Odéon). When the first post-war Japanese restaurant opened near the
Panthéon in 1958, few Parisians appreciated the unique qualities of this cuisine. Several years later, the Japanese community set up shop in rue Sainte-
Anne (behind the Opéra), but still only managed to attract tourists from back
home. Since then, sushi has come into its own. Riding the exotic wave of
'World Food', it satisfies all the criteria of a healthy diet. Rich in vitamins C and
B2, chock-full of protein and slow sugars, each of these small Japanese rolls
contains a mere 40 or 50 calories. Light but sophisticated, they make a tantalising snack at any time of the day. Home-delivery and catering chains have
sprung up everywhere to satisfy the growing demand. According to purists,
some providers don't think twice about using machines to make their product –
is the fine art of sushi preparation in danger? The only way to get back that
original sushi taste is to learn how to make them yourself. Every month, the
Centre Culturel Franco-Japonais runs a course for that very purpose.

Centre Culturel Franco-Japonaise
8-10, passage Turquetil, 75011 Paris
☎ 01 43 48 83 64

Map: 2 H7
Métro: Étienne Marcel

Smoking throughout

Le Loup Blanc
International

☎ 01 40 13 08 35
42, rue Tiquetonne, Montorgueil

If clients keep coming back to this predominantly but not exclusively gay restaurant, which is always crowded and smoky, it's because of the waiters' friendly smiles. In a well-lit dining area combining earth tones, Alain and his helpers will treat you to a range of inventive and inexpensive dishes: meat and fish marinated with herbs and spices (cardamom, star anise, marjoram, liquorice) and then grilled. For accompaniments,you can choose from a variety of vegetables and grains, according to your appetite and the season: caponata, red lentils, quinoa (a South American grain), creamed corn (a must) or carrots with cumin. Our favourites are the chicken with cumin and sumac, Sechuan pork, veal cooked in beer with juniper berries and skirt steak with oregano. On Sunday, you can choose one of three generous brunches for under 100FF.

main: 67FF-111FF
dessert: 32FF
MC V

Open: Mon-Thurs 7.30pm-midnight, Fri 7.30pm-12.30am, Sat 7.30pm-1am, Sun 11am-5pm; reservations advisable

---

Map: 2 G7
Métro: Sentier

Smoking throughout

Rêve d'Asie
Vietnamese

☎ 01 42 36 11 21
9, rue Mandar, Sentier

The owner of the Rêve d'Asie, a relaxed and friendly old gent, makes no effort to advertise his restaurant. He doesn't need to; this little Vietnamese eatery fills up quickly with locals who have turned it into their cafeteria. In fact, if you hadn't heard about the place, you wouldn't be inclined to go in and try it. The décor is a bit tired, but the atmosphere is calm, and the main attraction is the excellent Chinese-Vietnamese food. From the varied menu you might choose a potage aux asperges et au crabe (asparagus and crab soup) followed by poulet á la citronnelle (chicken with lemongrass). The Vietnamese specialities, like crabe farci (stuffed crab), are made on the premises. It goes without saying that they're mouthwatering. Big pleasures at little prices. Off you go then, you won't be disappointed. But don't tell too many people.

starter: 30FF-45FF
main: 40FF-60FF
dessert: 30FF
AE CB V

Open: Mon-Fri 11am-2am, Sat lunch; reservations not accepted

Le Tambour
French

☎ 01 42 33 06 90
41, rue Montmartre, Étienne Marcel

Map: 2 G7

Métro: Étienne Marcel, Les Halles

 Smoking throughout

 Pavement tables in summer

This country-in-the-city bistro is doing its bit to keep up the tradition of the restaurants that used to surround Les Halles market. You can get a solid meal here at any time of the day or night. The menu is extensive (though less so after 1am) and reassuringly familiar: soupe à l'oignon (onion soup), filets de harengs (fillets of herring), œufs mayonnaise... home-made foie gras and huîtres fraîches (fresh oysters) – even in the small hours – followed by the classic andouillette AAAAA (a variety of pork sausage), entrecôte à l'ail (rib steak with garlic), bavette à l'échalote (steak with shallots), pieds, jarrets ou travers de porc (pigs' trotters, shins or spare ribs). The huge, inventive salads are another good option and the home-made tarts a real treat. The night-owl owner, with his handlebar moustache and overalls, is an institution in the neighbourhood. As well as sustenance for the body, he provides dog-eared books for his clients to read.

starter: 35FF-80FF
main: 65FF-100FF
dessert: 40FF-45FF
Set menu: 55FF (lunch)
Plat du jour: 48FF (lunch)

Open: daily 24 hours; reservations not accepted

CB DC EC JCB MC V

Tana
Thai

☎ 01 42 33 53 64
36, rue Tiquetonne, Montorgueil

Map: 2 H7

Métro: Étienne Marcel

Entertainment: Live show Sat evenings

 Smoking throughout

In a street where restaurants try to outdo each other in originality, Tana probably gets the prize for eccentricity and sheer folly. Customers are greeted by sexy and vivacious 'waitresses' and immediately plunged into a highly exotic world where the extravagance of the 'hostesses' is equal to the dishes on offer. Not for the inhibited, perhaps, this Thai den seems more likely to appeal to a male clientele, although the fairer sex is naturally welcome. Rhinestones and glitter are brought out on Saturday nights for a show that it's best to know nothing about beforehand. Foodwise, the subtle, aromatic flavours of the mixed hors d'oeuvre for two, the crevettes sautées au basilic (sautéed shrimps with basil), the soupe de poulet á la citronnelle (chicken and lemongrass soup) and the poisson vapeur dans sa feuille de banane (steamed fish served in a banana leaf) all impart the tastes of Thailand.

starter: 36FF-55FF
main: 58FF-120FF
dessert: 30FF-35FF

Open: daily 7.30pm-11pm; reservations advisable (Sat evenings)

CB EC MC V

2ᵉ ARRONDISSEMENT

2ᵉ arrond

Le Tire-bouchon
French

☎ 01 42 21 95 51
**22, rue Tiquetonne,
Montorgueil**

Map: 2 H7
Métro: Étienne Marcel, Les Halles

Smoking throughout

With its copper-plated bar, kitsch overhead fans and exposed beams, Le Tire-bouchon looks like a cosy apartment. This is a place where you feel good and, even better, eat well. Start your meal with a delicious terrine de chevreuil et sa purée d'oignons (venison terrine with puréed onion), followed by a confit de canard pommes à l'ail (confit of duck with garlic potatoes) prepared in the traditional way, before finishing in style with a tarte aux figues (fig tart) studded with bilberries and enhanced by a touch of cinnamon. The service is fast and efficient. At lunchtime, businessmen and local retailers mix easily in this friendly and elegantly fashionable environment. The chef likes to point out that he bases his dishes on whatever produce has just arrived at the market. You can tell.

starter: 38FF-67FF
main: 68FF-105FF
dessert: 30FF
Set menu: 98FF
Plat du jour: 60FF-65FF
(lunch)
V

Open: Mon-Sat noon-2.45pm, 8pm-11pm, Sun 8pm-11pm; reservations essential

Voyageurs du Monde
International

☎ 01 42 86 17 17
**51 bis, rue Saint-Anne,
Bourse**

Map: 2 D6
Métro: Pyramides, Quatre Septembre

Nonsmoking tables available

Voyageurs du Monde needs no introduction to locals. Parisian fans of faraway lands all know this welcoming establishment, where they can organise a tailor-made trip, buy a travel guide from the bookstore or find a rare and exotic present at the gift shop. Travel of the gastronomic variety is also catered for. The adjoining restaurant explores the cuisine of every continent in a single menu devoted to a different country each day. The décor could be a bit more exotic, but in a street where exclusively Japanese restaurants jostle for space, it's nice to find this little culinary Babel. However, it must be said that the result is not always equal to the bill.

Set menu: 110FF
CB EC MC V

Open: Mon-Fri noon-2.30pm; reservations advisable

3ᵉ Arrondissement

Arts et Métiers

Marais

République

Rue Beaubourg

3e Arrondissement

The third arrondissement contains a small corner of the Marais that has managed to remain friendly and picturesque. Noisy during the week, calm and languid on weekends, the opulent renovations of its period homes and the dictates of fashion haven't yet destroyed its soul. Rue du Temple and rue de Turenne move to the rhythm of clothing workshops, artisans and wholesalers. The tempo picks up along rue de Turbigo, rue Réaumur and blvd de Sébastopol, and is perfectly offset by the place de la République. Business calls at all hours and the blvds du Temple, des Filles-du-Calvaire and Beaumarchais barely manage to contain the hive of activity. Properties on rue des Archives, rue Charlot, rue de Saintonge and rue de Bretagne require neither artifice nor restoration to reveal their lovely bas reliefs, balustrades, courtyards and stairways. Suddenly, the tempo takes on an elegant nonchalance. The Musée Picasso and the Musée Carnavalet appear, and the Archives Nationales makes its presence felt. The rue de Rambuteau and rue des Francs-Bourgeois of the Marais are part of Paris's gay centre.

A 2 pas du dos
Modern French

☎ 01 42 77 10 52
101, rue Vieille-du-Temple, Marais

Map: 3 G6

Métro: Rambuteau

 Smoking throughout

 Pavement & terrace tables in summer

This trendy, gay-friendly establishment is frequented by people who work in fashion, advertising and TV. It's smooth and sophisticated but always welcoming, and success hasn't spoilt its tasty, well-balanced French cuisine. The menu changes every two months, and the dishes are accompanied by a variety of vegetables, simmered with Mediterranean flavourings. We gave serious consideration to the velouté de cèpes et son suprême de caille croustillant (mushrooms with quail), the selle d'agneau rôtie aux girolles et sa poêlée d'artichauts (roast lamb with girolle mushrooms and fried artichokes), and the noisette de saumon rôtie accompagnée d'une concassée de tomates au romarin et d'oignons confits (roasted salmon with tomatoes, rosemary and preserved onions). The desserts are prepared with just as much care. When you book, ask for a table upstairs (or on the terrace in summer), so you can enjoy the view of the Musée Picasso's gardens.

Open: Mon-Sat noon-2.15pm, 8.30pm-11pm, Sun noon-2.15pm (8.30pm-11pm 3rd & 4th Sundays of the month); reservations essential

Set menu: 135FF, 165FF
Plat du jour: 77FF (lunch)

V; €

Ambassade d'Auvergne
French (Auvergne)

☎ 01 42 72 31 22
22, rue de Grenier Saint-Lazare, Beaubourg

Map: 3 E3

Métro: Rambuteau, Arts et Métiers, Étienne Marcel

 Nonsmoking tables available

This 100-year-old 'embassy' located between Les Halles and the Centre Beaubourg has a friendly atmosphere and offers traditional recipes, among which the dishes from Puy-de-Dôme are rivalled only by those from Aveyron. The terrine d'agneau et sa vinaigrette aux cinq parfums (lamb terrine served with a five-flavour vinaigrette) and the émincé de choux verts aux petits lardons (thinly sliced green cabbage with bacon) are a tasty lead-up to the house speciality, which simply must be tried: la saucisse d'Auvergne à l'aligot (Auvergne sausage with potato and cheese purée). Served with Chanturgues (a red wine from Auvergne), this famous dish is a moment of pure gastronomy. The mousseline à la verveine (lemon verbena mousse) is a fitting conclusion to this magnificent feast. If the bill seems a bit steep, just close your eyes and think of the Auvergne.

Open: daily noon-2pm, 7.30pm-11pm; reservations advisable (especially evenings)

starter: 58FF-120FF
main: 89FF-120FF
dessert: 48FF
Set menu: 170FF

AE CB MC

3ᵉ ARRONDISSEMENT

Map: 3 D5
Métro: Arts et Métiers

Smoking throughout

Au Bascou
French (Basque)

☎ 01 42 72 69 25
38, rue Réaumur,
Arts et Métiers

Far from traditional festive surrounds, this regional eatery offers both the richness and sophistication of Basque cuisine. The owner, a knowledgeable wine waiter and renowned restaurateur, plans the varied and carefully updated menu around his region's best produce. The soupe de châtaignes (chestnut) et sa raviole foie gras and the millefeuille d'anchois (anchovy) are light and delicious, the charcuterie des Aldudes perfect. The subtle spice and garlic flavours of the dishes go well with an excellent Irouléguy (a local Basque wine). The axoa de veau façon Espelette (veal ragout with red chilli), the caneton (duckling) et sa croustade aux champignons and the marmitako de thon (tuna in a ragout of tomatoes, onions, peppers and white wine and served with potatoes) are faultless. For dessert, treat yourself to the brebis Ardi Gasna et sa confiture de cerises (ewe's milk cheese with cherry conserve).

starter: 55FF-115FF
main: 85FF
dessert: 40FF
Plat du jour: 85FF (lunch)

AE CB MC V

Open: Tues-Fri noon-2pm, Mon-Sat 8pm-11pm; reservations advisable

---

Map: 3 F6
Métro: Filles du Calvaire

Entertainment: Wine-tasting evenings

Smoking throughout

Le Baromètre
French

☎ 01 48 87 04 54
17, rue Charlot,
Marais

You can't fault this bistrot, with its classic décor and food. There's nothing surprising about the lunch menu, but everything is absolutely delicious. The hareng et ses pommes á l'huile (herring with potatoes and olive oil) is straightforward and fresh; the pot-au-feu présenté avec son bouillon et l'os á moelle (stew with broth and marrowbone) and the gratin d'andouillette dijonnaise (gratin of Dijon pork sausage) are everything they should be. The tarte tatin looked so appealing it disappeared before we could taste it. The clafoutis aux prunes (plum clafoutis) wasn't bad either. In the evening, it's the ideal spot to have a tartine and warm up your palate with one of the carefully chosen wines (all sold by the glass), before setting out to enjoy Paris by night.

starter: 20FF-35FF
main: 50FF-70FF
dessert: 26FF-35FF
Plat du jour: 70FF

CB V

Open: Mon-Fri 7am-9pm; reservations advisable

Chez Janou
French (Provence)

☎ **01 42 72 28 41**
2, rue Roger Verlomme, Marais

Map: 3 J9

Métro: Bastille, Chemin Vert, Saint-Paul

 Smoking throughout

 Terrace tables

For those who love light, southern-French cuisine, this is an ideal spot set in lovely surroundings, in a small, quiet street a stone's throw from the Place des Vosges. What more could you ask for? If you're lucky or have booked well in advance, you can sit on the terrace decked with garlands. Otherwise enjoy the traditional bistro atmosphere, which has been only slightly revamped with a formica bar and big mirrors. The fish is excellent, fresh and varied: bar au thym (bass with thyme), thon (tuna) à la provençale and rouget (mullet) à la tapenade. For those partial to offal, the foie de veau aux pommes (calf's liver with potatoes) is excellent. Tempting desserts include a creamy blanc-manger sur coulis de framboise (blanc mange in raspberry sauce) and a tarte aux figues (fig tart). The restaurant has recently had to expand to accomodate its ever-increasing clientele of gourmets.

starter: 26FF-64FF
main: 62FF-98FF
dessert: 36FF
Set menu: 88FF (lunch, weekdays only)
Plat du jour: 88FF

Credit cards accepted; €

Open: Mon-Fri noon-3pm, 8pm-midnight, Sat & Sun noon-4pm, 8pm-midnight; reservations advisable

Chez Nénesse
French

☎ **01 42 78 46 49**
17, rue Saintonge, Marais

Map: 3 F7

Métro: Filles du Calvaire

 Smoking throughout

The linen tablecloths and soft interior hues are straight out of an old Parisian cafe. You immediately feel at ease in this unpretentious, untrendy restaurant, where the food is relatively traditional but made with fresh, high-quality ingredients. The salade de mesclun au foie gras de canard (mixed green salad with duck foie gras) makes an excellent starter, followed by the fricassée de volaille aux morilles (poultry fricassee with morel mushrooms). Everything is exquisite, including the gratin de fruits rouges à la menthe fraîche (red berry crumble with fresh mint). Chez Nénesse is an oasis of simplicity and good taste in an area that can tend to lose the plot. A terrific place.

starter: 30FF-40FF
main: 70FF-85FF
dessert: 50FF-60FF
Plat du jour: 52FF (lunch)

CB EC MC V

Open: Mon-Fri noon-2.30pm, 7.45pm-10.30pm; reservations essential

Map: 3 F8

Métro: Filles du Calvaire,
Saint Sébastien Froissart

Nonsmoking tables
available

Les Épicuriens du Marais
French

☎ 01 40 27 00 83
19, rue Commines,
Cirque d'Hiver

Entering this restaurant, nothing immediately promises epicurean pleasure. But for these Epicureans, all that counts is the wholesome and traditional food they offer in abundance. If you're a hearty eater, choose the bisque d'étrilles et ses croûtons (crab soup with croûtons) or the salade de lentilles aux gésiers confits (lentil salad and preserved gizzards) to start, followed by any of the classics: cocotte de rognons de veau (casserole of veal kidneys), cuisse de canard en pot au feu (stewed duck drumsticks) or the tasty tajine d'agneau au gingembre (lamb tajine with ginger). Fish options are lighter: the caviar d'aubergines en pannequets de saumon fumé (eggplant caviar in smoked salmon pancakes) or the salade de filets de rouget Barbet au fenouil cru et agrumes (mullet fillet salad with raw fennel and citrus fruits) – just the right tanginess. All this, and the well thought-out wine list, featuring excellent burgundies and bordeaux, will convince you that Epicurus was no fool.

starter: 45FF
main: 90FF
dessert: 45FF
Set menu: 79FF (lunch),
129FF, 159FF (dinner)
Plat du jour: 60FF

MC V; €

Open: Mon-Sat noon-3pm, 7pm-11.30pm, Sun 7pm-11.30pm; reservations advisable

Gli Angeli
Italian

☎ 01 42 71 05 80
5, rue Saint-Gilles, Marais

Map: 3 J8

Métro: Chemin Vert

 Smoking throughout

 Pavement tables

One of the top 23 Italian restaurants in Paris, according to its three founding friends! The heady atmosphere, Latin lover accents, culinary expertise and sparkling kitchen certainly give credence to this claim, and attract regulars and local trendies alike. Try the mussel poivrade for starters, the taglierini à la roquette et au parmesan de Vénétie (taglierini with rocket and Venetian parmesan) for mains and the tarte à la ricotta for dessert. Or the calamaretti à la sauce piquante (baby squid with a spicy sauce), the foie de veau au vinaigre balsamique (calf's liver with balsamic vinegar) and the tiramisù. The flavours of Northern Italy have a special place in this wonderful, classic menu. The extensive wine list includes many Tuscan wines, of course: nobile de Montepulciano is the best, followed by the Brunello, but certainly don't overlook the Umbrian Rubesco or the Calabrian Cir.

starter: 45FF-85FF
main: 55FF-110FF
dessert: 40FF
Plat du jour: 70FF-110FF

V; €

Open: daily noon-2pm, 8pm-11pm; reservations advisable (especially later in the week)

Le Hangar
French

☎ 01 42 74 55 44
12, impasse Berthaud, Beaubourg

Map: 3 F3

Métro: Rambuteau

 Smoking throughout

 Veranda tables

It's a real surprise to cross the noisy rue Beaubourg and find this peaceful dead end street, with a restaurant that is nothing like its name suggests. Bare walls, exposed stone, green plants and large mirrors form a simple but elegant interior. This is taste-bud heaven, with exquisite, unusual dishes: for starters try the beautifully fresh tartare de saumon au basilic (salmon tartare with basil) and the fenouil (fennel) gratiné à la mozzarella; for mains, the dos de saumon poché avec courgettes à la vapeur (poached salmon with zucchini) or the risotto aux asperges et jambon de parme (asparagus and Parma ham). Finally, for dessert have the petit gâteau mi-cuit au chocolat (semi-baked chocolate cake) or the gratin de pêches aux amandes (peach and almond crumble). A great place to discover new flavours.

starter: 28FF-58FF
main: 62FF-128FF
dessert: 38FF-58FF

cash only; €

Open: Mon 7pm-midnight, Tues-Sat noon-3pm, 7pm-midnight; reservations advisable

Coming home for a restaurant meal

Going out for a slap-up meal, choosing the best table, listening in on your neighbours' conversation – those days are gone. No need to take your guests out to a restaurant, let the restaurant come to you. It all started when that piping-hot pizza first turned up on your doorstep while you were watching the footy on TV. Since then, letterboxes have been groaning under the weight of fliers. Allo Couscous, Matsuri-sushi, Les Sommets del'Himalaya... Scooters defy the road rules to bring you flavours from every corner of the globe, including spring rolls, Tex-Mex and tandoori. Traditional restaurants have also got in on the act. Blanquette de veau (veal stew) from Aux Pipalottes Gourmandes (9e arrondissement), bourriche d'huîtres (basket of oysters) from Écailler du Bistrot (11e arrondissement), carry de requin (shark curry) from Coco de Mer (5e arrondissement), muffins from Colombus Café (4e arrondissement) or thon grillé au pistou (grilled tuna with pesto) from Joe Allen's (1er arrondissement) – sumptuous fare that you can either take away or have delivered to your home. From 250FF per person, an increasing number of chefs will actually come into your kitchen and whip up a personalised dinner in two shakes of a lamb's tail. The Internet is also knocking at the door: from clicresto.fr to canalfood.com, specialist sites are attempting to replace existing home restaurant services, with varying degrees of success. Alloresto.fr will even organise a video night in your loungeoom: La fille sur le Pont, Apollo 13 or Seven ... enough to ruin your appetite!

Fast food

Les Sommets de l'Himalaya ☎ 01 44 59 37 76

Allo Couscous ☎ 01 43 45 80 88

Matsurit-sushi ☎ 01 40 26 11 13

Takeaway

Aux Pipalottes Gourmandes (home-made food)
49, rue Rochechouart, Paris 9e ☎ 01 44 53 04 53

Le Coco de Mer (home-made food)
111, rue Monge, Paris 5e ☎ 01 47 07 55 55

L'Écailler du bistrot
22, rue Paul Bert, Paris 11e ☎ 01 43 72 76 77

Joe Allen (home delivery only)
☎ 01 45 77 77 00

Colombus Café
25, rue Vieille-du-Temple, Paris 4e ☎ 01 42 72 20 25,
www.colombuscafe.com

Internet
www.alloresto.fr

www.clicresto.fr

www.canalfood.com

www.madameestservie.com

Home-cook chefs
www.chefadomicile.com

3ᵉ ARRONDISSEMENT

Le Marais-Cage
Caribbean

☎ **01 48 87 31 20/**
01 48 87 44 51
8, rue de Beauce, Marais

Map: 3 E6

Métro: Temple, Arts et métiers

  Smoking throughout

The name of this restaurant, which translates as the Swamp Cage, might have something to do with its location: hidden away in one of the deep and narrow streets of the labyrinthine Marais. Quality Caribbean food has been served here for 35 years. The rather ponderous facade and décor are not in the least exotic, but the owner couldn't be more courteous and attentive. The set menus are excellent value for money and give you as much choice as à la carte. Start with the assiette d'acras, de boudin, de crabe farci (platter of fish or vegetables fritters, sausage and stuffed crab), which also features the Féroce martiniquais (a subtle but powerful mix of salt cod, chives, avocado and Cayenne pepper). Continue with a colombo de porc (spicy pork stew) or a baccalaou (salt cod sautéed in a marinade of onions, pepper, chilli and tomatoes), and finish smoothly with the rum-flavoured crêpes Caraïbes (Caribbean crêpes), invented right here.

Open: Mon-Fri noon-2.15pm, Mon-Sat 7pm-10.30pm; reservations advisable

starter: 55FF-75FF
main: 85FF-115FF
dessert: 40FF-68FF
Set menu: 90FF and 140FF (lunch), 99FF, 155FF, 185FF (lunch & dinner)
Plat du jour: 70FF

AE CB DC EC JCB MC V

Opus lounge
Modern French

☎ **01 40 29 44 04**
5, rue Elzévir, Marais

Map: 3 H6

Métro: Saint Paul, Chemin Vert

Entertainment: Music Tues, Fri-Sun nights

  Nonsmoking tables available

The old Le Détour is now called the Opus, though the change is in name only. This restaurant-bar has stuck to a recipe that keeps customers coming back for more. Speaking of recipes, everything here – the menu, the French and international wines, the music, the atmosphere – seems to blend together beautifully. The décor combines minimalist and Baroque elements with a trace of North African influence – including soft lighting and red velvet seats. There are all sorts of reasons for going to the Opus: an afternoon drink or Sunday brunch, Friday night dancing to Latin rhythms, or the crevettes à la noix de coco et légumes sautés (shrimps with coconut and sautéed vegetables) and the exquisite aiguillettes de canard au curry rouge (duck in red curry).

Open: Tues-Sat 2pm-2am, Sun noon-2am; reservations advisable

starter: 40FF-45FF
main: 80FF-90FF
dessert: 35FF-40FF
Set menus: 100FF, 125FF, 155FF

MC V

Map: 3 F2
Métro: Étienne Marcel,
Rambuteau

Nonsmoking tables
available

Le Quincampe
Moroccan

☎ 01 40 27 01 45
**78, rue Quincampoix,
Beaubourg**

Minutes from the Centre Beaubourg, the Quincampe is one of those restaurants where the décor is as impressive as the cuisine. The entrance (reserved for nonsmokers) is a bit nondescript, but leads into a spacious, softly lit room, where exposed beams, white stone walls, comfortable worn-leather armchairs and kitsch sofas create a contemporary but deliciously cosy ambience. The chef hails from the other side of the Mediterranean and offers high quality Franco-Moroccan specialities in which orange blossom is an omnipresent ingredient. Enjoy the tajines au poulet, the keftas (meatballs) or the simultaneously crunchy and creamy pastilla aux blancs de poulet parfumés au curry (puff-pastry tart filled with curried chicken breast): the contents are as delicious as the container!

starter: 40FF-62FF
main: 52FF-90FF
dessert: 30FF-38FF
Set menu: 79FF (2 courses), 95FF (lunch only: three courses)
CB V

Open: Mon-Fri noon-2.30pm, Mon-Sat 7pm-11pm; reservations essential

Map: 3 F6
Métro: Filles du calvaire

Smoking throughout

Le Réconfort
French

☎ 01 42 76 06 36
**37, rue de Poitou,
Marais**

Le Réconfort opened seven years ago in the heart of the Marais, near to the Musée Picasso. Recently expanded to accomodate a growing clientele, it's still an intimate place. The ambience is wonderfully peaceful and the inventive French cuisine will make your mouth water. Starters include home-made foie gras, terrine de foie de volaille (chicken liver) or champignons rôtis au chèvre (roasted mushrooms with goat's cheese). For mains, check out morue caramélisée au vinaigre balsamique (caramelised cod), pastillade d'agneau au chévre (lamb), or filet mignon de porc aux senteurs de Garrigue (pork with wild herbs). Just when you're thinking it can't get any better, out come the desserts – crumble á la compote de vieux garçon (stewed fruit crumble), tian au miel et à l'orange (baked orange and honey) or glace au gingembre (ginger ice cream). The friendly atmosphere and quality cuisine all justify the restaurant's name, which means 'comfort'.

starter: 36FF-62FF
main: 82FF-105FF
dessert: 38FF-42FF
Set menu: 72FF, 92FF (lunch)
Plat du jour: 62FF
AE CB V

Open: Mon-Sat noon-2pm & 8pm-11pm; reservations advisable

Robert et Louise
French

☎ 01 42 78 55 89
64, rue Vieille-du-Temple, Marais

Map: 3 H6

Métro: Saint-Sébastien-Froissart, Filles-du-Calvaire

 Smoking throughout

This country inn from another era seems out of place in such a sophisticated neighbourhood. It's a dark den with a glowing hearth, carefully tended by Robert's stooped silhouette. Regulars come here for the excellent red meat, char-grilled on a lop-sided grill, accompanied by potatoes sautéed with garlic. Though he might seem absent-minded, Robert keeps a close eye on the cooking of his beloved cuts: côtes de bœuf, entrecôtes et contre-filets (rib of beef, ribsteak, sirloin steak) ... And the attentive Louise serves them up sizzling and just how you like them. If you arrive early you can choose the farmhouse table, right next to the fireplace with its mouthwatering smells. Everyone passes bottles around, and spirits rise as the levels drop. This is what Rabelaisian means.

starter: 25FF-125FF
main: 70FF-120FF
dessert: 25FF

cash only

Open: Mon-Sat noon-2pm, 7pm-10pm; reservations advisable (evenings)

Bars & Cafes – 3e

L'apparement Café 18, rue des Coutures Saint-Germain, Paris 3e, Marais
☎ 01 48 87 12 22 Métro: Filles-du-Calvaire (Map 3 G7)

Nestled behind the musée Picasso, at a merciful distance from the 'shopping highways' that rue des Francs-Bourgeois and nearby streets have become, this oasis of peace looks like a private living room. Not a single lapse of taste mars the studied untidiness: wood panelling, the odd banquette, parlour games here and there, dog-eared books (but not too dog-eared) and cool service (but not too cool).

Open: Mon-Fri noon-2am, Sat 4pm-2am, Sun 12.30pm-midnight; By the glass: beer 25FF, champagne 55FF; coffee 13FF; meals and snacks available; CB EC MC V

L'Attirail 9, rue au Maire, Paris 3e, Arts et Métiers ☎ 01 42 72 44 42 Métro: Arts et Métiers (Map: 3 D5)

With its famously cheap pots and free concerts almost every day (Gypsy rap, hard rock, Italian pop), this North African enclave in the heart of Chinatown attracts a large crowd of poor students. At an amazing formica bar, which snakes its way down one side of a long room covered with posters, manic but friendly customers are served by placid staff. A great, cheap spot to have fun.

Open: daily 10.30am-1.30am; By the glass: beer 12FF-17FF; coffee 6FF-7F; meals and snacks available; live concerts, plays; CB DC EC MC V

Le Bar á thym 182, rue Saint-Martin, Paris 3e, Beaubourg ☎ 01 40 27 89 33 Métro: Rambuteau, Étienne Marcel (Map: 3 E3)

This bar is fairly quiet during the day and has a spacious lounge with cool tones: the perfect spot for a breather after that shopping spree at the Halles or a marathon visit to the Centre Pompidou ... At night, local party types take over the dance floor. If you're peckish, try the savoury tarts, daily specials and fondant au chocolat. There are DJs and plays in the evening.

Open: Mon-Fri 11am-2am, Sat 6pm-2am; By the glass: beer 15FF, champagne 40FF; coffee 10FF; meals and snacks available; plays peformed Wed, DJs Fri & Sat; credit cards accepted

Le dépôt 10, rue aux Ours, Paris 3e, Sentier ☎ 01 44 54 96 96 Métro: Rambuteau, Étienne Marcel (Map: 3 E2)

When the gay Chinese film maker Liu Lingjian arrived in Paris he knew one word of French: 'Dépôt'! There is no question that it's *the* in gay meeting place. Each day hundreds of clients visit the bar, the disco and the backrooms. What can you say, except that this huge, anonymous establishment attracts all sorts of guys. Don't forget your condoms.

Open: daily 2pm-8am; By the glass: beer 20FF, champagne 50FF; gay tea dance every Sunday afternoon; CB, V

Le duplex 25, rue Michel Le Comte, Paris 3e, Haut Marais ☎ 01 42 72 80 86 Métro: Rambuteau, Arts et Métiers (Map: 3 F4)

A place in a category of its own: the music is eclectic, ranging from pop (The Eels) to dub (Massive Attack). The atmosphere is intellectual and arty, with exhibitions and a groovy laid-back clientele. There's a pleasantly languid and melancholy feel to it all. Open extra late on the weekend.

Open: Sun-Thurs 8pm-2am, Fri-Sat 8pm-4am; By the glass: beer 15FF (22FF after 10pm); coffee 6FF (10FF after 10pm); CB, V

One Way 28, rue Charlot, Paris 3e, Marais-rue de Bretagne ☎ 01 48 87 46 10 Métro: Filles du Calvaire (Map: 3 F7)

This long-established gay bar is frequented mainly by 'bears' – so called for their stout build – and others over 40. Not much time is wasted in subtle preliminaries here. The collection of caps hanging from the exposed beams will give you a clue: plenty of these guys are into leather.

Open: daily 5pm-2am; By the glass: beer 18FF; CB, V

L'Orange Café 10, rue des Haudriettes, Paris 3e, Marais ☎ 01 40 29 96 82 Métro: Rambuteau, Arts et Métiers (Map: 3 F5)

L'Orange Café offers a friendly atmosphere and frugal but vitamin-rich breakfasts from the crack of dawn (hence the name). A great idea in this shopping district, where local traders start the day here, come back for lunch and then return again after work to carry on unfinished conversations over an evening aperitif. The bar only closes when everyone has gone home to bed.

Open: Mon-Fri 7.30am-midnigh;, By the glass: beer 10FF-16FF, champagne 28FF; coffee 6FF; snacks available at lunchtime; CB V

The Quiet Man 5, rue des Haudriettes, Paris 3e, Rambuteau ☎ 01 48 04 02 77 Métro: Rambuteau (Map: 6 F5)

Finally, a real Irish pub, run by a real Irishman, with real Irish music. There's live traditional music in the basement every night, and the owner occasionally joins the band for a jam. On some nights, the customers even dance to the strains of the violin or the uilleann pipes.

Open: Sun-Thurs 5pm-2am, Fri & Sat 4pm-2am, By the glass: beer 14FF; coffee 8FF; snacks available; live Irish music every night; credit cards accepted

L'Utopia Bar 15, rue Michel-Le-Comte, Paris 3e, Marais ☎ 01 42 71 63 43 Métro: Rambuteau, Hôtel de Ville (Map 3 F4)

This playful, friendly women's bar has entertainment on most nights and for all tastes: theme nights, tarot, piano bar, karaoke, comedy or music acts, billiards and techno dance music. A great spot for jilted lovers, passing travellers in search of a wild night out or country girls staying in the big smoke. A fun, gay-friendly atmosphere is guaranteed.

Open: Mon-Sat 5pm-2am, By the glass: beer 18FF-20FF, champagne 40FF; coffee 10FF; meals and snacks available; web-bar; various entertainment

Web Bar 32, rue de Picardie, Paris 3e, République ☎ 01 42 72 66 55 Métro: République (Map: 3 D7)

Not far from the République, this bar was one of the capital's first cybercafés. A monthly program available at the door or from the bar's Web site lists an almost nonstop series of events. Entertainment isn't limited to cyberculture and includes film screenings (live concerts broadcast on a huge screen), storytelling and exhibitions of young artists. The atmosphere on some nights makes you totally forget the Web Bar's association with new technology.

Open: Mon-Fri 8.30am-2am, Sat & Sun 11am-2am; By the glass: beer 17FF, champagne 50FF; coffee 9FF; meals and snacks available; web-bar; various entertainment; credit cards accepted

3e ARRONDISSEMENT

Map: 3 G6

Métro: Saint Sébastien Froissart, Filles du Calvaire

Smoking throughout

La Rose des Sables

Moroccan

☎ 01 42 71 28 20
105, rue Vieille-du-Temple, Marais

Strolling along beside the garden of the Musée Picasso, you might not notice the wooden front of this tiny restaurant. It relies on word of mouth to get the clients in, and in they come, as you can see from the signed photographs of gourmet celebrities proudly displayed on the walls. You'll find all the classic dishes, prepared with loving care: the couscous, made with fine, light semolina, contains plenty of vegetables; the tajines (stews), served bubbling hot, give off aromas of cumin, saffron, white pepper and cinnamon. From the lunch menu, we recommend the tajine kefta aux œufs (spicy minced lamb tajine with eggs), cooked on a bed of finely sliced potatoes with cumin. The friendly service, the stucco and mosaic decor, and the traditional family cooking give you a good idea of Moroccan hospitality.

starter: 30FF-95FF
main: 80FF-120FF
dessert: 28FF-45FF
Set menu: 75FF (lunch)

CB MC V

Open: Mon-Fri 11.30am-2.30pm, Mon-Sat 7.30pm-11pm; reservations advisable

---

Map: 3 E4

Métro: Arts et Métiers, Rambuteau

Smoking throughout

LE TAXI JAUNE

French

☎ 01 42 76 00 40
13, rue Chapon, Arts et Métiers

A coat of yellow paint has given this huge old bistrot a bright new look. Artworks on the walls pay homage to New York's yellow cabs and draw on the advertising posters of the '50s. The owner is always ready with a smile and a joke. When the rest of the team aren't busy at the stove, you'll find them shelling peas at a table. It's a pleasure to drop in at any time of the day, for morning coffee, a glass of splendid Gaillac wine at the bar, or to sample the tasty, home-style cooking: saumon cru aux herbes (raw salmon with herbs), un magret de canard au sel (salted duck breast) or steak de thon au fumet de crustacés (tuna steak with seafood stock). We enjoyed the fricassée de pintade aux poires accompagnée de ses petits légumes de saison (guinea-fowl fricassé with pears and seasonal vegetables); the sweetness of the fruit brings out the other flavours.

starter: 30FF-68FF
main: 78FF-92FF
dessert: 30FF
Set menu: 84FF (lunch)
Plat du jour: 58FF (lunch)

CB DC EC MC V

Open: Mon-Fri 8.30am-2am; reservations advisable

4ᵉ Arrondissement

Hôtel de Ville

Île Saint-Louis

Marais

Bastille

4ᵉ Arrondissement

Centuries of history are inscribed on the façades and pediments of the fourth arrondissement. Narrow streets and alleys, porches and courtyards, art galleries and mansions abound, notwithstanding the recent influx of clothing shops. The short walk from Beaubourg to the place des Vosges is intoxicating at night. The historic Jewish quarter – starting in rue des Rosiers, then continuing along rue Sainte-Croix-de-la-Bretonnerie to rue du Temple – is now home to the capital's gay community. Re-entering the urban bustle as rue Saint-Antoine becomes rue de Rivoli, the small, dark streets of the Marais seem like a distant memory. But you only have to cross the street, at rue Saint-Paul or rue du Pont-Louis-Philippe, to experience something of the bourgeois but bohemian tranquillity of the Marais of the past. A bridge takes you across to Île Saint-Louis, peaceful during the day and in winter, overrun by tourists during the evening and in summer.

L'Alivi
Corsican

☎ 01 48 87 90 20
27, rue du Roi-de-Sicile, Marais

Map: 4 E6

Métro: Hôtel de Ville, St-Paul

 Pavement tables in summer

Nestled in a neighbourhood where celebrating is a serious pastime, the Alivi ('olive tree' in Corsican) deserves its fashionable status. Customers flock to this friendly restaurant, especially in the evening, for a taste of the flavoursome cuisine of the island. The ingredients are fresh and refined: the duo de sanglier (wild boar), cooked to perfection, is rivalled only by the cabri rôti (roast kid). Try these dishes with a Leccia wine to fully experience the pleasures of the 'île de beauté' (the 'beautiful isle', a phrase that appears on numerous Corsican 'vins de pays'). Brocciu cheese, charcuterie and basil feature strongly on the menu, which also offers the adventures of Asterix and Obelix in regional dialect. The guest book attached to the menu is somewhat irritating, but the surroundings and service are most enjoyable. A sunny place to start an adventure, or a haven to spend a vaguely melancholy evening.

Open: daily noon-2.30pm, 7pm-11.30pm; reservations essential (evenings, later in the week)

starter: 48FF-89FF
main: 86FF-132FF
dessert: 49FF-62FF
Set menu: 95FF (lunch on weekdays), 128FF

AE CB EC MC V; €

Amadéo
French

☎ 01 48 87 01 02
19, rue François Miron, Saint-Paul

Map: 4 E5

Métro: St-Paul

Entertainment: Opera night once a month

 Smoking throughout

Amadéo is still one of the best restaurants in the Marais. Claudio and Rémy have established a faithful clientele among lovers of opera, fine food and fun. The monthly opera performances are ingeniously staged and feature singers of exceptional talent. Although the chef changes his menu from season to season, it's always good. His assured, creative cuisine includes a fresh sardine and tomato tart with pesto sauce that is simply scrumptious. The pan-fried magret de canard with sweet spices and figs roastedwith vanilla is a delicious blend of flavours. For dessert, words can't do justice to the symphonie de chocolat et d'amareno aux groseilles givrées (chocolate and amareno symphony with frosted currants): you just have to try it. This irresistible restaurant will have you coming back for more.

Open: Tues-Fri noon-2pm, 8pm-11pm, Sat 8pm-11pm; reservations advisable

starter: 55FF
main: 105FF
dessert: 45FF
Set menu: 75FF, 95FF (lunch), 185FF (dinner)

CB EC MC V

4ᵉ ARRONDISSEMENT

Map: 4 C6
Métro: Hôtel de Ville

Smoking throughout

Au Gamin de Paris
French

☎ 01 42 78 97 24
51, rue Vieille-du-Temple, Marais

This old brasserie in the heart of gay Marais is a pleasant find for those exploring Paris on foot. It gives you an idea of what the neighbourhood used to be like. The dark walls are decorated with faded garlands and the high ceiling is rib-vaulted. The candles on the tables and the huge fireplace give the place a vaguely gothic feel. The produce is fresh and of high quality, but what they do with it is rather basic. The lads, however, provide prompt service. There's a broad range of meat and fish dishes to choose from, all accompanied with potatoes. The starters are a bit more adventurous, like the crottin de chévre et sa marmelade de figues (goat's cheese with fig marmalade), or the feuille de brick à l'ouef et à la menthe fraîche (Tunisian pancake with an egg and fresh mint). For dessert, try the little home-made tarts displayed on the counter.

starter: 30FF-115FF
main: 65FF-115FF
dessert: 20FF-42FF
Plat du jour: 60FF (lunch during the week)

V

Open: daily 8am-1am; reservations accepted

Map: 4 B3
Métro: Châtelet-Les Halles

Smoking throughout

Au Pied de Chameau
Moroccan

☎ 01 42 78 35 00
20, rue Quincampoix, Les Halles

Once you've crossed the threshold of this enchanting restaurant in the heart of the Les Halles, it's easy to imagine yourself in the middle of the Sahara. The walls are draped with a huge, beautiful tent, while oriental furniture and ornaments complete the artistic interior. The subtle dishes of traditional Moroccan cuisine include succulent, generous serves of couscous (chicken, lamb, merguez, kebab), tajines and other grills, served with a fine red wine from Fez. To follow, there's peppermint tea with pine nuts and various sweetmeats, including chunky, sweet Turkish delight. An evening at Au Pied de Chameau resembles an oriental banquet: the Arabian Nights décor, delicious food and impeccable service make for a special experience.

starter: 50FF-60FF
main: 95FF-145FF
dessert: 50FF
Set menu: 250FF

AE CB V

Open: daily 11am-2am; reservations advisable

4ᵉ arrondi

Auberge de Jarente

French (South-West)

☎ 01 42 77 49 35
**7, rue de Jarente,
Marais**

Map: 4 E7

Métro: St-Paul, Bastille

 Nonsmoking tables available

 Pavement tables in summer

This rustic inn was established 36 years ago by a family from Saint-Palais, on the border of the Béarn and Basque regions. The son has been at the helm for six years now, serving good family-style dishes, all home-made, except for the foie gras. The main attractions in the seafood department are the soupe de poissons (fish soup), chipirons au piment d'Espelette (squid with Espelette peppers) and filets de rougets à la coriandre et à l'ail (mullet fillets with coriander and garlic). If you're more of a landlubber, you can have confit de canard, pleurotes et pommes sautées (duck confit with pleurote mushrooms and sautéed potatoes) or cassoulet. Wines from the South-West are given pride of place: irouleguy, tursan, madiran, to name just a few. To finish, be unfaithful to Basque cuisine and indulge in a chocolate fondant.

starter: 35FF-62FF
main: 72FF-90FF
dessert: 25FF-45FF
Set menu: 78FF (lunch), 135FF, 185FF
Plat du jour: 78FF

CB V

Open: Tues-Sat noon-2.30pm, 7.30pm-10.30pm; reservations advisable

---

Baracane

French (South-West)

☎ 01 42 71 43 33
**38, rue des Tournelles,
Place des Vosges**

Map: 4 E9

Métro: Bastille, Chemin Vert

 Smoking throughout

A small corner of South-West France is friendly without being intrusive, deliciously refined without being inaccessible – welcome to Baracane! This 'bistrot de l'Oulette' has replaced the famous restaurant (now located in the 12e arrondissement) and is run by the same team, who provide service with a smile and a fantastic menu, all within walking distance of the gorgeous place des Vosges. You immediately feel at ease in this slightly noisy place, where provincial produce is elegantly presented with a personal touch. The salade de foies de volaille tièdes (warm poultry liver salad) matched with sherry is an absolute must; the onglet de veau poêlé (pan-fried veal onglet) is seasoned with gentian; the chef's magret de canard (fillet of duck breast) is unimaginably delectable. Film director Étienne Chatiliez was right: *le bonheur est dans le pré* ('happiness is in the field'), in a south-westerly one to be precise.

starter: 46FF-98FF
main: 70FF-120FF
dessert: 40FF-45FF
Set menu: 56FF, 85FF, 148FF, 238FF
Plat du jour: 86FF

CB V

Open: Mon-Sat noon-2.30pm, 7pm-midnight; reservations advisable

Map: 4 E6
Métro: St-Paul

Nonsmoking tables available

Le Bûcheron
Italian

☎ 01 48 87 71 31
9, rue du Roi de Sicile, Marais

As soon as you sit down at one of the little tables, a pot of fresh basil and a pair of scissors will appear before you: season your dishes as you please. A word of warning – the serves in this trattoria are copious, so rather than choosing a starter each, why not share the homemade antipasto: marinated mushrooms, peppers, artichokes and zucchini, plus bread rubbed with garlic. Then you'll be ready to get acquainted with the ricotta ravioli 'mezze lune', drizzled with cream and served with finely sliced mushrooms. As for dessert, tiramisú fans won't be disappointed here. The Sunday brunch is particularly memorable: an Italian-style colazione of marinated vegetables, scrambled eggs, lasagne, charcuterie, tiramisú, crêpes and Champagne!

main: 62FF-75FF
dessert: 35FF
Set menu: 110FF (Sunday brunch)
Plat du jour: 65FF
CB V; €

Open: Mon-Sun noon-3.30pm, Mon-Sat 7pm-10.45pm; reservations advisable

Map: 4 F8
Métro: Bastille

Smoking throughout

Café de la Poste
French

☎ 01 42 72 95 35
13, rue Castex, Saint-Paul

This is a little, old-style bistrot tucked away between the Bastille and the Marais and is popular with locals. Paintings brighten up the simple decor and the atmosphere is both restful and friendly. This is how life should be, with smells of good, simple cooking wafting in from the kitchen. There's not a menu as such, but every day you can choose from three starters, three mains and a pasta. Try the fricassée de saucisson à l'échalote (sausages with shallots), the anchois à l'orientale (Eastern-style anchovies) or the poivrons farcis (stuffed peppers), followed by canard rôti aux airelles (roast duck with berries), petit salé aux lentilles (salt pork with lentils), or succulent lasagnes au potiron de saison (pumpkin lasagna). It's always a pleasure to eat here, and never too expensive – the Café de la Poste delivers.

starter: 22FF-28FF
main: 55FF-69FF
dessert: 23FF-24FF
Plat du jour: 48FF & 56FF
CB MC V

Open: Mon-Fri noon-2pm, 7pm-10.30pm; reservations advisable

Le Chant des Voyelles
French

☎ 01 42 77 77 07
4, rue des Lombards, Beaubourg

Map: 4 C3
Métro: Hôtel de Ville, Rambuteau

 Smoking throughout

 Pavement tables

The Chant des Voyelles sits comfortably on the edge of the Beaubourg neighbourhood. If the somewhat flashy décor and loud music aren't to your taste, take a seat at the terrace, set up all year round in the pedestrian precinct of rue St-Méri and rue des Lombards. Inside, there are three spacious rooms, including two vaulted cellars. The cuisine is varied and the more innovative dishes work well. Tartare lovers will enjoy the *carte des trois tartares* (traditional, Italian-style and 'belle maman', served hot and au gratin), while discerning palates will be sorely tempted by the starter of marbré de foie gras et de chèvre frais (foie gras and fresh goat's cheese marbré). Classic dishes including pasta and pavé de bœuf au poivre (thick-cut steak with pepper sauce) feature alongside a divine chocolate terrine coated in creamy peppermint sauce. The service could do with some fine-tuning, but this is an occasional rather than regular shortcoming.

starter: 28FF-55FF
main: 55FF-95FF (except seafood)
dessert: 35FF
Set menu: 75FF
Plat du jour: 55FF

cash only

Open: daily 11.30am-3pm, 7pm-midnight (winter), 11.30am-midnight (summer); reservations advisable for groups

Le Coude Fou
French

☎ 01 42 77 15 16
12, rue du Bourg-Tibourg, Marais

Map: 4 D5
Métro: Hôtel de Ville

 Smoking throughout

This archetypal Parisian bistrot, warm, friendly and unpretentious, is full of atmosphere and people at all times of the day. At the end of a long, narrow room, past the bar, small tables are surrounded by naive frescoes in the style of early Rousseau. The food might not feature in the Guinness Book of Flavours (if such a book existed), but is scrumptious nonetheless. The tian d'agneau à la niçoise (lamb tian à la niçoise) is redolent of the South, while the pavé de sandre au gewurtzraminer (pike-perch steak with gewurtzraminer wine) melts in your mouth. Don't skimp on the wine: knowledgeable staff will help you select just the right drop. We'd like to be equally positive about the desserts, but unfortunately our fondant au chocolat was utterly tasteless.

starter: 46FF-120FF
main: 89FF-95FF
dessert: 32FF-46FF
Set menu: 100FF, 120FF (lunch), 145FF
Plat du jour: from 88FF

CB V

Open: restaurant: Mon-Sat noon-2.45pm, Sun noon-3pm, daily 7.30pm-midnight; bar: daily 24 hours (closed Sat 4pm-7pm); reservations advisable (evenings)

Map: 4 E9

Métro: Bastille

Nonsmoking tables available

De bouche à oreille
French

☎ 01 44 61 07 02

15, rue des Tournelles, Bastille, Place des Vosges

The well-chosen name of this restaurant translates as 'word of mouth'. It makes you think of the little secrets that friends share, touches that bring grace and harmony to daily life. Everything in the restaurant has been chosen and arranged with a schooled eye. The elegance of the food matches the décor, and the prices are very reasonable. Even the most finicky eaters will be charmed by the bloc de foie gras mi-cuit (semi-cooked), the cassoulet au confit de canard (duck), or the tarte tatin nappée de créme fraîche (fresh cream). Food and décor, it's all so beautifully set out you'll be tempted to buy something as a reminder of the cosy atmosphere. Perhaps a little milk jug picked up in a provincial antique shop – the owner will let you have it for a song.

starter: 55FF
main: 55FF
dessert: 34FF
Set menu: 67FF, 77F (lunch), 125FF (dinner)

CB MC V

Open: Tues-Thurs noon-4pm, Fri & Sat noon-3pm, 7pm-10.30pm, Sun (Oct-Mar) noon-4pm; reservations advisable Fri & Sat

---

Map: 4 E7

Métro: St-Paul

Smoking throughout

L'Épouvantail
French

☎ 01 40 29 03 03

6, rue Jarente, Marais

Armand doesn't know what he's going to write up on the slate menu until Laurence returns from the market with her spoils. She may, for example, make a salad with the artichokes, a soup with the pumpkin and serve the sea bream fillets with olive oil. The owners' friends have left their mark here: their photographs are exhibited on the walls, while their designs adorn the table mats. The menu proclaims 'the potato favours the boldest'. To work out what this cryptic message may mean, it seems you have to let yourself be tempted by the generous cuisine. The free-range chicken, cooked the way your grandma used to do it, is a favourite, and the home-made foie gras pan-fried with figs will have you coming back for more. The fondant au chocolat leaves a lasting impression, and as to the wines, let Armand's fancy be your guide.

starter: 45FF-60FF
main: 75FF-85FF
dessert: 38FF
Set menu: 139FF

CB EC MC V

Open: Mon-Fri 12.30pm-3pm, Tues-Sat 7.30pm-11pm; reservations advisable

Pick of pastries

Attention all chocoholics! The best macaron au chocolat (chocolate macaroon) in town comes from Ladurée, but if it's a princesse (praline-filled chocolate topped with meringue) you're after, get down to Peltier. If you're on a binge, Maison du Chocolat is ready and waiting with éclairs, mokambos (chocolate truffle mousse with raspberries) and togos (chocolate mousse with candied orange). The délice (praline-filled chocolate) at Millet is delicious and the suc-cès (nougatine macaroon) at Lenôtre ... successful, to say the least. You can't go wrong with the forêt noire (black forest cake) from Châtelain, the sachertorte from Stübli and the opéra from Mauduit or Lenôtre. If tarte au chocolat is your poison, try Café Français.

OK, time to talk fruit: the tartes aux pêches de vigne, au citron, aux pommes (wild peach, lemon and apple tarts) from Mulot are in a class of their own and the tartes aux fraises or framboises (strawberry or raspberry tarts) at Malitourne are top-notch. Dominique's makes a mean vatrouchka (cheese-cake with lemon-flavoured cream cheese and raisins) and the Pâtisserie Viennoise still excels at strudel aux pommes (apple strudel). The only place to go for a typically French fraisier (strawberry sponge with Kirsch syrup and but-ter cream) is chez Constant.

The mont blanc (vanilla-flavoured chestnut purée topped with Chantilly cream) is a great classic at chez Angelina, but has also been spotted at Carette's. Châtelain offers a barquette aux marrons (a boat-shaped pastry shell filled with chestnut purée), the macaron à la pistache (pistachio macaroon) is still the corner stone at Ladurée, but make sure you try the macaron au citron (lemon macaroon) at Levain du Marais. Millefeuille lovers won't be disappoint-ed by the offerings at chez Peltier or Constant. One of the most wickedly deli-cious galettes des rois (Twelfth-Night cakes) in Paris is to be had at chez Stohrer.

In the sticky bun category, stick to Fauchon's petit pain à la cannelle (cinna-mon roll), Lerche's kouglof (kugelhopf), Dalloyau's pain aux raisins (escargot) – the Café de Flore buys its cakes from here – Viallard's croissant aux aman-des (almond croissant) and the Flûte Gana's deliciously soft, fragrant brioches.

Angelina 226, rue de Rivoli, 1er; **Café Français** place de la Bastille, 4e; **Carette** 4, place du Trocadéro, 16e; **Châtelain** 203, ave Daumesnil, 12e; **Constant** 37, rue d'Assas, 6e; **Dominique** 19, rue Bréa, 6e; **Fauchon** 26, place de la Madeleine, 9e; **La Flûte Gana** 226, rue des Pyrénées, 20e; **Ladurée** 16, rue Royale, 1er and 75, ave des Champs-Élysées, 8e; **Lenôtre** 61, rue Lecourbe, 15e; **Lerche** 2, rue du Cardinal-Lemoine, 5e; Au Levain du **Marais** 32, rue de Turenne, 3e; **Malitourne** 30, rue de Chaillot, 16e; **La Maison du Chocolat** 19, rue de Sèvres, 6e; **Mauduit** 54, rue du Faubourg-Saint-Denis, 10e; **Millet** 103, rue Saint-Dominique, 7e; **Mulot** 76, rue de Seine, 6e; **La Pâtisserie Viennoise** 8, rue de l'École-de-Médecine, 6e; **Peltier** 66, rue de Sèvres, 7e; **Stohrer** 51, rue Montorgueil, 2e; **Stübli** 11, rue Poncelet, 17e; **Viallard** 23, rue du Rendez-Vous, 12e

Map: 4 B5
Métro: Rambuteau,
Hôtel de Ville

Smoking throughout

Le Felteu
French

☎ 01 42 72 14 51
**15, rue Pecquay,
Rambuteau**

For over 30 years, Marinette ran this bougnat in the heart of the Marais. (The bougnats used to be coal merchants' shops with small cafés.) These days the easy-going locals, who come for their fill of traditional French food, are charmed by the southern accent and sunny good humour of Marinette's successor. On a seat upholstered in the original moleskin, surrounded by dishes that conjure up France's finest gastronomic regions, you can tuck into the andouillette de chez Duval (pork sausage) or the enormous and memorable boudin aux deux pommes (two-apple sausage). The starters vary with the season: fricassée de champignons (mushroom), steaming potage de légumes (thick vegetable soup), harengs pommes á l'huile (herrings with potatoes and olive oil) or museau en salade (pork brawn salad). Each week the likeable and talkative owner selects wines from the South-East or South-West to complement the plat du jour. You'll leave perfectly satisfied without having emptied your wallet.

starter: 30FF-45FF
main: 65FF-85FF
dessert: 18FF-22FF
Set menu: 80FF
Plat du jour: 65FF

€ (by cheque)

Open: Mon-Sat noon-2.30pm & 7.30pm-10.30pm; reservations advisable Fri-Sat

Map: 4 D5
Métro: St-Paul

Smoking throughout

Courtyard tables

Le Fond de cour
French

☎ 01 42 74 71 54
**3, rue Sainte-Croix
de la Bretonnerie,
Marais**

The Fond de cour fronts on to a courtyard where you can eat in spring and summer. The rest of the year you have the choice of the glassed-in porch, the inside room or the cellar with its stone walls. The cuisine is classic French, but with creative touches. For starters, there's excellent home-made foie gras, escargots au beurre d'ail, salade gourmande and cassolette de poissons au safran (fish casserole with saffron). Follow up with faux-filet grillé sauce béarnaise (sirloin steak), steak de thon au pistou (tuna steak with pesto), or marmite de lapereau aux herbes (young rabbit stew with herbs). Finish off with a crème brûlée á la vanille Bourbon (caramelised custard with Bourbon vanilla) or profiteroles au chocolat. The ample wine list is well suited to the sophisticated cuisine of this welcoming and highly recommended restaurant.

starter: 75FF-85FF
main: 85FF-120FF
dessert: 50FF
Set menu: 170FF

AE CB V

Open: Mon-Sat 11am-2pm; reservations advisable

Galerie 88
French

☎ 01 42 72 17 58
**88, quai de l'Hôtel de Ville,
Hôtel de Ville**

Map: 4 E4

Métro: Hôtel de Ville

 Smoking throughout

 Pavement tables

Exposed beams, walls decorated with earthen-ware – including a superb antique from northern Pakistan – and comfortable bench seats all contribute to the atmosphere of this small restaurant that faces the Seine, a stone's throw from the Hôtel de Ville. The unpretentious, handwritten menu offers fresh ingredients at affordable prices. Several multiflavoured dishes, including the delicious Assiette 88 (tabbouleh, tapenade, guacomole, eggplant caviar, tomato, capsicum and cucumber), attract a loyal clientele. For those who enjoy the simple pleasures of pasta, the gnocchis aux trois fromages (gnocchi with three cheeses) and the tagliatelles à la sauce tomate maison (tagliatelle with the chef's tomato sauce) are invariably good. Try the fromage blanc au miel, raisins secs et amandes (cream cheese with honey, raisins and almonds) and the tarte amandine-poire (almond-pear tart) – both fortifying desserts – before the arrival of the very reasonable bill and peppermint tea.

starter: 25FF
main: 40FF-80FF
dessert: 25FF

cash only

Open: daily 10am-2am; reservations advisable (especially evenings)

Grand Appétit
Macrobiotic/vegan/vegetarian

☎ 01 40 27 04 95
**9, rue de la Cerisaie,
Bastille**

Map 4 G9

Métro: Bastille, Sully Morland

Lovers of high-energy health food, here's your chance to discover the benefits of macrobiotics. Set back from the Bastille, in a small, quiet street, Le Grand Appétit offers light fare such as miso soup and cereals as well as strength-building food (for big eaters only!). Find a table, then order at the bar. The menu is on a big blackboard and features delicious, filling dishes served with cereals, raw and cooked vegetables and seaweed. Not to be outshone, the desserts include a superb crème de noisette (hazelnut cream). The ingredients are 100% organic and cooked in filtered water, while the herbal tea of the day is available in unlimited quantities from a Thermos in the middle of the room. An added bonus: free advice on the most appropriate food for your body's needs. Adventurous diners make haste!

starter: 20FF-40FF
main: 30FF-60FF
dessert: 20FF-25FF
Set menu: 55FF-90FF
Plat du jour: 60FF

CB JCB V

Open: Mon-Thurs noon-3pm, Fri noon-2pm; reservations not accepted

4e ARRONDISSEMENT

Map: 4 G5
Métro: Pont Marie

Smoking throughout

Isami
Japanese

☎ 01 40 46 06 97
4, quai d'Orléans,
Ile Saint-Louis

Well known among lovers of Japanese food, Isami has recently made a name for itself as one of the capital's best and most affordable sushi bars. Japanese customers flock to this tiny, frequently packed restaurant – a sure sign of quality. Behind the bar, the somewhat sullen chef prepares impeccably fresh sushi and sashimi. Try the joh sushi moriawase, a comprehensive assortment of raw fish and seafood served with rice. Among the starters, each one as good as the next, the chawanmushi, ikura-oroshi and ika-natto are authentic Japanese specialities with atypical flavours. Gorgeous delicacies made with sea urchins and eels are especially popular.

starter: 30FF-150FF
main: 110FF-180FF
dessert: 20FF-50FF
Set menu: 110FF-180FF

CB EC MC V

Open: Tues-Sat noon-2pm, Tues-Sun 7pm-10pm; reservations advisable

Map: 4 E6
Métro: St-Paul

Smoking throughout

Pavement tables

Karine
French

☎ 01 42 72 14 16
16, rue Charlemagne,
Saint-Paul

Far from the fashions and finery of the Marais, but an integral part of the neighbourhood nonetheless, Karine and Laurent welcome you to their small family bistrot with a smile and without fuss. The menu offers traditional starters such as œufs mayonnaise and tomatoes with mozzarella, but fearless customers will go for the fromage de tête polonais. For mains, there's a choice between confit de poule (confit of chicken), jarret sur choucroute (knuckle with sauerkraut), bavette à l'échalotte (skirt steak with shallots) or a salade de tomates farcies au chèvre et gésiers confits (salad of stuffed tomatoes with goat's cheese and preserved gizzards), an original and successful combination of flavours. If you're still hungry, finish up with the delicious marquise au chocolat. A great local restaurant with extremely reasonable prices.

main: 52FF
Set menu: 69FF
Plat du jour: 52FF
cash only

Open: Mon-Fri 8am-midnight, Sat 8am-3pm; reservations not accepted

Le Piano dans la cuisine
French

☎ 01 42 72 23 81
**20, rue de la Verrerie,
Marais**

Map: 4 D4

Métro: Hôtel de Ville

Entertainment: singing
transvestites

 Smoking throughout

Like the name says, the piano is in the kitchen.
The kitchen produces simple food, and, as
you'll see, the piano is equally down to earth.
Choose from various salads, a soup or a terrine
for starters, then dorade (red sea bream), bar
(sea bass) or aloyau (sirloin of beef), to fill in
the time. But when the eating's over, you can
forget all about taste – the show that follows is
completely over the top. Transvestites dressed
to kill give spirited renditions of risqué songs by
Jacques Lantier and Colette Bernard, while
Mireille Mathieu and Nana Mouskouri are
subjected to unspeakable affronts. Naturally
the audience is invited to participate, and with
a bit of luck, it works. The programme changes
every month, but the prices remain very reasonable.

Open: until 10.30pm nightly; reservations essential

Set menu: 199FF; Sat &
public holidays (including
night before): 249FF

cash only

The Studio
Tex-Mex

☎ 01 42 74 10 38
**41, rue du Temple,
Marais**

Map: 4 C4

Métro: Hôtel de Ville

 Smoking throughout

 Courtyard tables in
summer

The Studio opens onto a listed 17th-century
courtyard, right next to the Café de la Gare and
the alluring Conservatory of Dance. There's no
denying that the surroundings and the local set
make this place what it is. Rather than being
an end in itself, the cuisine provides a pretext
to linger: one of the many cocktails, perhaps,
or desserts like the Black Joe (chocolate cake
with vanilla ice cream and coffee liqueur) and
the Capricho (cinnamon ice cream with wheat
crisps and almonds). The rest of the menu is
mostly Tex-Mex: nachos, tapas and chilli. The
weekend menu also includes three wholesome
brunches, a good option for avoiding the week-
night crush. There are sunny courtyard tables in
summer, if you still need a reason for coming.

Open: café: Mon 6pm-1.30am, Tues-Sun 12.30pm-1.30am;
reservations not accepted

main: 75FF-99FF
dessert: 36FF-48FF

AE CB EC MC V

Bars & Cafes – 4e

Alcantara Café 30, rue du Roi de Sicile, Paris 4e, Marais ☎ 01 42 74 45 00
Métro: St-Paul, Hôtel de Ville (Map: 4 E6)

This cosy place – perfect for a first date or a gas with the gals – has a reputation
for attracting a feminine crowd who would never have frequented such an establishment in the past. Let yourself go to the strains of Saturday night techno and,
occasionally, to the schmaltzy flights of Whitney Houston at happy hour.

**Open: 5pm-2am; By the glass: beer 18FF, champagne 45FF; live DJ (weekends);
CB V**

Amnésia 42, rue Vieille-du-temple, Paris 4e, Marais ☎ 01 42 72 16 94 Métro:
Hôtel de Ville, Saint-Paul (Map: 4 D6)

This cosy bar in the heart of the Marais is the perfect spot for an afternoon rendezvous. The clientele tends to be somewhat earnest and 'well bred'. Since opening a basement nightclub on weekends: the packed dance floor is the price of success. Pity about the '80s music.

**Open: daily 10.30am-2am; By the glass: beer 18FF (after 10pm 23FF), champagne
45FF (after 10pm 50FF); coffee 12FF; snacks (noon-4pm) and meals available;
CB V**

Cox 15, rue des Archives, Paris 4e, Marais ☎ 01 42 72 08 00 Métro: Hôtel de
Ville (Map: 4 C5)

This is body-builder territory. At night though, the proteinpackers lighten up and the
atmosphere is quite laid-back. The crowd spills out onto the footpath and gets
drunk on beer. The noise level is low and, if you can put up with the awful nonstop
dance music, you just might have a good time.

Open: daily 2pm-2am; By the glass: beer 18FF; coffee 10FF; cash only

L'Imprévu café 9, rue Quincampoix, Paris 4e, Beaubourg ☎ 01 42 78 23 50
Métro: Châtelet (Map: 4 C3)

Be prepared to travel in this roomy bar. There's a main room with a starry, vaulted
ceiling, which gives onto three smaller rooms, one of which is smoke-free.
Couches, armchairs, barber's chairs, leopard-skin seats – all begging to be sat in.
Choose from 24 cocktails, divided into five types, from weak to strong

Open: 11am-2am; By the glass: beer 17FF, champagne 40FF; cash only

Les Marronniers 18, rue des Archives, Paris 4e, Marais ☎ 01 40 27 87 72
Métro: Hôtel de Ville (Map: 4 D4)

Gay and straight customers mix happily at this local institution behind the Bazar de
l'Hôtel de Ville. A spacious terrace becomes home to people of leisure in spring.
Inside, two floors with 1950s-style tables, leather easy chairs and bizarre, spider-
shaped lamps offer a quiet, cosy setting for a drink or a bite to eat.

**Open: daily, 8am-2am; By the glass: beer 20FF, champagne 38FF; coffee 12FF;
meals and snacks available; live DJs; credit cards accepted**

Le Loir dans la théière 3, rue des Rosiers, Paris 4e, Marais ☎ 01 42 72 90
61 Métro: St-Paul (Map: 4 F5)

This salon de thé in rue des Rosiers is a divine spot for a weekend brunch. The
atmosphere is intimate and cosy and the big leather armchairs quickly get
snapped up. Try tartines, jam and savoury tarts or a delectable slice of cake.

**Open: Mon-Fri 11.30am-7pm, Sat & Sun 10am-7pm; coffee 12FF; meals available,
CB EC MC V**

Le Vieux Paris 72, rue de la Verrerie Paris 4e, Châtelet, Métro: Châtelet
(Map: 4 C3)

The old Paris of the classic movies lives on in this bar: yellow formica and brown leatherette, draught beer, accordion music, and tunes like they don't write 'em any-more. Drinking songs or dancehall standards, La Vie en Rose or Java bleue – it doesn't matter if you don't know the words, Madame Simone will give you a sheet with the words.

Open: Tues-Sat 11pm-dawn; By the glass: beer 20FF; accordion and singing; cash only

Okawa 40, rue Vieille-du-temple, Paris 4e, Marais ☎ 01 48 04 30 69 Métro: Hôtel de Ville, Saint-Paul (Map: 4 D6)

A bar where you can chat to your neighbour without scaring him off. The atmos-phere is friendly and girls are welcome. The flirting isn't heavy, drinks are half-price at happy hour (6pm-9pm) and you can have a laugh with Kiki, the waiter. Only one flat note: the music. Alysée fans will love it, but as for others...

Open: daily: noon-2am; By the glass: beer 16FF; meals and snacks available; credit cards accepted

Le Pick Clops 16, rue Vieille-du-Temple, Paris 4e, Marais ☎ 01 40 29 02 18 Métro: Hôtel de Ville (Map: 4 D5)

Le Pick Clops is blue on the outside, red on the inside and sports large picture windows that open out onto the street. This former bistrot has been revamped, but the original bar (running the full length of the room), formica cupboards and floor tiles have been preserved. The setting remains unpretentious. The clientele, which includes both regulars and passing trade, is hip but friendly.

Open: daily 8am-2am; By the glass: beer 19FF; coffee 12FF; snacks available; credit cards accepted

Le Quetzal 10, rue de la Verrerie, Paris 4e, Marais ☎ 01 48 87 99 07 Métro: Hôtel de Ville (Map: 4 D5)

This dark bar, one of the city's old gay haunts, gets very crowded after 2am and stays that way until ... very late. Watch out; the madcap atmosphere can quickly turn dodgy. On good nights (Friday), the Quetzal is great fun and you can actually strike up a spontaneous conversation. No posing allowed.

Open: Mon-Fri 1pm-4am, Sat & Sun 2pm-5am; By the glass: beer 18FF, cham-pagne 35FF; coffee 10FF; web-bar 1pm-8pm; credit cards accepted

Les Scandaleuses 8, rue des Écouffes, Paris 4e, Marais ☎ 01 48 87 39 26 Métro: St-Paul, Hôtel de Ville (Map: 4 D6)

Try and pick which girls have that sweet smell of scandal ... Barmaids keep a watchful but convivial eye on the rolling clientele and select music to fit the moment: intimate, voluble or more mischievous towards the end of the night. The atmosphere is relaxed and tattoos adorn – um, the wall – not the girls!

Open: daily 6pm-2am; By the glass: beer 23FF, champagne 40FF; coffee 13FF; theme nights, live music; CB V

Le Thermik 7, rue de la Verrerie, Paris 4e, Marais ☎ 01 44 78 08 18 Métro: Hôtel de Ville (Map: 4 D5)

During the week, only a handful of regulars frequent this bar,so it can be a bit depressing. Try the weekend instead, when the overheated basement is packed with people dancing to the type of music that Le Thermik has long promoted: '70s and '80s pop, Sheila, Sardou, Desireless ... Love it or hate it, the atmosphere is great. Upstairs, people chat and laugh.

Open: daily 5pm-2am; By the glass: beer 17FF, champagne 29FF; live DJ, dancing, games; cash only

4ᵉ ARRONDISSEMENT

Map: 4 B5
Métro: Rambuteau
Entertainment: exhibitions of photography & other art forms

Smoking throughout

main: 46FF (lunch), 55FF (dinner)
dessert: 18FF
Set menu: 82FF
Plat du jour: 46FF
CB EC MC V

Le Tapis franc
French

☎ 01 44 59 86 72
12, rue Pecquay, Marais

If Tapis Franc were a *tapis volant* (magic carpet), there'd be plenty of passengers. A stone's throw from the Rambuteau stalls, the locals have taken this place into their hearts. Alain's simple, flavoursome food is embellished with delicate, thoughtful touches. Guarded by the impassive Bernadette, a dining room covered with customers' holiday snaps (some better than others) comes alive to the sound of accordion music and the booming 'et voilààà' that accompanies the arrival of each meal. The tarte au chèvre (goat's cheese tart) has a staunch following both as a starter and as a main course. The menu also offers delicate œufs en meurette (eggs poached in a red wine sauce) and an exquisite magret de canard au miel (fillet of duck breast with honey). If you're cheesed off by chips, you'll love the side serves of potatoes (cut in half and grilled in the oven), braised endives and the chef's ratatouille.

Open: Mon-Fri noon-2pm, Mon-Sat 8pm-11pm; reservations not accepted (lunch), advisable (dinner)

Map: 4 G8
Métro: Bastille, Sully Morland

Smoking throughout

starter: 15FF-30FF
main: 40FF-60FF
dessert: 15FF-30FF
Set menu: 75FF
Plat du jour: 49FF
cash only

Le Temps des cerises
French

☎ 01 42 72 08 63
31, rue de la Cerisaie, Marais

The walls of this typically Parisian bistrot, situated between the Bastille and Marais neighbourhoods, are adorned with photos of Georges Brassens, Raymond Devos and Maxime Le Forestier, all of whom came here at one time or another for a drink or a meal. If the Temps des cerises offers an exceptionally friendly, relaxed atmosphere and impeccable service, it's thanks in no small part to the owner, Gérard Vimard. Customers come here at all times of the day for a coffee, a beer or a glass of one of the many wines (a different vintage is selected every week). The lunch menu features the best of simple, French family cooking: the œufs mayonnaise and the copious lapin en gibelotte (rabbit stewed in wine sauce with bacon, potatoes, mushrooms, garlic, onions and herbs) are outstanding. A great local institution devoted to food, wine and good company.

Open: cafe: Mon-Fri 7.45am-8pm; restaurant: Mon-Fri 11.30am-2.30pm; reservations not accepted

4ᵉ ARRONDISSEMENT

La Tertulia
Venezuelan

☎ 01 42 71 32 55
**4, rue Malher,
Marais**

Map: 4 E7

Métro: Saint-Paul

Entertainment: New exhibition of paintings every month

 Smoking throughout

A wonderful introduction to one of the lesser-known regional varieties of South American cuisine. The arepas (stuffed tortillas) or the salade La Tertulia with watercress and avocado are a must, while the soupe de potiron et de clémentine (pumpkin and clementine soup) or the pabellon con baranda, combining thinly-sliced beef, baked banana and avocado, are perfect examples of the originality of Venezuelan cuisine. Desserts like the green papaya or the quesillo (pineapple tart) are just two of the choices that reflect the excellent menu. La Tertulia not only promotes a neglected cuisine, it also doubles as an art gallery, organising monthly exhibitions of emerging Venezuelan painters. The small number of tables and welcoming atmosphere make this restaurant a perfect culinary and cultural embassy.

Open: Wed & Thurs noon-8pm, Fri &Sat noon-9pm, Sun 1pm-4pm (brunch); reservations advisable

starter: 12FF-38FF
main: 55FF-70FF
dessert: 16FF-28FF
Plat du jour: 38FF
CB V

4ᵉ ARRONDISSEMENT

Map: 4 F8
Métro: St-Paul

Smoking throughout

Vins des Pyrénées
French

☎ 01 42 72 64 94
**25, rue Beautreillis,
Marais**

Vins des Pyrénées is the sort of place you arrange to meet friends or happen to bump into them. Seven years ago it was still a wine cellar, and it has retained its old-style charm – wood panelling, zinc bar and original posters. It's not surprising that a crowd of locals have set up headquarters here. How could you tire of excellent French cuisine? The fish, meat and game are all equally good. The superb foie gras is worth a special mention, as well as the classic but top-notch pavé de rumsteak (thick rump steak). For dessert, treat yourself to a delicious crème brûlée à l'anis (aniseed-flavoured). On top of all this, the wine list offers a wide choice of famous and little-known estate wines. All in all, this place is warmly recommended.

starter: 41FF-81FF
main: 75FF-125FF
dessert: 36FF-50FF
Set menu: 80FF (lunch)
Plat du jour: 60FF

AE CB V

Open: Mon-Sat noon-3pm, 8pm-2am; reservations advisable

5e Arrondissement

Saint-Michel

Panthéon

Contrescarpe

Jussieu

5ᵉ Arrondissement

Home to the capital's most famous university campuses, this eternal student district has challenged prevailing social attitudes throughout history. Each university has its own field of enquiry, its own headquarters. Bookshops and libraries, cafes and restaurants are like annexes to these venerable institutions and are packed at all times of the day. People meet and linger at the terraces spilling out over place Saint-Michel or place de la Sorbonne. In rue de la Harpe, rue Mouffetard, rue de la Huchette or place de la Contrescarpe, restaurant windows display set menus appealing to customers' cravings for Mediterranean or Asian food. Movie buffs flock to rue des Écoles to see cinema classics while activists and sympathisers come together under the same banner at the Mutualité, chanting slogans and fighting the good fight. The Institut du monde arabe offers a glimpse of another continent and the Jardin des plantes, with its tropical greenhouses and its Muséum National d'Histoire Naturelle, opens new horizons in a bucolic, romantic setting.

Amore Mio
Italian

☎ 01 45 35 83 95
13, rue Linné, Jussieu

Italian food lovers will be impressed by the menu at this friendly restaurant. In addition to the classic range of pizzas, there are refined starters and antipasti (a dozen or so), such as the crostinis chauds sur mozzarella et lit d'anchois or the roulés d'aubergine gratinées au jambon de Parme (eggplant roulade). But the real star of theshow is the pasta, including the scupoles Alfredo and the ricottis aux pousses d'épinard (ricotta and baby spinach). A range of meat and fish dishes is also on offer. You'll definitely want dessert, including the panacotti, a crème brûlée with raspberry sauce, and the divine sabayon (zabaione). There is also a wide range of affordable wines. The decor is sophisticated and the staff extremely attentive. The only frustration comes from not being able to sample everything, but you can always come back.

Open: daily 11.30am-2.45pm, 7pm-10.45pm; reservations advisable

Map: 5 F7

Métro: Jussieu

 Nonsmoking tables available

 Pavement tables

starter: 36FF-56FF
main: 48FF-58FF
dessert: 29FF
Set menus: 69FF, 75FF, 85FF

AE V; €

Anahuacalli
Mexican

☎ 01 43 26 10 20
30, rue des Bernardins, Maubert

Mexican cuisine can offer both excellent and awful eating experiences. More often than not, it's the latter, to the point where some gourmets have declared war on this type of food. If there's any possibility of reconciliation, it has to be in the lovely surroundings of Anahuacalli, which translates as 'house by the water'. The ample menu takes you off the beaten track, starting with the delicate napolitos compuestos (cactus salad), the quesadilla de cuitlacoche (buckwheat turnovers) or the cocktail de crevettes (shrimp cocktail). The poulet et sa sauce d'amandes et noix de cajou (almond and cashew sauce), the gigot d'agneau mariné (marinated roast lamb) or the fajitas et leurs haricots lay strong foundations for peace talks. Doused in rompope (an eggnog-like drink), the chocolate cake looks like an Aztec pyramid and will have you raising a glass of Domecq red wine to Mexican cuisine.

Open: daily 6.45pm-11pm, Sun noon-3pm; reservations advisable

Map: 5 C5

Métro: Maubert Mutualité

Entertainment: Live Mexican music once a week

 Smoking throughout

starter: 40FF-125FF
main: 80FF-110FF
dessert: 25FF-45FF

CB DC EC JCB MC V; €

Map: 5 D5
Métro: Maubert Mutualité

Smoking throughout

Le Berthoud
French

☎ 01 43 54 38 81
1, rue Valette, Maubert

The Berthoud is on one of the calm, almost traffic-free streets of the Saint-Geneviève hill. Its discreet interior, with 'medieval' tapestries and wood panelling, hasn't changed in nearly 25 years. The décor might seem a bit old fashioned and middle class, but it doesn't stop the regulars coming back for more. And you're so warmly welcomed that once you're seated, you feel perfectly at home. At first glance, the menu looks familiar, but the food is tasty, and skillfully prepared with fresh, quality produce: bar grillé à l'estragon (grilled sea bass with tarragon), rognons de veau sautés grand-mère (sautéed veal kidneys), magret de canard à la sauce aigre-douce (duck breast with sweet and sour sauce). The ravioles de Royan au basilic (ravioli with basil) is delicious too. And even the butter is home-made! Let yourself be tempted by the 'nounours' ('teddy bear') desserts, made from an especially good chocolate ganache (blended butter and fresh cream flavoured with chocolate).

starter: 40FF-75FF
main: 85FF-105FF
dessert: 40FF-50FF
Set menu: 185FF
Plat du jour: 80FF-110FF

AE CB EC MC V

Open: Mon-Fri noon-2.30pm, Mon-Sat 7.30pm-11.30pm; reservations not accepted

---

Map: 5 F4
Métro: Panthéon
Entertainment: Impromptu live jazz

Smoking throughout

Terrace tables

Le Café de la Nouvelle Mairie
French

☎ 01 44 07 04 41
19, rue des Fossés-Saint-Jacques, Panthéon

With its polished bar, wooden chairs and logs by the door, the Café de la Nouvelle Mairie deliberately cultivates its traditional bistrot atmosphere. In summer, the terrace is a perfect spot to enjoy the charming little Place de l'Estrapade. In winter, you can move into the cosy interior and watch frozen students walk past while you sip your hot chocolate. Simple pleasures perhaps, but this place has something extra – its food. You might not realise just by looking at the menu, but the ordinary-sounding salade de roquefort et de parmesan is in fact a delicately-seasoned rocket salad with shaved cheese. The same goes for the quiche au fromage (with fourme d'Ambert cheese) and the quiche au jambon (with Parma ham). The tarte aux quetsches (plum tart) offers yet another nice surprise.

starter: 32FF-44FF
main: 50FF-69FF
dessert: 30FF

cash only

Open: Mon, Wed & Fri 8am-9pm, Tues & Thurs 8am-late; reservations not accepted

5ᵉ arrondi

Chez Lena et Mimile
French

☎ **01 47 07 72 47**
32, rue Tournefort, Mouffetard

Map: 5 G4

Métro: Monge, Censier Daubenton

  Smoking throughout

 Terrace tables overlooking a garden

One of the best terraces in Paris: overlooking a little park with murmuring fountain, you could be on a village square, with students strolling past. And the cuisine is excellent. In the evening a typically French menu includes an apéritif, wine and coffee. The flavoursome foie gras is a favourite starter; seize the rare opportunity to taste pieds de cochon farcis (stuffed pig's trotters) or the innovative marbré de pommes de terre, camembert et andouille (potato, camembert and pork sausage slice). Classic main dishes include the magret de canard au miel (duck breast with honey), or with a new twist: the gigot d'agneau à la crème de chorizo (leg of lamb with spicy Spanish sausage) or the delicate ravioles de pétoncles à la crème safranée (queen scallop ravioli with saffron-flavoured cream). Hats off to the desserts, too, like the poire au vin et sa glace au pain d'épice (pear cooked in wine with gingerbread ice cream).

Set menu: 98FF (lunch), 198FF (dinner)
Plat du jour: 70FF (lunch)
CB EC MC V

Open: Tues-Fri noon-2.30pm, Mon-Sat 7.30pm-11pm; reservations advisable

Le Coco de Mer
Seychelles

☎ **01 47 07 06 64**
34, blvd Saint-Marcel, Austerlitz-Gobelins

Map: 5 J8

Métro: Saint Marcel

 Nonsmoking tables available

 Veranda tables

All aboard for an island cruise! The Love Boat décor won't be to everyone's taste, although the wood panelling and creole music will appeal to some. In any case, the real show is on your plate, starring fish from the turquoise waters of the Indian Ocean. Raw or marinated for starters: carpaccio d'espadon fumé (smoked swordfish), the delicious tartare de thon frais au gingembre (fresh tuna tartare with ginger), and bourgeois mariné cru aux herbes et au citron vert (raw, marinated fish with herbs and lime). The 'découverte' or 'discovery menu' is a great option, allowing you to compare the flavours of requin au tamarin (shark with tamarind), espadon sauté au safran (swordfish sautéed with saffron) and vindail de dorade coryphène (dolphin fish). A touch of fresh chilli goes perfectly with these light, refined and colourful dishes. The mousse de mangue (mango mousse) is sheer heaven.

starter: 60FF-80FF
main: 98FF-110FF
dessert: 38FF-40FF
Set menus: 135FF, 170FF
AE CB DC EC MC V; €

Open: Tues-Sat noon-3pm, daily 7.30pm-midnight; reservations advisable

Map: 5 D5

Métro: Maubert Mutualité

Smoking throughout

El Palenque
Argentine

☎ 01 43 54 08 99
5, rue de la Montagne-Sainte-Geneviève, Quartier Latin

References to Argentine culture adorn the walls, with pride of place reserved for tangos and gauchos. The main culinary attraction is meat from the pampa, which is chargrilled and served on a platter. The local Angus beef is eaten in the form of churrasco (chargrilled steak), lomo (fillet steak) and its various derivatives. Garnished simply with salads and corn, the meat is tender, delectable and cooked to your taste. Whet your appetite first with a glass of clerico (a mix of wine and fresh fruit), which comes with traditional stuffed turnovers or black pudding. For dessert, try the unusual pâte de patate douce (sweet potato cake) or the dulce de leche (flavoured custard cream). The wine list includes offerings from Chile and Mexico as well as Argentina. The only disappointment was the unfriendly manner in which we were greeted: a surprising departure from traditional South American hospitality.

starter: 27FF-30FF
main: 56FF-105FF
dessert: 25FF-35FF

cash only

Open: Mon-Sat noon-2pm, 7.30pm-11.30pm (dinner served at 8pm & 10pm); reservations essential

Fogon Saint-Julien
Spanish

☎ 01 43 54 31 33
10, rue Saint-Julien-le Pauvre, Quartier Latin

Map: 5 B4

Métro: Saint Michel, Maubert Mutualité

 Smoking throughout

On the table is arroz negro, rice as black as the cast-iron dish in which it is served. From the Ebro delta near Barcelona or from the Calasparra mountains near Murcia, the rice is 'toasted' with tomato and spices, sprinkled with giant squid ink, adorned with small cuttlefish, shrimps and fish, then slowly cooked to perfection. Now that's a real Spanish paella! With saffron, for those who like it golden-coloured, or with vegetables, rabbit, chicken and seafood. The Castilian chef offers seven versions of this famous dish, which is so often not cooked as it should be. A full range of Spanish flavours is also on offer in the form of tapas. Unfortunately, the atmosphere is a tad snobbish and lacks the simplicity and friendliness of traditional bodegas.

starter: 45FF-140FF
main: 120FF
dessert: 50FF
Set menu: 190FF
Plat du jour: 60FF (lunch)

CB EC MC V

Open: daily noon-2.30pm, 7pm-midnight; reservations advisable

La Fourmi ailée
French

☎ 01 43 29 40 99
8, rue du Fouarre, Saint Michel

Map: 5 B4

Métro Saint Michel, Maubert Mutualité; RER: Saint Michel Notre Dame

 Smoking throughout

 Pavement tables

You're reading a good book by candlelight while a fire crackles in the hearth. No, you're not in the library of some stately old manor house, although the high walls are covered with bookshelves and pictures. Every element of the décor contributes to the intimate, romantic ambience of this restaurant. The food is simple but varied: salads or a decent chèvre chaud aux figues (warm goat's cheese with figs) to start, then a tourte au bœuf et aux herbes (beef pie with herbs) – tasty but a bit dry. Rather than choosing a standard dessert, why not try the innovative apfel strudel aux cèpes (apple strudel with cèpe mushrooms), since mushrooms are a speciality here. The bread is home-made and there are plenty of vegetarian dishes. It's a pity that the cuisine doesn't quite match the surrounds.

starter: 48FF-58FF
main: 58FF-82FF
dessert: 30FF-35FF
Plat du jour: 70FF

CB EC MC V

Open: daily noon-midnight (salon de thé), noon-3pm, 7pm-midnight (restaurant); reservations advisable (especially Fri & weekends)

Map: 5 G6

Métro: Place Monge

Nonsmoking tables available

Le Foyer du Vietnam
Vietnamese

☎ 01 45 35 32 54
80, rue Monge, Place Monge

The Foyer du Vietnam is a favourite meeting place among the capital's Vietnamese community. A long room with peeling walls (1930s Saigon-style) resonates with the conversation of Vietnamese customers and waiters. The hearty house specialities – 'Saigon' and 'Hanoi' soup (noodles, soybeans and pork flavoured with lemongrass, coriander and chives) – will satisfy the most voracious of appetites (all meals are available in either medium or large serves). Continue if you can, just for pleasure's sake, with the delectable, slightly crunchy raviolis aux crevettes (shrimp dumplings). Oilcloth-covered tables, plastic flowers and a small photo of Ho Chi Minh proudly displayed near the bar all contribute to the undefinable charm of this quiet Vietnamese restaurant.

starter: 16FF-49FF
main: 30FF-54FF
dessert: 13FF-26FF
Set menu: 50FF (student concession 40FF)

cash only

Open: Mon-Sat noon-2pm, 7pm-10pm; reservations not accepted

Map: 5 C4

Métro: Maubert Mutualité

Entertainment: Special theme nights held

Nonsmoking tables available

Hélices et Délices
French

☎ 01 43 54 59 47
8, rue Thénard, Maubert

Hélices et Délices translates literally as 'Propellers and Delights', but let's stick with the rhyme and rebaptise this restaurant Flights and Delights. In any case, with a name like this, you'd expect whacky decor with a multitude of planes and other whirligigs. We were almost disappointed to discover a restrained and tasteful setting, the only propellers in sight belonging to a handful of model boats and planes.The food is traditional and based on fresh ingredients mixing all sorts of spices and flavours and changing with the seasons. The salade d'automne aux figues (figs) makes a great starter, followed by the filet de carrelet aux pommes et au cidre (fillet of plaice with potatoes and cider). As a bonus, weekly theme nights allow customers to get together for a fine meal while discussing a range of topics from chocolate to oenology. A unique spot combining food for the body with food for thought.

starter: 40FF-65FF
main: 75FF-95FF
dessert: 35FF-40FF
Set menu: 85FF (lunch)
Plat du jour: 75FF

CB EC MC V

Open: Tues-Sat noon-2.15pm, 7.45pm-10.15pm; reservations accepted

Mavrommatis

☎ 01 43 31 17 17

Greek

Corner of rue Daubenton & rue du Marché-des-Patriarches, Place Monge

Map: 5 H5

Métro: Censier Daubenton, Gobelins

 Nonsmoking tables available

 Pavement tables

If your experience of Greek food in Paris is limited to those stalls for tourists in the Latin Quarter, it's definitely time you went to Mavrommatis. You'll discover just how varied and tasty the real thing is. This airy, well-lit establishment, with its large windows facing onto a little square, offers menus that are excellent value for money. It's hard to choose between the assortment of tarama (fish roe dip), aubergines fumées (baba ghanoush) and tzatziki (cucumber and yogurt with garlic and mint), on one hand, and the salade grecque (tomatoes, lettuce, peppers and feta cheese), on the other. It doesn't get any easier: a delicious moussaka or the crépines d'agneau sur lit de tomates, courgettes et pommes de terre (lamb tripe on a bed of tomatoes, zucchini and potatoes)? Wash it all down with some retsina and you'll be swearing there's nothing like Greek food.

starter: 40FF-68FF
main: 88FF-134FF
dessert: 38FF-45FF
Set menu: 120FF (lunch during the week), 160FF (dinner)

CB MC V; €

Open: Tues-Sun 12.30pm-2.15pm, 7pm-11pm; reservations advisable

---

Mirama

☎ 01 43 29 66 58/01 43 54 71 77

Chinese (Cantonese)

17, rue Saint-Jacques, Quartier Latin

Map: 5 B4

Métro: Saint Michel, Maubert Mutualité, Cluny-la-Sorbonne

 Smoking throughout

The Peking ducks in the window or the steel vats used for preparing stock might grab your attention, but chances are you'll walk straight past this small, unimposing restaurant. In a neighbourhood overrun by tourists, broke students and movie stars, Mirama isn't much to look at, but customers flock here for the authentic Chinese cuisine and, in the evening, often have to wait for a table. The main specialities are the canard laqué (Peking duck) and the soupe de raviolis aux crevettes (soup with shrimp ravioli). Not a frozen ingredient in sight: deliciously crunchy seasonal vegetables accompany shrimps as fresh and plump as they come. The crabe au gingembre (crab with ginger), served whole and steaming, has to be finished with your fingers, but what a feast it is!

starter: 30FF-47FF
main: 48FF-120FF
dessert: 28FF-36FF

CB MC V

Open: daily noon-11pm; reservations not accepted

Map: 5 F5

Métro: Cardinal Lemoine

Limited pavement tables

Les Quatre et Une Saveurs
Macrobiotic

☎ 01 43 26 88 80
72, rue du Cardinal Lemoine, Contrescarpe

Set back 30m from the place de la Contrescarpe and hidden behind a yellow blind, this bright restaurant is extremely popular among health-food lovers. Sophie Court's food is generous, colourful, varied and delicious. Her approach to macrobiotics is nonconformist: communal experience matters as much as individual health. All ingredients are fresh and guaranteed 100% organic to satisfy the demanding clientele. Whet your appetite with mû tea (16 plants and roots including clove, peony, thistle and liquorice) before enjoying the hearty, delectable assiette complète au seitan (cooked wheat gluten) served with artistically presented crudités (white radishes pickled in plum vinegar, seaweed, beans, rice and millet). If you manage to eat all this, you may have no room left for the mouthwatering desserts on display as you walk in.

starter: 28FF-36FF
main: 70FF-78FF
dessert: 34FF-38FF
Set menu: 130FF

MC V; €

Open: Tues-Sun noon-2.30pm, 7pm-10.30pm; reservations advisable (end of the week)

Map: 5 J6

Métro: Censier Daubenton

Smoking throughout

Le Refuge du passé
French

☎ 01 47 07 29 91
32, rue du Fer-à-Moulin, Mouffetard

Tucked away in the quiet Scipion square, this small, neighbourhood restaurant attracts numerous tourists with its 'music-hall' décor, including theatre posters and a collection of opera hats pinned to the ceiling. The Refuge du passé combines all the ingredients of the archetypal French restaurant, not the least of which are the owner's warmth and humour. A sensible menu offers popular regional specialities – chou farci (stuffed cabbage), tripoux (small bundles of sheep's offal and feet), magret de canard aux oranges confites (fillet of duck breast), blanquette à l'ancienne, blancs de poireau gratinés au cantal (leeks au gratin with cantal), navarin d'agneau (lamb stew with vegetables), bœuf miroton (slices of beef gently stewed with onions) – all cooked to perfection and served in generous portions. For dessert, make a beeline for the gorgeous crème glacée aux mirabelles caramélisées et flambées.

starter: 45FF-60FF
main: 95FF-110FF
dessert: 35FF-50FF
Set menu: 90FF

AE V; €

Open: Mon-Sat noon-2.30pm, 7.30pm-11pm; reservations advisable (evenings)

Le Réminet
French

☎ **01 44 07 04 24**
**3, rue des Grands-Degrès,
Maubert**

Map: 5 C5

Métro: Maubert Mutualité

 Smoking throughout

In the heart of old Paris, Le Réminet might be tiny but it's big on good food. By the light of chandeliers and candles, enjoy flavours subtly blended by a young chef who hasn't forgotten his childhood in Normandy but who also knows how to use spices. His mother used to prepare cockles and mussels with burnt onions, while he serves them in crisp, light millefeuille pastry. But since the menu changes with the seasons, maybe you'll have filets de sardine au cumin (sardine fillets with cumin) accompanied by tasty preserved eggplant. The board displays the often original plats du jour and the wines of the month (there are more to choose from on the menu). If you're good, you might be allowed to finish with the quenelles au chocolat (small mousses made with bitter chocolate, flavoured with sweet Banyuls wine and garnished with amarena cherries) or the beautifully soft bavaroise with lemon and fromage blanc.

starter: 60FF-80FF
main: 85FF-125FF
dessert: 45FF-55FF
Set menu: 85FF (Wed-Fri lunch), 110 FF (Wed-Thurs lunch, Sat dinner)
Plat du jour: 90FF-130FF

Open: Wed-Sun noon-2.30pm, 7.30pm-11.00pm; reservations advisable

CB EC V; €

Savannah café
World food/Mediterranean

☎ **01 43 29 45 77**
**27, rue Descartes,
Mouffetard**

Map: 5 E5

Métro: Cardinal Lemoine

 Smoking throughout

The Savannah café thrills your tastebuds and seduces your entire being with the colours of the sea and the sun. Customers are greeted with Mediterranean warmth, zebras inhabit a décor made for the capital's armchair travellers, and good music contributes to the fulfilment of all the senses. Since 1985, well before the tsunami of world food, Richard Sahlani has been offering cuisine centred on the Mediterranean but extending to the banks of the Brahmaputra and the suburbs of Acapulco. Try galettes de fromage de brebis (galettes with ewe's milk cheese), ceviche (raw fish marinated in lemon juice, a Peruvian speciality), Florentine-style raviolini, tagliatelle with eggplant, selle d'agneau au thym (saddle of lamb with thyme) and vegetable and fruit curry. Indulge in baklava, profiteroles and crème de lait for dessert. This restaurant is a godsend in an area overrun with tourist traps.

starter: 38FF-70FF
main: 76FF-86FF
dessert: 36FF-42FF

Open: Mon-Sat 8pm-10.30pm; reservations advisable

V; €

Bars & Cafes – 5e & 13e

Batofar 11, quai François Mauriac, Paris 13e, Quai de la Gare
☎ 01 56 29 10 00 Métro: Bibliothèque, Quai de la Gare (Map: 13 E8)

Batofar is well and truly a bateau-phare (lightship), a metallic, scarlet beacon for avant-garde night-owls. From the gangway to the ship's hold, house and electronica concerts and happenings take passengers on a voyage to the end of the night. Then the Otocar brings exhausted passengers safely back to port.

Open: Tues-Thurs 8pm-3am, Fri & Sat 8pm-4am; By the glass: beer 20FF, champagne 50FF; meals and snacks available; multimedia workshops, multidisciplinary events in summer, CB EC MC V

Café Oum Kalthoum 4, square Vermenouze, Paris 5e, Mouffetard ☎ 01 45 87 38 58 or 01 45 87 63 81 Métro: Censier-Daubenton (Map: 5 H5)

Samir Khamarou is a guy with a friendly smile. Poet, writer, director and skilful chef, he also established the first narghile bar in Paris. His café is dedicated to the mythic Oum Kalthoum and could be in Cairo, Baghdad or Damascus. Fruity narghile, cardamom coffee or karkade (a drink made from hibiscus flowers) are on offer in the small Arabic-Persian room downstairs.

Open: daily 12.30pm-2am; coffee 15FF; meals and snacks available; occasional readings of Iraqi literature and poetry; credit cards accepted, €

Café OZ 184, rue Saint Jacques, Paris 5e, Panthéon, Sorbonne ☎ 01 43 54 30 48 RER: Luxembourg (Map: 5 E3)

This Australian pub is in the heart of the Latin Quarter. Everything is made of wood, old 'Foster's' posters adorn the walls, and the décor and lighting evoke the ochre tones of the Australian landscape. Cocktails and (strictly Aussie) beers combine with soft jungle music to conjure up a mythical Outback.

Open: daily 4pm-2am; By the glass: beer 15FF, champagne 35FF; coffee 10FF; web-bar; football and other sporting events shown on TV; credit cards accepted (100FF minimum)

Comptoir Méditerrannée 42, rue du cardinal Lemoine, Paris 5e, Jussieu ☎ 01 43 25 29 08 Métro: Cardinal Lemoine (Map: 5 E6)

Halfway between the Panthéon and the Institut du monde arabe, Comptoir Méditerrannée is a delicious place to stop off. The entire spirit and art of Mediterranean living brighten this lovely, sun-yellow cafe. Kébbés (meatballs), felafels, crème de lait (milk ice cream), halawa (halva), sweets and aromas from Lebanon and elsewhere are served in a friendly atmosphere.

Open: Mon-Sat 11am-10.30pm; By the glass: beer 14FF; coffee 8FF; snacks available; CB EC MC V

El Alamein opposite 11, quai François-Mauriac, Paris 13e, Quai de la gare ☎ 01 45 86 41 60 Métro: Quai de la Gare, Bibliothèque François Mitterand (Map: 13 E8)

The site of a famous WWII battle, El Alamein, a small Egyptian fishing port, was also the birthplace of a legend that spoke of the coming together of the earthly and spiritual worlds. Lush vegetation and souvenirs of numerous voyages give this Parisian El Alamein a real soul with a quasi-mystical atmosphere.

Open: daily 6.30pm-2am; By the glass: beer 20FF, cocktails 50FF; concerts; cash only; €

Maison de la Vanille 18, rue du Cardinal Lemoine, Paris 5e, Jussieu ☎ 01 43 25 50 95 Métro: Cardinal Lemoine (Map: 5 D6)

With madras, a coconut palm and a fan, the hosts of this lovely Creole cafe have colonised the gloomy climes of Paris. Roberto explains to customers the finer details of cocoa and especially vanilla, his long-time passion. Mylène prepares sumptuous specialities – gâteau à la patate douce (sweet potato cake) and thé à la mauricienne (Mauritian-style tea with milk and cardamom).

Open: Tues-Fri 11.30am-7pm, Sat & Sun 2.30pm-7pm; Creole coffee 20FF; meals and snacks available; CB EC MC V; €

Le Merle Moqueur 11, rue de la Butte-aux-Cailles, Paris 13e, Butte aux Cailles ☎ 01 45 65 12 43 Métro: Place d'Italie (Map: 13 G2)

The Merle Moqueur is an integral part of rue de la Butte-aux-Cailles. This small bar's selection of flavoured rums (no fewer than 15) is one of its main attractions. Loud music detonates these explosive mixes that get customers dancing along to the sounds of Izouk as well as Herbert Léonard. A friendly atmosphere.

Open: Mon-Sat 8.30am-1am, Sun 9.30am-8pm; By the glass: beer 18FF; coffee 15FF; pinball machine and dancing; credit cards accepted

La Mosquée 39, rue Geoffroy-Saint-Hilaire, Paris 5e, Place Monge ☎ 01 43 31 38 20/01 43 31 18 14 Métro: Monge, Censier-Daubenton (Map: 5 G7)

Does Eastern magic work in a Western world? The answer is yes, the proof is at the Mosquée de Paris. Within its walls are a hammam, a winter lounge with a fountain and a cafe covered with tapestries and mosaics and painted in emerald and red tones. The perfect spot for a peppermint tea break. Afterwards, in the courtyard, be bewitched by the *Arabian Nights* rose bushes among the rocks.

Open: daily 9am-11.30pm; peppermint tea 10FF; meals and snacks available; dress code applies; CB EC MC V

Oya Café 25, rue de la Reine Blanche, Paris 13e, Les Gobelins ☎ 01 47 07 59 59 Métro: Gobelins (Map: 13 D3)

A place where you can play and even buy more than 250 parlour games and games of strategy from all over the world. The owners are more than happy to explain the rules in detail and warmly encourage customers to mingle. Oya Café is alcohol and smoke free. Get in on the game!

Open: Tues-Sun & public holidays 2pm-midnight; coffee 10FF; parlour games, games of strategy and occasional championships in these games; cash only

Le Pantalon Bar 7, rue Royer-Collard, Paris 5e, Panthéon, ☎ 01 40 51 85 85 Métro: Luxembourg (Map: 5 E3)

A tiny bar tucked away in a tiny street near the Panthéon, the Pantalon seems out of place in this chic part of town. The owner has moved the terrace inside, arguing that neighbours would be disturbed by the music. The price list is in keeping with this friendly refuge, a favourite among the hordes of local students.

Open: Mon-Sat 5.30pm-2am; By the glass: beer 15FF; coffee 8FF; snacks available; cash only

Le Salon Egyptien 77, rue du Cardinal Lemoine, Paris 5e, Place de la Contrescarpe ☎ 01 43 25 58 99 Métro: Cardinal Lemoine, Place Monge (Map: 5 F5)

People come here mainly to smoke narghile or kif. You can detect the soft, intoxicating aromas of apricot, honey, apple or strawberry as soon as you walk in the door. Snuggle into a pouffe and sip karkade or nibble on Eastern salads, fritters or pastries. For more intimacy, five small rooms adjoin the main lounge.

Open: daily 11am-2am; By the glass: beer 25FF; coffee 15FF; snacks available; Eastern music and belly dancer (certain nights); cash only

Map: 5 C5

Métro: Maubert Mutualité

Smoking throughout

Pavement tables

starter: 18FF-30FF
main: 42FF-50FF
dessert: 20FF-24FF
Plat du jour: 42FF-50FF

CB EC MC V (more than
120FF)

Saveurs d'Asie
Vietnamese

☎ 01 44 07 05 55
**31, place Maubert,
Maubert**

This is one of those lovely, simple spots where you can pop in for a quick taste of fragrant Vietnamese cuisine. Outstanding specialities include pho (beef soup with basil), cua hap (steamed stuffed crab) and the hearty yet refined bo bun (a warm salad with thinly sliced beef, rice vermicelli, lemongrass, fresh mint, soybean sprouts, raw carrot and cucumber, and crushed peanuts). In summer, a terrace situated below the street, away from the traffic, is the ideal spot for a sunny lunch. A small dining room with six tables offers customers a refuge in winter; alternatively, you can order takeaway or eat at the adjoining restaurant Kim Lien (which run Saveurs d'Asie).

Open: Mon-Sat noon-8pm; reservations not accepted

Map: 5 E3

Métro: Luxembourg

Smoking throughout

starter: 32FF-52FF
main: 45FF-95FF
dessert: 18FF-45FF

CB EC MC V

Tao
Vietnamese

☎ 01 43 26 75 92
**248, rue Saint-Jacques,
Quartier Latin, Luxembourg**

Taoism has influenced many traditional exercises, practices and arts, including the preparation of food. In any case, the cuisine at Tao, a tiny restaurant at the top end of rue Saint-Jacques, is absolutely delicious. The fried spring rolls are sensationally crisp, while the pan-fried shrimps, served on a bed of crunchy Chinese cabbage, taste perfect. The soupe de cheveux d'ange ('angel's hair soup') is accompanied by mushrooms flavoured with chicken stock. The refined, subtle, almost Zen décor and service are immensely appealing. Tao thoughtfully offers vegetarian versions of many dishes as well as different combinations of courses to suit every appetite.

Open: Mon-Sat noon-2.30pm, Mon & Wed-Sat 7.30pm-10pm; reservations advisable

Tashi Delek
Tibetan

☎ 01 43 26 55 55
4, rue des Fossés-Saint-Jacques, Panthéon

Located between the Panthéon and the Palais du Luxembourg, Tashi Delek is the first Tibetan restaurant in Paris. The light, recently redecorated interior with its rows of small tables has the intimate feel of a museum antechamber. From the middle of the room, the Dalai Lama smiles benevolently at customers while the standard and set-price evening menus attract novices and initiates alike. For starters, try the tangmok (ravioli and vegetable soup), followed by the delicious daril seu (grilled meatballs with garlic, ginger and rice) or the momok (large vegetable or meat dumplings). Wash everything down with traditional or salted-butter tea, and don't forget the desserts, including the delicious dressil (yoghurt with dried fruit).

Open: Mon-Sat noon-2.30pm, 7pm-11pm; reservations advisable (essential at end of week)

Map: 5 E3

Métro: Luxembourg (RER)

 Nonsmoking tables available

starter: 19FF-25FF
main: 37FF-66FF
dessert: 14FF-22FF
Set menu: 50FF-65FF (lunch), 105FF (dinner, drinks included)

AE CB DC EC JCB MC V

Le Tournebride
French (Auvergne)

☎ 01 43 31 42 98
104, rue Mouffetard, Mouffetard

The Tournebride's restaurant section is closed in the evening, so make sure you come here for lunch, when you can savour simple but well-prepared cuisine in the company of academics and journos from the nearby offices of *Le Monde*. Try the sauté d'agneau à l'estragon (lamb with tarragon), the andouillette à la crème de moutarde (andouillette with creamy mustard sauce), or the confit de canard (confit of duck with apples) avec pommes sarladaises. The salads are generous and the green beans deliciously crunchy, but the poultry gizzards in the salade landaise could be a bit warmer. In any case, the Tournebride's treasure is its bleu d'Auvergne (blue-veined cheese), straight from La Bourboule and alone worth the trip to rue Mouffetard. The beautifully presented aumônière (a pear-filled crêpe served with orange-flavoured cream) adds just the right touch of sweetness to the meal. You'll be a regular here before you know it!

Open: restaurant: Mon-Sat noon-3.30pm, bar: Mon-Sat 8am-2am; reservations not accepted

Map: 5 H5

Métro: Censier Daubenton

 Smoking throughout

 Pavement tables

starter: 26FF-29FF
main: 59FF-75FF
dessert: 26FF-30FF
Plat du jour: 59FF

AE CB EC MC V; €

Le Vivario
Corsican

☎ 01 43 25 08 19
**6, rue Cochin,
Quai de la Tournelle**

Map: 5 C6

Métro: Maubert Mutualité

Entertainment: Corsican nights with music

Smoking throughout

starter: 35FF-70FF
main: 55FF-120FF
dessert: 35FF-45FF
Plat du jour: 50FF-120FF

AE CB EC MC V

The oldest Corsican restaurant in Paris (according to the menu) knows how to look after its customers with a minimum of fuss. Expect a warm welcome, equally friendly surroundings and food to delight the most demanding taste buds. But the faint-hearted and health-food fanatics should beware: this is authentic fare and often comes in huge serves. Specialities from the 'Isle of Beauty' have pride of place, including cabri rôti (roast kid), tourte aux herbes du maquis (wild herb pie) and fiadone (sponge cake with lemon and Brocciu). The fressure de cabri (kid's fry) is a memorable starter, and we can't speak highly enough of the delectable veau aux olives dans sa belle casserole en cuivre (veal with olives served in a copper saucepan). Try one of the numerous Corsican wines on offer, or a Pietra (Corsican chestnut beer) with your meal. A fabulous restaurant.

Open: daily noon-2pm, 7.30pm-10pm; reservations advisable (evenings)

6e Arrondissement

Saint-Germain

Odéon

Saint-Michel

Luxembourg

6ᵉ Arrondissement

Bohemia and jazz have deserted its streets and basements, but the sixth arrondissement's reputation remains intact. Artists and writers, politicians and journalists, actors, musicians, and students still cross paths in the shadow of the École Nationale Supérieure des Beaux Arts, the Académie Française, the théâtre de l'Odéon and the Sénat. Many years ago, the arrival of the fashion industry upset local traditions and changed the general tenor of conversation. Since then, clothing and footwear shops exist alongside bookshops, art galleries, publishing houses, antique dealers and interior design boutiques. But while haute couture and prêt-à-porter make flirtatious neighbours, each sector keeps for the most part to itself. Cinemas still advertise their multiple screenings, making no distinction between new films and old classics, small works and big-budget extravaganzas. The statue of Danton at the carrefour de l'Odéon remains a favourite meeting spot: large crowds flocking to this landmark daily before invading the area's cafes, bars, terraces and restaurants. In the nearby rue de Seine, market stalls still groan under the weight of fresh fruit and vegetables, a reminder that village life here survives the passing fashions.

6ᵉ ARRONDISSEMENT

Au 29
Lebanese

☎ 01 46 33 75 92
**29, rue Dauphine,
Saint-Germain**

Map: 6 C8

Métro: Odéon

At this fabulous restaurant, Mediterranean dishes strongly influenced by Lebanese cuisine are prepared with fresh market produce and are constantly reinvented. There are no meze, but the seasonal menu features a new offering each week. Karim, the chef, recreates the entire spectrum of flavours from his childhood: his grandmother's salade d'artichauts et de fèves fraîches (artichoke and fresh broad bean salad), his uncle's soupe aux lentilles corail et à la tomate, his mother's aubergine confite farcie à la noix et parfumée au clou de girofle (eggplant stuffed with walnuts and flavoured with cloves), his neighbour's fattouch ('crumble'), as well as kebbé au potiron (meatballs with pumpkin), rascasse au fenouil (scorpion fish with fennel), agneau et riz aux cinq épices, blé à la grenade (crushed wheat with pomegranate) and poire à l'arak et au caroube (pear with arak and carob). Au 29 also boasts a magnificent wine and spirits list. A rare find indeed.

Open: Mon-Sat noon-2.15pm, 7pm-10.15pm; reservations advisable (Saturday)

starter: 38FF-60FF
main: 70FF-150FF
dessert: 23FF-48FF
Set menu: 68FF (lunch)

AE DC V; €

La Cafetière
Italian

☎ 01 46 33 76 90
**21, rue Mazarine,
Saint-Germain**

Map: 6 C8

Métro: Odéon, Mabillon

 Smoking throughout

Given the magnificent collection of enamelled coffee pots scattered throughout this restaurant, it could easily have been a salon de thé. But no, Italian food is the drawcard here, including the very fresh poêlée de langoustines (fried Dublin Bay prawns) with crunchy vegetables, or the sauté d'épinards (sautéed spinach) with saffron mussels. You can't go wrong with the tagliatelles de gambas et Saint-Jacques (tagliatelli with king prawns and scallops) and the risotto aux artichauts (artichokes) et scampi. If you're feeling more adventurous, try the lasagnes de légumes à la purée d'oignons recouvertes d'un foie gras poêlé (vegetable lasagna with onion purée covered with fried foie gras). The steep prices are standard in this part of Paris, but not too bad when you consider the fresh, high-quality produce, the inventive cuisine and the friendly staff.

Open: Tues-Sat noon-3pm, 7.30pm-11pm; reservations advisable

starter: 45FF-100FF
main: 70FF-100FF
dessert: 50FF
Set menu: 150FF (lunch)
Plat du jour: 90FF-110FF

CB EC MC V

Le Caméléon
French

☎ 01 43 20 63 43
6, rue de Chevreuse,
Montparnasse

Map: 6 J6
Métro: Vavin

Smoking throughout

This authentic bistrot will leave you with fond memories. Yves welcomes his clients with a warmth that has become legendary. The red-tile floor, the honey-coloured ceiling and the peaceful, friendly atmosphere make the place a little island of calm. The cook does all sorts of things well, especially the ravioles de homard (lobster ravioli) or the purée de pomme de terre (mashed potato), which is worth a visit in itself. His cuisine is traditional and always very tasty. The terrine de canard (duck terrine) is a first-rate starter. For mains, you can't go wrong with the selle d'agneau à la fleur de thym (lamb saddle with thyme flowers) or the saucisse fumée d'Auvergne (smoked Auvergne sausage). When it comes to dessert, don't even try to resist the mousse glacée au citron vert (lime mousse).

starter: 52FF-98FF
main: 88FF-120FF
dessert: 35FF-45FF

AE CB V

Open: Mon-Fri noon-2pm, 8pm-10.30pm, Sat 8pm-10.30pm; reservations advisable

La Caspienne
Persian

☎ 01 45 48 11 39
4, rue Stanislas,
Montparnasse

Map: 6 H5
Métro: Vavin, Notre-Dame-des-Champs

Nonsmoking tables available

Persia conjures up romantic visions, but Persian food is not well known in France. Cultures mingle on the menu of this restaurant, which combines specialities from Iran, India and Greece, just as they do on the shores of the Caspian sea, where Europe and Asia meet. The assorted hors d'oeuvre (tzatziki or cucumber and yoghurt with garlic and mint, tarama or fish roe dip, dolmas or vine leaves filled with meat and rice...) prepare the way for ragoûts d'agneau épicés (spicy lamb stews), sometimes sweetly flavoured, or brochettes of filet mignon, which go well with the wine from Crete. The bread is excellent, and so is the honey that accompanies the sheep's yoghurt and the oriental pastries.

starter: 32FF-48FF
main: 68FF-98FF
dessert: 30FF-34FF
Set menu: 82FF (lunch during the week & up till 8.30pm)

CB EC MC V

Open: Mon-Fri noon-2pm, Mon-Sat 7.30pm-11pm; reservations advisable

Le Cherche Midi
Italian

☎ 01 45 48 27 44
**22, rue du Cherche-Midi,
Saint-Germain**

Map: 6 E5

Métro: Sèvres-Babylone

 Smoking throughout

 Pavement tables

(VOL)

Since 1979, the kitchens of this bistrot-style restaurant have been busy from seven in the morning, preparing traditional, impeccably fresh Italian dishes. The regular clientele of discerning international diners expects no less. The pâtés are always home-made, the fish is never farmed, and the fruit tart is made with seasonal produce. Seafood and vegetables (especially mushrooms) have pride of place on the menu. Scallops, clams, cuttlefish and oronges (Caesar's mushrooms) are subtly combined with a wide variety of pasta. You'll also enjoy the classic escalope à la milanaise cuisinée à l'ancienne (escalope of veal cooked in the traditional Milanese fashion). The splendid wine list contains as many Italian as French wines (note the Duca San Felice and the Selegas de Sardaigne). Don't forget to book, as this restaurant is always full.

starter: 50FF-70FF
main: 78FF-100FF
dessert: 38FF
Plat du jour: 78FF

Open: daily noon-3pm, 8pm-11.45pm; reservations advisable

V; €

Chez Albert (p 90)

Chez Albert
Portuguese

☎ 01 46 33 22 57
43, rue Mazarine, Odéon

Map: 6 C8
Métro: Odéon

Smoking throughout

It's best to arrive on time, otherwise you might find you'll have to go on fantasising about that brandade de morue (creamed salt cod). Punctuality is a virtue here – the staff let you know this when you ring to book. But once you taste the food, you'll realise you did well to keep an eye on the time. The atmosphere is very pleasant, the cuisine is wholesome and the produce is fresh. There's an endless variety of fish specialities, especially morue, which comes in croquettes and in salad. You can also have a superb and generous viande á la planche (meat platter) for two, or arroz de mariscos, a no-frills paella abounding in seafood. The entrées, mainly seafood, are served like tapas, and there are all sorts of pleasant surprises among the Portuguese desserts. It's a good place for the family, a rare thing in the very flash neighbourhood of Saint-Germain-des-Prés.

starter: 30FF-120FF
main: 98FF-300FF
dessert: 36FF-50FF
Set menu: 95FF (until 8pm);
135FF
Plat du jour: 90FF
CB EC MC V

Open: Tues-Sat noon-2.30pm; 7pm-11.30pm; reservations not accepted

Chez Diane
French

☎ 01 46 33 12 06
25, rue Servandoni, Saint-Germain

Map: 6 F7
Métro: Saint Sulpice, RER: Luxembourg

Smoking throughout

Located in a little street just near the Luxembourg gardens and a stone's throw from the Senate, Chez Diane is one of the eating places favoured by members of that venerable institution, and not just because it's handy. This little restaurant resembles an antique shop with its wooden counter, framed pictures on the walls and charming old-world chandeliers. It goes all out to seduce the gourmet diner's taste buds: oeufs coques à la purée de morilles (soft-boiled eggs with a purée of morel mushrooms), pleurotes à la crème de foie gras (mushrooms with creamed foie gras), lotte au vinaigre balsamique (monkfish with balsamic vinegar), faisan rôti aux marrons et aux choux de Bruxelles (roasted pheasant with chestnuts and brussel sprouts). The fish cassoulet is a popular favourite, but it's also well worth considering the escalope of salmon with sweet vegetables, barely cooked and very subtly seasoned with a light curry sauce.

starter: 50FF-70FF
main: 100FF-130FF
dessert: 40FF-45FF
Set menu: 160FF
CB MC V

Open: Mon-Fri noon-2pm, Mon-Sat 8pm-11.30pm; reservations advisable (evenings)

Le Chipiron
French (South-West/Basque)

☎ 01 43 26 26 45
22, rue de Vaugirard, Odéon

Map: 6 F8

Métro: Odéon

Dress code applies

Although you'll see a view of Saint-Jean-de-Luz reflected in the big wall mirrors, it's the cuisine here, not the décor, that conjures up the Basque countryside in all its splendour. The owner is a fisherman's son, and he draws on traditional working-class recipes, like the marmitako des corsaires, a ragoût of tuna, potatoes, peppers and tomatoes. In the same vein, the chipirons à l'encre (squid with ink) is redolent of the wide open sea. The piquillos farcis à la morue (peppers stuffed with salt cod) make a perfect starter: sweet and flavoursome. The irouleguy and ochoa wines go well with these dishes. To finish, the fromage de brebis (sheep's cheese) and confiture de cerises (cherry conserve) are good local fare, like the inevitable gâteau basque, but you can always have the little pot of refreshing crème vanille (vanilla cream) instead.

starter: 35FF-89FF
main: 75FF-88FF
dessert: 36FF-40FF
Set menu: 98FF, 128FF
Plat du jour: 78FF

AE CB EC V

Open: Mon-Sat noon-2.30pm, 7pm-10.30pm; reservations advisable

Coffee Room
English

☎ 01 45 44 20 57
71, rue du Cherche Midi, Sèvres Babylone/St-Placide

Map: 6 G3

Métro: Sèvres Babylone/
  St-Placide

 Nonsmoking tables available

In this establishment – part salon de thé, part club – you can relax on a welcoming Chesterfield or sit down to lunch at an Art Deco table. Here you can enjoy a Madras curry: of finely sliced chicken on a bed of rice mixed with Corinthian raisins, just right for the middle of the day. The rôti de lapin farci aux pruneaux (roast rabbit stuffed with prunes) is not to be sniffed at either. There are homemade brownies and crumbles every day as well and among the 24 varieties of tea available, you're sure to find one to your taste. They think of everything here: there are papers for you to read, and to make things even more convivial, board games for you to play.

main: 57FF-75FF
dessert: 30FF
Set menu: 80FF, brunch
  120FF (weekends only)
Plat du jour: 59FF

CB V

Open: Mon-Fri noon-4pm, Sat noon-7pm, Sun 11am-7pm (serving brunch only); reservations accepted

Le Douze

International

☎ 01 56 24 32 84
12, rue Dauphine, Odéon

Map: 6 C8
Métro: Pont Neuf, Odéon

Smoking throughout

Le Douze is a rather unlikely combination of cabaret-nightclub and restaurant for night owls (including some of the celebrities who frequent this neighbourhood). Sit yourself down in the quaint, charming room at the back, where an Italian singer croons syrupy melodies. If it's already very late, a couple of fines de claire (oysters) will pick you up. Big spenders can get into the Iranian caviar. Then it's a choice between fish and meat. Both are well combined with mushrooms: try the coquilles Saint-Jacques aux girolles et basilic (scallops with chanterelle mushrooms and basil) or the côte de veau rôtie aux morilles (roasted veal with morel mushrooms). Adventurous diners may choose the pavé de saumon braisé au chou vert (braised salmon steak with green cabbage). Bring the feast to a fitting close with an excellent Saint-Marcellin goat's cheese or a dessert. Then you can go to bed late and full.

starter: 70FF-420FF
main: 90FF-145FF
dessert: 50FF-60FF

AE CB EC MC V

Open: daily 9pm-4am; reservations advisable

Indonesia

Indonesian

☎ 01 43 25 70 22
12, rue de Vaugirard, Luxembourg

Map: 6 F8
Métro: Odéon, RER: Luxembourg

Entertainment: Balinese dancing every second Friday evening

Nonsmoking tables available

At this Indonesian restaurant just opposite the Luxembourg gardens, the fragrance of incense and the rhythm of gamelans whisk you across land and sea in the twinkling of an eye. Wooden lattice work on the downstairs ceiling, along with traditional décor and furniture, evoke the gentle atmosphere of the Indonesian islands. Tables are covered with a dazzling array of dishes. The set menus (mixed platter or menu degustation) offer between five and nine courses, a perfect introduction to the archipelago's cuisine. The delicate flavour's saffron, strong spices of Java and a peanut sauce accompany chicken satays and mutton or fried beef with coriander. Desserts include a large selection of cakes and the slightly acidic fermented rice (not for first-timers!). There are 17 guest books, but the quality of the service can vary.

starter: 22FF-32FF
main: 40FF-51FF
dessert: 19FF-27FF
Set menu: from 51FF (lunch, vegetarian) to 149FF
Plat du jour: 51FF-89FF

AE CB DC EC JCB MC V

Open: Sun-Fri noon-2pm, daily 7pm-10.30pm; reservations advisable (evenings)

6ᵉ ARRONDISSEMENT

Korean Barbecue

Korean

☎ **01 42 22 26 63**
**1, rue du Dragon,
Saint-Germain**

Map: 6 C6

Métro: Saint-Germain-
des-Prés

   Smoking throughout

This is a high-standard and very friendly Korean grill room. After soup and a small salad for starters comes the inevitable barbecue: a plate piled with strips of finely sliced and marinated beef, which you get to cook yourself on the grill in the centre of each table. The meat is accompanied by rice and soy beans, and you can wash it down with jasmine tea or a Chinese beer. This is Korean cuisine at its best: simple and full of flavour. The commercially made desserts, however, are neither Korean nor memorable. The pleasant, well-ventilated room, the warm welcome and the generosity of the serves make this place a favourite with gourmets and hearty eaters alike.

Open: Mon-Sat 11am-2am; reservations advisable

starter: 75FF-85FF
main: 85FF-120FF
dessert: 50FF
Set menu: 170FF

AE CB V

La Lozère

French (Lozère)

☎ **01 43 54 26 64**
**4, rue Hautefeuille,
Saint-Michel**

Map: 6 D9

Métro: Saint-Michel

 Smoking throughout

A word of friendly advice: fast before dining here. This restaurant showcases the cuisine of the Lozère, where people take eating very seriously, so prepare for a gargantuan feast. For starters: an authentic pâté caussenard or a filet de truite fumée (fillet of smoked trout). Then on to the serious business: filet de veau rôti aux pruneaux (fillet of veal roasted with prunes), tripoux (small cushions of stuffed and seasoned tripe) or filet de truite au jambon cru ou maoucho (fillet of trout with raw ham or cabbage sausage), all accompanied by a good splash of Languedoc red. We have a soft spot for the aligot (puréed potatoes with fresh un-cured cheese), which is served every Thursday evening. Don't let the magnificent cheese platter trap you: save some space for the delicate poire rôtie aux oranges confites (baked pear with preserved oranges). The restaurant's harsh lighting is its only drawback.

Open: Tues-Sat noon-2pm, 7.30pm-10pm; reservations advisable

starter: 22FF-68FF
main: 62FF-178FF
dessert: 30FF
Set menu: 96FF (lunch),
131FF, 162FF (dinner)
Plat du jour: 69FF

CB EC MC V; €

Le Mâchon d'Henri
French (Lyon)

☎ 01 43 29 08 70
**8, rue Guisarde,
Saint-Germain**

Map: 6 D7
Métro: Mabillon, St-Sulpice

Smoking throughout

This tiny *mâchon* (in Lyons, a restaurant serving light meals) combines the cuisine of Lyons with Mediterranean flavours, to satisfy the most voracious of appetites. The menu and specials board offer no less than 18 starters, including poivrons grillés à l'huile d'olive (grilled capsicum with olive oil), chèvre frais et sa tapenade (fresh goat's cheese with tapenade) – an absolute must – and terrine de courgettes et son coulis de tomates (zucchini terrine with a tomato coulis). The filet de rascasse (fillet of scorpion fish) is perfectly grilled and served with a slightly tart sorrel sauce. Regional dishes such as the saucisson de Lyon and the sumptuous boudin noir aux pommes en l'air (black pudding with apple) come in generous serves. The owner keeps a vigilant eye on the tables, looking after everyone's smallest needs. Rustic décor (exposed beams, stone walls and bistrot tables) and gratified customers make this little mâchon an easy place to get used to.

starter: 35FF-40FF
main: 70FF-80FF
dessert: 30FF-40FF

cash only

Open: daily 12.30pm-2.30pm, 7pm-11.30pm; reservations advisable

La Milonga
Argentine

☎ 01 43 29 52 18
**18, rue Guisarde,
Saint-Germain**

Map: 6 D7
Métro: Mabillon

Entertainment: Argentine folklore on Saturday evenings

Smoking throughout

There's no end of restaurants in Saint-Germain-des-Prés, but the Milonga's different: it will send you on a long journey. As you cross the threshold, you're in Argentina: boleadoras (a hunting weapon), rebenques (riding crops) and reproductions of pictures by Molina Campos set the scene. Begin exploring with the humita (corn paste on a corn leaf), empanadas (meat pasties) or a delicate pascuali (savoury tart). But the real pride of Argentinian cuisine is of course its meat. The tender, tasty offerings here come from the pampa: bife de lomo (fillet steak), bife ancho (entrecôte), travers de port (pork spareribs), agneau au miel (lamb cooked with honey). The meat is grilled over a wood fire and, in most cases, accompanied simply by potatoes, so as not to distract your taste buds from the country's number one speciality. For a sweet finish to your trip, try the dulce de leche, or custard cream.

starter: 35FF-85FF
main: 80FF-155FF
dessert: 28FF-38FF
Set menu: 75 FF, 85FF (lunch); 89FF, 118FF, 145FF, 165FF (dinner)

AE CB V

Open: Tues-Fri noon-2.30pm, daily 7.30pm-midnight; reservations advisable

Orestias
Greek

☎ 01 43 54 62 01
4, rue Grégoire-de-Tours, Saint-Germain

Map: 6 D8

Métro: Odéon, Mabillon

 Smoking throughout

Whether in honour of the Macedonian city or the son of Agamemnon, clients beat a path to the door of Orestias for a budget meal. On the ground floor, the hunting trophies and cut-glass chandeliers don't really go with the lively, un-stuffy atmosphere. There are Greek dishes on the menu, but the cuisine is very cosmopolitan with couscous, paella, and châteaubriand. This might seem odd, but it's a way of giving the numerous regulars more variety. If you want to eat Greek food, don't bypass the starters of tarama, excellent vine leaves and tzatziki. You could continue with keftedes (meat balls). A bottle of armanti wine from Crete would go well with all this. For dessert, it's a toss up between the confiture de rose (rose conserve) and the crème caramel. Founded in 1928, this is a place where regulars and travellers are equally at home.

Open: Mon-Sat noon-2.30pm, 5.30pm-11.30pm; reservations not accepted

starter: 11.50FF-34.50FF
main: 34.50FF-63.50FF
dessert: 6.90FF-23FF
Set menu: 41FF, 48FF

AE CB EC V

Le Petit Saint-Benoit
French

☎ 01 42 60 27 92
4, rue Saint-Benoit, Saint-Germain

Map: 6 C6

Métro: Saint-Germain-des-Prés

 Smoking throughout

 Pavement tables

Since 1901 this eatery has changed hands only three times, and the regular clientele remains faithful in return. It has the atmosphere of an old bistrot and serves traditional, family-style food. The offerings change every day (this is probably the last place in Paris where you'll see Roneoed menus), and the only fixture is the hachis Parmentier (shepherd's pie). Will you find pâté de campagne (country pâté) and truite meunière (trout coated in flour and fried in butter)? Cannette rôtie au jus (roast duckling) or filet mignon de porc au miel (pork fillet with honey)? It doesn't really matter, because the quality of the food never fails. On top of which, here in the heart of posh Saint-Germain-des-Prés, a bottle of premier cru Champagne costs only 180FF. What more could an upper-crust client need?

Open: Mon-Sat noon-2.30pm, 7pm-11pm; reservations not accepted

starter: 15FF-25FF
main: 55FF-70FF
dessert: 20FF-30FF

cash only

Map: 6 D7

Métro: Mabillon

Smoking throughout but clients are asked to moderate their smoking; no cigars

Pavement tables

Le Petit Vatel

French/International

☎ 01 43 54 28 49

5, rue Lobineau, Saint-Germain

In this Lilliputian room with its cream and maroon décor, a varied clientele gathers around the family-style Mediterranean cuisine of the globe-trotting proprietor, who's a great source of information about Paris and its history. The eclectic menu confirms the French saying 'travel develops taste': in summer, try the soupe au citron, a Mayan recipe modified for European palates; there's also a herb salad (mint, parsley and coriander) and home-made terrine. The sautée d'agneau (sautéed lamb) takes on the moussaka, and the tome crayeuse de Savoie (a crumbly alpine cheese) goes up against the chocolate cake, made to a recipe that hasn't changed in 50 years. You can either choose one of the wines on the list, mainly from the South-West (excellent value for money), or the wine of the month, for example, the Tursan des Landes – a discovery the proprietor was quick to share.

starter: 20FF-30FF
main: 55F
dessert: 20FF-30FF
Plat du jour: 55FF

cash only; €

Open: Tues-Sat noon-3pm, 7pm-11pm; reservations not accepted

Map: 6 C8

Métro: Odéon

Nonsmoking tables available

Pavement tables

Le Restaurant des Beaux Arts

French

☎ 01 46 33 20 73

80, rue Mazarine, Odéon

The mouldings on the ceiling, the red-and-white checked tablecloths and the familiar creak of parquetry make this unpretentious place a haven of conviviality. We like to take refuge in the upstairs room with a few friends to enjoy a pan-fried entrecôte with red wine sauce, a fillet of pork with turmeric or a tarte tatin with generous chunks of hot apple. There's just one thing that doesn't take us back to our childhood: the wine list. It's the strong point of the restaurant: the choice is exceptionally wide, the wines are sold at cost price, and they are classified by region of origin and by grade of wine. A good reason to spend another hour or two at the table.

starter: 45FF-50FF
main: 82FF-95FF
dessert: 35FF-48FF
Set menu: 85FF (lunch during the week)
Plat du jour: 70FF

CB DC EC JCB MC V

Open: daily 12.15pm-2pm, Mon-Fri 7pm-10.30pm, Sat & Sun 7pm-11.30pm; reservations advisable

6e ARRONDISSEMENT

Sans Frontières
Persian

☎ 01 45 48 87 67
19, rue du Regard, Montparnasse

Map: 6 F4

Métro: Saint-Placide

Nonsmoking tables available

Retro ceiling fans keep the air moving, slatted teak blinds filter the light, and gigantic fake tropical plants spring up here and there. In other words, a relaxing colonial decor awaits you. Since culinary style sets little store by borders, the menu subtly mingles Greek and Middle Eastern flavours. Grilled aubergine, caviar and vine leaves mix it with borani epfnadj (endive-like spinach with cheese and garlic). As for the mains, it's no easy task to pin down their origin, whether it's the lamb curry with spinach, still simmering on your table in its copper casserole, or the borg (brochette of beef marinated in lemongrass and coriander). Retsina, honey baklava and halva add a touch of sweetness to this caravan of delights.

Open: Mon-Fri noon-2.30pm, Mon-Sat 7.30pm-10.30pm; reservations advisable

starter: 32FF-48FF
main: 69FF-90FF
dessert: 30FF-34FF
Set menu: 79FF (lunch), 95FF, 120FF (dinner)

CB V

La Sieste
French

☎ 01 43 26 28 05
16, rue de la Grande-Chaumière, Montparnasse

Map: 6 J5

Métro: Vavin

Smoking throughout

This restaurant was established by two partners, one from Corsica, the other from Toulouse. Customers can expect a complimentary glass of sangria, but not before opening time (8pm – that's the South for you). Mirrors and candles create a quiet, even romantic atmosphere. The long dining room is tastefully decorated and the service lives up to the sumptuous food: ravioles aux champignons à la sauce au jus de truffe (mushroom ravioli accompanied by a sauce made with truffle juice); croustillant de sardines marinées (crispy marinated sardines); rumsteck argentin grillé aux épices (grilled Argentine rumpsteak with spices); and profiteroles aux pruneaux (profiteroles with prunes). La Sieste is a great find in an area dominated by overpriced brasseries. The seasonal menu changes four times a year, while the customers are as regular as they come.

Open: Mon-Fri noon-2.30pm, Mon-Thurs 8pm-11pm, Fri & Sat 8pm-11.30pm; reservations essential towards end of the week

starter: 39FF-65FF
main: 74FF-105FF
dessert: 30FF
Set menu: 69FF (lunch)

CB EC MC V

Map: 6 C8

Métro: Odéon, Saint-Michel

Smoking throughout

La Soummam
North African/French

☎ 01 43 54 12 43
25, rue des Grands Augustins, Saint-Germain

The left bank of the Seine is a long way from the North African home of the Berbers. But here, in this restaurant decorated with carpets, pottery and artworks, you can taste tammek-foult, a couscous of steamed vegetables accompanied by milk curds. There's also the veal tajine with olives, artichokes, prunes and other vegetables. Meanwhile, at the next table, someone will be opting for œuf (egg) mayonnaise followed by blanquette de veau (veal stewed in a lemony white sauce). In the Berber part of the menu, you'll find the proprietor's speciality, the 'remonte-moral' ('spirit-raiser') – with eggs, onions, spicy sausage and tomatoes – which fulfils the therapeutic promise of its name. The hasban are unique too: semolina croquettes flavoured with mint and served with vegetables and chickpeas. The Algerian wines – red or light rosé from Medea – make for very pleasant drinking. And before the ritual tea, why not give in and have a makrout, blended from semolina, dates, honey and mint?

starter: 22FF-45FF
main: 67FF-115FF
dessert: 24FF-48FF
Set menu: 65FF (lunch), 89FF, 102.50FF, 152.50FF
(lunch & dinner)
AE CB DC EC V

Open: Mon-Sat noon-2.30pm, 7pm-11.30pm; reservations advisable in the evening

7ᵉ Arrondissement

Saint-Germain

 Tour Eiffel

Invalides

Quai d'Orsay

7^e Arrondissement

It has the reputation of being rather staid. At first glance, its formal beauty and conventional manners give an impression of restraint and distance. But the seventh's world of elaborate ironwork, flashing gold leaf and hewn stone has an extravagance all of its own. Watching over the city by night, the Eiffel Tower's slender silhouette dominates the Paris skyline. At its feet, the Seine flows in a gracious curve and the smooth lawns of the Champ de Mars stretch away. Somehow it always feels like Sunday in the alleys of this park, with its sweeping prospects and precise design. To the east, the well-to-do and sleepy rue de l'Univer-sité, rue Saint-Dominique and rue de Grenelle make their calm way down to the Boulevard Saint-Germain, leaving behind the bright dome of Les Invalides. Here it seems there's a Ministry on every block. The National Assembly is over by the river, the hôtel de Matignon (the Prime Minister's residence) in the rue de Varenne. On Quai Anatole France, the Musée d'Orsay, housed in the impressively cavernous shell of an old railway station, displays paint-ings from the 19th century. This is, after all, the seventh arrondissement, where history lives on in the present.

Le 7e Sud
Mediterranean

☎ **01 44 18 30 30**
**159, rue de Grenelle,
Invalides**

Map: 7 D5

Métro: Invalides, La Tour
Maubourg

 Nonsmoking tables
available

The tone here is cosmopolitan. Le 7e Sud specialises in bringing together the full gamut of Mediterranean flavours. The décor has a warm, eastern feel, especially in the vaulted cellar downstairs. Customers organise their own culinary itinerary, starting, for example, with light-as-a-feather fritellis calamares grecs (Greek-style calamari), creamy Tunisian ojja or soup of the day. For mains, you can have a stopover in Italy with rigatoni ricotti au jambon de Parme (rigatoni with Parma ham), a tajine in the purest Moroccan tradition or a mixed kebab on a bed of baby beans from the market. This is a great spot to meet up with friends: the food comes in generous serves, so you can let the others have a taste of your meal while leaving an elegant sufficiency for yourself. The more traditional desserts are prepared according to time-honoured methods: behold the warm, creamy centre of the fondant au chocolat.

starter: 40FF-55FF
main: 64FF-92FF
dessert: 45FF
Plat du jour: 92FF

AE V; €

Open: Mon-Sat noon-4pm, 7pm-midnight, Sun noon-5pm;
reservations advisable

Apollon
Greek

☎ **01 45 55 68 47**
**24, rue Jean-Nicot,
Invalides**

Map: 7 E5

Métro: Invalides, La Tour
Maubourg

 Smoking throughout

 Pavement tables

The warm buzz of Greek conversation is an indication of this restaurant's popularity among the capital's Hellenic community. The blue décor is dominated by a central, open kitchen, typical of restaurants in Greece. A procession of hors d'œuvres with dry, sparkling names makes its way to the tables: tzatziki, dolmadakia, ktipiti. The tiropitas (small cheese turnovers) are straight out of Zeus' kitchen. These starters are followed by the famous souvlakis or giouvesti, a lamb-based dish whose ingredients remain a mystery to us but which is absolutely delectable. For dessert, the yaourt maison au miel et aux pignons de pin (chef's yoghurt with honey and pinenuts) adds just the right touch of sweetness. The retsinas and Cretan wines help bring back memories of past holidays.

starter: 45FF-73FF
main: 75FF-120FF
dessert: 35FF-45FF
Set menu: 85FF (lunch),
138FF (dinner)

cash only

Open: Mon-Sat 11.30am-3pm, 7pm-11pm; reservations
advisable

Au Sauvignon
French

☎ 01 45 48 49 02
80, rue des Saints Péres, Saint-Germain

Map: 7 J7
Métro: Sèvres-Babylone

Smoking throughout

Pavement tables & covered terrace

At the corner of rue de Sèvres and rue des Saints Pères, the Sauvignon has chosen to keep it simple: snacks and quality wine. It seems to be a winning combination; at lunchtime clients take this little bistrot by storm. It's a fair bet the sandwiches made from Poilâne bread (to complement the wines) have something to do with it. Try fillings of rillons de Touraine (pork pieces), cou d'oie farci (stuffed goose neck), terrine pur porc (pure pork terrine), rillettes (meat pastes), andouille de Vire (smoked pork sausage) or saucisse ou jambon d'Auvergne (sausages and ham from the Auvergne). All the ingredients have been carefully chosen to make you forget that sad old café standard, the ham sandwich. Cheese lovers needn't feel left out either; there's an excellent Saint-Marcellin de Barthélemy, among others. Feel at ease among picturesque rural and vineyard scenes and enjoy the efficient service.

main: 27FF-129FF
dessert: 34FF
Set menu: 70FF

CB EC MC V

Open: Mon-Sat 8.30am-10pm; reservations not accepted

Aux délices du Shezuen
Chinese

☎ 01 43 06 22 55
40, Ave Duquesne, École Militaire

Map: 7 E7
Métro: St-François Xavier, École Militaire

Nonsmoking tables available

Pavement tables

This is definitely the place to taste Chinese food in all its sophistication. A short walk from Les Invalides, this rather opulent restaurant specialises in Sichuan cuisine, which is among the spiciest in China. The décor is a cut above your average Chinese restaurant and the rounded contours of the room give it an intimate feel. The welcome is warm, and the service courteous and discreet. Among the starters, don't miss soupe de raviolis aux crevettes (shrimp dumpling soup), which is one of a kind. The menu also features guotieh (fried dumplings) and jiaotze (steamed dumplings). The meat is tender and flavoursome; try bœuf aux écorces d'oranges (beef with orange peel) or sauté d'agneau à la ciboulette (sautéd lamb with chives). To finish, let yourself be tempted by the unusual sorbet au gingembre (ginger sorbet). Don't fall for the menu conseillé (suggested menu) – it's a bit dull.

starter: 39FF-80FF
main: 45FF-200FF
dessert: 30FF-80FF
Set menu: 96FF
Plat du jour: 80FF

AE CB

Open: daily noon-2pm, 7pm-10pm; reservations advisable

Banga de Mayotte
Creole

☎ 01 45 66 84 44
33, rue Rousselet,
Invalides

Map: 7 G8

Métro: Duroc

 Smoking throughout

You enter this minuscule restaurant through a narrow hallway and courtyard. Not easy to find, but worth the trouble for those wishing to sample the culinary delights of Mayotte (Mahore in English), a tiny island paradise to the north-west of Madagascar. The dishes borrow heavily from Creole cuisine: delicious, fresh sambos (small flaky pastries stuffed with beef, herbs and spices), rougail de saucisses (sausage rougail), cari de poulet au lait de coco (chicken curry with coconut milk) and banana baked in its skin then sprinkled with rum. While the choice is limited and the food simple, this place is worth a visit if only for the owner's sunny welcome. There's nothing like a quick trip to the tropics to cheer yourself up on a rainy day.

main: 55FF
dessert: 20FF
Set menu: 90FF
Plat du jour: 55FF

cash only

Open: Mon-Fri noon-2.30pm, Tues-Sat 8pm-11pm; reservations advisable

Chez l'Ami Jean
French (Basque/South-West)

☎ 01 47 05 86 89
27, rue Malar,
Invalides

Map: 7 D5

Métro: La-Tour-Maubourg,
  Invalides, Pont-de-l'Alma
  (RER)

 Smoking throughout

Although dark and cramped, Chez l'Ami Jean is full of atmosphere. Photos of rugby players and chisteras (a type of wicker basket used in the Basque game of pelota), a hearty welcome and the laid-back ambience transport you to the Basque country as soon as you walk through the door. The mixed clientele includes politicians, journalists and personal friends of the owner, who all come to soak up the friendly atmosphere. The food reflects the surroundings: pleasant and unpretentious. Basque-style eggs or chicken, piperade (tomatoes and sweet green peppers served with a delicious slice of quickly seared Bayonne ham), fromage de brebis à la confiture de cerises noires (ewe's milk cheese with black cherry conserve) or gâteau basque (a type of custard-filled tart) are among the Basque specialities that dominate the menu. A fabulous, affordably priced restaurant and a good place to fight off the winter cold in this posh neighbourhood.

starter: 35FF-80FF
main: 60FF-120FF
dessert: 25FF-50FF
Set menu: 99FF
Plat du jour: 80FF

CB EC MC V; €

Open: Mon-Sat noon-3pm, 7pm-10.30pm; reservations essential

Café crème

Some people have it in bed, some in the kitchen, some wolf it down, some give it a miss because they're just not hungry; and others prefer the local cafe. Strong coffee or black tea, croissants or buttered toast, fresh news and the first light of dawn: breakfast starts each and every day.

While the romantic cafe breakfast is still with us, the working-week business breakfast has proved particularly popular, saving time (it doesn't cut the day in half and never drags on), energy (it's light, so you avoid that post-lunch fatigue) and money (it's less expensive than a full-blown meal). Business breakfasts are usually served between 8am and 9am, so they need to be booked the day before. There are many venues catering to different sectors (banking, finance, business or communications) and their agendas.

Breakfast at a luxury hotel costs no less than 170FF to 270FF per person. The George V, the Plaza Athénée, the Ritz, the Crillon and the Raphaël (see the feature entitled 'Window on the bars of luxury hotels' in the next chapter) each has its own atmosphere and a menu crammed with enticing offerings. From continental or health-food breakfasts to American or buffet-style spreads, each caters to the needs of its customers and offers food that could be considered worthy of a gourmet lunch. At George V, for example, the Japanese-style breakfast (onseg eggs, miso soup, tofu, dried seaweed, vegetables in vinegar, rice and green tea) is prepared by an experienced chef and often proves a great comfort to homesick Japanese unable to stomach the thought of yet another continental breakfast.

The breakfasts available from caterers such as Hédiard, pastry chefs like Ladurée or bakers in the league of Chez Paul are both tasty and tasteful. Apart from the cost (half the price of breakfast at a luxury hotel) and the more informal aspect, it's the sight and smell of warm buns and other delicacies that really whets the appetite.

Hédiard 21, place de la Madeleine, 8e ☎ 01 43 12 88 99

Ladurée 16, rue Royal, 8e ☎ 01 42 60 21 79

Chez Paul 77, rue de Seine, 6e ☎ 01 55 42 02 23

La Cigale
French

☎ 01 45 48 87 87
11 bis, rue Chomel,
Saint-Germain

Map: 7 H7
Métro: Sèvres Babylone

 Nonsmoking tables available

 Pavement tables

For the past seven years, Gérard Idoux – the undisputed 'soufflé master of Paris' and a man of great taste – has won the hearts (and taste-buds) of a loyal clientele. His secret lies in the fusion of sophistication and simplicity, both in the dining room and in the kitchen. He is also a generous person, whose passion for food is reflected above all in his meticulous choice of ingredients. Depending on the season, customers can choose from between 60 to 80 savoury or sweet soufflés. The soufflés aux morilles (morel mushrooms), aux oursins (sea urchins) and au potiron (pumpkin) are autumn favourites. In summer, don't miss the soufflé aux abricots (apricot soufflé), which is redolent of Roussillon. The menu changes monthly and constantly attracts new regulars.

Open: Mon-Fri noon-2.30pm, Mon-Sat 7.30pm-11pm; reservations advisable

starter: 38FF-41FF
main: 59FF-119FF
dessert: 38FF-59FF
Plat du jour: 115FF

CB MC V

Clémentine
French

☎ 01 45 51 41 16
62, ave Bosquet,
École Militaire

Map: 7 D6
Métro: École Militaire

 Nonsmoking tables available

The slate outside tells you straightaway to expect 'cuisine de terroir et de tradition' ('traditional country cooking'). Pull aside the heavy curtain hanging in the doorway and you've arrived chez Clémentine. The lady of the house looks after the customers while her partner takes charge of the stove. Common sense and simple, harmonious combinations of flavours characterise the mouthwatering menus, hand-written in chalk on the wall. Dishes such as the jambon de pays grillé aux échalotes (grilled country ham with shallots) and the rognons de veau à la moutarde (veal kidneys with mustard) are lovingly prepared and invariably prompt the customers to exclaim: 'C'est bon!' Which is all the reward the owner could want.

Open: Mon-Fri noon-3pm, 7pm-10pm, Sat 7pm-10pm; reservations not accepted

starter: 53FF-73FF
main: 89FF
dessert: 35FF
Set menu: 129FF

CB EC MC V

7ᵉ ARRONDISSEMENT

7 arrondi
7arrondi

Le Clos des Gourmets

☎ 01 45 51 75 61

French

**16, ave Rapp,
Champ de Mars, Tour Eiffel**

Map: 7 C5

Métro: Alma Marceau

Dress code applies

Smoking throughout

Pavement tables in summer

In a neighbourhood with as many embassies as posh restaurants, Le Clos des Gourmets stands apart. The customers are just as well-heeled and there's nothing particularly original about the decor but finding reasonably-priced cuisine with this much style in such an area could be classified mission impossible. After working with the best, the young chef Arnaud Pitrois is going it alone, and with fabulous results. There's moussaka d'agneau en pastilla (lamb moussaka served as a pastilla, with eggplant pulp, orange blossom and fresh coriander); tête de cochon croustillante, pommes rattes écrasées au beurre demi-sel (crispy pig's head and ratte potatoes mashed with lightly-salted butter); noix de Saint-Jacques poêlées au sésame, risotto au vieux parmesan (fried scallops with sesame and risotto with aged parmesan); fenouil confit aux épices, sorbet citron et basilic. Top quality ingredients, subtle flavours, food cooked to perfection and a regularly updated menu – you can't do better than that.

Set menu: 175FF (135FF (Tues-Fri for two-course lunch))

CB EC MC V

Open: Tues-Sat noon-2pm, 7.30pm-10.30pm; reservations essential

---

La Fontaine de Mars

☎ 01 47 05 46 44

French (South-West)

**129, rue Saint-Dominique,
Tour Eiffel**

Map: 7 D5

Métro: École-Militaire

Smoking throughout

Pavement tables

La Fontaine de Mars occupies the corner of a small square with covered archways and an imposing fountain from which the restaurant takes its name. Since the 1930s, Parisians and foreigners alike have come here for the cassoulet aux haricots tarbais (cassoulet with Tarbes beans) and the magret de canard (fillet of duck breast). The bench seats and red checked tablecloths are still the same and the restaurant is never empty. At lunch and dinner, lively conversation accompanies the clink of knives and forks. If you're not already converted to the joys of cottage farm produce, try the confit de canard gersois (duck from the Gers), served with potatoes sautéed in duck fat and tossed in parsley. The madiran Bouchecassé 95 goes extremely well with this dish. Monsieur and Madame Boudon have been at the helm of La Fontaine for ten years and love talking about the origin of their ingredients.

starter: 55FF-135FF
main: 70FF-135FF
Set menu: 90FF (lunch)

AE CB MC V

Open: daily noon-3pm, 7.30pm-11pm; reservations essential

Il 34
Italian

☎ 01 45 55 80 75
34, rue de Bourgogne,
Invalides

Map: 7 G5

Métro: Varenne, Invalides

  Smoking throughout

The simple yet intimate interior, the irreproachable service, the stylish cuisine and the wine list make Il 34 (pronounced 'trenta quattro') one of the most elegant Italian restaurants in Paris. Predictably, various sorts of pasta figure on the short, classic menu, but there are also delicious antipasti (notably the very tasty Parma ham and mozzarella), primi piatti (including pappardelle with preserved zucchini and tomatoes) and some subtle variations on veal – the meat that rules in Italy. Everything is done with flair. There are not many wines available here, but the wines that are offered are well chosen (for example a lovely Nobile de Montepulciano), which explains the relatively high prices. Customers include lovers of Italian food and politicians – the National Assembly being just a short walk away.

starter: 70FF-140FF
main: 80FF-160FF
dessert: 50FF

CB EC MC V

Open: Mon-Fri 12.30pm-2.30pm, daily 7pm-11pm; reservations advisable (evenings)

Le Télégraphe
French

☎ 01 42 92 03 04
41, rue de Lille,
Musée d'Orsay

Map: 7 J5

Métro: Rue-du-Bac, RER
Musée d'Orsay

 Nonsmoking tables available

 Garden tables

Le Télégraphe has a great atmosphere and sumptuous cuisine. This top-notch restaurant is situated in a Belle Époque residence originally built to accommodate single women employed by the Postes, Télégraphes et Téléphones. The current owner has faithfully preserved the building's old-style charm, especially inside – Art Deco fans will love the high ceilings and gorgeous mosaics. There's also a garden, totally removed from the bustle of inner Paris, where you can enjoy lunch or dinner when the sun comes out. The food is just as attractive as the décor. The chef brings a personal touch to stylish and beautifully presented dishes such as the carpaccio de foie gras, the bavette d'aloyau (top sirloin of beef), the noix de veau poêlée (fillet of veal) and the poire rôtie au caramel (baked pear with caramel).

starter: 65FF
main: 120FF
dessert: 50FF
Set menu: 195FF
Plat du jour: 150FF

AE D V

Open: Mon-Fri noon-2.30pm, 7.30pm-midnight, Sat 7.30pm-midnight, Sun; reservations essential (towards end of the week)

Bars & Cafes – 6e & 7e

Le 10 10, rue de l'Odéon, Paris 6e, Odéon ☎ 01 43 26 66 83 Métro: Odéon (Map: 6 E8)

For years and years now this handily located little pub has been attracting a friendly crowd of students, many from other countries. Sangria is the number one drink here, and la chanson française is the favoured music. Soft lighting, smoke-browned posters and a little cellar room make this an ideal place for plotting the next revolution or conquering a lonely heart.

Open: daily 5.30pm-2am; By the glass: beer 18FF (after 9pm 23FF); cash only

A la cour de Rohan cour du commerce Saint-André, 59-61, rue Saint-André-des Arts, Paris 6e, Saint-Germain-des-Prés ☎ 01 43 25 79 67 Métro: Odéon, Saint-Michel (Map: 6 D8)

Tucked away in the historic Saint-Germain neighbourhood, this cosy, unassuming salon de thé is on an alley where the revolutionaries used to get together, notably Marat and Guillotin. In the salon, nothing matches: the china is partly English, partly from Limoges; there are rattan chairs, and others upholstered in 'medieval' velvet or leatherette. The scents of filtered coffee, pounded cocao and pastries baking waft around upstairs and down. Note: this place is nonsmoking.

Open: daily noon-7.30pm, Fri & Sat noon-midnight (Apr-Oct); By the glass: champagne 38FF; coffee 20FF; meals and snacks available; credit cards accepted

Le café des lettres 53, rue de Verneuil Paris 7e, St Germain ☎ 01 42 22 52 17 Métro: Solférino, RER: Musée d'Orsay (Map: 7 J5)

Inside the magnificent Hôtel d'Avejan, which also houses the Centre national des lettres (a state literature council) and the Maison des écrivains (a writers' centre), Le Café des Lettres is a marvellously tranquil place. The tucked-away location and quiet talk give it a calm and intimate feel. When the weather's fine, you can enjoy the flavours of Scandinavian, French and Indian food on the charming terrace. A perfect place to unwind and let your thoughts wander.

Open: Mon-Fri 9am-11pm, Sat 11am-11pm, Sun noon-4pm; By the glass: beer 30FF, champagne 50FF; coffee 14FF; meals available; CB EC MC V

Café du musée Rodin 77, rue de Varenne, Paris 7e, Invalides ☎ 01 44 18 61 10 Métro: Varenne (Map: 7 F6)

A serene beauty pervades the garden of the Rodin Museum. Sculptures appear here and there among the roses or along the pathways lined with lime trees. As you walk in (entry to the garden alone is 5FF) you can see the bowed head of Le Penseur (The Thinker) and La Porte de l'Enfer (The Gates of Hell). If the weather's good, you can have a drink and a snack at one of the tables hidden behind the trees.

Open: Tues-Sun 10am-6pm (Apr-Sept), 10am-4.30pm (Oct-Mar); coffee 10FF; snacks available; credit cards accepted

Café Thoumieux 4, rue de la Comète, Paris 7e, Quai d'Orsay ☎ 01 45 51 50 40 Métro: La Tour Maubourg, Invalides (Map: 7 E5)

This bar à tapas is attached to the restaurant of the hôtel Thoumieux. A bit of a hike from the bustle of rue Saint-Dominique's shops, its single, long room is nevertheless rarely empty. The neighbourhood's well-heeled young people seem to enjoy the Iberian ambience. Scrumptious platters of tapas (Spanish-style hors d'œuvres) go perfectly with a San Miguel or a flavoured vodka (no fewer than forty different varieties are on offer, including chocolate and watermelon).

Open: Mon-Fri noon-2am, Sat 5pm-2am; By the glass: beer 20FF, champagne 38FF; coffee 12FF; meals available; credit cards accepted

Coolin's 15, rue Clément, Paris 6e, Odéon ☎ 01 44 07 00 92 Métro: Mabillon, Odéon (Map: 6 D7)

This Irish pub offers a friendly refuge from the somewhat cold atmosphere of the Saint-Germain market. English-speaking expats come here to chat over a pint and nibble on food from back home. The giant screen is not an object of beauty but, when there's a football match, you can feel those Irish heartbeats throbbing in unison, and your beer suddenly tastes quite different.

Open: daily 9am-2am; By the glass: beer 19FF; coffee 7FF-12FF; meals and snacks available; occasional performances of traditional Irish music; credit cards accepted

Cubana Café 47, rue Vavin, Paris 6e, Montparnasse ☎ 01 40 46 80 81 Métro: Vavin (Map: 6 J5)

The spirit of Cuba hangs in the air of this bar-restaurant, intertwined with curls of smoke in the smoking room, where customers loll about in old leather armchairs and contemplate oil paintings of daily life on the island. Later in the evening, set yourself up at the bar – the cheerful banter of Franck, Alban and Ludivine will keep you going until dawn.

Open: daily noon-3pm, 7pm-3am; By the glass: beer 19FF, champagne 43FF; coffee 11FF (after 10pm 22FF); meals available; cash only

Les Étages Saint-Germain 5, rue de Buci, Paris 6e, Odéon ☎ 01 46 34 26 26 Métro: Odéon (Map: 6 C8)

In an old-fashioned Parisian setting overlooking a lovely terrace, customers can have a drink, salad or brunch on one of the colourful étages or levels of this small bar. Not a must, perhaps, but a friendly place nonetheless, and more original than some of the area's better-known brasseries.

Open: daily 11am-2am, By the glass: beer 20FF; coffee 15FF; snacks available; literary afternoon on Thursdays; SLAM (hip-hop, rap poetry); credit cards accepted

La Paillote 45, rue Monsieur le Prince, Paris 6e, Odéon ☎ 01 43 26 45 69 Métro: Odéon, RER: Luxembourg (Map: 6 E8)

Small lamps cast a dim red light on the Paillote's bamboo décor, giving this place the feel of an exotic speak-easy. Nightbirds of different feathers come to perch here well into the wee hours, sipping cocktails in couch hammocks and putting some swing in their spleen, with the help of 'the largest collection of jazz records in Paris'.

Open: daily 9pm until dawn; By the glass: beer 38FF, champagne 56FF; CB EC MC V

7ᵉ arrondi

Map: 7 J5
Métro: Rue du Bac

Smoking throughout

Veggie
Vegetarian

☎ 01 42 61 28 61
**38, rue de Verneuil,
Solférino, Musée d'Orsay**

This is just like being in the countryside. The rear of the shop is stacked with crates of potatoes and carrots still covered in earth. Try the invigorating carrot juice before moving on to the scrumptious potage aux poireaux et poti-marron (leek and squash soup), ratatouille de poivrons avec tomates et olives (capsicum ratatouille) and tambouille de riz et patates douces avec des grains de maïs frais (rice with sweet potatoes and fresh corn kernels). The food is served simply in cardboard containers, while a handful of chairs and plastic barrels serve as a dining room. For dessert, even the most spartan of customers will love the barely sweetened compote de pommes aux pruneaux (stewed apple with prunes) and the amazing fig cream. The menu is updated daily and the extremely affordable food is priced according to weight. This is a fantastic spot for light, healthy food.

starter: 20FF
main: 40FF
dessert: 20FF
Plat du jour: 40FF

cash only

Open: Mon-Fri 10.30am-3pm, 4.30pm-7pm; reservations not accepted

8e Arrondissement

Champs-Élysées

Madeleine

Monceau

Saint-Lazare

8e Arrondissement

This arrondissement was born under a lucky star. Its avenues radiate from l'Étoile, bathing in the glow of fame. First among them is the Champs-Elysées. From the Arc de Triomphe to the Place de la Concorde, the 'Elysean Fields' rule unchallenged. On New Year's Eve and after major sporting victories there's always a party on the Champs. Like a splendid, regal hostess, the avenue receives its guests, makes them mingle and moves them along. And the guests keep coming. Just a short walk away, the ave Montaigne haughtily displays its designer wares. Motor boats are moored by the pont de l'Alma. And members of the jet-set go shopping in the ave George-V and the rue du Faubourg Saint-Honoré. Here fashion, art and luxury hotels go hand in hand. Only the finest are on display, as in the neighbourhood's theatres and museums. Grand Palais or Petit Palais? The door is wide open, just go in and have a look. The adventure continues with a walk among the office buildings from rue Royale to the place de la Madeleine. When you reach Gare Saint-Lazare, the feel changes and another journey begins. The languidly romantic Parc Monceau belongs to a more mysterious world.

Bangkok Café
Thai

☎ **01 43 87 62 56**
28, rue de Moscou, Gare St Lazare

Map: 8 C8

Métro: Rome, Place de Clichy

 Smoking throughout

 Pavement tables

Manu has gone from mixing plaster (he did the Thai-style decor himself) to mixing drinks (this young, dynamic owner currently looks after the bar). Some customers may be happy just to sip a Singha or a mei kwei lue, but Thailand is renowned for its sophisticated, colourful and varied cuisine – which is an apt description of the fare on offer at the Bangkok Café. Gourmets will love the som tam thaï (green papaya salad) or the yam neugne (beef with sweet herbs) and go into raptures over the simple porc au caramel (pork with caramel) or the massaman neuwe (beef curry). The dishes are decorated with petals and usually accompanied by rice with saffron or coconut milk. If you have a sweet tooth, you won't mind using chopsticks to sample the tapioca or the riz noir au lait de coco (black rice pudding with coconut milk).

starter: 54FF-68FF
main: 68FF-120FF
dessert: 35FF-52FF
Set menu: 89FF (lunch), 170FF (dinner)

AE CB DC EC MC V; €

Open: Mon-Fri 11am-2am (lunch noon-3pm, dinner 7pm-midnight), Sat 5pm-2am; reservations advisable (end of week)

Le Bec rouge
French (Alsace)

☎ **01 45 22 15 02**
33, rue de Constantinople, Villiers

Map: 8 C7

Métro: Villiers, Europe

 Smoking throughout

Le Bec rouge is a real find, offering delicious, time-honoured cuisine while remaining open to new ideas. In a traditional setting, which manages to avoid being kitsch, you can choose between two plats du jour. Dishes like the duo de poissons aux légumes (fish duo with vegetables) are not typical of the Alsace region; others, such as the hearty baeckeofe (three meats cooked with potatoes and vegetables) are regional standards. For starters there's marbré de poireaux au foie gras sucré (leek with sweet foie gras) or the semi-cooked foie gras and marc de gewurtz jelly. For mains, there's choucroute royale (sauerkraut), bibelakasse à base de fromage blanc et de raifort (a traditional dish based on cream cheese and horseradish), entrecôte au pinot noir and travers de porc au miel de sapin (pork spare ribs with pine honey). These last two are particularly tasty. Finish off with an Alsatian coffee (marc de gewurtz, coffee and crème fraîche). Yop'la.

starter: 40FF-75FF
main: 70FF-120FF
dessert: 40FF-45FF
Set menu: 98FF (excluding public holidays), 120FF, 148FF

AE CB EC MC V

Open: Mon-Sat noon-2pm, 7.30pm-10.30pm; reservations advisable

8ᵉ ARRONDISSEMENT

Map: 8 F4
Métro: Georges V

Smoking throughout

Chez les Filles
French

☎ 01 45 62 58 38
36, rue Washington,
Friedland

Just when you thought you'd seen and tasted everything Paris had to offer ... Chez les Filles is like nowhere else, and that's exactly what gives this place its charm. You eat facing the wall, the kitchen sink or, with a bit of luck, at two folding tables. Instead of a menu, your friendly hostesses Florence and Anne offer a range of plats du jour. You book your meal, not your table. On the day we visited, regulars could choose between gnochetta (gnocchi with tomato and oregano) and a delicious bœuf carottes au thym et au laurier (beef with carrots, thyme and bay leaves). Just like eating at home. And all that for a modest sum, in the chic 8th arrondissement. What do you say? Merci, les filles!

main: 35FF-45FF
dessert: 12FF-15FF
Plat du jour: 35FF-45FF

cash only

Open: Mon-Fri noon-4pm; reservations not accepted

Map: 8 D3
Métro: Ternes, Courcelles

Smoking throughout

Le Daru
Russian

☎ 01 42 27 23 60
19, rue Daru,
Place des Ternes

'The oldest Russian restaurant in Paris'? The competition might have something to say about this claim, but who cares? A hop, skip and a jump from rue Daru's charming Orthodox church, the food here is as Russian as it gets. The borsch aux choux rouges et aux betteraves (borsch with red cabbage and beetroot), served with a tender *piroshki*, is a great way to start. To follow, it's a toss-up between the hearty assiette Orlov (salmon rillettes, flavoured herring and blinis with crème fraîche) and agneau Luli (minced lamb marinated with cumin then crumbed), served with the traditional kacha (small buckwheat pancakes). Finish in style with a slice of vatrouchka, a cream-cheesecake flavoured with lemon, that melts in your mouth. The warm décor, which is traditional without being kitsch, is an ideal foil for the discreet, professional service.

starter: 45FF-150FF
main: 80FF-160FF
dessert: 40FF-45FF
Set menu: 130FF,
170FF (lunch)

AE V

Open: Mon-Sat noon-3pm, 7.30pm-10.30pm; reservations advisable

Window on the bars of luxury hotels

Ever been tempted to walk into the bar of a luxury hotel? Go for it! They're open to the public and not nearly as intimidating as you might think. Everything from the contents of your glass to the contents of the room seems carefully designed to blend in. Wood panelling, comfortable armchairs, soft lighting and an opulent bar are standard features. The atmosphere is hushed, intimate and elegant, and every bar feels like a special retreat, sheltered from the hustle and bustle of the outside world. Whether it's at the Ritz, the George V, the Plaza, the Lutétia, the Crillon or the Raphaël, a bar will often recall the famous writers, artists, businessmen and media personalities who have enjoyed spending time there. Hemingway's observation about the bar at the Ritz holds as true today as always: 'You come here in the hope of forgetting, meeting and discovering'.

Crillon 10, place de la Concorde, 8e ☎ 01 44 71 50 00

George V 31, ave Georges V, 8e ☎ 01 49 52 70 00

Lutétia 45, blvd Raspail, 6e ☎ 01 49 54 46 46

Plaza Athénée 25, ave Montaigne, 8e ☎ 01 53 67 66 00

Raphaël 17, ave Kléber, 16e ☎ 01 53 64 32 00

Ritz 15, place Vendôme, 1er ☎ 01 43 16 30 30

Elliott
American

☎ **01 42 89 30 50**
166, blvd Haussmann, Monceau

Who said American restaurants have to be noisy and full of skimpily clad waitresses shifting hamburgers? You can forget that stereotype at Elliott, where the aim is to reconcile French and American cuisine. The décor is sophisticated: authentic old-style bench seats upholstered in moleskin and with sepia photos of baseball legends. The serving staff are gracefully cool but also very attentive. You could almost be in a Frank Capra film. And the best of it is, the food lives up to the setting. Among the American dishes, eggs benedict (poached eggs, toasted muffin, grilled bacon and hollandaise sauce) is a favourite with business types at lunch and aficionados in the evening. The gambas (king prawns) or the fraise melba (strawberry melba) will delight those who swear by French cuisine. Wine lovers will appreciate the rounded flavour of the Copperidge cabernet or chardonnay.

Open: Mon-Sat noon-3pm, 8pm-2.30am, Sun noon-5pm; reservations essential for lunch, advisable for dinner

Map: 8 E5

Métro: St-Philippe-du-Roule

Entertainment: DJ Thursday evenings, clairvoyant readings Friday & Saturday evenings

 Nonsmoking tables available

 Pavement tables

starter: 42FF-48FF
main: 63FF-118FF
dessert: 38FF-43FF
Set menu: 99FF (Sunday brunch)
Plat du jour: 90FF

AE CB EC MC V; €

8e ARRONDISSEMENT

Map: 8 F2
Métro: Charles de Gaulle-Étoile

Nonsmoking tables available

Sheltered interior courtyard

Le Flora Danica
Scandinavian

☎ 01 44 13 86 26
**142, ave des Champs-Élysées,
Champs-Élysées**

Right on the Champs-Élysées, Le Flora Danica has a quiet, concealed courtyard, a lovely place to be on a sunny day. After recent renovations, the look is contemporary Danish. The salmon is a long-standing speciality and is prepared in a variety of ways: marinated in dill and served raw (almost preserved) in a thick cut, seasoned with a mustard dressing; grilled on one side; hot-smoked; pickled; and as a fondue ... Imported straight from Denmark, it tastes nothing like the salmon that most of us are used to. Other musts include the fried herrings and the filets de renne aux fruits des bois (fillet of reindeer with wild berries), which is tender and has a rich game-like flavour. Don't forget to sample the Danish desserts. Both curious gourmets and lovers of fine food won't be disappointed.

starter: 58FF-145FF
main: 92FF-195FF
dessert: 42FF-60FF
Set menu: 175FF
Plat du jour: 100FF-200FF

CB DC EC JCB MC V; €

Open: daily noon-2.30pm, 7.15pm-11.30pm (24 hours in summer); reservations advisable

---

Map: 8 F7
Métro: Miromesnil

Smoking throughout

Granterroirs
French

☎ 01 47 42 18 18
**30, rue de Miromesnil,
Saint-Augustin**

Not your average lunch spot, Granterroirs is located in the business district of Saint-Augustin and resembles a huge delicatessen. The owner, Jean-François Gimenez, lovingly selects the best local produce the French provinces have to offer (more than 600 products). Customers sit on benches at a huge table in the middle of the room, where casual eating and conversation are guaranteed. There are five daily specials instead of a menu, including a range of gourmet tarts and platters. The assiette Périgourdine (mixed green salad dressed with olive oil from Provence and balsamic vinegar, fresh foie gras and preserved gizzards) and the tarte provençal (eggplant, Rocamadour cheese, olive oil and herbes de Provence) confirmed our suspicions: the French countryside tastes like heaven.

main: 35FF-45FF
dessert: 30FF-34FF
Set menu: 139FF

CB DC EC JCB MC V

Open: Mon-Sat noon-3pm; reservations not accepted

Le Huitième Sud
French

☎ 01 47 20 81 18
13, rue de la Trémoille,
Franklin Roosevelt

Caroline, the proprietor of Le Huitième Sud, likes to joke: 'We came here to brighten up the neighbourhood'. They've succeeded: there's nowhere else like this in the 8th arrondissement. Caroline and her acolytes don't offer set-price menus or meals à la carte, but a series of plats du jour: savoury tarts, mixed salads, pasta, steamed vegetables, terrines, all served with a smile. You'll soon discover that the pleasures of the tart can be infinitely varied: from chicken to curry to orange crab. If it's all too confusing, there's the tasty and substantial terrine de thon et son coulis de tomates (tuna terrine with tomato coulis). Choosing a dessert can be a wrench too: crumble, fromage blanc aux framboises (cream cheese with raspberries) or tarte bananes-noix de coco (banana and coconut tart). The Spanish-style décor reinforces the feeling of wellbeing that comes over you upon entering Le Huitième Sud.

Open: daily 9am-11.30am; noon-4pm; reservations advisable (can be made up until 1pm)

Map: 8 H4

Métro: Franklin Roosevelt

 Nonsmoking tables available

 Pavement tables

Plat du jour: 52FF-70FF

CB DE EC JCB MC V

Lô Sushi
Japanese

☎ 01 45 62 01 00
8, rue de Berri,
Étoile

Pure lines and spatial harmony characterise the decor at Lô Sushi. This is contemporary Japan, where design and technology dominate. Set into white walls that create a calm, sophisticated atmosphere, television screens show nonstop previews of recently released films and fashion parades organised by Lô Channel, the restaurant's own broadcaster. The service is not traditional, there's no pausing between courses, and no surprises either because you can see what you're choosing. The meal starts with a feast for the eyes: customers sit around a carousel and try to identify the food under the transparent lid of each dish as it crosses the room. The dexterity of the chefs is fascinating to watch, as they cut, slice and fill the sushi with salmon or tuna, the maki with avocado and the temaki with crab or cucumber. A stunning initiation rite for newcomers to Japanese cuisine.

Open: daily noon-12.30am; reservations advisable

Map: 8 F3

Métro: Georges V

 Nonsmoking tables available

starter: 15FF-50FF
main: 15FF-50FF
dessert: 15FF-50FF

AE CB V; €

8ᵉ ARRONDISSEMENT

Map: 8 G4

Métro: Charles de Gaulle-Étoile

Nonsmoking tables available

La Maison de l'Aubrac
French

☎ 01 43 59 05 14
37, rue Marbeuf,
Champs-Élysées

The Maison de l'Aubrac is proud of its region's beef, which comes in every conceivable form: steak, pavé de rumsteck (thick-cut rump), bavette (flank steak). Served with salad and sautéed potatoes, the meat is delicious – firm and tender at the same time. Other delectable offerings include the magret de canard (fillet of duck breast) and the traditional saucisse-aligot (sausage with a mash of potato, garlic and melted cheese). Renovated last summer, this restaurant attracts a mixed clientele including office workers, trendies and movie buffs. At lunchtime, it's absolutely packed. Customers wait at the enormous bar before being seated at one of the enclosed booths in the main dining room. If possible, avoid the nonsmoking area, which is laughably small.

starter: 50FF-80FF
main: 80FF-140FF
dessert: 30FF-40FF
Plat du jour: 80FF-100FF

AE CB V

Open: daily 24 hours; reservations not accepted

9^e Arrondissement

Havre-Caumartin

Cadet

Grands Boulevards

Pigalle

9ᵉ Arrondissement

It's as if the ninth arrondissement was doing its best to confuse you, just for fun. The smart set and the riff-raff, and foodies and big feeders all rub shoulders here. It's not in the least uncommon to find wildly different establishments just across the road or round the corner from each other. Leaving the Opéra or Drouot's, in the southern part of the arrondissement, you can wander and window shop on the boulevards. Department stores and little boutiques jostle for space on blvd Haussman and blvd des Capucines. On rue de Provence, rue Richer and rue du Faubourg-Montmartre, fast-food outlets and restaurants are crammed into every bit of space, and you'll hear a babel of languages. The northern part of the arrondissement has a rough and ready charm – there's the famously seedy Pigalle, and the restless place de Clichy. On Place Gustave-Toudouze the shops, cafes and restaurants are a colourful feast for the eye. Between Pigalle and the church of the Trinity, the New Athens district with its beautiful Greco-Roman architecture has a singular elegance. This little corner of Paris, full of grand houses and private gardens, has long been favoured by artists.

Addis Abeba
Ethiopian

☎ **01 42 80 06 78**
56, rue Notre-Dame-de-Lorette, Pigalle

An Ethiopian restaurant is something of a novelty, and in Pigalle of all places! It's also surprising to discover that you sample the local fare with your hands, although cutlery isn't strictly forbidden. Everyone digs into the huge dish of injera – a kind of grain pancake served with each course – doing their best not to make a mess. Your culinary safari might begin with blé concassé au beurre et piment (cracked wheat with butter and chilli) or mousse au lentilles (lentil mousse) and continue with Ethiopian tartare – cooked or raw. The mixed platter, which includes beef, lentils, spinach, cheese and cabbage, allows you to range over the extraordinary flavours of this cuisine. Don't miss the coffee ceremony: the mocha is grilled in front of you before being brewed. The décor is somewhat lacking in character, but the real change of scenery takes place where it counts: on your plate.

Open: daily noon-3pm, 7.30pm-11.45pm; reservations advisable (especially weekends)

Map: 9 E5
Métro: St-Georges

 Smoking throughout

starter: 30FF
main: 59FF-110FF
dessert: 28FF-30FF

CB MC V

L'Auberge du Clou
Modern French

☎ **01 48 78 22 48**
30 ave de Trudaine, Pigalle

L'Auberge du Clou opened in the late 19th century, when regulars included Courteline, Satie and Toulouse-Lautrec. You can still see the traces of a magnificent fresco that Lautrec painted in the cellar. The copper bar in the large dining room emphasises the provincial inn atmosphere. The food combines excellent country cooking with inventive, cosmopolitan flavours. The unbeatably priced set menu changes weekly. Culinary delights at the time of our visit included poulpe á galicienne (Galician-style octopus), brioche tiède au sésame et chorizo (warm sesame and chorizo brioche), a perfectly seasoned tajine de chinchard aux petits légumes (scad tajine with baby vegetables), mascarpone mousse and a tuile au cacao (cocoa and almond biscuits). A varied main menu ranges from fond d'artichaut au foie gras tiède (artichoke heart with warm foie gras) to sauté de porc aux palourdes (sautéed pork with clams). The cellar holds some fine international vintages as well as a well-chosen selection of organic wines.

Open: Tues-Sat noon-2pm, 7.30pm-11.30pm; reservations advisable

Map: 9 C7
Métro: Pigalle, Anvers

 Smoking throughout

 Terrace tables in summer

starter: 39FF-78FF
main: 84FF-120FF
dessert: 32FF-44FF
Set menu: 98FF, 75FF (lunch)
Plat du jour: 85FF-110FF

CB EC MC V; €

Aux Berges du Sud
Corsican

☎ 01 48 00 80 30
**4, rue Saulnier,
Lafayette, Folies Bergères**

Map: 9 G8
Métro: Cadet
Entertainment: Range of popular musical acts on Friday nights

Smoking throughout

Pavement tables in summer

In a room with thick stone walls, customers are treated to dishes, prepared by the owner himself, from Corsica and the Mediterranean region. The menu is seasonal and changes three times a year. The soupe corse cuit au four (Corsican soup cooked in the oven) and the cabri au miel (kid with honey) are available until February. The filets de rouget à la proprianaise (Propriano-style fillets of mullet), flamed with myrtle and raspberry vinegar, are a gorgeous summer dish. In winter, Brocciu cheese is served in a chestnut pancake, while in the summer, it's the star of a sumptuous salad. San Michele reds, whites and rosés are available throughout the year and go well with this cuisine. The host is a lover of fine music as well as food, and organises weekend soirées featuring performers from Corsica and elsewhere.

starter: 55FF-78FF
main: 55FF-120FF
dessert: 35FF-40FF
Set menu: 78FF (lunch)
Plat du jour: 50FF-65FF

CB EC V; *chèques déjeuner* (lunch vouchers)

Open: Mon-Fri noon-3.30pm, 7pm-11pm, Sat 7pm-11pm; reservations advisable on weekends

---

Aux Pipalottes Gourmandes
French

☎ 01 45 26 34 23
**1, rue Chaptal,
Saint-Georges, Pigalle**

Map: 9 C4
Métro: Pigalle, St-Georges

Smoking throughout

Pavement tables in summer

The owner buzzes around this hive of activity where old posters line the walls. Table two has ordered the lapin graine de moutarde et herbes de la garrigue (rabbit with mustard seed and wild herbs), table six is trying the filet de sandre au beurre blanc et fondue de poireaux (pikeperch fillet with a beurre blanc sauce and leek fondue), while table seven has settled on the refreshing salade de chou au curry et à la vinaigrette au cumin (cabbage salad with curry and cumin vinaigrette). There's a great wine list, including some interesting estate wines. Desserts such as the tatin de figues caramélisées (fig tarte tatin) and the pastilla au chocolat (chocolate tart) combine the traditional with the exotic. After a lively lunch hour, the theatre world takes over in the evening, with actors and audience mingling happily together. At interval, the regular clientele get in on the act!

starter: 32.90FF-59.90FF
main: 59.90FF-79.90FF
dessert: 39.90FF-42.90FF
Set menu: 69.90FF,
79.90FF, 99.90FF,
149.90FF (lunch),
99.90FF, 129.90FF,
149.90FF (dinner)
Plat du jour: 50FF-65FF

CB EC MC V

Open: Mon-Fri noon-2.30pm, 7pm-11.30pm, Sat 7pm-11.30pm; reservations advisable

Le Bistro de Gala
French

☎ **01 40 22 90 50**
45, rue du Faubourg-Montmartre, Grands Boulevards

Map: 9 G7
Métro: Le Peletier

   Smoking throughout

Movie posters are displayed on the panelled walls of the dining room and there's a huge fresco of Charlie Chaplin behind the bar. The traditional cuisine served in this movie-buff décor isn't just an act, though. The set menu offers dishes based on fresh market produce: tapenadede rouget-grondin (gurnard tapenade); croustillants de boudin, compote depommes aux épices et salade mesclun (crispy black pudding, stewed apple with spices and mixed green salad); marmite de joues de cochon, petits oignons caramélisés (pig's cheeks with caramelised baby onions); cuisse de lapin rôti à la fleur de thym, pâtes fraîches (roast leg of rabbit with thyme blossom). Among the desserts, check out the delicious tarte fine aux figues (fig tart) or the trio de sorbets (home-made, like the bread). This is beautifully pre-pared food. The chef, Thierry Jack-Roch, worked at two renowned restaurants (Au Dodin Bouf-fant and Chez Jean, rue Saint-Lazare) before taking over this stylish and welcoming bistrot.

Set menu: 160FF, 180FF, 210FF (tasting menu)

AE CB DC EC MC V

Open: Mon-Fri noon-2.30pm (last orders), Mon-Sat 7pm-11.30pm; reservations advisable

Casa Olympe
French (Mediterranean)

☎ **01 42 85 26 01**
48, rue Saint-Georges, Saint-Georges

Map: 9 E5
Métro: St-Georges

    Smoking throughout

The name alone evokes the warmth of southern France, crickets, the smell of thyme and rose-mary, and a dash of olive oil on fresh fish. The association is reinforced when you walk into the small, stylish restaurant with yellow-ochre walls, closely arranged tables and old furniture. Celebrities and less famous regulars come for the friendly atmosphere and are warmly greeted by Olympe Versini, chef and author of a cook-book. With only a quick glance at the menu, we know the Mediterranean isn't far away. The marinated sardines are perfectly seasoned, while the chef's speciality – thon au lard et aux oignons (tuna with bacon and onions) – simply melts in your mouth. The desserts are more traditional but use fresh, seasonal ingredients.

Set menu: 210FF

AE CB EC MC V

Open: Mon-Fri noon-2pm, 8pm-11pm; reservations advisable

To food or not to food?

'Le fooding'? It means the art of appreciating not only the contents on your plate but also what's going on around you: ambience, décor, scene. The term was coined by a journalist in autumn 1999, and it's a combination of 'food' and 'feeling'. Although not in the dictionaries yet, it's already on the lips of all cool Parisians. There was even a week-long festival at the beginning of December 2000, with exhibitions at Colette's and a competition with prizes for the best 'fooding' spots of the moment.

But what is it exactly? The funny thing is, no one seems to know. The 'foodeur' frequents places as different as le Spoon, le Georges, l'Alcazar, le Bon, le Thiou or le Café Ruc. It seems that food is not really a big part of 'le fooding'. After all, the true fashion victim is much more concerned with appearances than tastes. So paying through the nose for mediocre food in a really trendy spot has got to be better than eating a superb meal somewhere uncool.

Map: 9 G4

Métro: Chaussée d'Antin

Nonsmoking tables available

Chez Catherine
French

☎ 01 45 26 72 88
65, rue de Provence, Chaussée d'Antin

A stone's throw from the big department stores, Chez Catherine combines the lovely, old-fashioned décor of a traditional Parisian bistrot with an innovative menu. Maryse creates sumptuous and sometimes unusual flavours using the best provincial ingredients. Memorable dishes include the ravioles aux cèpes (ravioli with cep mushrooms), the fricassée de sot-l'y-laisse (chicken oyster fricassee), the gâteau de céleri à l'émincé de jambon de Bayonne (celery pudding with finely sliced Bayonne ham), the perdreau entier flambé à l'armagnac (whole partridge flamed with Armagnac brandy), the canard colvert aux figues (wild duck with figs) and the croustillant de figues et caramel au beurre demi-sel (fig and caramel 'crunch'). The wine does justice to the exquisite food. Like many restaurants in the area, Chez Catherine is not cheap, but you can't put a price on pleasure like this.

starter: 58FF-75FF
main: 90FF-255FF
dessert: 45FF-50FF
Plat du jour: 110FF

CB EC MC V

Open: Mon-Fri noon-2.30pm, Tues-Fri 7pm-midnight; reservations advisable

Chez Jean

French

☎ **01 48 78 62 73**
**8, rue Saint-Lazare,
Trinité**

Map: 9 F6

Métro: Notre Dame de Lorette

 Nonsmoking tables available

This stylish gourmet restaurant is within the range of most budgets and has just the right dose of sophisticated but friendly ambience. Dark-red bench seats liven up the otherwise large, quiet dining room, which looks a bit like a yacht with its mahogany panelling and polished brassware. The revolving door comes as a surprise, but once you're through, you can expect a warm welcome. The owner does the rounds of the tables, ensuring that customers are happy. And they're more than happy: for starters, fricassée of langoustines (scampi) served with a julienne of vegetables, followed by magret de canard rôti au miel et ses navets et échalotes confites (honey-roasted fillet of duck breast served with preserved turnips and shallots) and, to finish, a scoop of scrumptious vanilla ice cream between two crunchy, chocolate-coated meringues. An inspired touch that might leave you thinking you really shouldn't have...

Open: Mon-Fri noon-2pm, 7.30pm-10.30pm, Sat 7.30pm-11pm; reservations advisable

starter: 60FF
main: 130FF
dessert: 60FF
Set menu: 185FF (lunch), 195FF (dinner)
Plat du jour: 130FF

AE CB EC MC V; €

Les Diamantaires

Lebanese/Armenian

☎ **01 47 70 78 14**
**60, rue Lafayette,
Cadet**

Map: 9 F7

Métro: Cadet

Entertainment: Singers Tues-Sat from 9pm

 Smoking throughout

Mountains of marble, lashings of gilt, pastel walls, plaster statues and a white piano create a flashy setting, perfect for an operetta about the East. You almost expect a belly dancer to suddenly appear in this old restaurant frequented by Greek furriers, Armenian jewellers and Lebanese businessmen. In the evening, the Kazarian brothers sing; on the weekend, you can't even hear yourself think. The authentic cuisine includes Armenian specialities, which are difficult to find elsewhere in Paris. It's hard to choose among the variously priced platters of meze, the dorade grillée au fenouil (sea bream with fennel), chich taouk, marmite du pêcheur mikrolimano (fish stew), gambas au four (oven-baked king prawns) and moussaka aux aubergines. The only disappointment was the service, which could have been a bit friendlier.

Open: Mon-Sun noon-2.30pm, 8pm-11pm; reservations advisable (towards end of the week)

starter: 40FF-65FF
main: 70FF-145FF
dessert: 30FF-50FF
Set menu: 78FF, 98FF, 150FF

V; €

Map: 9 G7

Métro: Grands Boulevards, Cadet

Smoking throughout

El Mauresque
Moroccan

☎ 01 48 24 42 99
3, rue Cadet (end of courtyard), Grands Boulevards

Tucked away at the back of a courtyard, this lovely Moroccan restaurant pays great attention to food and customers alike. Eastern panelling and soft lighting offer an exotic décor, which makes up for the isolated location, and creates a pleasant setting in which to sample dishes prepared entirely by women: small pastilla pastries with pigeon meat, spices and sugar; stuffed sardines; a variety of couscous; but, above all, the tajines (spicy casseroles), including pigeonneau farci aux abricots et aux pruneaux (stuffed squab with apricots and prunes), veau maigre émincé à la cannelle, au safran et aux coings (finely sliced lean veal with cinnamon, saffron and quinces), or the more traditional lamb and chicken tajines with grapes, onions and preserved lemons. To finish, delectable sweet pastries and mint tea. The bill is reasonable, and you leave with the owner's best wishes.

starter: 30FF-55FF
main: 80FF-115FF
dessert: 15FF-40FF
Set menu: 89FF (lunch)

CB EC MC V

Open: Mon-Fri noon-2pm, Mon-Sat 7pm-10pm; reservations advisable

---

Map: 9 G7

Métro: Grands Boulevards, Le Peletier, Cadet

Smoking throughout

Courtyard tables

le fermette d'Olivier
Organic

☎ 01 47 70 06 88
40, rue du Faubourg-Montmartre, Grands Boulevards

Don't expect a little thatched cottage tucked away in the heart of Paris. Situated at the back of a minuscule courtyard, la fermette d'Olivier is more of a '60s-style eatery with homey dining room and Formica décor. It still makes a nice change, perhaps because of the warm welcome you receive from the gentle couple who run the place. At lunchtime, regulars make themselves at home and, without a moment's hesitation, order the assiette zen (zen platter), a hearty dish comprising all kinds of grains (bulghur wheat, brown rice, semolina and buckwheat), vegetables and a fillet of fish. If you make it through this delicious meal, unseasoned except for a dash of oil, you're ready for the tarte zen (a prune tart sprinkled with coconut). For drinks, try the home-made apple juice, a mysterious and utterly delectable concoction.

starter: 33FF-35FF
main: 55FF-85FF
dessert: 22FF-24FF
Set menu: 60FF, 75FF, 80FF, 98FF

CB EC MC V

Open: Mon-Fri noon-3pm, 7pm-10pm; reservations advisable

9e arrond

I Golosi
Italian

☎ **01 48 24 18 63**
**Corner of passage Verdeau and 6,
rue de la Grange-Batelière,
Grands Boulevards**

Map: 9 H7

Métro: Grands Boulevards,
  Richelieu Drouot, Le
  Peletier

 Nonsmoking tables
available

The menu at I Golosi is updated weekly and concentrates on true Italian gourmet food rather than the ubiquitous pasta. Through the window, in a spotless kitchen, you can see chickens being plucked and meals meticulously arranged, which puts you in just the right mood. The chef uses high-quality traditional ingredients, sometimes in unique combinations: radis émincés et copeaux de fromage de chèvre poivré de Sicile (thinly sliced radishes and shaved peppered goat's cheese from Sicily) or raviolis au potiron (pumpkin ravioli). The mortadella imported direct from Bologna and the marinated anchovies are absolute musts. At lunchtime, businessmen and local antique dealers come here for the stylish, cheerful atmosphere, while at night there's a more mixed clientele. Well known among wine buffs, this restaurant offers a range of more than 500 Italian wines (also available from the adjoining shop).

Open: restaurant: Mon-Fri noon-2.30pm, 7.30-midnight, Sat noon-2.30pm, bar: Mon-Fri noon-midnight; reservations essential

starter: 45FF-70FF
main: 70FF-110FF
dessert: 50FF-55FF

CB EC MC V

9e ARRONDISSEMENT

Map: 9 D2
Métro: Liège

Smoking throughout

Il Sardo
Italian (Sardinian)

☎ 01 48 78 25 38
**46 bis, rue de Clichy,
Clichy**

The traditional décor of this small neighbourhood restaurant is proof that you should never judge a book by its cover. It's always crowded, and you can see the cooks at work. The quality of the food confirms these good omens. Try the delicious salade d'artichauts sur lit de speck avec roquette et parmesan (artichoke salad served on a bed of speck with rocket and parmesan), fines tranches d'espadon assaisonnées (thin slices of seasoned swordfish), petits gnocchis sardes au blé dur avec tomates fraîches, gambas et épinards (Sardinian gnocchi made from durum wheat, with fresh tomatoes, king prawns and spinach), filets de sole aux aubergines, palourdes et vin blanc (sole fillets with eggplant, clams and white wine), and the sabayon glacé sur lit de crème anglaise (frozen zabaione on a custard base). The owner adds to the authentic flavour of Il Sardo, embracing or winking at customers and translating the daily specials written on the board in Italian.

starter: 55FF-75FF
main: 60FF-120FF
dessert: 35FF-40FF
Set menu: 90FF (lunch)
Plat du jour: 120FF

AE CB EC MC V

Open: Mon-Fri noon-2.30pm, 7.30pm-11pm, Sat 7.30pm-11pm; reservations essential

---

Map: 9 D3
Métro: Blanche, St-Georges

Smoking throughout

Lorenzo
Italian

☎ 01 48 74 39 25
**50, rue Blanche,
Trinité, Pigalle**

Light filters in through Venetian blinds onto the scarlet upholstery reflected in the mirrors, the ceiling fans are ready to spin, and all you have to do is sit down and order one of the specialities: l'escalope Parmigiana, gratinée à la fondue d'artichaut, or Gina Lollobrigida's favourite, penne all'arrabiata. But an antipasto can be an indulgence too – including the delicious légumes grillés réhaussés de provolone (grilled vegetables with provolone cheese), a generous and very stylish serve of zucchini, peppers and eggplant. The wine list is written up on a slate and frequently revised. Having partaken of these good things, your main problem will be choosing between the crème brûlée à l'amaretto and the tiramisú. La dolce vita.

starter: 24FF-68FF
main: 52FF-110FF
dessert: 28FF-45FF

AE CB EC MC V

Open: Mon-Sat noon-2.30pm, 7pm-10.30pm; reservations advisable

Menthe et Basilic
French (Provence)

☎ **01 48 78 12 20**
6, rue Lamartine,
Saint-Georges,
Notre Dame de Lorette

Map: 9 F8

Métro: Cadet

 Smoking throughout

The simple Provençal décor of wood, stone and warm tones immediately puts you in a good mood. This neighbourhood restaurant promotes the reputation of its chef, Stéphane Michot – with good reason. You'll hesitate between the brochette d'escargots et sa fondue de poireaux (snail kebab with a leek fondue) and the terrine de foie gras mi-cuit maison (the chef's own semi-cooked foie gras terrine). In either case you'd miss the Tatin de tomates et sa chantilly au basilic (tomato tatin with a basil sauce), a speciality registered with the National Patent and Trademark Office. Equally delectable main courses include the suprême de sandre et son sabayon au poivre et à la tomate (pikeperch with pepper and tomato zabaione) and the sauté d'agneau et son nid de ratatouille (sautéed lamb served in a basket of crunchy ratatouille imbued with the colours of southern France). The fondant au chocolat chaud (warm chocolate fondant) has never been so deliciously worthy of its name.

starter: 56FF-95FF
main: 85FF-129FF
dessert: 47FF-50FF
Set menu: 79FF (lunch),
121FF, 161FF (dinner)
Plat du jour: 79FF

CB EC MC V

Open: Mon-Fri noon-2.30pm, Mon-Sat 7pm-10.30pm; reservations essential towards end of week

---

Mi Ranchito
Colombian

☎ **01 48 78 45 94**
35, rue de Montholon,
Lafayette

Map: 9 F8

Métro: Cadet

Entertainment: Theme
nights held

 Nonsmoking tables
available

In this small, quiet restaurant decorated with traditional artefacts, customers can sample the delights of Colombian cuisine – something of a rarity in Paris. The menu offers a wide range of specialities at extremely reasonable prices. For starters, guacamole and marinated shrimps feature alongside empanadas (stuffed fritters accompanied by a zippy sauce seasoned with chilli and lemon). There's also Yuca corriada (manioc cooked in a sauce and served with tomatoes and cheese). For mains, there is a variety of fish, beef and chicken dishes served with manioc, tortillas, plantain bananas and rice. The latter is sometimes cooked in banana leaves or coconut milk: an original combination matching the sweetness of the Caribbean with the ruggedness of the Andes.

starter: 25FF-75FF
main: 60FF-90FF
dessert: 25FF-40FF
Set menu: 65FF (lunch),
98FF (dinner & weekends)
Plat du jour: 45FF

cash only; €

Open: Sun-Fri noon-3pm, daily 7pm-midnight; reservations advisable

Map: 9 H5

Métro: Chaussée d'Antin
La Fayette

Nonsmoking tables
available

Le New Balal
Indian/Pakistani

☎ 01 42 46 53 62
**25, rue Taitbout,
Opéra**

The décor is worthy of the *Thousand and One Nights*, somewhere between Art Deco and colonial trading post. The cuisine offers a rainbow of flavours, the degree of spiciness varying according to the region of origin. Start exploring with the raita, a very refreshing blend of cucumber, yoghurt and cumin. Then try the bater tandoori for the subtle flavour of partridge in a delicate sauce. The very mild eggplant curry (bringal) makes a delicious complement to the lamb biriani, which has rice, almonds and 25 spices. Choose a bottle of Brouilly to accompany these dishes. In the realm of desserts, try the kulfi ice cream, with vanilla, rose, pistachio and almond flavours. And it would be unthinkable to leave without having a cup of deliciously spiced Darjeeling tea.

starter: 26FF-130FF
main: 50FF-140FF
dessert: 30FF
Set menu: 69FF (lunch),
99FF, 129FF
AE CB DC MC V; €

Open: daily noon-2.30pm, 6.45pm-midnight; reservations advisable

Le Roi du Pot au Feu

French

☎ 01 47 42 37 10

34, rue Vignon, Havre Caumartin

Map: 9 H1

Métro: Havre Caumartin, Madeleine

 Smoking throughout

 Pavement tables (2 only) in summer

For starters, a glass of red at tables decked out in checked cloths and serviettes. A few gherkins and a bowl of broth to whet your appetite, and behold the kingdom of pot-au-feu! The fresh market vegetables are served piping hot on a large plate, the slowly cooked meat melts in your mouth and the bone marrow, seasoned with a touch of cooking salt and spread on toast, is simply scrumptious! The other offerings – the chef's terrine, leeks à la vinaigrette, hachis parmentier (chopped beef with potatoes), crème caramel, apple tarte tatin or chocolate mousse – are traditional fare and less noteworthy. Still, Le Roi du Pot au Feu has an incredible reputation; the walls are covered with famous autographs and international newspaper reviews. People no doubt appreciate this restaurant's authenticity and rustic simplicity, as well as its typical Parisian bistro atmosphere, 1930s décor and efficient service.

Open: Mon-Sat noon-10.30pm; reservations not accepted

starter: 25FF-40FF
main: 90FF-110FF
dessert: 40FF-50FF
Plat du jour: 90FF

CB EC MC V

Tea Folies

International

☎ 01 42 80 08 44

6, place Gustave-Toudouze, Pigalle

Map: 9 F8

Métro: St-Georges

Entertainment: Exhibition openings (drawings) every six weeks, Monday night

 Nonsmoking tables available

 Terrace tables

Nestled in the beautiful place Gustave-Toudouze, in the discreetly hip New Athens neighbourhood on the edge of Pigalle, Tea Folies has instant appeal. Attractive pale beechwood tables, simple, modern décor and trendy but extremely attentive staff create a favourable impression. Sample one of the many savoury tarts (including the legendary chicken pie), enticing platters (cheese and herb ravioli, tuna salad, thinly sliced serrano ham that melts in your mouth) and British-style desserts (sultana scones with butter, cheesecake etc) that complement the quiet but friendly atmosphere. The icing on the cake is a lovely terrace where lucky customers can sit on a sunny day.

Open: Tues-Sat 10am-11.30pm, Sun & Mon 10am-7pm; reservations advisable

starter: 25FF-60FF
main: 58FF-95FF
dessert: 42FF-45FF
Set menu: 75FF
Plat du jour: 58FF

AE CB V

9ᵉ ARRONDISSEMENT

Map: 9 F6

Métro: Notre Dame de Lorette, Cadet

Smoking throughout

starter: 55FF
main: 110FF
dessert: 45FF
Set menu: 170FF, 135FF (lunch)
Plat du jour: 110FF
CB V

Velly
French

☎ 01 48 78 60 05
52, rue Lamartine, Cadet

Alain Brigant, the chef of this discreet and elegant restaurant a short walk from the church of Notre-Dame-de-Lorette, cut his teeth at the Bristol, the Manoir de Paris and chez Fauchon. So there's nothing amateurish about Velly. Attractive bench seats upholstered in black moleskin, an authentic period bar and appealing Art Deco ornaments put customers in the right frame of mind for indulging in the culinary pleasures on offer. As an starter, the miel du croustillant de chévre (warm goat's cheese) teases the taste buds deliciously and prepares the way for the paupiettes de sole rôties au romarin (rolled fillets of sole roasted, or rather transfigured, with rosemary). One reservation: the attractive if pricey wine list doesn't let you order by the glass or even by the pichet (jug).

Open: Mon-Fri noon-2pm, 7.30pm-10.45pm; reservations advisable

10e Arrondissement

République

Faubourg Saint-Denis

Canal Saint-Martin

Gare de l'Est

10ᵉ Arrondissement

Two sorts of foot traffic give this arrondissement a distinctive atmosphere. The canal
banks draw leisurely strollers, while travellers
part and are reunited on the platforms of the
gare du Nord and gare de l'Est. Each arrival
and departure announced over the loudspeak-
ers produces a burst of frenetic activity. Outside, the cafes and brasseries do a brisk
trade, catering to travellers and locals. Nearby,
the blvd de Magenta rushes like a swollen
river, the noisy, impatient crowd spreading
through the adjoining streets and pouring out
onto the place de la République. On rue des
Petites Écuries and rue du Château d'Eau,
mouth-watering smells of exotic and local
cuisine will tempt you to linger. The atmosphere is calmer. By the time you reach the
Canal Saint-Martin, easing along between the
Quai de Jemappes and the Quai de Valmy with
their rows of plain and chestnut trees, the
bustle will seem a world away. Barges appear,
pass silently, then vanish behind a lock. Little
iron bridges and walkways span the still water.
This was once the Paris of Marcel Carné's
films, but it is changing. Run-down until recently, the bistrots are now getting into the
groove.

La 25e Image
French

☎ 01 40 35 80 88
**9, rue des Récollets,
Canal Saint-Martin**

Map: 10 F6

Métro: Gare de l'Est,
Jacques Bonsergent

 Smoking throughout

 Pavement tables

The original, painted-tile ceiling of this former bakery is still intact and, along with brightly coloured ceramic tables, evokes the delicate charm of a bygone era. The 25e Image is appropriately located just near the romantic Canal Saint-Martin and offers simple, authentic cuisine in keeping with the lovely surrounds: tarte aux légumes et au chèvre (vegetable and goat's cheese tart), endives au jambon (endive with ham), rôti de porc purée (roast pork with mash) or a copious salade savoyarde (Reblochon cheese tartines, grilled cubes of bacon, crème fraîche and hot potatoes). To finish, the tarte tatin, tiramisú and marquise au chocolat are irresistable and present gourmets with an unbearable choice.

starter: 35FF
main: 50FF-65FF (lunch),
   60FF-85FF (dinner)
dessert: 20FF-28FF (lunch),
   25FF-33FF (dinner)
Set menu: 90FF (lunch)
Plat du jour: 50FF-65FF
   (lunch), 60FF-85FF
   (dinner)
CB EC MC V

Open: Mon-Fri 9am-3pm, 6.30pm-midnight; reservations advisable

L'an II
French

☎ 01 40 40 70 76
**9, rue du Faubourg du Temple,
République**

Map: 10 J7

Métro: République

Entertainment: Occasional
   live jazz nights

 Nonsmoking tables
available

 Pavement tables

The two owners have surmounted the cramped dimensions of this restaurant and even had fun devising an alternative form of grandeur for it. Lively and interesting, they have transformed the an II into a window onto art and culture. From special previews of arthouse films to exhibitions of photography or handmade jewellery, there's room for every conceivable type of artistic expression. Foodwise, this small restaurant proudly sticks to traditional French fare. Lovingly-prepared dishes include the escalope à la crème fraîche accompagnée de pommes de terre sautées as well as daily specials and gorgeous fruit tarts made with seasonal ingredients. Take note for when you're next in the area.

starter: 30FF-38FF
main: 65FF-75FF
dessert: 25FF-30FF
Plat du jour: 56FF
MC V

Open: Mon-Fri 6.30am-11pm; reservations advisable (lunch)

L'Apostrophe
French

☎ 01 42 08 26 07
23, rue de la Grange-aux-
Belles, Canal Saint-Martin

Map: 10 F7

Métro: Colonel Fabien

Entertainment: Cabarets,
concerts Fri & Sat nights

Smoking throughout

Pavement tables

starter: 13FF-16FF
main: 55FF-70FF
dessert: 15FF-17FF
Set menu: 52FF
Plat du jour: 42FF

AE CB EC MC V

At lunchtime, regulars shout to each other across the tables, chew the fat with the chef or tease the waitress. It's hard not to like this local institution, with its unbeatable prices and large picture windows that let you soak up the first rays of sun. The food is respectable, filling and even has a creative touch, like the carrot pudding flavoured with mushrooms for starters. The classic pepper steak with crispy fries can't be faulted, while desserts like the rich and flavoursome chocolate mousse are also up to scratch. You won't want to leave this lovely, peaceful spot.

Open: Mon-Fri 11.30am-4.30pm; reservations advisable

Le Bistro des Oies
French

☎ 01 42 08 34 86
2, rue Marie et Louise,
République

Map: 10 G7

Métro: Goncourt, Jacques
Bonsergent

Entertainment: Occasional
acoustic performances

Nonsmoking tables
available

Pavement tables on
quiet street

starter: 26FF-82FF
main: 54FF-82FF
dessert: 25FF
Set menu: 58FF (weekday
lunch), 92FF (weeknights
and weekends – some
dishes extra)
Plat du jour: 54FF

CB MC V

This friendly, laid-back neighbourhood bistrot has quiet pavement tables and cheap set-price menus for both lunch and dinner. Cheese can be ordered either by the portion or the platter. Those not hungry enough for a main course can order a platter-style entrée such as charcuterie and foie gras, brie fondant en salade or terrine de chèvre et crudités relevées au vinaigre de xérès (goat's cheese terrine and crudités seasoned with sherry dressing). The main courses are imbued with the flavours of the French countryside: confit de canard au sel de Ré (confit of duck with salt from the island of Ré), hampe de bœuf poêlé sauce camembert (fried flank of beef with camembert sauce) and gigoton d'agneau rôti au romarin (roast lamb with rosemary), served with delicious mash. For those with particularly lofty tastes, there's the filet d'oie à l'orange et à la cannelle (fillet of goose with orange and cinnamon)...

Open: Tues-Fri noon-2.30pm, 7pm-10.30pm, Sat noon-2.30pm, 7pm-11pm; reservations advisable

From Pondicherry to Paris

Over the past 20 years a little India has sprung up in Paris between rue du Faubourg Saint Denis and blvd de Sébastopol. In a narrow street covered with a dilapidated glass roof, customers take in the intoxicating aromas of cardamom and ginger emanating from a myriad of Indo-Pakistani restaurants. Known as passage Brady, the site owes its name to a shopkeeper who promoted the passage after its inauguration in 1828. For many years it was occupied by the textile industry and began falling into ruin when, in the early 1970s, an Indian from the former French trading post of Pondicherry decided to open a small restaurant on Brady's old stamping ground. Within a few years, five new restaurants (mostly Pakistani) were open for business. The passage is also home to grocery stores, several hairdressing salons and an Indian-video shop. The glass roof is to be renovated – none too soon – by the city council, which has decided to preserve the charm of this unique place.

Le Cambodge
Cambodian

☎ **01 44 84 37 70**
10, ave Richerand, Hôpital Saint-Louis

Map: 10 G7

Métro: Goncourt

Entertainment: Senegalese musician Tuesday nights, magician Wednesday

 Smoking throughout

 Terrace tables (heated in winter)

This out-of-the-ordinary place is located in a quiet street between the Hôpital Saint-Louis and the quai de Jemmapes. The name is written in big white letters on a spanking new façade, so you won't get lost. Inside, in cramped but welcoming surroundings, you can indulge in enormous rouleaux de printemps (spring rolls), bo bun (rice noodles with beef, small spring rolls and vegetables) or the pique-nique cambodgien (rice vermicelli and sautéed beef, which you wrap in lettuce leaves). The menu also encourages special requests: each customer is considered unique and can modify a dish to suit his or her taste. The food is home-made, a sure sign of authenticity, and the are staff run off their feet. A favourite spot among students, the Cambodge is always packed. Try to get there before 9pm so you don't have to wait for a table.

Open: daily noon-2.30pm, 8pm-11.30pm; reservations not accepted

starter: 17FF-40FF
main: 32FF-50FF
dessert: 20FF-37FF
Plat du jour: 56FF

CB MC V; €

Map: 10 D3

Métro: Gard du Nord, Poissonièere, RER: Gare du Nord

Smoking throughout

Pavement tables

Chez Casimir
French

☎ 01 48 78 28 80
**6, rue de Belzunce,
Gare du Nord**

The Casimir in question comes from the Tarn region and is totally unrelated to the small orange monster of the same name known to children all over France. While there's probably nothing to appeal to a monster on offer at Chez Casimir, you can be sure of fresh, top-quality ingredients and a menu that changes several times a week. We were treated to a richly flavoured crème froide de champignons (cold cream of mushroom soup), served with tiny croutons in a huge tureen, just like at home. Not a skerrick left! This was followed by an épaule d'agneau rôtie sur l'os (roasted shoulder of lamb), cooked with a generous helping of garlic cloves, which simply melted in the mouth. We left a well-gnawed bone! Among the less reliable desserts, the baked figs were tasteless, but the pain perdu aux poires (French toast with pears) was unforgettable.

starter: 30FF-35FF
main: 80FF
dessert: 30FF-35FF

cash only

Open: Mon-Fri noon-2pm, 7pm-11pm; reservations essential

Map: 10 D3

Métro: Gare du Nord, Poissonière, RER: Gare du Nord

Smoking throughout

Chez Michel
French

☎ 01 44 53 06 20
**10, rue de Belzunce,
Gare du Nord**

This Parisian institution was on its last legs when Thierry Breton brought it back to life with the flavours of Armorica. Since then, the hip set of the 10th arrondissement has been falling over itself to check out his generous and stylish cuisine, served in traditional bistrot surrounds. The menu might be set, but the mind wanders and hesitates as you nibble on delicious baby periwinkles: lasagne de chèvre et artichaut breton au pistou (goat's cheese, Breton artichokes and pesto) or millefeuille de betteraves et foie gras poêlé (beetroot and pan-fried foie gras); chapon fermier rôti et sa purée à l'andouille (roast free-range capon with andouille sausage purée) or rognons de veau pommes grenaille et ail confit (veal kidneys with new potatoes and preserved garlic); brandade de haddock des fumoirs malouins et dos de cabillaud rôti (brandade of smoked haddock and roast cod) or something from the hunter's magnificent bag? And to finish, kouing-aman fondant or the creamy Paris-Brest?

Set menu: 185FF

CB EC MC V

Open: Tues-Sat noon-2pm, 7pm-midnight; reservations essential

Le Coin de verre
French

☎ **01 42 45 31 82**
38, rue Sambre-et-Meuse, Belleville

Map: 10 F9
Métro: Belleville, Colonel Fabien
Entertainment: Cabaret nights

 Smoking throughout

First, you'll need to find rue Sambre-et-Meuse, just near attractive rue Sainte-Marthe. Then you'll have to wait at the door with the red curtain, not for permission to enter, but to give the owner time to finish his conversation and arrive from the back room of the restaurant (with its open fireplace and wooden tables). Once you're seated in this friendly establishment, it's all yours: charcuterie or cheese platters, poutargue méditerranéeene (pressed, smoked and finely sliced mullet roe), salade savoyarde (with warm smoked sausage and Cantal cheese) and the chef's clafoutis. Hot meals should be ordered two days in advance. The wine list takes you from one end of France to the other and includes everything from Gamay Touraine to Pommard. Customers are treated like family, and when the red curtain closes behind you, you'll be thinking about coming back as soon as possible.

starter: 35FF-50FF
main: 35FF-60FF
dessert: 16FF-20FF
Plat du jour: 60FF

Open: Mon-Sat 8pm-midnight; reservations advisable

cash only

Da Mimmo
Italian (Neapolitan)

☎ **01 42 06 44 47**
39, blvd Magenta, République

Map: 10 G5
Métro: Jacques Bonsergent

 Nonsmoking tables available

 Pavement tables in summer

Customers have been coming here from all over for the last 15 years to sample Domenico Sommella's authentic Neapolitan cuisine (if you like the food, see his recently published book). Neither the neighbourhood, the setting nor the prohibitive prices are enough to keep fans away. Naples is the birthplace of pizza – try one with rocket and forget about the pizzas of the past! To follow, there's a choice of antipasti, including petits saucissons au fenouil (baby sausages with fennel) and mozzarella di buffala fumée (smoked). For mains, there's a profusion of fish and clams (palourdes, tellines), abundant use of white truffles, pasta mista corta de Naples (the city that gives such a perfect taste to all these dishes), gatò de patate, chevreau au four (oven-baked kid), cive di rape for connoisseurs and minestra maritata at Christmas. Santa Madonna, Italian cuisine is absolutely divine!

starter: 45FF-75FF
main: 65FF-200FF
dessert: 50FF-60FF
Set menu: 120FF

Open: Mon-Sat noon-2.30pm, 7pm-11.30pm; reservations advisable (evenings)

MC V; €

10e ARRONDISSEMENT

Map: 10 E3

Métro: Gare de l'Est

Smoking throughout

L'Enchotte
French

☎ 01 48 00 05 25
**11, rue de Chabrol,
Gare de l'Est**

This typical Parisian wine bar is located opposite the Halle Saint Quentin, as straight as the crow flies from the gare de l'Est. The friendly atmosphere, tasteful furniture, traditional bar and period wooden chairs create a comfortable, rustic feel, while finely crafted wooden serviette rings add a family touch. The food lives up to the surrounds. For starters, the saumon à la niçoise (niçoise-style salmon) summons all the flavours of the Mediterranean, while the médaillon de faux-filet (beef tenderloin medallions), served with a fabulous sauce, will win over the most wary of palates. A wine bar worthy of the name, L'Enchotte offers a large, well-chosen selection of beverages and value for money.

starter: 38FF-65FF
main: 70FF-100FF
dessert: 30FF-35FF
Set menu: 115FF

AE CB EC MC V

Open: Mon-Fri noon-2.30pm, 7.30pm-10.30pm; reservations advisable

Le Galopin

French

☎ **01 53 19 19 55**

**34, rue Sainte Marthe,
Sainte-Marthe**

Map: 10 F9

Métro: Colonel Fabien,
Belleville

Entertainment: Singer-gui-
tarist Sat & Sun 8.30pm-
9.30pm, 11pm-midnight

 Smoking throughout

The enticing smiles of Ophélia and Nathalie will draw you into this small bistrot-style restaurant in the place Sainte Marthe. These former English and history teachers have set up a school for more culinary pursuits, indoctrinating the entire neighbourhood in the process. Teachers' pets come for lunch *and* dinner, while the whole class is serenaded by Willy at the end of the week. The menu changes daily according to what's available at the market. Beef carpaccio might replace a vegetable feuilleté for starters, while a magret de canard à l'orange (fillet of duck breast with orange) is ousted by thon au beurre blanc (tuna with beurre blanc). Gourmets won't want to leave without trying the home-made ice cream in summer and the plum clafoutis in winter.

starter: 40FF
main: 72FF-88FF
dessert: 28FF
Set menu: 69FF (lunch),
85FF (dinner)
Plat du jour: 72FF-88FF

CB EC MC V

Open: Mon-Fri noon-2.30pm, 8pm-11pm, Sat & Sun 8pm-midnight; reservations advisable (especially dinner)

Le Parmentier

French

☎ **01 42 40 74 75**

**12, rue Arthur-Groussier,
Saint-Louis**

Map: 10 G8

Métro: Goncourt

 Smoking throughout

The outside isn't much to look at, but the inside is immediately reassuring: linen servi-ettes, beautifully set tables and discreet décor. This small neighbourhood restaurant has the air of a well-run bistrot, and the owners obviously love their job. Busy at lunch and restful in the evening, Le Parmentier offers a cuisine of consummate sophistication. Subtle starters include polenta au morbier (polenta with Morbier cheese), anchois marinés (marinated anchovies) or champignons au cerfeuil (champignons with chervil). For mains, the daube à la provençale (Provence-style braised beef) is perfectly marinated, while the classic filet de bœuf au poivre (fillet of beef with pepper sauce) is also first rate. If you're not really in the mood for a meat dish, try the ravioli or the spicy goujonnettes de rascasse au curry (scorpion fish fillets with curry). Orange crepes or creamy crème brûlée are a perfect end to a perfect meal, followed by coffee and petits fours.

starter: 34FF
main: 60FF
dessert: 34FF
Set menu: 80FF (lunch),
128FF, 150FF (dinner)
Plat du jour: 60FF

CB EC MC V

Open: Mon-Fri noon-2.30pm, Mon-Sat 7pm-10.30pm; reservations advisable

Métro: Bonne Nouvelle

Smoking throughout

Pavement tables

Phénix Café
French

☎ 01 47 70 35 40
4, rue du Faubourg Poissonnière, Bonne Nouvelle

The owner of the Phénix Café is passionate about conserving the heritage of this turn-of-the-century bistrot. Behind the 100-year-old façade, waiters in aprons look after lovers of genuine bistrot fare: saucisson lyonnais (boiled Lyon sausage with warm potatoes and shallots), jambon d'York braisé (braised York ham), assiette de cochonailles (charcuterie platter), selle d'agneau à la provençale (Provence-style saddle of lamb), truffade (a potato cake with Cantal cheese) or pied de porc sauce gribiche (pig's trotters with a vinaigrette of hard-boiled egg yolks, gherkins and capers). This unpretentious, exquisite cuisine is prepared according to classic recipes, while the salads and desserts are in the same league. The son of a wine grower and a knowledgable oenologist in his own right, the owner is planning to open a wine shop next to the restaurant. He also collects wine-growing paraphernalia with a view to turning the place into a bacchanalian museum. What a great idea!

starter: 39FF-60FF
main: 48FF-66FF
dessert: 26FF-32FF
Set menu: 69FF (lunch only)
Plat du jour: 60FF
CB EC MC V

Open: Mon-Fri noon-3pm, 7.30pm-11.30pm; reservations advisable (for more than two people)

10e rrond

Pooja
Indian

☎ 01 48 24 00 83
**91, passage Brady,
Gare de l'Est**

Map: 10 G3

Métro: Strasbourg St-Denis,
Château d'Eau

 Nonsmoking tables available

Incense, spices, jewellery and saris – the heart of Paris' Little India is passage Brady, near the Gare de l'Est. There are plenty of Indian restaurants in this covered passageway, but the quality of Pooja's cuisine stands out. 'Pooja' means prayer; it's also a serene-sounding first name given to girls. Umesh Bhatt and his team honour the name, sharing their love of Indian food. The classic menu is livened up with some innovative touches. So for starters you can choose between the traditional samosas and gost tikka (marinated diced lamb). And as well as the various tandoori dishes for mains, there is murgh madras (chicken curry). Don't deprive yourself of naan (bread) and lassi (yoghurt drink) as accompaniments. The weariest diners will be grateful for this benediction of flavours.

starter: 24FF-99FF
main: 62FF-75FF
dessert: 25FF-28FF
Set menu: 45FF (vegetarian lunch), 65FF (lunch), 89FF, 125FF

CB DC EC JCB MC V

Open: Tues-Sun noon-2.30pm, 7pm-11pm; reservations advisable (weekends)

Le Réveil du Xe
French

☎ 01 42 41 77 59
**35, rue du Château-d'Eau,
République**

Map: 10 G4

Métro: Château d'Eau,
République

Entertainment: Wine tastings with vineyard owners

 Smoking throughout

 Pavement tables

Le Réveil du Xe, which takes its name from a late-19th-century left-wing newspaper, offers the simplicity and conviviality of a traditional neighbourhood wine bar. You can have a snack at the bar or lunch in the dining room packed with customers and bric-a-brac from the Auvergne. Produce from this gastronomic region dominates the menu: terrines, tripoux (small parcels of highly seasoned sheep's or calf's tripe), truffade (a potato cake with Cantal cheese), pounti (a hash of bacon, Swiss chard and onions bound with milk and eggs) and cheese, of course... Dinner on Tuesday nights is quite expensive (but well worth it). Daniel Vidalenc knows his wines and can recommend anything from an estate vintage or a highly drinkable beaujolais to a heady côtes-du-rhône or a côtes d'Auvergne (drunk young and chilled). This bistrot is an authentic, historic institution, where hearty, flavoursome family cooking is celebrated in a friendly atmosphere.

starter: 20FF-35FF
main: 54FF-72FF
dessert: 25FF-30FF
Plat du jour: 54FF

V

Open: Wed-Mon 7.30am-8.30pm, Tues 7.30am-9.30pm (lunch served until 2.30pm); reservations advisable (Tues nights)

Bars & Cafes – 10e & 12e

Le Baron Bouge 1, rue Théophile-Roussel, Paris 12e, Aligre ☎ 01 43 43 14 32 Métro: Ledru Rollin (Map: 12 C3)

This old Parisian wine shop and bar is an obligatory watering hole at the exit of the marché d'Aligre. It is also an ideal spot to refill your 'Cubitainer' with one of the owner's large selection of wines. Try the scrumptious Corsican charcuterie or the goat's cheese while you're here.

Open: Mon 5pm-10pm, Tues-Thurs 10am-2pm, 5pm-10pm, Fri & Sat 10am-10pm, Sun 10am-3.30pm; By the glass: beer 12FF; snacks available; cards accepted

Centre culturel Pouya 48 bis, Quai de Jemmapes, Paris 10e, Canal Saint-Martin ☎ 01 42 08 38 47 Métro: République (Map: 10 H7)

Persian musical instruments, carpets, benches and low tables adorn this little salon de thé on the banks of Canal Saint-Martin. You can sip Kurdish cardamom tea or nibble on a salad or some cake, but that's about it for Iranian specialities. Tequila and whisky are also available. The perfect place for a change of air.

Open: daily 10am-2am; coffee 10FF; snacks available; cash only

Chez Adel 10, rue de la Grange-aux-Belles, Paris 10e, Canal Saint-Martin ☎ 01 42 08 24 61 Métro: Colonel Fabien, Jacques Bonsergent (Map: 10 G6)

People come here at lunchtime for a quick bite to eat (salads, egg and mayonnaise ...). In the evening, the part-Parisian part-Eastern décor of this simple bistrot is transformed into a shambolic soundscape. Concerts, poetry readings and short plays bring together a highly diverse crowd. Check out the program in the free monthly magazine LYLO.

Open: Mon-Fri 10am-2am, Sat 5pm-2am, Sun 6pm-10pm; By the glass: beer 18FF; coffee 6FF; meals available; concerts, poetry readings, plays; cash only

Chez Jeannette 47, rue de Faubourg St-Denis, Paris 10e, Strasbourg St-Denis-Château d'eau ☎ 01 47 70 30 89 Métro: Strasbourg St-Denis (Map: 10 G3)

Multicoloured neon lights illuminate Chez Jeannette day and night. You'd swear the interior hasn't changed since the belle époque, apart from modern furniture in the latest bad taste. This huge place has a relaxed atmosphere, a mixed clientele and exceptionally friendly staff.

Open: Mon-Sat 7am-9pm, Sun 9am-2pm; meals and snacks available; AE CB DC EC JCB MC V

China Club 50, rue de Charenton, Paris 12e, Ledru Rollin ☎ 01 43 43 82 02 Métro: Ledru Rollin (Map: 12 B3)

This stylish, cosy place evokes the 'Roaring 20s' and the novels of F. Scott Fitzgerald. Great Gatsbys sip martinis while lounging about in black leather chesterfields. Upstairs, the last nabobs savour coffee and rare cigars in the smoking room, while on weekends, jazz bands seduce the customers.

Open: Sun-Thurs 7pm-2am, Fri & Sat 7pm-3am; By the glass: beer 25FF, champagne 72FF; coffee 17FF, 35FF; meals and snacks available; concerts Fri & Sat; credit cards accepted

De La Ville Café 34, Blvd de Bonne-Nouvelle, Paris 10e, Faubourg Saint-Denis ☎ 01 48 24 48 09 Métro: Strasbourg St-Denis (Map: 10 H2)

Don't look for the sign, there isn't one. On this long, popular boulevard, good news like De La Ville Café doesn't have to be publicised. The monumental interior is a dazzling combination of baroque and contemporary design. Heavy-duty lamps, furniture and concrete are subtly interwoven with Second Empire relics: wrought iron, stained glass and a sumptuous marble staircase. A real lcoup de théâtre!

Open: Mon-Sun 11am-2am; By the glass: beer 16FF, champagne 50FF; coffee 11FF; snacks available; DJ Thurs nights; CB EC MC V

Le Panier 32, rue Sainte-Marthe, Paris 10e, Sainte Marthe ☎ 01 42 01 38 18 Métro: Belleville, Colonel Fabien (Map: 10 F9)

The unpredictable atmosphere – sometimes akin to Rimbaud's drunken boat, at other times friendly and relaxed – combined with the personality of the regulars and impromptu songs give the Panier an element of surprise. The makeshift décor, warm tones and rickety chairs create a cosy, hip feel.

Open: Tues-Sun 4pm-2am; By the glass: beer 12FF; coffee 8FF; snacks available; occasional street songs; credit cards accepted

La Patache 60, rue de Lancry, Paris 10e, Canal Saint-Martin, ☎ 01 42 08 14 35, Métro: Jacques-Bonsergent, Gare de l'Est (Map: 10 G6)

Monsieur Vito is a real character. He's been running this place from behind the bar for the past 11 years. There are yellowing photographs and an outdated jukebox, while the flue of a coal-fired stove cuts the room in two, separating the 'stage' from the 'wings'. The Patache is something of a mecca for pub-style theatre, and drama is never far from the bar!

Open: daily 6pm-2am; By the glass: beer 12FF-14FF; snacks sometimes available; theatre acts; cash only

Pictural café 40, blvd de la Bastille, Paris 12e, Bastille ☎ 01 43 40 49 97 Métro: Bastille (Map: 12 B3)

Contemporary painting has pride of place at Pictural café. Once a month, Stéphane takes on the role of curator, organising openings and exhibitions. The customers at this popular cultural institution are like one big family: 'boulistes' from the Port de l'Arsenal play cards, students bury themselves in rare books and, in the evening, the singers from the Opéra Bastille strut their stuff

Open: Mon-Fri 7.30am-late, Sat & Sun 11am-late; By the glass: beer 16FF, champagne 43FF; coffee 12FF; meals and snacks available; web-bar; art exhibition, games, DJ twice a month, dancing; credit cards accepted

Raimo 59-61, blvd de Reuilly, Paris 12e, Daumesnil ☎ 01 43 43 70 17 Métro: Daumesnil (Map: 12 F6)

This café, specialising in ice cream and not far from the Coulée verte, is an obligatory stop on many Sunday walks and a favourite meeting place for young and old. Mr Raimondo makes his ice creams with love, according to secret family recipes. They all taste wonderful, with traditional flavours as well as newer ones: ginger, maple syrup or blood orange. A byword among gourmets since 1947, Raimo has managed to preserve its traditions and its unique charm.

Open: Tues-Sun 9.30am-noon; By the glass: champagne 31FF; coffee 13FF; snacks (lunch) available, credit cards accepted

Le Zorba 8, rue de Belleville, Paris 10e, Belleville ☎ 01 42 39 68 68 Métro: Belleville (Map: 10 G10)

A favourite meeting spot both before and after a hard day's night of partying, this Belleville bar and betting shop is an authentic neighbourhood institution. Momo – the man of 30,000 ties – and Akim rule this small, unpretentious roost.

Open: daily 5am-2am; By the glass: beer 10FF; coffee 6FF; cash only

Map: 10 F9

Métro: Colonel Fabien, Belleville

Entertainment: Occasional weekend jazz concerts

Smoking throughout

Tables in the square

starter: 35FF-56FF
main: 70FF-110FF
dessert: 35FF-45FF

CB V

Le Sainte Marthe

French

☎ 01 44 84 36 96
**32, rue Sainte Marthe,
Sainte Marthe**

In a small square sheltered from cars and crowds, Le Sainte Marthe provides a meeting place for the hip set from Belleville and the Canal Saint-Martin. An old bar, a little terrace (heated in winter), Art Deco furniture and occasional strains of jazz set the tone. But it's the cuisine more than the atmosphere that attracts customers. The young, talented and creative chef has devised a delectable menu that includes tartare d'espadon au gingembre (swordfish tartare with ginger), carde d'agneau rôti à la fleur de thym (roast lamb with thyme blossom) and soupe de fraises à la menthe et à l'orange (strawberry soup with mint and orange). The magret de canard (fillet of duck breast) is an absolute must. Traditionally prepared with honey, then mango, it's served here with figs and vegetables. Le Sainte Marthe is worth a visit just for the chocolate moelleux, a truly sublime dessert.

Open: Mon-Fri 5pm-2am, Sat & Sun noon-2am; reservations advisable (especially evenings)

11ᵉ Arrondissement

Charonne

Bastille

Oberkampf

Voltaire

11^e Arrondissement

The courtyards and alleyways of the 11th arrondissement used to belong to craftsmen and labourers. When you went into a building or a dead-end street off rue du Faubourg-Saint-Antoine, rue de Charonne, or rue de la Roquette, you'd find workshops, factories and warehouses. Cabinet makers, joiners, gilders, luthiers, dressmakers, lacemakers: a whole range of crafts, each with its characteristic activities and sounds, each adding notes to the familiar cacophony. In the area between Nation, Bastille, République and Belleville, there was always a mix of things going on. There still is, it's just that the things have changed. Along rue Oberkampf and rue de Charonne, cool cafes and restaurants have multiplied, spilling over into rue de la Folie-Méricourt, rue Saint-Maur and rue Jean-Pierre-Timbaud. It's a replay of what happened a while back in rue de la Roquette and the ad-joining streets. Artists, lofts, bohemia – this is where it began. Fashion followed with big name designers and unknowns setting up shop. But the old spirit lives on. The 11th has managed to preserve its charm. It's true there are new dress codes and new attitudes, but people still march from République to Bastille, demonstrating that there's strength in unity.

A l'Ami Pierre
French

☎ 01 47 00 17 35
**5, rue de la Main-d'Or,
Charonne**

Map: 11 H5

Métro: Ledru Rollin

 Smoking throughout

Marie-Jo, the owner of this authentic neighbourhood wine bar, has been serving drinks, with her cheeky Parisian humour, for 10 years. When a table in the long, narrow room became free, we sat down with a magnificent Givry 1998 de Bourgogne – heaven on earth – and a sumptuous osso buco. The Madiran and Saint-Émilion wines are in the same league, as are the bavette à l'échalotte (skirt steak with shallots) and the côte d'agneau au roquefort (lamb chops with Roquefort cheese). After the homemade fondant au chocolat, Marie-Jo offered us a delicious calva at the bar. This warm, friendly place makes you want to hang out with the regulars.

Open: Tues-Sat 10am-1.45am; reservations advisable

main: 50FF-60FF
dessert: 33FF
Plat du jour: 60FF

CB V

A la bonne franquette
Moroccan

☎ 01 43 48 85 88
**151, rue de la Roquette,
Père Lachaise**

Map: 11 F7

Métro: Voltaire, Philippe-Auguste

 Smoking throughout

 Outdoor tables

It doesn't look much from the outside, but A la bonne franquette is a local institution. Situated between the Voltaire and Père Lachaise neighbourhoods, this popular bar doubles as a small, unpretentious restaurant at lunch and dinner times. Customers come here to eat *à la bonne franquette*, that is, for a simple, casual meal. The Franco-Arabic setting (posters of old Paris and eastern landscapes by Toulouse-Lautrec) is in keeping with the menu, which offers the best of French charcuterie and meat dishes alongside Moroccan specialities such as tajines and hearty couscous with kebabs, lamb or merguez. With its cheap, delicious food and unfussy service, A la bonne franquette has attracted a loyal following and a great reputation.

Open: Mon-Sat 11am-2am; reservations not accepted

starter: 75FF-85FF
main: 85FF-120FF
dessert: 50FF
Set menu: 170FF

AE CB V

11ᵉ ARRONDISSEMENT

Map: 11 G6

Métro: Charonne

Entertainment: Magic show alternating with wine tastings on Wed evenings

Smoking throughout

L'Armagnac
French

☎ 01 43 71 49 43
104, rue de Charonne, Charonne

Fortunately, Armagnac's late 19th century café setting – just one of this place's many charms – remains intact. Local inhabitants and workers come here to hang out: the bar's open from 7.30am to 2am during the week and you can also get a good feed. The menu is simple, offering 'quick snacks' such as hot tartines on Poilâne bread, various savoury tarts and a hearty, traditional daily special. On Friday at lunchtime, you can indulge in oysters direct from the producer. For dessert, gourmets will adore the delectable fresh figs in spiced wine or the crème brûlée (as good as your grand-mother's!). On Wednesday nights, a magic show alternates with wine tastings, bringing a festive atmosphere to this friendly spot.

main: 39FF-60FF
dessert: 23FF-27FF
Plat du jour: 56FF

CB MC V

Open: restaurant: daily noon-3pm, 7pm-11pm; bar: Mon-Fri 7.30am-2am, Sat 10.30am-2am, Sun 10.30am-11pm; reservations not accepted

---

Map: 11 C4

Métro: Parmentier, Oberkampf

Smoking throughout

Outdoor tables

Astier
French

☎ 01 43 57 16 35
44, rue Jean-Pierre Timbaud, Oberkampf

Located in a somewhat fashion-conscious neighbourhood, this restaurant remains faithful to the tradition established by its founder, Madame Astier, more than fifty years ago. The décor is slightly austere, the staff efficient and the wine list fabulous. The set menu offers four courses and is updated on a daily basis. There's no picking at one's meal here – whether you choose the bulots (whelks) à l'ailloli or the terrine de biche maison (the chef's venison terrine) for starters, the mignon de porc rôti aux langoustines (roast tenderloin of pork with langoustines) or the filet de rouget poêlé à la crème d'olive (pan-fried fillet of mullet with olive purée) for mains, the food is invariably lavish and sophisticated. Next, a huge cheese platter takes up the entire table. Though don't pass over the enticing desserts at the bottom of the menu.

Set menu: 115FF (lunch), 145FF (dinner)

CB EC MC V

Open: Mon-Fri noon-2pm, 8pm-11pm; reservations essential

Astier

Au P'tit Cahoua
Moroccan

☎ 01 47 00 20 42
24, rue des Taillandiers, Bastille

Map: 11 G4

Métro: Bastille

 Smoking throughout

This authentic restaurant offers a welcome change of surroundings in the often overrated Bastille neighbourhood. The Moroccan décor and soft lighting create an atmosphere imbued with nostalgia for North Africa. Customers can satisfy without fuss their cravings for briks (a type of filled fritter), méchoui (spit-roasted meat, usually lamb or mutton), couscous and spices. The salad of smooth eggplant seasoned with coriander and cumin, the tajine d'agneau aux poires fraîches et miel d'acacia (lamb tajine with fresh pears and acacia honey – a delicate combination of sweet and savoury) and the salade d'oranges à la cannelle (orange salade with cinnamon) are delectable examples of this cuisine's subtle flavours. The service is appropriately simple and efficient. Round off the evening with a glass of peppermint tea.

Open: daily 12.30pm-2.30pm, Sun-Thurs 7.30pm-11pm, Fri & Sat 7.30pm-midnight; reservations advisable

starter: 45FF
main: 80FF-130FF
dessert: 40FF
Set menu: 65FF (lunch)
CB V

Au Trou Normand

French

☎ 01 48 05 80 23
9, rue Jean-Pierre Timbaud, Oberkampf

Map: 11 D2
Métro: Oberkampf

Smoking throughout

You don't come here to 'dine out' but to 'have a bite at Mme Magguy's'. Listed in all the guidebooks, *the* cafeteria of the 11e arrondissement offers tables covered with checked oilcloth, Pyrex glasses, more-than-reasonable prices and a convivial atmosphere in which customers share tables and chat with each other like old friends. The food is in keeping with the surrounds: simple and generous. There are no fewer than 35 starters to choose from including avocat crevettes (avocado and shrimps); œufs mayonnaise; and saucisson à l'ail (garlic sausage). Mains include various cuts of beef (tournedos, steak, skirt) and other meat dishes, served with authentic home-made chips. And since this restaurant isn't called the Trou Normand for nothing, pep yourself up before you leave with a café-calva!

starter: 10FF-16FF
main: 29FF-39FF
dessert: 9FF-18FF
Plat du jour: 29FF, 30FF, 39FF

cash only

Open: Mon-Fri noon-2.30pm, Mon-Sat 7.30pm-11.30pm; reservations not accepted

Au village

African (Senegalese)

☎ 01 43 57 18 95
86, ave Parmentier, Oberkampf

Map: 11 D4
Métro: Parmentier
Entertainment: live African music

Nonsmoking tables available

If you think this restaurant on the grand avenue Parmentier looks just like all the others, you're in for a surprise. In a small, narrow room with soft lighting, the décor transports customers to an African village. The atmosphere is warm, friendly and even a bit hip. Perched above the tables, a kora or bala player performs Myriam Makeba tunes and other African ballads. Newcomers to African cuisine can choose from a range of classic Senegalese dishes as well as set menus for all appetites. For starters, try the traditional aloco (fried plantain bananas with red sauce), followed by the delicious, lightly spiced fish yassa or the hearty beef mafé (with peanut sauce). For dessert, check out the amazing thiakry (semolina and cream cheese salad).

starter: 30FF-40FF
main: 70FF-95FF
dessert: 25FF-35FF
Set menu: 98FF, 135FF, 195FF
Plat du jour: 85FF (Tues, Wed & Thurs)

CB EC MC V

Open: daily 8pm-2am; reservations advisable (towards end of week)

Ave Maria
Afro-Brazilian

☎ 01 47 00 61 73
1, rue Jacquard, Oberkampf

Map: 11 D4
Map: 11 D4
Métro: Parmentier

 Smoking throughout

 Pavement tables

New kid in town Ave Maria is sure to brighten up the bottom end of rue Oberkampf. This place is like a Brazilian or African canteen, a chic, imaginary and colourful Greasy Joe's, a Spanish inn combining flavours of the southern hemisphere. The menu follows the chef's roaming imagination: Jardin de Goa, Voyage à Itaca, Women on top de Bahia, le Togolais... hearty, hybrid and harmonious dishes. If you choose Africa, you might be treated to the bœuf mijoté aux noyaux de palmes rouges (beef stew with red palm seeds), served with cassava and baby white eggplant. Tropical fruit, wild, un-known grasses and heavenly vegetation provide a lush garnish and an extra touch of exoticism. The music livens up towards the end of the night. As you sip your mojito at the bar, you just might surprise yourself by dancing.

Open: daily 8pm-midnight; reservations not accepted

starter: 50FF
main: 58FF-74FF
dessert: 38FF

cash only

Le Bali Bar
Thai

☎ 01 47 00 25 47
9, rue Saint-Sabin, Bastille

Map: 11 G3
Métro: Saint-Sabin

 Smoking throughout

Despite its name, the Bali Bar isn't a bar and has no Indonesian connections. The young chef, Oth Sombath, formerly of the Blue Ele-phant and the Asian, has been working at this Thai restaurant since last September. The oriental décor is reminiscent of a colonial trading post and has completely transformed what used to be a hairdressing school. The menu features numerous multiflavoured dishes. For starters, the assortment of chef's speciali-ties is the restaurant's star attraction. With its rich combination of spices, the curry is also a must. For dessert, the sweet-savoury sod sai, steamed in a banana leaf, is simply stunning. The Bali Bar's welcoming atmosphere and sumptuous cuisine make for an extremely enjoyable outing.

Open: Mon-Fri 11am-2am, Sat 6pm-2am; reservations advisable

starter: 37FF-55FF
main: 67FF-220FF
dessert: 35FF-37FF
Plat du jour: 65FF (lunch)

AE CB DC EC MC V

11ᵉrrondᵉ

Map: 11 H5
Métro: Ledru Rollin

Smoking throughout

Pavement tables

Le Bistrot du Peintre
French

☎ 01 47 00 34 39
116, ave Ledru-Rollin, Bastille

It's hard to know whether customers come here primarily for the food or the surroundings. The mouldings and the wood and glass panelling are glorious, if somewhat faded in spots, and the quintessentially Parisian atmosphere adds to the appeal of this busy bistrot, which is packed from noon onwards. The menu is based on fresh market produce and includes beautifully presented specials such as the subtle velouté de potiron aux moules et coques (pumpkin soup with mussels and cockles), and the sun-drenched filets de rougets à la badiane (mullet with badian). The pièce de bœuf au gratin de roquefort (beef au gratin with Roquefort cheese) is excellent, a well-balanced dish that has nonetheless been the downfall of many a chef. The generous tartines are also a popular item.

main: 22FF-92FF
dessert: 16FF-38FF
MC V

Open: Mon-Sat: 7am-2am, Sun 10am-2am (meals from noon); reservations advisable

---

Map: 11 C3
Métro: Oberkampf

Smoking throughout

Bistrot Florentin
Italian

☎ 01 43 55 57 00
40, rue Jean-Pierre Timbaud, Oberkampf

Imagine yourself somewhere in Tuscany, in a restaurant with mustard-coloured walls and sea-green tablecloths, the regulars giving each other a peck on the cheek before ordering their favourite pasta and catching up on the latest news over a couple of glasses of chianti. Grilled, finely seasoned eggplant for starters, tiramisù as light as a feather for dessert. Between these two courses, a wide choice of mains. The penne à la crème d'artichaut et aux truffes (penne with cream, artichokes and truffles) is superb. The ravioli aux épinards et au fromage, sauce aux cèpes (spinach and cheese ravioli with a cep mushroom sauce) won't disappoint. But despite the owner's Italian accent, this isn't Tuscany – Bistrot Florentin, in the mega-trendy neighbourhood of Oberkampf, is well and truly in Paris.

starter: 24FF-75FF
main: 45FF-95FF
dessert: 30FF-35FF
Set menu: 65FF
(weekday lunch)
Plat du jour: 80FF
CB V

Open: Mon-Fri 12.15pm-2pm, Mon-Sat 8pm-11pm; reservations advisable

Bistrot Guillaume
French

☎ 01 47 00 43 50
5, rue Guillaume-Bertrand, Saint-Maur

Map: 11 D5

Métro: St-Maur

  Smoking throughout

This smart 'bistrot', close to the flashy rue d'Oberkampf, has a dozen tables with gingham tablecloths arranged around a polished wooden bar. Add a few Venetian dolls, a touch of greenery and background music from Vivaldi to Abba... The ravioles de saumon crème ciboulette (salmon, cream and chives) or the fortifying salade Guillaume will tickle your tastebuds for starters. For mains, the menu offers a range of traditional provincial dishes enhanced by the chef's imagination: andouillette, jarret de porc sur choucroute (pork knuckle with sauerkraut), but also chou farci au saumon (stuffed cabbage with salmon),and mignon de porc au cidre (tenderloin of pork with cider). A surprising sweet and sour magret de canard aux griottes et pommes (fillet of duck breast with morello cherries and potatoes) is superb. A small corner of the menu is reserved for traditional but delectable desserts and the wine list is short but well chosen. As an added bonus, you can expect friendly, attentive service.

starter: 38FF-55FF
main: 64FF-88FF
Set menu: 68FF (lunch), 98FF, 128FF
Plat du jour: 40FF-58FF

AE CB MC V

Open: Mon-Fri noon-2.30pm, 7pm-11pm, Sat & Sun 7pm-11pm; reservations not accepted

Blue Bayou
Cajun

☎ 01 43 55 87 21
111, rue Saint-Maur, Oberkampf

Map: 11 C4

Métro: Parmentier, St-Maur

Entertainment: Concerts and theme nights

  Smoking throughout

Upstairs from the Blue Billard bar, this restaurant – the only one of its kind in Europe – offers the full Cajun experience. At the top of a knotty wooden staircase, a huge log cabin reveals rough-sawn tables and chairs, old stovepipes and the famous alligator, all of which come straight from the banks of the Bayou. The seasonal menu changes three times a year and features simple, original cuisine which more than satisfies. For starters, you can't go past the gorgeous écrevisses (crayfish). Mains range from traditional jambalaya (chicken, sausage and rice) and gombos (gumbo with seafood or duck and vegetables) to rarer specialties such as croustillant de crabe à la mue (crispy crab out of its shell). With the help of Cajun music, the owners 'let the good times roll' well into the small hours. Sunday brunch is a great outing for family and friends.

starter: 49FF-69FF
main: 75FF-90FF
dessert: 40FF
Set menu: 89FF, 119FF (Sunday brunch)
Plat du jour: 55FF

AE CB DC EC JCB MC V; €

Open: Mon-Sat noon-3pm, 7pm-2am (orders taken until 10.30pm), Sun 11am-3.30pm (brunch); reservations advisable

Boca chica

Spanish

☎ 01 43 57 93 13
**58, rue de Charonne,
Bastille**

Map: 11 H5

Métro: Ledru Rollin, Charonne

Entertainment: Live music on Sunday nights

Smoking throughout

Courtyard tables

Although not too far from the Bastille, this restaurant-bar specialising in tapas could be in Barcelona. Boca chica has pleasant surroundings, a relaxed, friendly atmosphere and is accessible via a paved courtyard where you can have lunch or dinner, weather permitting. On Sunday nights, a Spanish band transforms the restaurant into a vast concert hall while customers help themselves to lashings of paella. The menu offers traditional dishes such as pavé de bœuf (thick-cut steak), steak tartare, brochette de viande (meat kebab), fonte d'agneau (lamb) and an assortment of fish, but the main attraction here is the chef's speciality, the mixed tapas. Those who love Iberian snacks and sultry nights will be in their absolute element.

starter: 65FF-85FF
main: 70FF-90FF
dessert: 35FF
Set menu: 170FF

AE CB V

Open: Mon-Sat 11am-2am; reservations advisable

Boteco

Brazilian

☎ 01 43 57 15 47
**131, rue Oberkampf,
Oberkampf**

Map: 11 C5

Métro: Ménilmontant

Smoking throughout

Pavement tables

The Brazilian *boteco* is like the Spanish *bodega*, a place that offers a happy mix of drink, food and music. You might like to start here with a house cocktail such as the batida de coco (coconut milk and cachaca rum) or choose from the large selection of dark and white rums from Brazil, Guadeloupe and Cuba. Foodwise, there's Brazil's national dish, feijoada (black beans, pork and sausages) or, for more inquisitive palates, picadinho, a striking tartare dish sprinkled with cachaca. For dessert, try the delicious chocolate terrine coated in sweet aurriverde sauce. That leaves the music: MPB radio is broadcast over the PA, but if you're lucky, you might get to see Brazilian expats improvising to a bossa rhythm. Football is also part of the décor. Shorts, shoes and shirts in Boteco's colours hang above the long wooden tables.

main: 42FF-68FF
dessert: 22FF
Set menu: 55FF, 76FF
(Mon-Fri until 6pm)

cash only

Open: daily 9am-2am (restaurant noon-midnight); reservations essential (six or more people)

Le C'amelot
French

☎ 01 43 55 54 04
50, rue Amelot, Bastille

Map: 11 F3
Métro: Chemin Vert, Bréguet Sabin, Richard Lenoir

 Smoking throughout

This small gourmet bistrot has done everything right and, as far as the food is concerned, is on a par with the top restaurants. The owner, former chef at the Ambassadeurs (Hôtel de Crillon), has created an intimate and unpretentious atmosphere that highlights the finesse of his cuisine. For starters, the tarte feuilletée de sardines marinées et confit d'oignons (pastry tart with marinated sardines and onion confit) is a delicious discovery. The agneau de Lozère rôti, de l'ail en chemise et des haricots coco mitonnés au jus (roast lamb cooked with whole, unpeeled cloves of garlic and cocoa beans slowly simmered in the juice) offers a perfect combination of flavours (the beans get top marks). The bottle of côtes-roannaises wine, although young, does justice to the sardines and the lamb. The contrasting tartness of rhurbarb with vanilla makes a subtly refreshing dessert.

main: 70FF-80FF
Set menu: 180FF

CB MC V

Open: Tues-Sat noon-2.30pm, 7pm-midnight; reservations essential (evenings)

Café Cannelle
Moroccan

☎ 01 43 70 48 25
1 bis, rue de la Forge Royale, Bastille

Map: 11 J5
Métro: Bastille, Faidherbe-Chaligny

 Smoking throughout

While there's no dearth of Moroccan restaurants in Paris, they don't all have the moucharabieh, the mosaic tables, the warm and well-cared-for décor or, most importantly, the smiling owners of Café Cannelle (any restaurant named after a spice has to be good). Start with a briouat de poulet à la fleur de safran (saffron chicken in puff pastry) before savouring the tajine d'agneau aux poires et au miel d'acacia (lamb tajine with pears and honey) – some customers come just for this exquisite dish – and wash it all down with a cuvée du Président. Couscous (including the 'Zagora', with marinated lamb kebabs), eastern pastries and salade d'oranges à la cannelle (orange salad with cinnamon) also feature on the menu of this intimate, convivial restaurant. A lovely spot to let time pass as you sip your peppermint tea.

starter: 36FF-69FF
main: 75FF-95FF
dessert: 40FF-45FF

CB DC EC MC V

Open: Tues-Sun noon-3pm, 8pm-midnight; reservations advisable

La Cale aux Huîtres

Oyster bar/Japanese

☎ 01 48 06 02 47
**136, rue Saint-Maur,
Oberkampf**

Map: 11 C4

Métro: Goncourt, Couronnes

Entertainment: Occasional live music

A flashing lighthouse at the door, a huge wave in the window and an owner clad in a sailor's jersey bring the sea to a neighbourhood where just about anything goes. Customers are squashed up close together at big wooden tables. Set course for the oysters, freshly arrived from the Vendée, eaten with a squeeze of lemon, buttered rye bread and a glass of dry white. Devise your own meal according to how you like your fish: grilled or raw, with tuna tartare... Also on board, a range of sushi, sashimi and maki. The salade aux algues et aux concombres (seaweed and cucumber salad) is simple, but with the right seasoning, goes perfectly with the authentic décor. The desserts are nothing special, so take advantage of the oysters, which can be ordered one, half a dozen or as many as you like at a time!

main: 65FF-78FF
dessert: 25FF
Set menu: oyster menu 92FF-120FF, maki menu 80FF, sushi menu
Plat du jour: 65FF-75FF (grills)
AE CB EC MC V; €

Open: Tues-Sat noon-2.30pm, 7pm-midnight; reservations essential (evenings)

Cartet

French (Lyon)

☎ 01 48 05 17 65
**52, rue de Malte,
République**

Map: 11 C2

Métro: République, Oberkampf, Goncourt

Smoking throughout

Lovers of Lyons' cuisine have been coming to Cartet since 1936. This tiny, 20-seat restaurant is lovingly decorated like an old provincial house. The owner recommends various dishes with a friendly smile. If she suggests the terrine de maquereau maison (the chef's mackerel terrine), don't hesitate... accompanied by a Bugey white, this makes a deliciously fresh starter. The bœuf à la ficelle (beef poached in a rich meat and vegetable broth) comes with bone marrow and gorgeous gratin dauphinois, and is a paragon of flavour and tenderness. Try this dish with an excellent côtes-du-rhône Saint-Estève. Then finish in style with œufs à la neige or choux à la crème (cream puffs).

starter: 42FF-65FF
main: 150FF-165FF
dessert: 62FF
cash only

Open: Mon-Fri 12.30pm-2.30pm, 7.30pm-9.30pm; reservations advisable (especially evenings)

Chardenoux
French

☎ **01 43 71 49 52**
Cnr 1, rue Jules-Vallès and 23,
rue de Chanzy,
Faidherbe

This old bistrot opened in 1904 and retains its beautiful if slightly tarnished Art Nouveau décor. Expect a warm welcome and quiet atmosphere, but make sure you bring an appetite. This is French family cooking at its best, starting with the tête de veau sauce gribiche (calf's head served with a mayonnaise-style sauce) or the crème de lentilles à l'ail et à l'huile d'olive (a deliciously creamy consommé of lentils, garlic and olive oil served cold). Cooked to your taste, the magret de canard rôti (roast fillet of duck breast) comes with crispy skin and vegetables that are lovingly prepared without being overly elaborate. The wine list includes offerings from all over the French countryside, from the drinkable to the exceptional. To finish, gourmets will be transported by the chocolate mousse with orange purée.

Open: Mon-Fri noon-2pm, Mon-Sat 8pm-10.30pm; reservations advisable

Map: 11 H6

Métro: Faidherbe-Chaligny, Charonne, Boulets-Montreuil

 Smoking throughout

starter: 35FF-120FF
main: 75FF-125FF
dessert: 40FF-55FF
Plat du jour: 80FF-125FF

AE EC MC V

Chez Ramulaud
French

☎ **01 43 72 23 29**
269, rue du Faubourg
Saint-Antoine,
Nation

With its peaceful, antiquated atmosphere, this enormous place is reminiscent of one of those famous provincial restaurants. Countless details evoke the good old days – the original chequered tile floor, the cheese 'cage' next to the imposing 1950s fridge, the cast iron radiators and the large checked serviettes. For starters, you can try a different soup each day, unless you'd prefer the œufs cocotte aux champignons de saison (eggs with seasonal mushrooms) or the chef's terrine. For mains, it's hard to choose between the dos de morue et sa purée d'aubergine (fillet of cod with eggplant purée) and the carré d'agneau en croûte d'herbe et son gâteau de pomme de terre (loin of lamb in a herb puff pastry case). The tarte au citron and the fondant au chocolat are home-made, of course. Don't forget to look up and admire the superb collection of Art Deco centre lights while you're sipping your coffee.

Open: Mon-Fri noon-3pm, 8pm-11pm, Sat 8pm-11pm, Sun noon-3pm; reservations advisable

Map: 11 J7

Métro: Nation, Faidherbe-Chaligny

Entertainment: Open-air dancing accompanied by barrel organ

 Smoking throughout

 Pavement tables

starter: 30FF-45FF
main: 59FF-95FF
dessert: 38FF-40FF
Set menu: 67FF (2 courses), 140FF (dinner)
Plat du jour: 59FF

AE V

Map: 11 B3

Métro: Goncourt

Entertainment: Live accordion & piano music

Smoking throughout

Chez Raymonde
French

☎ 01 43 55 26 27
**119, ave Parmentier,
Goncourt**

Yannick and Benoît did their training around the Bastille before setting up this unique spot combining gastronomy with choreography. Bourgeois and bohemian customers alike come here to dance the paso doble and other ballroom favourites. As soon as everyone is seated, Benoît draws the red curtains and stands by the door. This gives the musicians their cue, and the night kicks off with Benoît and Yannick pirouetting in the centre of the room to the strains of an accordion and piano duo. Watch the gamest customers follow the chef onto the dance floor while you savour the skillfully prepared cuisine. The single set menu, subject to seasonal change, proves that the chef cooks just as well as he dances the tango.

Set menu: 185FF

AE CB DC EC MC V

Open: Wed-Sun 8pm-10.30pm, Sun 1pm-4.30pm (Oct-Mar); reservations essential

---

Map: 11 D2

Métro: Filles-du-Calvaire

Smoking throughout

Pavement tables

Clown Bar
French

☎ 01 43 55 87 35
**114, rue Amelot,
République**

Close by the Cirque d'Hiver (Winter Circus), the Clown Bar is aptly named. Superb early 20th century crockery features clowns from the golden age of circuses. The dual clown-Parisian bistrot theme pervades the entire décor, from the floor tiles and furniture to the old circus posters on the wall. Into the ring then, starting with a great wine list dominated by burgundies and côtes-du-rhône (often served in half-bottles or by the glass). The traditional charcuterie platter is substantial and goes well with a half-bottle of brouilly, while the Parmentier de boudin aux pommes (black pudding Parmentier with apple) is deservedly one of the restaurant's most popular dishes. Top marks also for the double crème brûlée (one with vanilla, the other with mandarin), which you can either enjoy for its dual flavours or share with a friend!

starter: 32FF-68FF
main: 68FF-85FF
dessert: 38FF-42FF
Set menu: 88FF (lunch),
120FF (dinner)
CB V (150FF minimum)

Open: daily 12.15pm-3pm, 7pm-midnight; reservations advisable

Cocoa Café
French

☎ 01 43 57 89 03
3, ave de la République, République

Map: 11 C2

Métro: République

 Smoking throughout

 Pavement tables

The name alone heralds the delicious coffee and chocolate colours of the Cocoa Café. Cane armchairs, dark-red velvet bench seats, murals, a superb library and the softest of lighting complete the minimalist but warm décor. The food is original with a distinct Asian influence. The coquilles Saint-Jacques au piment doux sur lit de roquette (scallops with capsicum on a bed of rocket) are mouthwatering, and the étouffée de poisson au curry vert à la vapeur (steamed fish in green curry) is equally delectable. For dessert, the rosewater crème brûlée is an absolute must. You'll keep coming back to the Cocoa Café, for Sunday brunch, afternoon tea or dinner with friends.

Open: daily 8.30am-2am; reservations not accepted

starter: 45FF-75FF
main: 70FF-110FF
dessert: 45FF
Set menu: 78FF (lunch)
Plat du jour: 65FF

CB MC V

Clown Bar

11errond

Map: 11 J7
Métro: Nation
Entertainment: Special nights: wine harvest, accordion, disco

Smoking throughout

Pavement tables

La Dame brune
French

☎ 01 40 24 09 38
287, rue du
Faubourg Saint-Antoine,
Nation

The real Dame Brune watches discreetly from one of the many picture frames hanging on the walls of this small tavern, which is straight out of an old working-class Parisian neighbourhood. But isn't that the owner? There *is* a likeness, if you look closely... The menu holds another surprise – along with classic bistrot fare such as andouillette (small pork sausage) and magret de canard (fillet of duck breast), you can order baby boudins antillais (a type of Carribean sausage) and lamb colombo! The brunette with the magnetic smile has something for everyone. For starters, you also have a choice between Scandinavian salmon rillettes and the more southern flavours of tomates séchées et chèvre frais (sun-dried tomatoes and fresh goat's cheese), unless you'd prefer the traditional salade de gésiers confits (preserved gizzard salad). Save some room for one of the copious, typically French desserts.

starter: 35FF-60FF
main: 45FF-115FF
dessert: 35FF-50FF
Set menu: 75FF, 85FF (lunch), 120FF, 135FF (dinner)
Plat du jour: 65FF (lunch), 85FF (dinner)
CB EC MC V

Open: Tues-Sat 9am-3pm, 6pm-11pm; reservations advisable

Map: 11 H5
Métro: Ledru-Rollin
Dress code applies
Nonsmoking tables available

Dame Jeanne
Modern French

☎ 01 47 00 37 40
60, rue de Charonne,
Charonne

Prepare yourself for a veritable banquet at this luxury restaurant. Well-chosen southern colours add warmth to a conventional, classical décor. The menu includes risotto aux champignons et à la volaille (mushrooms and poultry), pièce de bœuf grillée gros sel sauce Foyot (grilled beef with cooking salt and foyot sauce) and effeuillée de raie au vinaigre balsamique (skate with balsamic vinegar). The dishes are skillfully prepared, beautifully presented and full of flavour. Desserts such as the chocolate cake with cocoa sorbet are exceptional. The chef emphasises quality over quantity, and the food here is distinguished by its finesse. Dame Jeanne offers something for everyone, including vegetarians, who can order from a 'seasonal fruit and vegetables' menu. Attentive, professional service makes dining in this temple of good food an even more enjoyable experience.

Set menu: 98FF, 120FF, 128FF, 148FF, 178FF
MC V

Open: Mon-Sat noon-2pm, 7pm-11pm, Fri & Sat 7pm-11.30pm; reservations advisable (evenings)

Dans la cuisine
French

☎ 01 43 38 70 18
51, rue de la Fontaine au Roi, Oberkampf

Map: 11 C4

Métro: Goncourt

Entertainment: Theme nights for festivals like Halloween

 Smoking throughout

The small dining room looks like a Spanish bar, with red and yellow walls covered in garlands and kitsch furniture from secondhand shops – a place where you immediately feel at home. Grandma's food is prepared right in front of you, behind a large bar. The owner extols her cook's virtues with a grin: 'Our fish is delicious!' OK, we believe you! Go with the filet de cabillaud au curry (fillet of cod in curry), which is tastier than the pintade au chou (guinea-fowl with cabbage). But first refresh your palate Lyons-style with cervelle de canut cheese (served in a strainer with herbs). For dessert, the fondant comes with plenty of chocolate. Dans la cuisine offers respectable food with good ingredients (top marks for the Ré salt, the olive oil and the bread) and a warm, friendly welcome.

starter: 32FF
main: 53FF
dessert: 25FF
Plat du jour: 53FF

CB EC MC V

Open: Tues-Fri noon-2.30pm, Wed-Sat 8pm-11.30pm; reservations advisable

Les Domaines qui montent
French

☎ 01 43 56 89 15
136, blvd Voltaire, Voltaire

Map: 11 F5

Métro: Voltaire

Entertainment: Beaujolais nouveau festival, exhibitions

 Smoking throughout

You enter two worlds at once at 136 boulevard Voltaire. Through the first door, you'll find a cellarman recommending cheap, underrated wines. Then, at the back of the shop, there's a small restaurant, a kind of cross between a bistrot and a guesthouse. It gets busy at lunchtime as customers sit down to savour the delights of provincial French cooking. The warm welcome, the dish of Échiré butter and the bread on the table augur well. First impressions are confirmed when the starters arrive – flavoursome soupe de poissons de l'île de Ré (fish soup) or delicious 'pâtés épatants du Nord'('perfect pâté from the North'). For mains, the specials board features a petit salé aux lentilles (salted pork with lentils), cassoulet au confit (preserved meat) and brandade de morue (salt cod). Flavour and simplicity are the key ingredients at this original restaurant.

starter: 30FF-40FF
main: 49FF
dessert: 22FF
Plat du jour: 49FF

AE CB DC EC MC V

Open: Tues-Sat 10am-8.30pm; reservations advisable

11ᵉ ARRONDISSEMENT

L'Écailler du Bistrot
French

☎ 01 43 72 76 77
**22, rue Paul Bert,
Charonne**

Map: 11 H6

Métro: Faidherbe Chaligny,
Charonne

Smoking throughout

If there's a heaven for oyster lovers, it has to be here, at the Écailler du Bistrot. The menu includes every conceivable recipe for this shellfish. The only thing missing is the sound of the sea and the squawk of seagulls. This bistrot has undeniable charm and style. The quality of the ingredients is exceptional, from the oysters and shrimps to the chef's smoked salmon and spider crabs. The ubiquitous hareng pommes à l'huile (herrings marinated in oil with potatoes) is transformed into a masterpiece. The thon cru mariné à l'huile de sésame (raw tuna marinated in sesame oil) and the ravioles de gambas au jus d'étrilles (ravioli with king prawns and a sauce made from velvet swimming crabs) are particularly noteworthy. Subtle flavours also characterise the desserts – try the chocolate terrine with basil, an extraordinary combination and fitting conclusion to a blissful taste experience.

starter: 50FF-130FF
main: 68FF-135FF
Set menu: 85FF (lunch)

CB EC MC V

Open: Tues-Sat noon-2.30pm, Mon-Sat 7.30pm-11.30pm; reservations advisable

Extra Old Café
International

☎ 01 43 71 73 45
**307, rue du
Faubourg Saint-Antoine,
Nation**

Map: 11 J8

Métro & RER: Nation

Smoking throughout

Pavement tables

This old, spacious neighbourhood bar has been converted into a happening place with a new 'second-hand' look and loud music. It also has plenty to offer the average customer – nice, cheap food for all tastes and appetites, quick service around the clock and pleasant picture windows. The menu includes cold or hot tartines, hearty salads and cheese or charcuterie platters, as well as proper meals such as entrecôte marchand de vin (steak poached in red wine with shallots and onions), fricassée de poisson au curry (fish curry) or cheeseburgers. The food is simple and delicious if not particularly original. Snacks are served until 1am, which makes this an ideal spot to meet either before or after going out.

starter: 32FF-49FF
main: 40FF-75FF
dessert: 25FF-35FF
Set menu: 55FF (lunch)
Plat du jour: 65FF-72FF

CB EC MC V

Open: daily noon-3pm, 7pm-11pm, bar 7am-2am; reservations advisable

La Folie Milon
Modern French

☎ **01 43 70 01 76**
**33, ave Philippe-Auguste,
Nation**

Map: 11 H8

Métro: Nation (RER)

Entertainment: Monthly photo exhibitions

 Nonsmoking tables available

You enter the Folie Milon through a heavy wooden door. The décor is extremely plain and somewhat disappointing, despite being livened up by monthly photo exhibitions. Appearances can be deceptive though and, in the greyness of Paris' east end, this restaurant produces bright, colourful meals with the help of the fruits and exotic spices of southern cuisine. Certain combinations of flavours, such as the thon grillé à la noix de coco (grilled tuna with coconut), are a little surprising, while others will have you drooling instantly. The salade de foies gras chauds au pimiento (warm foie gras salad with pimiento – a mild, subtle spice from Jamaica) is a sumptuous dish and will delight the most discerning palates. The meal ends sweetly with dessert and an extremely reasonable bill.

starter: 30FF-90FF
main: 40FF-90FF
dessert: 30FF-40FF
Set menu: 85FF

CB MC V

Open: Tues-Sat noon-2.30pm, 8pm-10.30pm; reservations advisable (evenings)

Les Galopins
French

☎ **01 47 00 45 35**
**24, rue des Tallandiers,
Bastille**

Map: 11 G4

Métro: Bastille

 Smoking throughout

 Terrace tables

Not far from the Place de la Bastille, Les Galopins is a refreshing change from the hip restaurants of this neighbourhood (where people go to be seen rather than for the pleasure of eating). This lovely, quiet place has simple, plain décor and customers are greeted warmly with a kir. The menu features an impressive range of starters and mains in the best tradition of French cuisine: poêlée de pétoncles (pan-fried queen scallops); magret de canard (fillet of duck breast); coeur de rumsteck (tenderloin rumpsteak); and compotée d'agneau aux aubergines (lamb and eggplant ragout). The wine list is short but enticing. For dessert, you don't need a huge appetite to enjoy the tuile aux pêches (winged almond biscuit with peaches) or the delicious nougat glacé et son coulis de framboises. Everything is impeccable. You'll sip your coffee as slowly as possible to make this gourmet outing last.

starter: 35FF-45FF
main: 66FF-79FF
dessert: 30FF
Set menu: 72FF
Plat du jour: 50FF

V

Open: Mon-Fri noon-2.30pm, Mon-Sat 7.30pm-11.30pm; reservations advisable

Map: 11 C4

Métro: Parmentier,
Couronnes

Smoking throughout

Haïku
Macrobiotic/organic

☎ 01 56 98 11 67
**63, rue Jean-Pierre Timbaud,
Oberkampf**

Abdel Haq, Haïku's young chef, studied macro-biotics in the United States before being in-spired by the London chain Wagamama to open this restaurant with its relaxing yellow walls. His healthy, organic cuisine is highly original and creative. The first surprise is the iced green tea served as an appetiser. Next, the chef's spe-ciality – pasta made from semiwholemeal flour then sautéed or served as a soup. Pasta à la sicilienne (fresh sardines, onion, raisins and pine nuts) and soupe de pâtes au poulet à la sauce coco et curry (pasta soup with chicken and a cocoa-bean curry sauce) are offered alongside basmati rice with vegetables and tofu for vegetarians. Desserts include a delectable vanilla and cardamom sweet. You'll feel light but satisfied when you leave, as focused and beautiful as the Japanese poetic form from which this restaurant takes its name.

starter: 15FF-30FF
main: 51FF-72FF
dessert: 20FF-35FF
V; €

Open: Mon-Fri noon-2.30pm, Mon-Sat 7pm-10.30pm; reser-vations not accepted

L'Homme Bleu

L'Homme Bleu
North African

☎ 01 48 07 05 63
55 bis, rue Jean-Pierre Timbaud, Oberkampf

Map: 11 C4

Métro: Parmentier

Entertainment: Occasional musicians

 Pavement tables

People are falling over themselves to book a table at the Homme Bleu, Parisian restaurant and self-appointed ambassador of the famous Berber nomads of North Africa. This desert is packed! The open kitchen, where you can see women concocting aromatic delicacies, augurs well. Under the authentic Tuareg tent or in the Moroccan-style vaulted cellar, customers are served dishes of exceptional finesse and inventiveness, such as the tajine combining prunes, pears, almonds, orange and cinnamon. Eggs, chicken, fish and mutton are braised and served with vegetables in traditional covered clay pots. If you're not overly hungry, you might prefer to sample the delicate flavours of the chicken pastilla, sealed in a light fritter. For dessert, you won't be able to resist the magnificent platter of eastern pastries or the almonds, pistachios, honey and orange blossom.

Open: Mon-Sat 5pm-2am; reservations essential

starter: 35FF-60FF
main: 65FF-110FF
dessert: 35FF

cash only

Jours de Fête
French/Creperie

☎ 01 40 21 70 34
115, rue Oberkampf, Oberkampf

Map: 11 C5

Métro: Ménilmontant, Parmentier

 Smoking throughout

Imagine a collection of Christmas lanterns and kitsch decorations set against gleaming oilcloths and whitewashed walls. Add a permanently jolly owner to the picture and you'll understand why this small restaurant is called 'Jours de fête' ('feast days' or 'holidays'). The menu here is brimming with ideas. In addition to basic galettes (buckwheat crêpes) with one or two ingredients – appropriately named 'simplettes' or 'doublettes' – there's the galette aux coquilles Saint-Jacques, ciboulette et crème fraîche, flambée au whisky (with scallops, chives and crème fraîche) and the galette aux trois fromages (with emmental, roquefort and goat's cheese). At lunchtime, an extremely reasonable set menu offers customers a savoury galette, a sweet crêpe and a drink. Pommeau and cider, of course, are part of the feast. An authentic restaurant in a neighbourhood that is sometimes less so.

Open: Tues-Fri noon-3pm, Tues-Thurs 6pm-midnight, Fri 6pm-2am, Sat noon-2am, Sun 2pm-midnight (hours do vary so check first); reservations not accepted

main: 30FF-52FF
dessert: 14FF-32FF
Set menu: 55FF

cash only

11e ARRONDISSEMENT

Map: 11 C4

Métro: Parmentier, Couronnes

Entertainment: Art exhibitions

Smoking throughout

Juan et Juanita
Modern French/ Mediterranean

☎ 01 43 57 60 15
82, rue Jean-Pierre Timbaud, Oberkampf

This purple and green restaurant really catches your eye. The huge dining room is absolutely lovely and has a feminine and new-age feel. A seasonal, wayfaring menu travels between grandma's cottage and exotic culinary destinations, gathering herbs and spices from the Mediterranean along the way. The results of this wanderlust include a variety of salads with subtle taste and colour combinations, and raw marinated salmon with citrus fruit, an exquisite offering served in a small jar. For mains, the Arabic flavours of tajine d'agneau aux abricots secs (lamb tajine with dried apricots) feature alongside mignon de porc au raifort (tenderloin of pork with horseradish) and souris d'agneau (knuckle-joint of lamb). The same roaming spirit is reflected in the desserts: soupe de mangues et sa glace vanille (mango soup with vanilla ice cream) or figues rôties au vin (baked figs in wine) are a fitting way to end this enchanting gourmet voyage.

starter: 30FF-49FF
main: 70FF-80FF
dessert: 25FF-35FF
Set menu: 89FF
(two courses)
CB EC JCB MC V; €

Open: Tues-Fri 8pm-midnight, Sat & Sun 8pm-1am (closes 2am); reservations advisable

---

Map: 11 F2

Métro: St Sébastien Froissart, Chemin Vert

Smoking throughout

Les Jumeaux
French

☎ 01 43 14 27 00
73, rue Amelot, Oberkampf

There are places that reveal their secrets slowly: Les Jumeaux ('The Twins'), with its plain décor, is one of them. The first surprise is the unaffectedness and attentiveness of the twin brothers in question, one of whom works in the kitchen while the other waits on the tables. Next, a discreet sense of whimsy is reflected in the crockery, which is different for each person and each course. Finally, the creative, lovingly prepared food is simply to die for. Start with the galette de foie gras chaud aux oignons et citrons confits (buckwheat crêpe with warm foie gras and preserved onions and lemons) – this crunchy, sophisticated and flavoursome entrée is pure heaven. Move on to the extraordinary combination of flavours offered by the coquilles Saint-Jacques à la purée de pois cassés, sauce pamplemousse rose (scallops with a purée of split peas and pink grapefruit sauce), before finishing with a sumptuous mousse au chocolat noire au jus de café et zestes d'orange.

Set menu: 150FF (lunch: two courses), 185FF (dinner: three courses)
AE CB DC EC MC V; €

Open: Tues-Sat noon-2pm, 7.30pm-10.30pm; reservations advisable

Kasaphani
Cypriot

☎ **01 48 07 20 19**
**122, ave Parmentier,
Oberkampf**

Map: 11 B3

Métro: Goncourt

 Smoking throughout

This restaurant, sporting an impressive array of indoor plants, bears the name of the Cypriot village where its owners were born. The village's motto, encouraging you to drink your fill but to stay happy, explains the convivial atmosphere of its Parisian namesake. Along with Lebanon, Cyprus can lay claim to the best mezes of the Mediterranean region. The menu offers two banquets of small or large mezes, each comprising more than 15 different dishes. Your table will be covered in no time with small ramekins of poulpes au vin (octopus stewed in wine), brochettes d'olives grillées (grilled olive kebabs), sheftalias (pork sausages), moussaka, tarama, stuffed lamb and quail – you won't know where to begin. A few more sips of retsina and a small sweet such as the paix des dieux ('peace of the gods') and you'll think you're in Cyprus.

Open: Tues-Sun noon-2pm, 7.30pm-10pm; reservations advisable

starter: 25FF-65FF
main: 65FF-105FF
dessert: 28FF
Set menu: 92FF

AE CB V

Khun Akorn
Thai

☎ **01 43 56 20 03**
**8, ave de Taillebourg,
Nation**

Map: 11 J9

Métro: Nation

 Nonsmoking tables available

 First-floor terrace & pavement tables

Have coriander, honey, lemongrass, lime, chilli and garlic lost their ability to surprise you? Then you haven't been to Khun Akorn, an oasis of sophistication. This temple of Thai gastronomy will thrill the most blasé tastebuds with a menu featuring subtle combinations of flavours and classic Thai dishes alongside spectacularly successful innovations. Among the traditional dishes, the soupe de crevettes pimentées à la citronnelle (shrimp soup seasoned with lemongrass), the beef and chicken satays – with scrumptious peanut sauce – and the 'paniers d'or' (rice pasta with minced pork) are outstanding. Among the more innovative offerings, savour the fruits de mer grillés sauce barbecue maison (grilled seafood with the chef's barbecue sauce) – this will instantly dispel any preconceptions you may have about barbecue sauce – or the 'larmes de tigre' (grilled fillet of beef marinated in honey and herbs). The menu explains that the tiger 'is crying because he wants some more'.

Open: Tues-Sun noon-2pm, 7.30pm-11pm; reservations advisable

starter: 40FF-70FF
main: 75FF-95FF
dessert: 30FF

AE CB DC EC MC V

Map: 11 D2

Métro: Oberkampf, Filles-du-Calvaire

Smoking throughout

Le Kitch
French

☎ 01 40 21 94 14
10, rue Oberkampf, Oberkampf

It's quite possible to enjoy kitsch and good taste at the same time. Here, the former is on the wall and the latter on your plate. When this small restaurant isn't packed, the chef takes your order himself. His French cuisine incorporates Mediterranean flavours based on fleur de sel, balsamic vinegar, olive oil or cinnamon. He'll definitely recommend one of his specialities: in winter, the soupe de fèves chaude (hot broad bean soup), the blanquette or the stuffed cabbage; in summer, the warm goat's cheese and the manchons de poulet couscous banane (chicken with banana and couscous); for dessert, his famous chocolate soufflé. The wines are nothing special – try one of the punches instead; they're strong and delicious. The friendly, relaxed welcome attracts both local and foreign customers and the bill (which arrives rolled up in a hair curler) is always reasonable.

starter: 34FF-70FF
main: 58FF-70FF
dessert: 19FF-32FF
Plat du jour: 58FF (lunch)

cash only

Open: Mon-Fri 10am-4pm, daily 5pm-2am (orders taken until 11.30pm); reservations advisable

---

Map: 11 G4

Métro: Bréguet Sabin

Smoking throughout

Lire entre les vignes
French

☎ 01 43 55 69 49
38, rue Sedaine, Bastille

This is definitely one of our favourite restaurants. The open-plan kitchen on the left, just as you walk in the door, always makes you feel like you're at a friend's house. Pascaline, the heart and soul of the place, is absolutely lovely. Her smile, the way she greets you and her reproachfulness when you leave something on your plate make eating here a delightful experience. The décor has the charm of a country cottage. Foodwise, the velouté aux choux (cabbage soup) and the terrine de poireaux (leek) are terrific starters that can be followed, if you're feeling nostalgic, by the delicious hachis Parmentier with olive oil, served on a wooden board. Try a bottle of organic wine with your meal. If you make it to dessert (and you'll need to be a good eater), the chocolate mousse, approaching perfection, awaits. Lire entre les vignes is a real oasis of conviviality.

starter: 42FF
main: 60FF-95FF
dessert: 38FF
Set menu: 85FF (lunch)
Plat du jour: 60FF

CB MC V

Open: Mon-Fri noon-2.30pm, 7.30pm-10.30pm, Sat 7.30pm-11pm; reservations advisable

La Main d'Or
Corsican

☎ 01 44 68 04 68
133, rue du Faubourg Saint-Antoine, Ledru-Rollin

Map: 11 J5

Métro: Ledru Rollin

 Nonsmoking tables available (book in advance)

Pavement tables

A long dining room with exposed stone walls and a choir singing in the background set the tone at this staunchly Corsican establishment. La Main d'Or serves authentic island cuisine. Try, for example, the sturza preti (a subtle combination of spinach and fine brocciu cheese imported direct from the producer), the chausson fourré aux blettes et à l'oignon (turnover filled with Swiss chard and onion), the traditional omelette with brocciu or the jambon sec (dried ham, matured for two years). The good impression created by these starters is confirmed by the tian de veau aux olives (veal ragout) and the daube au vin de Toraccia (meat braised in wine). The fiadone – a sponge cake made with brocciu and lemon – will convince you that the Corsicans also know how to be *bons vivants*.

Open: Mon-Sat noon-3pm, 8pm-11pm; reservations advisable (especially weekends)

starter: 30FF-85FF
main: 50FF-105FF
dessert: 40FF
Set menu: 69FF (lunch)
Plat du jour: 85FF (95FF-105FF for the eel and wild boar)

CB EC DC JBC MC V

Menekse
Turkish/Kurdish

☎ 01 40 21 84 81
7, passage de la Main-d'Or, Charonne

Map: 11 H5

Métro: Ledru Rollin

 Smoking throughout

In a narrow street sheltered from the hubbub of the nearby Saint-Antoine neighbourhood, this Kurdish restaurant has a small, elegant dining room adorned with bluish tones and a few photos of the homeland. Young, laid-back customers come here to savour the chef's inventive and copious specialities. The dilan – a great assortment of flavours and aromas including lamb cutlets, chicken, eggplant, minced meat and yoghurt with garlic – goes well with a light Yakut. Lovers of fresh hors d'œuvre will swoon over the platter of meze (chickpea purée, tarama, crushed tomatoes with chilli and capsicum, oak leaves). To finish, the chef's dessert offers a succulent panorama of eastern sweets: baklava, Turkish delight, halva, oven-baked apples with cinnamon, and semolina with pinenuts and icecream.

Open: Mon-Fri 11.30am-3pm, Mon-Sat 7pm-11.30pm; reservations advisable on weekends

starter: 28FF-48FF
main: 46FF-79FF
dessert: 20FF-38FF
Set menu: 55FF, 62FF (weekday lunch), 95FF

MC V; €

11^e

Map: 11 D3

Métro: Oberkampf

Smoking throughout

Le Piano Fou
French

☎ 01 40 38 40 03
35, rue Oberkampf, Oberkampf

A lamp catches our attention as we wander idly past this small restaurant, wedged in between two blocks of flats. Through the narrow glass door, a long room with candles suspended from the ceiling, rough-painted yellow walls and friezes has a Provençal atmosphere. Southern herbs and flavours predominate: pot-au-feu with tarragon and carrots with cumin. Fresh steamed vegetables: simplicity above all else! The food comes in generous serves. The pavé de biche (venison steak) is stuffed with the chef's foie gras and served with a sauce périgourdine (demi-glace sauce with foie gras purée and truffles). The desserts are difficult to resist. Set course for the île flottante (egg whites as light as a feather floating on custard and topped with the chef's caramel sauce). Don't miss this simple, intimate and delectable little spot.

starter: 40FF-58FF
main: 70FF-98FF
dessert: 25FF
Set menu: 65FF
(weekday lunch)
Plat du jour: 70FF

CB EC MC V; €

Open: Tues-Thurs noon-2pm, Mon-Thurs 8pm-11pm, Fri & Sat 8pm-11.30pm; reservations advisable (especially weekends)

Map: 11 J5

Métro: Ledru Rollin, Faidherbe-Chaligny

Dress code applies

Entertainment: Live music every night from 11pm

Smoking throughout

le Réservoir
International

☎ 01 43 56 39 60
16, rue de la Forge-Royale, Saint-Antoine

Don't even think about coming here for a romantic dinner because this is a place to party. Stationed behind a heavy door, the bouncer scrutinises you closely. Once you're through, you're allowed into an impressive, cave-like space where small candles reveal a shabby baroque décor and an imposing concert stage in the centre of the room. Check out the other customers and extremely hip surrounds while you peruse the menu, which offers 'world' food in keeping with the background music. Our ricotta, basil and green tomato ravioli arrived without delay and was better than expected. The daurade au tian d'aubergines et de tomates (sea bream with eggplant and tomato tian) is also a hit with its deliciously crunchy skin and fresh herbs. The banana flambé was a bit disappointing but, when the music begins and the atmosphere livens up, such little flaws are soon forgotten.

starter: 45FF-105FF
main: 70FF-115FF
dessert: 45FF-50FF

AE CB EC MC V

Open: Mon-Thurs 8pm-2am, Fri & Sat 8pm-4am, Sun (bar only) 8pm-2am; reservations advisable

La Sanaga
African

☎ 01 43 14 95 00
24, rue de la Fontaine-au-Roi, République

Map: 11 C3

Métro: Goncourt

Entertainment: Live entertainment Sunday lunchtime

 Smoking throughout

A young, friendly Cameroonian woman named Victoire – Vicky for short – greets customers at the Sanaga seven days a week. If the restaurant is closed, knock on the door – there's always someone on duty. Don't be misled by the simple décor (reproductions of paintings, tourist posters promoting Cameroon) – the excitement is on your plate. For starters, the miondo (a stick of manioc flour in a banana leaf) is absolutely stunning. For mains, try the mbongo tchobi – one of the house specialities comprising fish served with a delectable black sauce (made from no less than 12 spices) and sweet potatoes – your tastebuds won't believe it! This is authentic cuisine from the Cameroonian countryside: it's even rumoured that you eat better here than in the best restaurants of Douala or Yaoundé.

Open: Mon-Sun 11am-2am; reservations not accepted

starter: 35FF-55FF
main: 65FF-120FF
dessert: 30FF
Set menu: 170FF

AE CB V

Le Serpent qui Danse
French

☎ 01 43 70 28 27
51, rue de Montreuil, Faidherbe

Map: 11 J7

Métro: Faidherbe-Chaligny

 Smoking throughout

Customers are greeted by the strong, appetising aroma of raclette (a type of cheese fondue) as they enter this small neighbourhood restaurant, a place that brings together charcuterie, Baudelaire and cheese. The (toy) snake – from one of the *Fleurs du mal* poems – is wrapped around a column in the middle of the dining room. Since 1993, Bruno has been offering the same fare while jazz or the Frères Jacques play in the background. The raclette is the star attraction and served in the traditional manner – until you've had your fill! Noncheese-buffs have numerous alternatives, including a range of salads, au gratin de saumon fumé (smoked salmon) or a pavé de bœuf (thick-cut steak) served with broccoli. This agreeable eatery also serves a creamy tiramisù and chocolate fondant, both home-made.

Open: daily noon-2.30pm, 7.30pm-11pm; reservations not accepted

main: 34FF-90FF
dessert: 20FF-35FF
Set menu: 68FF (lunch)

CB EC MC V

11ᵉ ARRONDISSEMENT

Map: 11 G3
Métro: Bastille,
Bréguet Sabin

Entertainment: Exhibitions
of paintings and
photographs

Smoking throughout

Le Sofa
French

☎ 01 43 14 07 46
**21, rue Saint-Sabin,
Bastille**

Glimmering red sheens set the tone at the Sofa, where everything encourages you to relax. At happy hour, try an excellent Saint-Chinian or a cranberry juice, and don't hesitate to sink into the white sofa, admire the exhibition and devour the alluring menu. Varied and stylish starters include the roulade chinoise aux légumes (Chinese roulade with vegetables) and the foie gras maison aux épices douces (the chef's foie gras with mild spices), both of which are utterly delectable. More-traditional main courses, such as the pintadeau rôti aux échalotes confites (roast guinea fowl with preserved shallots) or the tartare de bœuf coupé au couteau (steak tartare 'cut with a knife') are enhanced by exotic flavours and well-matched colours. The chef, Cidalia Alvès, bases her daily specials on seasonal market produce. The Sofa hasn't been open for long but has already attracted a loyal clientele.

starter: 47FF-69FF
main: 72FF-79FF
dessert: 25FF-33FF
Plat du jour: 75FF

CB EC MC V; €

Open: Tues-Sat 6pm-late (orders taken until 11.30pm); reservations advisable

---

Map: 11 H9
Métro: Alexandre Dumas

Smoking throughout

Le Sot-l'y-laisse
French

☎ 01 40 09 79 20
**70, rue Alexandre Dumas,
Nation**

This neighbourhood restaurant opened nearly five years ago and takes its name from the tender portion of meat hidden near the parson's nose of the chicken (which *sots* or 'fools' leave behind in their ignorance). The Sot-l'y-laisse boasts a staunchly loyal clientele. Bright walls decorated with bunches of grapes and wine lists provide a simple, friendly setting. You sense that the staff work here out of pleasure and sheer love of food. Indeed, the owner is also the chef. The menu changes with seasonal market produce and might include such delectable starters as crème de potiron (pumpkin soup) and brochettes de Saint-Jacques aux pruneaux (scallop and prune kebabs), followed by filet de rouget poêlé au poireau confit (pan-fried fillet of mullet with preserved leek) or poulet fermier au romarin (free-range chicken with rosemary). For dessert, the ananas rôti au ganache de chocolate blanc (roast pineapple with white chocolate ganache) is a delicious surprise.

starter: 30FF-52FF
main: 62FF-75FF
dessert: 32FF-35FF
Set menu: lunch: 69 FF (2
courses), 98FF
(3 courses)
CB EC MC V

Open: Mon-Fri noon-2pm, Mon-Sat 8pm-10pm; reservations advisable

La Toccata

Italian (Neapolitan)

☎ 01 40 21 04 59
52, ave de la République, Oberkampf

Map: 11 D4

Métro: Parmentier

Entertainment: Theme nights: Neapolitan songs, readings, scopa

 Nonsmoking tables available

 Pavement tables in summer

Don't leave this restaurant without meeting Ciro, the owner, a kind man who loves talking about the history of European cuisine, scopa (a Neapolitan card game) and his home town, Napoli! Neapolitan cuisine still bears traces of the French occupation, and makes abundant use of seafood – il piatto del guarracino (the local bouillabaisse), il 'sote' misto de cozze e vongole (mussels and clams) and sardines in escabèche. Also to die for: the fusili al 'ragù' (ham, white bacon, onion, meat and red wine, cooked for six hours). The chef's 'baba' al limoncello, available towards the end of the week, will take you straight to heaven. Occasional theme nights are organised with Neapolitan singing, scopa championships and readings of Italian authors.

Open: Mon-Sat 7pm-midnight; reservations advisable (towards end of week)

starter: 46FF-56FF
main: 56FF-99FF
dessert: 32FF-40FF
Set menu: 110FF
Plat du jour: 65FF

AE DC V; €

Le Villaret

French

☎ 01 43 57 75 56
13, rue Ternaux, Oberkampf

Map: 11 D3

Métro: Parmentier

 Smoking throughout

The staff at the Villaret are always friendly, always available. By way of introduction, the velouté de cèpes (cep mushroom soup) à la mousse de foie gras or the solette au beurre citronné (baby sole with lemon-flavoured butter) are guaranteed to make you weak at the knees. Each dish is a symphony of flavours, conducted by a chef who changes his menu each day. Will you get a chance to savour the gigot d'agneau de Lozère rôti et son gratin de topinambours (roast lamb with Jerusalem artichokes) or the poitrine de veau aux trompettes de la mort et cocos frais (breast of veal with fresh 'trumpet of death' mushrooms and coco beans)? Who knows? Each day brings its own pleasures. For dessert, the ananas confit aux épices avec un croustillant au romarin et un sorbet à la mangue (candied pineapple with spices, a rosemary biscuit and mango sorbet) is simply unforgettable.

Open: Mon-Fri noon-3.30pm, Mon-Sat 7.30pm-1am; reservations essential

starter: 50FF-85FF
main: 80FF-150FF
dessert: 45FF
Set menu: 120FF, 150FF (lunch)
Plat du jour: 90FF

CB EC MC V

Bars & Cafes – 11e

L'Ancienne menuiserie 29, rue des Trois Bornes, Paris 11e, République, Oberkampf ☎ 01 43 14 98 91 Métro: Parmentier (Map: 11 C4)

This quiet bar has a long room with high ceilings, and really did used to be a menuiserie (joiner's workshop). Customers are greeted with a poem, then seated amid old objects done up by the owner, whose personality permeates the original, artistic décor. This is an ideal spot to spend or finish the night in peace.

Open: daily 3.30pm-1.30am; By the glass: beer 15FF, champagne (bottle) 280FF; coffee 10FF; snacks available; credit cards accepted (from 100FF)

L'Aram bar 7, rue de la Folie-Méricourt, Paris 11e, between Oberkampf and Voltaire ☎ 01 48 05 57 79 Métro: Saint-Ambroise (Map: 11 E4)

A few streets away from the cool bars of the Oberkampf neighbourhood, this is definitely not one of those places where drinking is the main attraction. Plenty of other things happen at this unusual venue: exhibitions, theatre performances, community TV broadcasts and clairvoyant readings. Even without all the entertainment, l'Aram bar is worth discovering for its friendly service and slightly kitsch décor.

Open: Mon-Sat noon-2am, Sun 4pm-2am; By the glass: beer 13FF, champagne 40FF; coffee 7FF; snacks available; theatre, clairvoyants, debates broadcast on community TV, exhibitions (artworks for sale), games; cash only; €

L'Autre Café 62, rue Jean-Pierre Timbaud, Paris 11e, Oberkampf ☎ 01 40 21 03 07 Métro: Parmentier (Map: 11 C4)

This friendly bar attracts an increasing number of regulars. A great place to work, you can plug in your laptop anywhere around the room. Food is served at all hours. A springboard for young artists, the Autre Café organises exhibition openings, film screenings and philosophical afternoon teas for children. A small lounge upstairs is available for more intimate conversations.

Open: Mon-Fri 9am-1.30am, Sat, Sun & public holidays 11.30am-1.30am; snacks available; various art oriented entertainment; credit cards accepted

Blue Billard 111, rue Saint Maur, Paris 11e, Oberkampf ☎ 01 43 55 87 21 Métro: Goncourt, Parmentier (Map: 11 C4)

Located below Cajun restaurant Blue Bayou, the Blue Billard offers a friendly bar with comfortable stools and a great selection of beverages. The pool room out the back has about 10 tables and no, it's not the house cocktail speaking, the rugs really *are* blue. Rhythm and blues, old rock classics and hipper sounds keep that Yankee atmosphere happening.

Open: daily 11am-2am; By the glass: beer 22FF, champagne 45FF; coffee 10FF; theme nights; credit cards accepted; €

The Bottle Shop 5, rue Trousseau, Paris 11e, Bastille, ☎ 01 43 14 28 04 Métro: Ledru Rollin (Map: 11 J5)

Unlike your average thoroughfare with its hurried clientele, the Bottle Shop brings together regular customers who know each other well. The friendly clamour of Anglo-Saxon conversation is just as big a drawcard as the contemporary art, books and cocktails. This is a perfect mix between an American pub and a French café, a place where you feel good.

Open: daily 11.30am-2am; By the glass: beer 15FF; coffee 8FF; snacks & meals (lunch) available; games available; CB V; €

Le Café du passage 12, rue de Charonne, Paris 11e, Bastille ☎ 01 49 29 97 64 Métro: Bastille (Map: 11 H4)

Wine buffs will appreciate this chic, somewhat exclusive bar, where customers take the time to savour a Côte Roti or one of the other Loire vintages from the wide range on offer. Conversation is easy in the quiet atmosphere of this friendly place, which is bang in the middle of the Bastille neighbourhood.

Open: Sat 12.30pm-2am, Sun-Fri 6pm-2am; By the glass: champagne 42FF; coffee 11FF; snacks available; credit cards accepted

Cannibale Café 93, rue Jean-Pierre Timbaud, Paris 11e, Couronnes ☎ 01 49 29 95 59 Métro: Couronnes (Map: 11 B5)

Don't be scared, no one's going to eat you! The name of this cafe was inspired by a dada manifesto and one of Goya's paintings. In fact the place couldn't be more welcoming, with its grand rococo-style bar topped with worn zinc, spotted mirrors, peeling mouldings, wood panelling, Formica tables and red leatherette bench seats. You can come with a bunch of friends or on your own to sip a drink, have brunch, read the papers or just daydream.

Open: Mon-Fri 8am-2am, Sat & Sun 9am-2am; By the glass: beer 13FF, 15FF; champagne 38FF; coffee 7FF-10FF; meals and snacks available; CB EC MC V; €

Le Cithéa 112-114, rue Oberkampf, Paris 11e, Oberkampf ☎ 01 40 21 70 95 Métro: Parmentier, Ménilmontant (Map: 11 C5)

Far into the night, when all the other bars of the Oberkampf neighbourhood throw in the towel, the true night owls converge on the Cithéa. Avoiding nightclubs, they come here to drink, chat or dance to the expert DJ sets. Earlier in the evening, you can hear good live music.

Open: daily 10pm-5.30am; By the glass: beer 35FF, champagne 65FF; live music Wed-Sun, DJ after the concerts & Mon-Tues, music all night, dancing; credit cards accepted

Les couleurs 117, rue Saint Maur, Paris 11e, Oberkampf ☎ 01 43 57 95 61 Métro: Parmentier, Rue St-Maur (Map: 11 C4)

A heady mix of colour, smell and warmth emanates from this small bar squeezed in between rue Oberkampf and rue Jean-Pierre Timbaud. Customers are plunged into a South American ambience by the music, the décor, the aroma of hot cinnamon wine and the cocktails and biscuits on the bar. You'll hear as much Spanish as French spoken in this friendly, inexpensive spot.

Open: daily 3pm-2am; By the glass: beer 13FF; coffee 7FF; concerts (program available at the bar); cash only

Favela Chic 18, rue du Faubourg du Temple, Paris 11e, République ☎ 01 40 21 38 14 Métro: République (Map: 11 C2)

If crowds, music, noise and fashionable venues are your thing, you'll love Favela Chic. This big, colourful place has paintings and kites on the walls, large tables and a serious attitude towards partying. It's difficult to get a table after 8.30pm and, at 9.30pm, the bar is packed with people trying to get a drink. But the real action starts at midnight when customers start dancing on the tables...

Open: Mon-Sat 8.30pm-12.30pm; meals available, CB EC MC V

Les Funambules 12, rue Faidherbe, Paris 11e, Charonne ☎ 01 43 70 83 70 Métro: Faidherbe-Chaligny, Charonne (Map: 11 J6)

Like many other small cafes in the east end of Paris, the Funambules has been transformed into a fashionable bar. The original architecture provides character and authenticity. On summer evenings beautiful people occupy the terrace. The rest of the year customers take shelter inside under the stunning coffered ceiling and soft lighting, and enjoy a cocktail at the bar or a snack in the back room.

Open: Mon-Sat 7.30am-2am, Sun 10am-8.30pm: By the glass: beer 16FF, champagne 45FF; coffee 11FF; meals and snacks available; credit cards accepted

La Grosse Caisse 6, rue de la Main d'Or, Paris 11e, Charonne ☎ 01 49 23 05 91 Métro: Ledru Rollin (Map: 11 H5)

Fashion-free and uncompromising, the Grosse Caisse is a wild spot that brings together regular customers from all walks of life. This small, out-of-the-ordinary bar creates a dynamic atmosphere grounded in the local neighbourhood and its street life. The customers and owners have as much fun playing table football together as they do chatting at the bar. An enjoyably intense experience.

Open: Tues-Sat 6pm-2am, Sun 3pm-10pm; By the glass: beer 13FF, Pére Labat rum 12FF; exhibitions, plays, dancing; cash only

Le Lèche vin 13, rue Daval, Paris 11e, Bastille ☎ 01 43 55 98 91 Métro: Bastille (Map: 11 G3)

A divine surprise in a crass and vulgar neighbourhood. This joyous shambles of religious bric-a-brac, with its electric pietà, Pope John XXIII plates and Last Supper bathmat, stands out thanks to its amusing and attentive staff (worth mentioning in Paris) and its excellent easy-listening music. But beware, the Devil is not far away, lurking in the toilets. Will you yield to temptation?

Open: Mon-Thurs 6pm-1.30am, Fri & Thurs-Sat 6pm-2am, Sun 5pm-midnight; By the glass: beer 17FF, champagne 35FF; coffee 10FF; credit cards accepted

Léopard Café 149, blvd-Voltaire, Paris 11e, Charonne ☎ 01 40 09 95 99 Métro: Charonne (Map: 11 G6)

The Léopard was once a standard bistrot, but it has been done up with all sorts of recycled bric-a-brac to give it a bright, underground look: fairy lights in yogurt pots, wall lamps made from funnels, oil-bottle chandeliers. Here they know how to put on a show without planning it: theatre, music and video viewings are improvised in a relaxed, fun atmosphere. The clients are a real mixture, like the de\'cor, but they're always ready to celebrate the pleasures of getting together — often with a glass of 'monkey's brains' (vodka, Bailey's and grenadine).

Open: Mon-Sat 9am-2am: By the glass: beer 11FF; coffee 10FF; snacks & meals available; exhibitions (artworks for sale), musical and theatre performances, video viewings, dancing from time to time; credit cards accepted

Les marcheurs de planète/Le Resto Zinc 73, rue de la Roquette, Paris 11e, Voltaire ☎ 01 43 78 90 98 Métro: Voltaire (Map: 11 G4)

The owners of this small, friendly and simple bar really look after their customers. The warm welcome is characteristic of a place that the most stalwart regulars like to call home. Share a cheese platter, listen to Brassens or World Music, read Charlie Hebdo and you'll soon feel at home.

Open: Tues-Sat 5pm-2am, By the glass: beer 12FF; coffee 10FF, meals and snacks available, concerts four times a month, exhibitions, credit cards accepted (from 100FF)

Pause Café 41, rue de Charonne, Paris 11e, Charonne ☎ 01 48 06 80 31 Métro: Ledru Rollin (Map: 11 H4)

At meal times, this bar operates mostly as a restaurant, but you can still take advantage of the large terrace for a drink during the day or a weekend brunch.

Some distance from the Bastille, the Pause Café is frequented mainly by local inhabitants and workers. If you're after a more authentic bar-restaurant, try the Bistrot du Peintre just opposite, which is owned by the same person.

Open: Mon-Sat 7.45am-2am, Sun 9am-8pm; By the glass: beer 16FF, champagne 35FF; coffee 11FF; meals and snacks available; credit cards accepted

La Renaissance 87, rue de la Roquette, Paris 11e, Place Voltaire ☎ 01 43 79 83 09 Métro: Voltaire (Map: 11 F5)

Regulars drop in for a late breakfast, a drink or a meal at one of the pavement tables. For brave souls who enjoy tartare, this dish is something of a house speciality. The Renaissance is a simple, unaffected place whose customers always look forward to coming back.

Open: Mon 8.30am-8pm, Tues-Sat 8.30am-midnight, Sun 9.30am-8pm; By the glass: beer 15FF, champagne 50FF; coffee 12FF; meals & snacks available; cash only

Le Robinet Mélangeur 123, blvd de Ménilmontant, Paris 11e, Ménilmontant ☎ 01 47 00 63 68 Métro: Ménilmontant (Map: 11 C6)

What's with the name: 'the mixer tap'? There's an old-fashioned model of this plumber's fitting proudly displayed in the middle of the little oblong room. But it might also have something to do with the reasonably priced drinks the staff keep pouring, the quirky and friendly mix of people who frequent the place, the easy flow of the conversation and the atmosphere that is always at just the right temperature. All this and good food too: it's hard not to gush!

Open: Mon-Sat 5pm-2am; By the glass: beer 12FF, 16FF; coffee 8FF; meals and snacks available; credit cards accepted)

Le Sérail 10, rue Sedaine, Paris 11e, Bastille ☎ 01 43 38 17 01 Métro: Bastille (Map: 11 G3)

Le Sérail invites its patrons to embark on a journey. Hesitant at first, you step into an attractive Parisian bistrot, with a painted glass ceiling, framed pictures and chandeliers. The intimate atmosphere puts you at ease. Then the initiation begins. A caravan weaves its leisurely way through the labyrinth of obstacles. Bidding the West farewell, it leads the willing nomads on to a surprising Moroccan oasis. A total change of scenery!

Open: Mon-Sat 11.30am-2pm, Sun 4pm-2am; By the glass: beer 18FF, champagne 40FF; coffee 12FF; meals and snacks available; Oriental dancer Wed, Fri; credit cards accepted

Le Troisième Bureau 74, rue de la Folie-Méricourt, Paris 11e, bottom end of Oberkampf ☎ 01 43 55 87 65 Métro: Oberkampf, Parmentier

This small bar has a regular clientele and serves scrumptious meals from 60FF to 80FF. A quiet spot, even when things liven up at apéritif time. The Troisième Bureau has remained simple, true to itself, oblivious to the passing fashions of Oberkampf.

Open: daily noon-2am; By the glass: beer 16FF; coffee 10FF; snacks & meals available; credit cards accepted

Map: 11 G5
Métro: Charonne

Smoking throughout

Waly Fay
African

☎ 01 40 24 17 79
**6, rue Godefroy-Cavaignac,
Charonne**

Did you realise that Africa begins at the Bastille? Its flavours do, at any rate: apart from a few colourful paintings, the carefully designed simplicity of the décor at Waly Fay evokes nothing of Africa as you might imagine it. A rather hip crowd flocks here for African cuisine with a West Indian influence (acras), served to the strains of soul and jazz. For starters, the pepe soup (fish soup) is deliciously smooth and highly spiced. For mains, the tiep bou dienn (rice with fish), the fish n'dole and the maffe (meat served with a slowly simmered peanut sauce) are all recommended by the staff, making it a difficult choice. Go for the copious beef maffe with rice and aloco (fried plantain bananas) – the caramelised taste of cooked banana is a perfect foil for all the punchy spices.

starter: 35FF-40FF
main: 55FF-120FF
dessert: 30FF-35FF

MC V

Open: Mon-Sat 8pm-11pm; reservations advisable

12e Arrondissement

Gare de Lyon

Bastille

Bercy

Daumesnil

l'Aubergeade (p 184)

12ᵉ Arrondissement

There's plenty here for modern architecture
fans: the Bastille opera house, the Paris-Bercy
sports and concert stadium, the Ministry of
Economy and Finance. These architectural
innovations are the outward signs of rapid
changes taking place in this quiet sector of
Paris. The southern part of the arrondissement, which borders on the Bois de Vincennes,
is fairly well-to-do, like the suburb of Saint-
Mandé just beyond the ring road. On the weekend, hordes of cyclists and soccer players
head for the Bois. But walkers can also clear
away the cobwebs with a stroll along the
Coulée Verte, a green footpath along the ave
Daumesnil viaduct. At the foot of the arches,
shops, art galleries and cafes have opened up
one by one. On the other side of the Gare de
Lyon, you can take a break in the very pretty
parc de Bercy, where an orchard, a vegetable
patch and a garden have replaced the old wine
market. In spite of the renovation of Bercy (the
latest addition is a huge cinema complex), the
12th seems strangely frozen in time. And
that's probably what gives it charm.

Les Amis des Messina

Italian (Sicilian)

☎ 01 43 67 96 01
204, rue du Faubourg Saint-Antoine, Bastille

Map: 12 D3

Métro: Faidherbe-Chaligny

 Smoking throughout

 Pavement tables in summer

Ignacio Messina, a young Sicilian chef from Cefalù, has just opened his first restaurant and Les Amis des Messina has been an overnight success. The décor is stylish with clean lines, there's the inevitable *squadra Ferrari* flag as well as an open kitchen. Ignacio's Sicilian-speaking cousin looks after the customers. Sicilian flavours are modified here for French palates. Among the antipasti, enjoy discovering the boulettes farcies (stuffed meatballs) – Palermo's speciality. The moules à la tomate et à l'ail (mussels with tomato and garlic) are also noteworthy. For mains, the escalopes farcies aux aubergines are a huge hit, while the entrecôte au romarin (rib steak with rosemary) is also an absolute winner. Friday is fish day at Messina, so those sardines had better behave... A menu dégustation offers great value for money.

Open: Mon-Fri noon-2.45pm, 8pm-11pm, Sat 8pm-11.30pm; reservations advisable (towards end of the week)

starter: 38FF-82FF
main: 58FF-98FF
dessert: 38FF
Set menu: 190FF
Plat du jour: 80FF

MC V; €

Athanor

Romanian

☎ 01 43 44 49 15
4, rue Crozatier, Aligre-Gare de Lyon

Map: 12 D4

Métro: Reuilly Diderot

Entertainment: Performance of baroque music twice a month

 Smoking throughout

 Pavement tables

The puppets, red curtain and warm-coloured tapestries are reminiscent of a theatre set. Seagull and snail figurines appear here and there while candles glow on the mauve-coloured straw placemats. In this fairy-tale décor, the banquet begins with a large choice of vodkas. A lovely, tipsy feeling takes hold... While baroque music plays in the background, let yourself go as you savour the Eastern flavours of blinis served with tarama (fish roe dip) and herrings in cream. Seasoned freshwater fish are the chef's speciality, along with popular Romanian dishes such as sarmalé (stuffed cabbage). There's also a 'surprise' menu that changes according to the market produce available on the day and the inspiration of the chef. A culinary kingdom ruled by imagination, fantasy and finesse.

Open: Mon-Sat noon-3pm, 7pm-midnight, Sun noon-3pm; reservations advisable

starter: 45FF-65FF
main: 90FF-110FF
dessert: 40FF-60FF
Set menu: 90FF, 130FF, 170FF
Plat du jour: 59FF (lunch)

AE CB EC MC V; €

l'Aubergeade

French

☎ 01 43 44 33 36
17, rue de Chaligny,
Faidherbe Chaligny, Reuilly Diderot

Map: 12 D4

Métro: Reuilly-Diderot

Smoking throughout

Pavement tables

Exposed beams and yellow walls give this small restaurant a warm, comfortable feel. First impressions are confirmed by the simple and friendly welcome. The food is what you'd expect of traditional French cuisine: delicious and generous. Foie gras, escargots (snails), salade de lardons avec oeufs pochés (salad with bacon and poached eggs) and the eggplant and mozzarella salad make excellent starters. To follow, equally sterling classics include noix (scallops) de Saint-Jacques à la provençale, os à moelle (marrowbone) avec toast, pommes de terre farcies au jambon (potatoes stuffed with ham) or aile de raie aux câpres (wing of skate with capers). With the assured flavours, and lovingly prepared and presented food, you'll leave this great neighbourhood restaurant on a high.

starter: 57FF-70FF
main: 70FF-97FF
dessert: 24FF-33FF
Set menu: 59FF, 69FF
(lunch), 89.50FF, 99FF,
135FF (dinner)
Plat du jour: 48FF

AE CB DC EC MC V

Open: daily noon-2pm, 7pm-10.30pm; reservations advisable (evenings)

Les bombis

French

☎ 01 43 45 36 32
22, rue de Chaligny,
Reuilly Diderot

Map: 12 D4

Métro: Reuilly-Diderot

Smoking throughout

Pavement tables

As the food arrives, your olfactory organs thrill to a delicate aroma. You raise your fork in almost feverish anticipation... It's even better than you imagined while devouring the menu! A 'new neighbourhood-bistrot' ambience, red and ochre tones and tiny star lights create a friendly setting, but it's the food you come back for. The cassoulet d'escargot forestière à la crème de munster au cumin (snail casserole à la forestière with cream of cumin Munster cheese) is unforgettable: the name isn't long enough to describe all the perfectly matched flavours of this dish! As for the brandade à la niçoise, this classic offering has been deliciously updated with the flavours of olives and oranges. Finally, words can't describe the craquelin praliné et cerises amarena confites (praline craquelin with glacé amarena cherries). Let's just say it's not easily forgotten...

starter: 20FF (lunch), 45FF-
65FF (dinner)
main: 50FF (lunch), 75FF-
95FF (dinner)
dessert: 20FF (lunch), 35FF-
45FF (dinner)
Set menu: 75FF (lunch)
Plat du jour: 50FF (lunch)

CB EC MC V

Open: Tues-Fri noon-2pm, 8pm-10.30pm, Sat 8pm-11pm, Mon 8pm-10.30pm; reservations essential

Café Barge
French

**☎ 01 40 02 09 09
Port de la Rapée,
Gare de Lyon**

Map: 12 B5

Métro: Gare de Lyon
('E' exit)

Entertainment: DJs every
night and salsa every
second Sunday

 Smoking throughout

 Outdoor seating on
barge & terrace

A barge moored to the Port de la Rapée, modern Eastern décor and a variety of menus throughout the year, each one devoted to a particular country – La Barge has a unique way of celebrating stationary travel! A young and friendly team has just taken over this restaurant, giving it new life. The cuisine, influenced by the destination of the moment (eg, Mediterranean, North Africa, Russia), the salsa nights and the attentiveness of the host, Roland, make this an enjoyable outing. Don't hesitate to come just for a drink, either at the sheltered terrace on the quay if it's a sunny day, or on board. Below deck (check it out when you go to the toilet) the sound of the water lapping at the portholes is very relaxing.

Open: restaurant: Sun-Fri noon-3pm, daily 8pm-11.30pm, (weekends to midnight), bar: 9am-2am; reservations advisable

Set menu: 99FF, 139FF
(lunch), 139FF, 180FF
(dinner)

AE CB DC EC MC V

Chez Régis
French

**☎ 01 43 43 62 84
27 ter, blvd Diderot,
Gare de Lyon**

Map: 12 C4

Métro: Gare de Lyon

 Smoking throughout

There should be more places like Chez Régis. The young owner (Régis) has done everything right since taking over this attractive Parisian bistrot (established in 1908), from preserving and highlighting the authentic décor, to playing great background jazz and devising a menu with unbeatable value for money in this area. The quintessential flavours of fresh, carefully selected ingredients are emphasised in simple, perfectly cooked dishes. We had an apéritif at the bar with the regulars, before sitting down to an appetiser of baby ravioli that simply melted in the mouth. To follow, an excellent magret de canard a sel de Guérande (fillet of duck breast with Guérande sea salt) and a perfect, warm tarte tatin. Along with the organic bread and some fine wines, this is enough to make Chez Régis a real (re)treat for *bons vivants*.

Open: daily noon-3pm, 7pm-11pm; reservations advisable

starter: 35FF
main: 65FF
dessert: 35FF
Set menu: 110FF
Plat du jour: 65FF

AE CB DC EC MC V

Map: 12 D4
Métro: Gare de Lyon

Smoking throughout

Pavement tables

Comme Cochon
French

☎ 01 43 42 43 36
**135, rue de Charenton,
Bastille**

We were intoxicated by a strange and equally enjoyable sensation at Comme Cochon, as if we could faintly taste the colours and flavours of a Paris that knows no time. The images parading before us at this traditional bistrot belong to every era, and the blackboard featuring a carefully handwritten menu faithfully testifies to stories and conversations from all walks of life. Only the paintings on the wall, by a local artist, keep us in the present. Fine vintages, numerous and inexpensive, feature on a wine list that evokes new images – those of the good life. Good food also makes an important contribution to the charm of this place. The house specialities are paleron aux endives meunières (beef served with endives) and ganache de chocolat noir aux grillotines (dark chocolate ganache).

starter: 35FF-65FF
main: 70FF-100FF
dessert: 30FF-40FF
Set menu: 75FF (lunch)

V

Open: Mon-Sat 8am-2am; reservations advisable (towards end of the week)

Map: 12 B5
Métro: Quai de la Gare,
Gare de Lyon

Smoking throughout

Barge-terrace in
summer

La Compagnie du Ruban bleu
Modern French

☎ 01 43 41 11 55
**Port de la Rapée,
Gare de Lyon**

The young owners of this barge-restaurant are international wine merchants and have even partnered up recently with an English oenologist to help them ferret out small, original vintages from every corner of the globe. To complement the Chilian, Californian or South African wines, their talented chef combines exotic flavours with French provincial produce in his highly inventive, delectable cuisine: foie gras rôti aux épices et au carpaccio d'ananas (foie gras and pineapple carpaccio), salade de roquette au filet d'autruche (rocket salad with ostrich), plancha d'espadon et crème légère au réglisse (grilled swordfish with a light liquorice sauce) or braisé de kangourou au lard fumé et vitelotte (braised kangaroo with smoked bacon and vitelotte potatoes). The Compagnie du Ruban Bleu offers great service and value for money. Our only two qualms are the opening hours (restricted to lunch in winter) and the overly formal atmosphere (due perhaps to the excessive use of teak in the décor).

starter: 55FF
main: 135FF
dessert: 50FF
Set menu: 165FF, 210FF

AE CB EC MC V; €

Open: May-Sept: Mon-Fri noon-3pm, Mon-Sat 8pm-11pm; Oct-Apr: Mon-Fri noon-3pm (evenings & weekends for group bookings); reservations advisable

La Coulée d'Or
Corsican

☎ **01 44 87 99 37**
17, rue Michel Chasles,
Gare de Lyon

Map: 12 B4

Métro: Gare de Lyon

Entertainment: Live Corsican music four times a year (reservations essential)

 Smoking throughout

From a distance, the Coulée d'Or looks like just another brasserie. What makes this place different is the owners' passion for Corsica, the Isle of Beauty to which they longingly return each year. Back in Paris, their love of island cuisine manifests itself in honest, provincial fare rather than highly wrought gourmet food. The menu is subject to seasonal change and features tasty appetisers such as the crêpe à la châtaigne fourrée au brocciu et herbes du maquis (chestnut crêpe filled with brocciu and wild herbs). To follow, the pavé de sanglier au poivre (thick-cut steak of wild boar with pepper sauce) is amazingly tender. For dessert, go for the chestnut tiramisù rather than the cake, which is less original. The quality of the ingredients no doubt accounts for the high prices. Customers are greeted warmly and can order cheese or charcuterie platters at all hours.

Open: Mon-Sat 11.45am-2.30pm, 8pm-10.30pm, Sun 11.45am-2.30pm; reservations not accepted

starter: 28FF-42FF
main: 68FF-98FF
dessert: 34FF-82FF
Set menu: 68FF (lunch: starter + main or main + dessert)
Plat du jour: 65FF (lunch)
AE CB EC MC V

L'Ébauchoir
French

☎ **01 43 42 49 31**
45, rue de Cîteaux,
Bastille

Map: 12 D3

Métro: Faidherbe Chaligny

 Nonsmoking tables available

 Pavement tables in summer

The first thing that strikes you about this typical bistrot is the convivial atmosphere. Warm colours, small wooden tables, naive frescoes, regular customers and young, smiling staff make this an enjoyable place to eat. The genuine Parisian bistrot fare is lovingly prepared and enhanced by some bold innovations. Ample starters include the médaillon d'espadon à l'émulsion de vanille et noisette (swordfish with an emulsified vanilla and hazelnut sauce) and the foie gras de canard poêlé aux girolles (pan-fried duck foie gras with chanterelle mushrooms). But concentrate on the mains, which combine tradition with discreet originality. The filet d'espadon au beurre de citron et gingembre (fillet of swordfish with lemon and ginger butter) and the jarret de veau braisé à l'ancienne (braised knuckle of veal à l'ancienne) will delight your tastebuds. You pay for wine by the glass, which is a bonus. A great place to indulge yourself, though not always inexpensive.

Open: Tues-Sat noon-2.30pm, Mon-Sat Mon 8pm-11pm; reservations advisable

starter: 30FF-90FF
main: 80FF-100FF
dessert: 30FF-40FF
Set menu: 70FF (lunch)
CB EC MC V

12ᵉ arrondi

Map: 12 C4

Métro: Ledru Rollin, Gare de Lyon

Smoking throughout

L'Encrier
French

☎ 01 44 68 08 16
55, rue Traversière, Bastille

A stone's throw from the hanging gardens of the Coulée Verte, the Encrier is perfectly situated for a gourmet break. A perennially popular spot, you can nonetheless expect a relaxed atmosphere and a warm welcome. For starters, the classic salmon tartare alternates on the menu with less-common dishes such as cervelle des canuts (a herbed cheese from Lyon) or pear with Roquefort cheese. To follow, try the bar entier grillé (whole grilled bass), tender entrecôte (rib steak) or delicate joues de cochon aux épices (pig's cheeks with spices). The desserts remain sensible: nougat glacé (nougat ice cream) or sabayon (zabaione). A variety of inexpensive set menus served with the 'vin du moment', an open-view kitchen, exposed beams and a large picture window make this a lovely place to eat.

Set menu: 65FF (lunch), 78FF, 90FF, 108FF (dinner)
Plat du jour: 48FF

CB EC MC V

Open: Mon-Fri noon-2.15pm, Mon-Sat 7.15pm-11pm; reservations not accepted

---

Map: 12 E5

Métro: Montgallet

Smoking throughout

Jean-Pierre Frelet
French

☎ 01 43 43 76 65
25, rue Montgallet, Daumesnil

Near a seedy block of flats, this restaurant seems oddly out of place. As you arrive, a series of architectural prints set the tone. Everything here is based on a subtle mixing and matching of materials: wickerwork for the armchairs, steel for the subdued lighting, and an equally stylish and discreet menu moving skillfully between innovation and tradition. The poêlée de gigot (pan-fried lamb) is served with pear tart, the vichyssoise garnished with crayfish and the crêpe doused with delicious orange butter. The foie gras mousseline, bordered with a spinach sauce, is stratified like a cliff-face but light as a brioche, and strikes a masterly balance between sophistication and provincial tradition. Your whole dining experience is a work of art signed by Jean-Pierre Frelet, host and builder of flavours.

starter: 48FF-75FF
main: 98FF-145FF
dessert: 42FF-48FF
Set menu: 105FF (lunch), 150FF (lunch & dinner)
Plat du jour: 75FF (lunch), 85FF (dinner)

CB EC MC V

Open: Mon-Fri 12.30pm-2.30pm, 8pm-10.30pm, Sat 8pm-10.30pm; reservations advisable

12ᵉ ARRONDISSEMENT

La Liberté
French

☎ 01 43 72 11 18
192, rue du Faubourg Saint-Antoine, Faidherbe Chaligny

Map: 12 D4

Métro: Faidherbe-Chaligny

Entertainment: Live music Thursday evenings, painting exhibitions

 Smoking throughout

 Pavement tables

This diminutive, modest, all-yellow bar has several guises but remains one of a kind. In the morning, coffee is served in small Pyrex glasses. At lunchtime, from Monday to Friday, customers can choose one of three original and copious *plats du jour*. Fifi and François, affectionate and gruff, will cook you up a treat with fresh market produce – mixing herbs and baby vegetables, testing sauces, getting excited, making recommendations, and making sure you enjoy your food. Vegetarian meals are also available on request. This honest, jovial fare reflects the chefs' personalities. Bruno, the owner, is a wine buff, and you can taste vintages from small growers either by the glass or by the measure. From 7pm, aperitif time sets the tone for the rest of the evening. The premises also houses an artists' association and a new talent is displayed every week. Utter contentment reigns.

Open: daily 9am-1.30am; reservations not accepted

main: 48FF
dessert: 18FF
Plat du jour: 48FF

Credit cards accepted; €

L'Oulette
French (South-West)

☎ 01 40 02 02 12
15, place Lachambeaudie, Bercy

Map: 12 E7

Métro: Cour Saint-Émilion, Bercy

 Nonsmoking tables available

 Sheltered pavement tables

The Oulette, or 'little saucepan' in the traditional language of the Languedoc region, is a ray of sunshine in this gloomy neighbourhood. In a setting dominated by 'suits', Marcel Baudis and Alain Fontaine, head chef and wine waiter respectively, are masters in the art of satisfying meat, fish and wine buffs. From the *menu du marché*, the soupe de poisson (fish soup), with crème de coquillages au safran (cream of shellfish flavoured with saffron), is sweet and creamy. The *plat de saison*, a suprême de pintade farci d'un hachis de trompettes de la mort et d'échalotes (guinea-fowl stuffed with finely chopped 'trumpet of death' mushrooms and shallots), strikes just the right note. Try the parfait glacé de vanille Bourbon au rhum (iced parfait with Bourbon vanilla and rum) and choose among coffees from all over the planet. The Oulette also offers provincial produce at its gourmet delicatessen and a home catering service for those special dinner parties.

Open: Mon-Fri noon-2.15pm, Mon-Sat 8pm-10.15pm; reservations advisable

starter: 96FF
main: 138FF
dessert: 58FF
Set menu: 170FF, 280FF

AE CB DC MC V; €

Partie de campagne
French

☎ 01 43 40 44 00
Bercy Village, Cour Saint-Émilion, Chai no. 36, Bercy

Map: 12 D7
Métro: Cour St-Émilion

Smoking throughout

Pavement tables

Feeling nostalgic for those weekends in the country? In a former wine and spirit storehouse on the cour Saint-Émilion, Partie de campagne ('country outing') offers customers an oasis of conviviality in this new Parisian neighbourhood. Hurried businessmen and bucolic strollers from the Jardin de Bercy get acquainted at a large communal table, set up at the back of a room with old beams and restored stone walls. Cassoulet, pies and carrot soup, as well as lasagne and crumble, feature on a varied menu that includes several beautifully prepared classics. To finish, savour the fresh tarte aux figues fourrée à la pistache (fig tart with pistachio filling), which simply melts in your mouth. And if you *really* loved it, Partie de campagne also has takeaway...

starter: 35FF
main: 50FF-75FF
dessert: 15FF-38FF
Plat du jour: 55FF

CB EC MC V

Open: Mon-Sat 8am-midnight; reservations not accepted

Pataquès
French (Provence)

☎ 01 43 07 37 75
40-42 blvd de Bercy, Bercy

Map: 12 D6
Métro: Bercy

Nonsmoking tables available

Garden terrace tables

The fragrance of fruit bursting with sun, the flavour of olive oil and rosemary ... memory, taste and pleasure are sometimes so intertwined that just reading the menu at Pataquès is like being invited on a nostalgic trip to the heart of Provence. Inside the restaurant, high yellow walls are as bright as the brightest of summer days; outside, a heated garden terrace, as lovely in summer as in winter, brings back memories of long, lazy summer nights. Soupe au pistou (soup with vegetables, vermicelli, herbs and parmesan), bouille de rascasse (scorpion fish soup) and dorade (sea bream) à l'anchoïade offer a perfect excuse to linger. A hearty Provençal brunch is served on Sundays and public holidays until 4pm, which just leaves time for a siesta before the traditional evening pastis.

starter: 50FF
main: 80FF
dessert: 40FF
Set menu: 75FF (lunch), 155FF (dinner)
Plat du jour: 80FF

AE CB V

Open: Mon-Sat noon-2.30pm, 7pm-11pm (Sunday brunch 11am-4pm); reservations advisable

Sardegna a Tavola
Italian (Sardinian)

☎ 01 44 75 03 28
**1, rue de Cotte,
Marché d'Aligre**

Meet Antonio Simbula, Sardinian, bon vivant and fabulous chef. With mountain herbs and other produce imported from his native Sardinia (even salt and bread), along with ingredients from the nearby Aligre market, he creates family style cuisine enriched by Spanish, Egyptian and Italian influences. A generous serve of olives and sautéed potatoes makes a delicious starter and goes well with a glass of Vernaccia. To follow, close your eyes and wait... Carpaccio de cheval ou de poutarge (carpaccio of horse or of poutargue, a type of sausage made from dried mullet roe), Sardinian gnocchi with mint and almonds, marinade de mérou au verjus (marinated grouper with verjuice), tagliatelle with prawns and orange, salade de langouste (rock lobster salad), pâtes à l'encre (pasta with squid ink): daily specials that speak for themselves to a gourmet clientele. In other words, Sardegna a Tavola offers excellent value for money and is a place to note in your diary.

Open: Tues-Sat noon-2pm, Mon-Sat 7.30pm-11pm; reservations advisable (evenings)

Map: 12 C4

Métro: Ledru Rollin

 Nonsmoking tables available

starter: 60FF-130FF
main: 65FF-140FF
dessert: 35FF
Set menu: 90FF (lunch)
AE V; €

Sì señor!
Spanish

☎ 01 43 47 18 01
**9, rue Antoine-Vollon,
Bastille**

This Spanish restaurant, which opens onto the lovely Trousseau Square, has the opening hours and intimate atmosphere of a Parisian bistrot, but both the bright décor (yellow walls, red bench seats and ceramic tiles at the bar) and the chefs definitely have Iberian origins. The menu offers a wide range of tapas (including stuffed capsicum, tortillas, loin of pork and charcuterie), although you might prefer a copious daily special such as the sauté de veau pimenté (sautéed veal with spices) or the tender entrecôte d'Argentine (Argentinian rib steak). If this whets your appetite, try the melon soup or the natilla (semolina and vanilla cream flavoured with cinnamon) for dessert. Let the friendly, knowledgeable waiters recommend one of the numerous and inexpensive Spanish or South American wines. In summer there are pavement tables, just like you'll find in Spain. Olé!

Open: Tues-Sat noon-3pm, 7.30pm-11pm; reservations advisable

Map: 12 C3

Métro: Ledru Rollin

 Smoking throughout

Pavement tables

starter: 24FF-84FF
main: 72FF-98FF
dessert: 19FF-36FF
Set menu: 72FF, 85FF
  (lunch), 90FF, 120FF
  (dinner)
Plat du jour: 65FF (lunch),
  70FF-85FF (dinner)
CB EC MC V

Viaduc Café

Map: 12 B3

Métro: Ledru Rollin, Bastille

Smoking throughout

starter: 35FF-60FF
main: 60FF-110FF
dessert: 30FF-45FF
Set menu: 85FF
(lunch Mon-Fri)
Plat du jour: 75FF

cash only

Swann et Vincent
Italian

☎ 01 43 43 49 40
**7, rue Saint-Nicolas,
Ledru Rollin**

Swann and Vincent are the children of the owner of this terrific Italian restaurant, which looks just like an old bistrot. Customers are greeted without fuss and served by unpretentious staff. If the weather's nice, ask for a table by the window: the sunlight fills this part of the room. The waiter starts by bringing you a basket of home-made olive and sweet herb bread, which is simply amazing. This is followed by celery soup with a dash of olive oil, lovely if somewhat overpriced. The escalope with lemon and al dente vegetables is delicious, but the pasta dishes are also worthy of attention. You musn't finish without indulging in the tiramisú. As for that olive bread...

Open: daily noon-2.45pm, Sun-Wed 7.30pm-11.45pm, Thurs-Sat 7.30pm-12.15am; reservations advisable

La Table d'Aligre
French

☎ 01 43 07 84 88
11, place d'Aligre,
Marché d'Aligre

Map: 12 C4

Métro: Ledru Rollin

 Smoking throughout

In this spacious, sunny spot overlooking the picturesque place d'Aligre, the chef, who used to work at the old Connivence (just a few streets away), set up shop a year ago with the same enticing, inexpensive cuisine. Bursting with daring, mouthwatering flavours and updated on a seasonal basis, the menu includes clafoutis de champignons aux figues violettes (clafoutis with mushrooms and purple figs) – an interesting idea – Toro de poissons (Basque-style bouillabaisse) and tournedos de canard et sa crème de bacon (duck tournedos with cream of bacon – a delicious combination including celery, walnuts and onions). Chocaholics will make a beeline for the 'tout chocolat' platter: rich chocolate custard, crisp and creamy mille-feuille and a deep dark sorbet... At night, table-cloths and candles engender a more intimate atmosphere.

Open: daily noon-2pm, 8pm-11pm; reservations advisable (towards end of the week)

starter: 30FF (lunch), 42FF (dinner)
main: 62FF (lunch), 72FF (dinner)
dessert: 30FF (lunch), 42FF (dinner)
Set menu: 72FF (lunch), 90FF (lunch + drink & coffee), 104 FF, 124FF (dinner)
Plat du jour: 72FF

CB EC MC V

Viaduc Café
French

☎ 01 44 74 70 70
43, ave Daumesnil,
Gare de Lyon

Map: 12 C4

Métro: Gare de Lyon

Entertainment: Sunday jazz, noon-4pm

 Smoking throughout

 Pavement tables & enclosed terrace

After browsing in the craft shops and strolling along the promenade of the Viaduc des Arts, take a break at Viaduc Café, either at the terrace or inside, underneath an impressive vaulted ceiling of pale-coloured stone. The soft lighting, comfortable chairs and quiet atmosphere are relaxing and make you forget about the occasionally slow service. On Sunday you can enjoy a sumptuous brunch while listening to live jazz. The menu offers a wide range of stylish and delicious dishes, such as the Saint-Marcellin rôti au lard sur salade (roast Saint-Marcellin with bacon, served on a bed of salad), the ravioles aux cinq fromages (ravioli with five cheeses) and the effiloché de haddock en mousseline de pommes de terre (thinly sliced haddock with potato mousseline). The poule à la crème à l'ancienne (chicken à l'ancienne) is simpler, but no less succulent. To finish, the fondant au chocolat amer (bitter chocolate fondant) is an absolute must.

Open: daily 9am-4am; reservations advisable

starter: 27FF-69FF
main: 78FF-124FF
dessert: 36FF-44FF
Set menu: 125FF, 135FF (brunch)

CB EC MC V

Map: 12 F7

Métro: Daumesnil, Michel Bizot

Nonsmoking tables available

Les Zygomates
French

☎ 01 40 19 93 04
7, rue de Capri, Daumesnil

In an anonymous street, this former charcuterie doesn't grab your attention, but don't walk by. Roaring 1920s décor, playful reflections in the slightly mildewy mirrors and discreet service put you immediately at ease. Hors d'oeuvres arrive quickly and are reassuring: marbré de poireaux et joues de porcelet (leek and piglet's cheeks 'marble'), ravioles d'escargot en meurette (ravioli with snails in red wine sauce) and croustillant de calamars à la tomate (crispy squid with tomato). Presentation is attractive and flavours carefully matched: try the magret de canard aux trompettes de la mort (fillet of duck breast with 'trumpet of death' mushrooms) or the crépinette de faisan au chou et foie gras (pheasant crepes with cabbage and foie gras), although this dish can be a bit sparing on the last ingredient. The blancmanger aux fruit rouges (blancmange with red berries), or the chef's sweets assortment, make a fitting end to the meal. Not always perfect, Les Zygomates occasionally reaches great heights.

starter: 40FF-60FF
main: 65FF-100FF
dessert: 35FF-50FF
Set menu: 80FF (lunch),
130FF (dinner)

CB EC MC V

Open: Mon-Fri noon-2pm, Mon-Fri 7.30pm-10.45pm; reservations advisable (evenings)

13^e Arrondissement

Les Gobelins

Place d'Italie

Butte aux Cailles

Quartier Chinois

13^e Arrondissement

Ave d'Italie used to be a real eyesore, and the place d'Italie a major traffic intersection. Today, the thirteenth arrondissement is one of the capital's most colourful and dynamic areas. The Italian quarter is being renovated and, with its spanking new footpaths, the eponymous avenue has become human once again. On the quays, modern architecture scales new heights with the monumental bibliothèque François Mitterrand. The nearby quai de la Gare is still cherished by all artists who dream of liberty. The stylishness of the neighbouring fifth arrondissement extends to the Gobelins, while further south, between ave d'Italie and ave de Choisy, the succession of Asian restaurants, stalls and shops in the capital's version of Chinatown gives passersby the illusion of having imperceptibly changed continents. The thirteenth arrondissement is also proud of its history. A working-class district if ever there was one, it's home to both a place Nationale and a blvd Auguste-Blanqui, a pairing propitious to the reconciliation between anarchism and patriotism. At the butte aux Cailles, the jewel in the thirteenth's crown, people still sing revolutionary songs from the time of the Paris Commune.

L'Audiernes
French

☎ 01 44 24 86 23
22, rue Louise-Weiss, Nationale

Map: 13 E6

Métro: Chevaleret

 Nonsmoking tables available

 Pavement tables

Let's be upfront about this neighbourhood – it's got nothing going for it. Caught between Bercy and the Bibliothèque François Mitterrand, Nationale is struggling to find an identity. The Audiernes has no such problem. Contemporary décor with a designer touch attracts local office workers to this brasserie. If you don't mind dining in the company of suits from the adjoining branch of the Department of Economy and Finance (who may have just been scrutinising your tax declaration), then check out the delicious, if hardly original, brasserie fare, including bœuf à l'échalote (beef with shallots), pavé de rumsteck (thick-cut rumpsteak), faux-filet (beef sirloin) and a range of main-course salads with clever names. The tender, well-selected cuts of meat come in generous serves. There's also a terrace where you can sit on a sunny day.

Open: restaurant: Mon-Sat noon-3pm, bar: noon-9pm; reservations not accepted

starter: 22FF-70FF
main: 43FF-100FF
dessert: 22FF-40FF

AE MC V

Map: 13 D3
Métro: Les Gobelins

Smoking throughout

Au Petit Marguery
French

☎ 01 43 31 58 59
9, blvd du Port Royal,
Les Gobelins

This restaurant, run by the Cousin brothers, is one of the best places in Paris for game. So it's important to book during the autumn months if you want to dine on pheasant, venison or wild boar. Surrounded by belle époque décor, with pink walls and pink lampshades, you'll discover the purée de perdrix au genièvre (partridge puréed with juniper). As it melts in your mouth, you'll be surprised by its delicate but powerful flavour. The lièvre à la royale (boned hare stuffed with foie gras) really is fit for kings. You can also choose from seafood dishes such as the perfectly tender coquilles Saint-Jacques (scallops), poached à la Provençale with onions, tomatoes and herbs. More surprises await you with the desserts. The Grand Marnier soufflé is an aesthetic triumph. To top it all off, the service is efficient and friendly. First class.

Set menu: 165FF (weekday lunch), 215 FF, 450FF
AE CB EC MC V

Open: Tues-Sat noon-2.15pm, 7.30pm-10.15pm; reservations advisable

Map: 13 F3
Métro: Place d'Italie

Smoking throughout

L'Avant-Goût
Modern French

☎ 01 53 80 24 00
26, rue Bobillot,
Butte aux Cailles

What a place! Right near the Butte aux Cailles, this restaurant now has a solid reputation, maintained by its well-entrenched but unstuffy clientele. Each dish is lovingly prepared. For starters, we recommend the delicious ravioles de thon et de morue avec velouté de crustacés (tuna and cod ravioli with a velouté sauce). And for mains, how about the sanglier de sept heures et sa polenta croustillante (seven-hour wild boar with crunchy polenta)? Cooked to perfection, the meat is exquisitely tender. For dessert, you won't be disappointed by the moelleux au chocolat, served with vanilla ice cream. Above all, the food is beautifully presented. Lack of space makes it difficult to whisper sweet nothings to a special friend, and prompts the only false note in this chorus of praise. The last mouthful of dessert left us convinced that this particular *avant-goût* ('foretaste') is more moreish than most!

starter: 45FF
main: 85FF-105FF
dessert: 40FF
Set menu: 63FF (lunch), 150FF, 190FF
CB V

Open: Tues-Sat noon-2pm, 8pm-10.45pm; reservations essential

Le Bambou
Vietnamese

☎ 01 45 70 91 75
70, rue Baudricourt,
Quartier Chinois

Map: 13 G5

Métro: Tolbiac

 Smoking throughout

If you know about the Bambou, it's either by word of mouth, because you live in the area, or because you happened to be walking past. Otherwise, the stark tiles and lighting give this restaurant the same appearance as all the others that line the streets of the Chinese quarter. The only thing that grabs your attention is the queue outside the door. Most of the food is unexceptional, but there are several outstanding dishes: the salade de papaye au porc, aux crevettes et méduses (papaya salad with pork, shrimps and jellyfish) and the classic bò bun are lovely starters. The brochettes de viande et de crevettes grillées (grilled meat and shrimp kebabs), served with large helpings of salad, are also delicious; on the other hand, the brochettes de crevettes à la canne à sucre (shrimp kebabs with sugar cane) lacked flavour.

starter: 20FF-40FF
main: 38FF-72FF
dessert: 18FF-38FF

CB EC MC V

Open: Tues-Sun 11.45am-3.30pm, 6.45pm-10.45pm; reservations advisable (not accepted on weekends)

La Bonne Heure
Organic/vegetarian

☎ 01 45 89 77 00
72, rue du Moulin-des-Prés,
Butte aux Cailles

Map: 13 G3

Métro: Tolbiac

 Smoking throughout

Just a short walk from the Butte aux Cailles, this is a simple place, a bit like a family dining room, that serves organic vegetarian food. Each day the chef supplements the menu with a savoury tart (mushroom or onion) plus a plat du jour, such as gratin de poisson (fish gratin) or poêlée de légumes (pan-fried vegetables). The carnival of colours and flavours on your plate deserves to be accompanied by the biodynamic Ventoux wine recommended here. To round the meal off sweetly, chocolate lovers will plump for the gâteau au chocolat, but the tarte aux reines-claudes à l'amande (greengage and almond tart) and the figues gratinées à la vanille (vanilla fig crumble) are so good you'll dream about them.

starter: 30FF-35FF
main: 50FF-68FF
dessert: 16FF-24FF
Plat du jour: 48FF, 55FF

CB EC V

Open: Tues-Sun noon-2.30pm, 7pm-10.30pm; reservations advisable

Les Cailloux
Italian

☎ 01 45 80 15 08
**58, rue des Cinq Diamants,
Butte aux Cailles**

Map: 13 F2
Métro: Corvisart

Smoking throughout

This new kid on the Butte aux Cailles has been an unequivocal success. Les Cailloux offers a bright, modern setting with grey and earth tones, low lamps on the tables, all-Italian staff and northern Italian recipes based mostly on pasta. The tomato purée is imported, the ricotta comes from Naples and the pasta from De Cecco's. The fabulous wine list features French and Italian vintages for under 200FF, which you can also take away. For lunch, the inexpensive set menu consists of a starter, a main course and a glass of wine, and is changed daily. Treat yourself to rocket salad with ricotta, tagliata de filet de bœuf, pâtes au tourteau et aux artichauts (pasta with crab and artichokes) or pâtes aux calamars et à la sauge (pasta with squid and sage). For dessert, the coffee-flavoured affogato makes a nice change from tiramisù. Everything is done with brio and good taste. This *is*, after all, an Italian restaurant!

starter: 33FF-48FF
main: 52FF-88FF
dessert: 30FF-35FF
Set menu: 80FF

AE MC V; €

Open: Tues-Sat 12.30pm-2.30pm, 7.30pm-11pm; reservations advisable

Chez Jacky
French

☎ 01 45 83 71 55
**109, rue du Dessous-des-Berges,
Nationale**

Map: 13 F7
Métro: Chevaleret,
Bibliothèque François
Mitterrand

Dress code applies

Smoking throughout

If you belong to some hip, postmodern set, be on your way! Chez Jacky is a serious, traditional restaurant with thoughtful service and a nice, old-fashioned provincial atmosphere. The three brothers in charge know how to find good regional produce and present it with great panache, even if originality isn't their cardinal virtue. You can set your heart with confidence on the tête de veau (calf's head), the noisette d'agneau (lamb), or the rognons (kidneys). The compote de lapereau maison sur un lit de mesclun niçois (the chef's compote of young rabbit served on a salad of mixed niçois greens) makes a terrific starter. The presentation of the desserts is assured, although the timbale de mousse au chocolat aux zestes d'orange (chocolate mousse with orange peel) wasn't quite up to scratch: the balance of chocolate and orange flavours needed some fine tuning.

starter: 88FF-168FF
main: 88FF-158FF
dessert: 48FF
Set menu: 188FF
Plat du jour: from 88FF

CB V

Open: Mon-Fri noon-2.30pm, 7.30pm-10.30pm; reservations advisable

Les Décors
French/European

☎ **01 45 87 37 00**
18, rue Vulpian, Glacière

Map: 13 E2

Métro: Glacière, Place d'Italie

  Nonsmoking tables available

Gorgeous traditional food is prepared behind the '*décors*' (scenes) at this fine restaurant. The white-tiled floor, paintings of rural scenes, and floral tablecloths add a Swiss touch to the dining room. Customers are greeted warmly and offered a menu revealing one nice surprise after another. Specialities include morel mushrooms, truffles and foie gras, cuisses de grenouilles (frogs' legs), filets de perchettes (fillets of baby perch), tête de veau sauce ravigote (calf's head with ravigote sauce) and pavé de bœuf Rossini (thick-cut steak Rossini). The chef, Christine Sonnefraud, is of Flemish origin. After 20 years experience, she obviously knows her stuff. It's difficult not to swoon over the œufs brouillés aux truffes (scrambled eggs with truffles), the filet mignon de porc aux cêpes et röstis (pork filet mignon with cep mushrooms and rösti – a kind of Swiss potato cake) and the tarte aux mûres (blackberry tart). Fresh ingredients, simple and perfectly cooked dishes – nothing but the best.

starter: 53FF-88FF
main: 68FF-150FF
dessert: 32FF-58FF
Set menu: 73FF (lunch), 99FF, 138FF, 159FF
Plat du jour: 49FF (lunch)

AE CB DC EC MC V

Open: Mon-Sat noon-2.30pm, Tues-Sat 7.30pm-10.30pm; reservations advisable

---

Entotto
Ethiopian

☎ **01 45 35 41 94**
143-5, rue Léon-Maurice-Nordmann, Denfert-Rochereau

Map: 13 E1

Métro: Glacière

 Smoking throughout

This Ethiopian restaurant looks like nothing much from the outside – management certainly hasn't tried to build a reputation on appearances. Even inside, it's almost spartan, with just a few photos of Abyssinian emperors and covers from old copies of *L'Illustration* to brighten up the décor. The cuisine is a different matter though, being full of character and authentically exotic. For starters, try the doro wott (chicken, berberé – a kind of pepper – and spices). Then you could treat yourself to a superb beyayenetou entotto, a dish that combines two kinds of meat (beef and guinea fowl) and five vegetables, offering a unique blend of textures and flavours. The injera (Ethiopian flat bread) that comes with the mains is an essential part of the experience. It's smooth to the touch and adds to the rare pleasure of eating with your fingers.

starter: 42FF-48FF
main: 90FF-102FF
dessert: 42FF-46FF

CB EC MC V

Open: Tues-Sat 9.30am-10.30pm; reservations not accepted

Impérial Choisy
Chinese

☎ 01 45 86 42 40
32, ave de Choisy,
Quartier Chinois

Map: 13 H5
Métro: Porte de Choisy

Smoking throughout

In the heart of Chinatown, an area packed with Asian restaurants, the Impérial Choisy has played its cards well. Not much to look at, it's the food that grabs your attention here. The décor in this popular family eatery is starting to show its age, but customers can expect meals with assured flavours and textures as well as a good range of particularly original specialities. The copious crevettes à la vapeur aux haricots noirs de soja (steamed shrimps with black soya beans) are served with a strong but not over-whelming sauce that will thrill your tastebuds. This restaurant may give you the confidence to check out more-exotic dishes on subsequent visits, such as the langues de canard au sel et au poivre (ducks' tongues with salt and pepper), the salade de méduse (jellyfish salad) or even the holothuries aux abalones et champignons (sea cucumbers with abalones and mushrooms).

starter: 23FF-55FF
main: 25FF-130FF

cash only

Open: daily noon-11pm; reservations advisable (especially weekends)

Le Jardin des Pâtes
French

☎ 01 45 35 93 67
33, blvd Arago,
Gobelins

Map: 13 D2
Métro: Les Gobelins

Smoking throughout

Pavement tables

Pasta and more pasta, yes, but *this* pasta ... OK, let's stop right there. Forget the compar-isons. This restaurant offers lovingly prepared, fresh pasta unlike anywhere else. The pasta is made from barley, buckwheat, rye, wheat or rice – bringing back forgotten flavours and textures – and is served with fresh ingredients, which leaves a delicious taste in your mouth. The barley pasta with salmon, crème fraîche, seaweed and leeks is a lovely dish. The spe-cialities are all organic and the desserts, which are simple but perfect, are home-made. The setting is just right, with a small but welcoming dining room brightened up with colourful pic-tures and 'Grass roots'-style furniture. The little terrace works magic on a sunny day.

starter: 19FF-48FF
main: 42FF-77FF
dessert: 25FF-29FF

CB V

Open: Mon-Sat noon-2.30pm, 7pm-11pm; reservations advisable (evenings)

Exotic origins

Plants from the Americas were the first to give French vegetables variety, including the humble potato, which the Spanish discovered in Peru in 1532. Along with corn, *papas*, as they were called, were the staple food of the Peruvians. Back in Europe, the precious tuber spread from Spain to Italy and Germany, where Parmentier first encountered it, infiltrating England by other routes. The tomato also came from Peru and appeared in Europe in the 16th century, spreading from Italy. It seems that the Cucurbiticeae family (squash, marrows, zucchini and pumpkin) originated in Peru too. Another American vegetable, the bean, conquered Christopher Columbus in Cuba, and Jacques Cartier at the mouth of the Saint-Laurent. The Jerusalem artichoke, cultivated by native North Americans, was adopted by the French in the 17th century under the name 'Canadian artichoke'. And did you know that the ancestors of European strawberry plants were brought back from Chile and North America in the 18th century? As for chilli (the only major spice to have come out of the New World) the Mexicans have been growing it since about 5000 BC.

Looking to the other continents: cucumber comes from ancient India; melons from southern Africa (although Asian growers increased the size of their fruit by selection); bananas from South-East Asia; and edible apples from Turkey, along with cherries and chestnuts. Orange, lemon, mandarin and apricot trees all originated in China, as did the peach tree, the symbol of immortality, which is depicted on many Chinese art objects.

Lao Douang Chan
Lao/Vietnamese

☎ 01 44 24 80 80
161, ave de Choisy,
Quartier Chinois

Map: 13 F4
Métro: Place d'Italie

Smoking throughout

Why choose this particular restaurant rather than one of the many others on ave de Choisy? Definitely not for the small, cramped dining room, the paunchy stucco Buddha on the counter or the genuine floodlit waterfall cascading down the wall. You come here for a dish known as bo bun, the star of a lavish menu featuring countless noodles, soups and specialities from Laos and Vietnam. Simultaneously hot and cold, tender and crisp, bitter and sweet, copious and light, bo bun is an extraordinary taste experience. Try the other offerings another time. The desserts deserve a special mention – they dazzle all the senses. Check out the sousa aux trois trésors or the taro with betel before you leave.

starter: 20FF-45FF
main: 35FF-55FF
dessert: 20FF-35

cash only

Open: Wed-Mon noon-3pm, 7pm-10pm; reservations advisable

Menabe l'Île Rouge
Madagascan

☎ 01 45 65 04 11
33, rue Damesme,
Place des Peupliers

Map: 13 H4
Métro: Tolbiac, Maison Blanche

Smoking throughout

Menabe l'Île Rouge isn't just a good little restaurant, it's also a friendly meeting place for lovers of Madagascar. The pleasant atmosphere owes nothing to the forgettable décor – it's entirely due to the master of ceremonies, who cooks, serves and dispenses information. He's a passionate ambassador for his native island, always ready with a book for you to look through or a helpful tip for the traveller. The adventure begins straight away here, with the food. Unbeatable prices and menus that offer unfamiliar flavours, such as boeuf aux brèdes malgaches, beef with a Madagascan herb that has a strange 'cooling' effect. Don't miss the seiches au lait de coco (cuttlefish cooked in coconut milk), which is deliciously sweet. The accompaniments include achards de légumes parfumés (spicy vegetable pickle), as well as koba and parakevy (types of fritters). For dessert there are delicious tropical fruits available.

starter: 5FF-20FF
main: 35FF-45FF
Set menu: 45FF (lunch),
65FF, 90FF (150FF for
group bookings on Sunday
& public holidays)
Plat du jour: 35FF-45FF

CB EC MC V

Open: Mon-Sat noon-2pm, 7pm-10pm; reservations essential

Le Pet de lapin
French

☎ 01 45 86 58 21
**2, rue Dunois,
Jeanne d'Arc**

Map: 13 F7

Métro: Chevaleret,
  Nationale

  Smoking throughout

  Pavement tables

You might describe something worthless with the popular French expression 'ça ne vaut pas un pet de lapin' (literally, it's not worth a rabbit's fart). Pet de lapin is a strange name then for a restaurant that, without being pretentious, offers exceptional fare. Some of the wine could be classified as a national treasure (the oldest bottle dates from 1904!) and is simply unaffordable (700FF-2,300FF). However, the menu at this spacious, peaceful establishment is within the range of most budgets. The salade de feuilles d'épinard aux lardons (salad of spinach leaves and bacon), the échine de porc à la moutarde de Meaux (loin of pork with Meaux mustard), the faux-filet sauce poivre vert (beef sirloin with green pepper sauce) and the chocolate mousse with orange peel would bring many Parisian restaurants down a peg or two. In autumn, the game menu will delight lovers of flavoursome meat. In summer, you can eat outside in a tiny, relatively peaceful square.

Open: Tues-Sat noon-2pm, 8pm-10pm; reservations advisable (evenings)

starter: 25FF-69FF
main: 49FF-129FF
dessert: 26FF-45FF
Set menu: 69FF (except
  Saturday nights)

AE CB V

Pho 14
Vietnamese

☎ 01 45 83 61 15
**129, ave de Choisy,
Quartier Chinois**

Map: 13 G4

Métro: Tolbiac

 Smoking throughout

 Pavement tables

Feel like a bit of local colour? This is the place to find it. There's a range of simple, well-prepared dishes, but it is the Vietnamese soups that are the main attraction for a predominantly Asian crowd. In a rowdy cafeteria-like atmosphere, you can savour soupe tonkinoise, the famous 'pho' made with beef, meatballs or chicken, and served with soy sauce and coriander. Nothing fancy, but it does the trick – you'll leave satisfied and invigorated. Among the handful of desserts, the surprising haricots rouges au lait de coco (red beans with coconut milk) and the dessert aux trois couleurs (three-coloured dessert) deserve an honourable mention. The staff are young and relaxed. Keep the address handy for when you next need a good no-frills meal.

Open: daily 8am-11pm; reservations not accepted

starter: 32FF
main: 32FF-41FF
dessert: 16FF-20FF

cash only

13e ARRONDISSEMENT

Restaurant Tricotin
Chinese/Thai

☎ 01 45 84 74 44
01 45 85 51 52
15, ave de Choisy,
Quartier Chinois

Map: 13 J5
Métro: Porte de Choisy

Smoking throughout

This restaurant is right at the end of ave de Choisy, in the heart of Chinatown. It's nothing much to look at with its plain furniture and unimaginative décor; Tricotin is like a cafeteria where various communities mingle. The smaller Thai section offers tasty food at unbeatable prices. The dishes come seasoned with peppers, lemongrass or salt and pepper, and the menu seems infinite. For starters it's hard to choose between the unusual salads (spicy beef or green pawpaw) and the flavoursome soups. The mains are of the same standard. Try the crabes mous au poivre et sel (soft crabs with salt and pepper), the poisson au lait de coco (fish in coconut milk) and, as an accompaniment, the riz gluant (sticky rice) or riz à l'ananas (fried rice with shrimps, cashews and fresh pineapple pieces – sufficient for two).

starter: 10FF-23FF
main: 24FF-50FF
dessert: 12FF-23FF
Plat du jour: 45FF

CB, MC, V

Open: daily 9am-11.30pm; reservations advisable

Le Samson
French

☎ 01 45 89 09 23
Cnr rue Samson &
rue Jean-Marie-Jego,
Butte aux Cailles

Map: 13 F3
Métro: Place d'Italie,
Corvisart

Smoking throughout

It shouldn't be all that hard to create a good restaurant. First, put together a varied menu that is simple but full of pleasant little surprises, such as tender, golden poulet fermier (free-range chicken), perfectly complemented by a gratin de chou-fleur au curry (curried cauliflower gratin) or hareng mariné au piment de Guadeloupe (marinated herring with Guadeloupe peppers), which is spicy – but not too spicy. (The desserts are less inventive than the mains.) Next, make sure the interior is uncluttered – big wooden tables, a zinc bar and a few pictures to give it warmth – and looks out onto the street through large bay windows. Finally, keep the prices down and make the set menus great value. Simple as that. It might just become one of your haunts.

starter: 30FF-55FF
main: 55FF-85FF
dessert: 22FF-40FF
Set menu: 55FF (lunch),
70FF, 80FF
Plat du jour: 55FF

cash only

Open: Mon-Sat noon-2.30pm, Mon-Fri 7.30pm-11.30pm; reservations advisable

Sinorama
Chinese

☎ 01 53 82 09 51
**135, ave de Choisy,
Quartier Chinois**

Map: 13 G4
Métro: Tolbiac

 Smoking throughout

Why the cinematic name? Probably because a skilful chef creates popular meals just as a director puts together a successful film... At peak hour, customers fall over each other to get a table at this top-notch Chinese restaurant. The décor isn't terribly original, but it avoids the obligatory kitsch. The menu is a Prévert-style inventory and includes a staggering 938 choices, which defies all Cartesian logic. The specialities take you off the beaten track and include the well-matched flavours of the copious farci aux trois trésors à la sauce de soja noir (farci with 'three treasures' and black soy sauce) as well as the slightly fatty but tender and delicious canard aux prunes et au taro (duck with plums and taro). The raviolis pékinois à la poêle (pan-fried Pekinese dim sum) melt in your mouth. Estomac de poisson farci (stuffed fish stomach) is also available.

starter: 25FF-95FF
Set menu: 55FF, 58FF
(except weekends and
public holidays), 220FF
CB EC MC V

Open: daily noon-3pm, 7pm-2am; reservations advisable (evenings)

Sukho Thaï
Thai

☎ 01 45 81 55 88
**12, rue du Père-Guérin,
Place d'Italie**

Map: 13 F3
Métro: Place d'Italie

 Nonsmoking tables available

Most of the customers here are either Thai tourists passing through or expats living in Paris – a sure sign of quality. Sukho Thaï offers authentic Thai cuisine, with just the right amount of spice and style, at extremely reasonable prices. The salade de bœuf à la citronnelle (beef salad with lemongrass), canard sauté épicé au poivre frais (sautéed duck seasoned with fresh pepper), crevettes sautées au basilic (sautéed shrimps with basil) and cassolette de gambas aux vermicelles (cassolette of king prawns with noodles) served with deliciously sticky rice are all sumptuous. The meals are as sophisticated as the décor and are served generously in elegant Thai crockery. Sukho Thaï has established its reputation by word of mouth. It's absolutely packed in the evening and the owner is often run off his feet, so reservations and patience are essential. Well worth the effort.

starter: 20FF-55FF
main: 45FF-105FF
dessert: 25FF-45FF
Set menu: 58FF, 69FF
(lunch), 95FF, 115FF
MC V

Open: Mon-Sat noon-2.30pm, 7pm-10.30pm; reservations essential (evenings)

Map: 13 D2
Métro: Gobelins

Smoking throughout

Vy Da
Vietnamese

☎ 01 47 07 37 75
**15, blvd de Port-Royal,
Les Gobelins**

In this unpretentious restaurant, 50m from the Escurial Cinema, newcomers are initiated into the cuisine of Hué, Vietnam's old imperial city. Until quite recently the menu was entirely in Vietnamese, and the desserts still haven't been translated. Trust Madame Nguyen and her daughter to choose from the menu on your behalf – you won't be disappointed. The galettes, papillotes, bouchées and rouleaux de riz aux crevettes (ricepaper rolls with shrimps) are steamed in banana leaves and go well with a Xuy Moï Perrier (with salted plums) or an artichoke-leaf tea. The crêpe de Hué and the porc grillé avec pâté de crabe (grilled pork with crab pâté) are outstanding. Generous serves, cheap prices and the exotic 'made in Hué' cachet make Vy Da a great favourite among Vietnamese expats.

starter: 11FF-42FF
main: 35FF-85FF
dessert: 13FF-20FF

cash only

Open: daily 11am-3pm, 5pm-10pm; reservations not accepted

14e Arrondissement

Montparnasse

Alésia

Denfert-Rochereau

Cité Universitaire

14ᵉ Arrondissement

Parc Montsouris, the cimetière du Montparnasse, place de la Catalogne, place Denfert-Rochereau: the fourteenth arrondissement has a lot going for it. The extraordinary Cité universitaire – a lush oasis reserved for country and overseas students – acts as a buffer between parc Montsouris and the external ring road. The somewhat cold elegance of rue Froidevaux, which runs alongside the beautiful cimetière du Montparnasse (home to the remains of Sartre and Gainsbourg, among others) contrasts with the neon signs and nightlife of the aptly named rue de la Gaîté. Pedestrians have the run of rue Daguerre, whose market, shops and bars attract friendly hordes on the weekends. Further south, a young, dynamic residential area, full of restaurants and bistrots, stretches between ave du Général-Leclerc and blvd Brune. This is one of those apparently anonymous places where you can feel the city's heartbeat. Bargain hunters flock to the clothing shops of rue d'Alésia, which runs through the entire arrondissement. Less flamboyant than the Latin Quarter, less hip than Bastille and less audacious than Bercy, the unpretentious fourteenth arrondissement has perhaps struck a better balance than most.

Le 14 juillet il y a toujours des lampions...
French

☎ **01 40 44 91 19**
99, rue Didot,
Glacière

Map: 14 F4

Métro: Plaisance

  Smoking throughout

For over seven years now, Stéphane Reynaud, lover of fine food and good living, has been at the helm of this bubbling restaurant. Sitting at one of the wooden tables under the high ceiling, you could be at a friend's place. The welcome is warm, the conversation lively, and the menu – written up on large slates – promises a personal and creative cuisine with traditional roots. Dishes include terrine de canard aux cèpes et confiture d'oignons (duck terrine with cèpe mushrooms and onion jam), l'ossau iraty (sheep's milk cheese from the Pyrenees) cooked with potatoes, onions, bacon cubes, honey and fresh cream, and Saint-Jacques et gambas au lard au beurre de crustacés (scallops and king prawns with bacon). The service is efficient and friendly, and the lunch menu is worth a special mention – it's excellent value for money.

starter: 28FF-55FF
main: 78FF-120FF
dessert: 38FF
Set menu: 69FF (weekday lunch)
Plat du jour: 80FF (fish)
CB EC MC V; €

Open: daily noon-2.30pm, 7pm-11pm; reservations advisable

Aquarius
Vegetarian

☎ **01 45 41 36 88**
40, rue de Gergovie,
Plaisance-Pernety

Map: 14 E4

Métro: Plaisance, Pernety

 Nonsmoking rooms available

This vegetarian restaurant, which was the first of its kind to open in Paris, is a pleasant place that offers meals inspired by traditional French cuisine. From the classic chèvre chaud (warm goat's cheese) to the ravioles de Romans (French-style ravioli), the starters are substantial and give you a first taste of the chef's skill. In the main courses, meat has been replaced with tofu or seitan (a paste made from wheat gluten cooked in an aromatic broth). You can enjoy lasagne, cassoulet or tartiflette (a baked potato and cheese dish) without missing out on authentic flavours. The desserts are a gourmet's delight. Succumb to tarte aux fruits (fruit tart) or pavé au chocolat parfumé à l'orange (chocolate cake flavoured with orange). Organic wines are on offer to accompany these vegetarian feasts. The furthermost of the three rooms, where smoking is permitted, opens out onto a little garden that is pleasantly cool in summer.

Set menu: 65FF
Plat du jour: 60FF
CB DC EC MC V

Open: Mon-Sat noon-2.30pm, 7pm-10.30pm; reservations advisable

Au Vin des Rues
French (Beaujolais/Lyon)

☎ 01 43 22 19 78
**21, rue Boulard,
Mairie du 14e,
Denfert-Rochereau**

Map: 14 D7
Métro: Denfert Rochereau,
Mouton Duvernet
Entertainment: Live
accordion Thurs nights

Smoking throughout

Pavement tables

This wine bar takes its name from the beautiful book by Doisneau and Bob Giraud. Lovely, generous dishes from the Beaujolais and Lyons regions are served with inexpensive wines carefully selected at the vineyard itself. For starters, charcuterie and terrines (including amazing rillettes with a cinnamon flavour), followed by quenelles (dumplings), a delicious poulet aux écrevisses (chicken with crayfish) and onglet à l'échalote (beef with shallots) transport you to the banks of the Saône. The lunch and dinner both menus change daily. The prices, the warm welcome, the setting and loyal, happy customers help make this place an emblematic Parisian bistrot.

starter: 30FF-80FF
main: 62FF-120FF
dessert: 32FF-44FF
Plat du jour: 70FF

V

Open: Tues-Sat 10am-midnight; reservations advisable Wed, Thurs & Fri nights

Azulejos
Portuguese

☎ 01 43 20 93 04
**7, rue Campagne-Première,
Port Royal**

Map: 14 B8
Métro: Raspail

Smoking throughout

This restaurant is home to lovers of Portuguese cuisine and *fados* (popular songs about unrequited love). It has a slightly faded setting, decorated with posters and, of course, *azulejos* (glazed ceramic tiles). Don't miss the owner's speciality: cataplana de lotte aux fruits de mer, named after the deep cooking pot in which it is prepared. A pork or clam version of this dish is also available. The morue a Braz (pieces of cod with fried potatoes and scrambled eggs) – more popular than the cataplana and just as flavoursome – is served on a terracotta plate and exemplifies the traditional home cooking on offer. The croquettes de morue et de salade, washed down with vinho verde, avaleva or casal garcia, make a delicious snack for those with smaller appetites. The riz au lait à la cannelle (rice pudding with cinnamon) rounds off the meal with a lovely burst of sweetness.

starter: 28FF-68FF
main: 75FF-140FF
dessert: 28FF-45FF
Set menu: 85FF (lunch)
Plat du jour: 58FF

AE CB EC MC V

Open: Mon-Sat 9am-3.30pm, 7pm-11.30pm; reservations advisable (evenings)

Le Bistrot des Pingouins

French

☎ 01 43 21 92 29
79, rue Daguerre,
Denfert-Rochereau

Map: 14 D6

Métro: Denfert Rochereau

 Nonsmoking table available

 Terrace tables

You may wonder why penguins would set up shop on such a busy street. And yet there's not a flightless bird to be seen in this spacious, comfortable and well-lit room. The starters are delicious: brick de chèvre chaud à la menthe (warm goat's cheese in a fine Tunisian pancake with mint), saumon mariné à la coriandre (marinated salmon with coriander), or, better still, compote de lapereau et oignons confits (slow-cooked young rabbit stew with preserved onions). You should then be ready to take on a tasty steak tartare with coriander and french fries (unfortunately not home-made), or a filet de canard aux agrumes (fillet of duck with citrus fruits). You can't go wrong with the salads, which are varied and balanced. The crème brûlée with strawberries for dessert will help you forget the minor shortcomings of the mains (accompaniments and cooking times), and the charming staff compensate for the factory-like feel of this large establishment.

starter: 19FF-39FF
main: 59FF-89FF
dessert: 29FF-40FF
Set menu: 67FF (3 courses)
Plat du jour: 48FF

CB DC EC JCB MC V

Open: Mon-Fri noon-3.15pm, Mon-Sat 7pm-2am (meals served until 11.30pm or midnight); reservations advisable

Café d'Enfer

French

☎ 01 43 22 23 75
22, rue Daguerre,
Denfert-Rochereau

Map: 14 D7

Métro: Denfert Rochereau

 Nonsmoking tables available

 Terrace tables

Outside, there's the friendly bustle of a shopping strip; inside, designer décor that manages to remain warm and welcoming. Situated in rue Daguerre, Café d'Enfer attracts a hip-but-human crowd. Enjoy the soft lighting and chairs as you peruse a menu that has an undeniably personal touch with dishes such as pavé de gigot poêlé à la crème de basilic (pan-fried lamb steak with creamy basil sauce); pavé de foie de veau poêlé sauce miel et coriandre (pan-fried calf's liver with honey and coriander sauce); filet de dorade royale crème de safran (fillet of sea bream with creamed saffron); and petit bar entier grillé huile d'olive (whole grilled baby bass with olive oil). These delectable dishes, all prepared with fresh produce, are beautifully presented. A heated terrace allows customers to enjoy the pedestrian precinct in both winter and summer.

Set menu: 150FF
Plat du jour: 60FF

AE CB V; €

Open: Mon-Sat 9am-midnight, Sun 10.30am-3.30pm; reservations advisable

Map: 14 E4

Métro: Plaisance

Smoking throughout

Les Caves de Solignac
French (South-West)

☎ 01 45 45 58 59
9, rue Decrès, Alésia

The name evokes a small restaurant tucked away in a vaulted cellar with exposed stone walls. Far from it, Les Caves de Solignac is simply close-set tables, a few framed posters and a bar chock-full of liqueurs. You stumble across this place either by chance or because you know that such restaurants often serve the best regional cuisine in town. The food here is full of character and authenticity, just like the owner. Try the magret de canard (fillet of duck breast), salade de gésiers (salad with gizzards), canard confit (confit of duck) and foie gras. The South-West has pride of place here. The owner is a seasoned traveller on the highway of flavours, journeying from small farm to vineyard in search of the best provincial produce for the kitchen in Paris.

starter: 40FF-60FF
main: 85FF
dessert: 40FF-50FF
Set menu: 110FF (lunch), 167FF (dinner)
Plat du jour: 85FF

MC V

Open: Mon-Fri noon-2pm, 7.30pm-10pm; reservations advisable

Map: 14 B6

Métro: Vavin, Edgar Quinet

Nonsmoking throughout

Pavement tables

Dietetic Shop
Vegetarian

☎ 01 43 35 39 75
11, rue Delambre, Montparnasse

In this little no-fuss restaurant, you can choose your meal from the kitchen in the middle of the room. Among the cold dishes, there's a home-made vegetable pâté, caviar d'algues marines (seaweed caviar) with pasta and an assortment of raw vegetables or lentils served with smoked tofu and raw vegetables. The range of hot dishes is broad and includes soups, grains and pulses, pies and tarts, couscous and more innovative specialities, such as tarte aux graines germées (sprout tart). The owner makes the filets de sardines crues marinés au citron (raw sardine fillets marinated in lemon juice), but the demand has been so great she's had to limit herself to offering them on Tuesday and Wednesday. Fruit and vegetable juices are also available. The unusual 'hard cocktail' combines fresh fruit, grated ginger and nutmeg. The desserts change daily, and range from the traditional clafoutis and tartes à la crème to seaweed and fruit.

starter: 27FF-39FF
main: 42FF-57FF
dessert: 19FF-29FF
Set menu: 45FF
Plat du jour: 45FF

AE EC MC V; €

Open: Mon-Sat noon-3pm, Mon-Fri 7pm-10.30pm; reservations not accepted

Les Gourmands
French (South-West/Catalonia)

☎ 01 45 41 40 70
**101, rue de l'Ouest,
behind Montparnasse**

Map: 14 D4

Métro: Pernety

  Smoking throughout

Forget about Paris in this little corner of the French provinces. Exposed beams, stone and roughcast walls, linen tablecloths and serviettes create a simple, warm atmosphere in keeping with the hostess' welcome. Cuisine from the South-West and French Catalonia (the chef's birthplace) features prominently on the mouthwatering menu. Sumptuous starters include an escalope de foie gras frais poêlée (pan-fried escalope of fresh foie gras), a ragoût d'escargots à la catalane (snail ragout) and cœurs de canard sautés déglacés au vinaigre de Banyuls (sautéed ducks' hearts deglazed with Banyuls vinegar). The suprême de poulet fermier, served with a stunning sauce Roussillon (supreme of chicken with a black olive, bacon and cep mushroom sauce) and the côte de cochon sauce aux morilles (pork chop with a morel mushroom sauce), served with potatoes sautéed in goose fat, left us feeling full and happy. We'll come back for the desserts – these gourmands really know how to look after gourmets!

Set menu: 112FF (2 courses), 152FF (3 courses), 192FF (4 courses + salad)

AE CB EC MC V

Open: Tues-Sat noon-2pm, 7.30pm-10pm; reservations advisable

L'O à la Bouche
French

☎ 01 56 54 01 55
**124, blvd du Montparnasse,
Montparnasse**

Map: 14 B7

Métro: Vavin

 Nonsmoking tables available

 Pavement tables

This restaurant lives up to its name ('Mouthwatering'), and the kitschy decoration reinforces the message that pleasure reigns here. L'O à la Bouche attracts enthusiastic Parisians as well as travellers. The cuisine is boldly creative, combining fish and meat, cheese and seafood, while the wine list is limited to a few carefully chosen bottles, including a very pleasant sancerre red. The terrine de foie gras de canard (duck foie gras terrine), with purple fig jam and lamb's lettuce, is a special treat to be savoured in tiny mouthfuls – as is the pavé de cabillaud poêlé à la moelle (fresh cod steak pan-fried with bone marrow), served with creamy lentils, which combines contrasting flavours to perfection. The tarte fine aux pommes caramélisée (caramelised apple tart), which you need to order at the start of the meal, is yet another triumph.

starter: 82FF-98FF
main: 120FF-135FF
dessert: 50FF-58FF
Set menu: 140FF (lunch), 195FF (dinner)

AE CB JCB MC V

Open: Tues-Sat noon-2.30pm, 7pm-midnight; reservations advisable

Bars & Cafes – 14e & 15e

Au Roi du café 59, rue Lecourbe, Paris 15e, Vaugirard ☎ 01 47 34 48 50
Métro: Volontaires, Sèvres Lecourbe (Map: 15 E8)

With its 1910 architecture, this place dates from the heroic age of the local
bistrot and still has an old-time feel. There's almost nothing modern, except for
the bar's name emblazoned in blue neon on one wall. Regulars gather at the
counter to pay their respects to the wine list (written up on a slate). The atmosphere is lively in the dining room too, where generous traditional dishes are
served.

Open: daily 6am-2am; By the glass: beer 11FF, champagne 35FF; coffee 6FF;
meals & snacks available; credit cards accepted

Le Bistrot Bourdelle 12, rue Antoine-Bourdelle, Paris 15e, Montparnasse
☎ 01 45 48 48 59 Métro: Falguière, Montparnasse Bienvenüe (Map: 15 E9)

The décor owes nothing to Bourdelle's chisel: posters of retro B-grade movies, old
advertisements, vintage skateboards and an improvised chapel in the toilets ...
anything goes! This joyful oasis casts a spell on all who enter its realm. How can
one feel so good, so quickly, and be so utterly incapable of tearing oneself away?
Maybe it's those magic happy hours.

Open: Mon-Wed 10.30am-1am, Thurs-Sat 10.30am-2am; By the glass: beer 10FF,
champagne 38FF; coffee 6FF; snacks & set menu meals available; occasional concerts during the Fête de la Musique; cash only; €

Le Breguet 72, rue Falguière, Paris 15e, Pasteur ☎ 01 42 79 97 00 Métro:
Pasteur (Map: 15 E8)

For five years, the Breguet has been trying to breathe some life back into this isolated stretch of rue Falguière. Its old neighbourhood bistrot façade is easily
missed in the surrounding torpor. A few model flying machines remind regulars
that the Breguet used to be a make of airplane. Drinks here are as cheap as the
atmosphere is lively, colourful and unfussy.

Open: Mon-Fri 5pm-1.30am, Sat 6pm-2am; By the glass: beer 12FF; coffee 6FF;
snacks available; credit cards accepted

Le Café de la Place 234, rue d'Odessa Paris 14e, Montparnasse ☎ 01 42
18 01 55 Métro: Edgar Quinet (Map: 11 B6)

100% bistrot! Oil paintings, enamel plaques, wooden tables, chairs and floor: this
attractive establishment has managed to preserve the charm of old
Montparnasse. Playing up to the good-natured crowd, the jovial, apron-clad waiters distribute charcuterie platters and half bottles of wine. In the morning, the
sunny terrace is a good place to break for coffee and have a read of the paper.

Open: Mon-Sat 7.30am-2am, Sun 10am-10pm; By the glass: beer 22FF, champagne 40FF; coffee 14FF; meals & snacks available; 14th of July dance;
CB EC MC V

La Chopotte 168, rue d'Alésia, Paris 14e, Alésia ☎ 01 45 43 16 16 Métro:
Plaisance (Map: 14 E4)

The owner of the Chopotte is proud of his wine bar's typically 'Gallic' character. A
genuine working-class atmosphere and superb regional wines including Cahors,
Côtes de Blayes and Beaujolais are offered alongside tartines – duck scratchings
or rillettes on Poilâne bread – and, on Thursday nights, a range of plats du jour
with a South-Western influence (reservations advisable!).

Open: Tues-Fri 7am-8pm, Thurs 7am-10.30pm, Sat 8am-4pm; By the glass: beer
12FF, champagne 28FF; coffee 11FF; snacks & meals (lunch & Thurs night) available; cash only; €

Le Cristal 163, Ave de Suffren, Paris 15e, Sèvres-Lecourbe ☎ 01 47 34 47 92
Métro: Sèvres Lecourbe (Map: 11 E9)

Nestled between the seventh and 15th arrondissements, this unpretentious bar breathes a bit of life into a neighbourhood known for its chic quietness. Like any self-respecting beer joint, customers order at the bar and drink standing up or perched on bar stools. The evening happy hour and Thursday night DJ sets make Le Cristal a popular place, especially among young locals.

Open: Mon-Wed 9am-1am, Thurs & Fri 9am-2am, Sat 6pm-2am; By the glass: beer 11FF, champagne 35FF; coffee 6,50FF; meals available; DJ Thurs nights; credit cards accepted

L'entrepôt 7/9, rue Francis-de-Pressensé, Paris 14e, Alésia ☎ 01 45 40 60 70, Métro: Pernety (Map: 14 D4)

You don't just stumble upon the Entrepôt – this hangar-like place is one of the area's few hip bars. Also a restaurant, cinema and concert venue, this unique spot livens up the neighbourhood and boasts a staunchly loyal clientele. On sunny days, the garden is another argument for becoming one of the regulars.

Open: Sun-Fri 10am-2am, Sat 6pm-2am; By the glass: beer 14FF, champagne 50FF; coffee 9FF; meals available; web-bar; cinema, jazz, world music; CB EC MC V; €

Le Magique 42, rue de Gergovie, Paris 14e, Alésia ☎ 01 45 42 26 10 Métro: Pernety (Map: 14 D4)

No covers here: this place is totally committed to the idea of the singer as original artist. Twenty years ago, Martine and Marc Havet took over an old dive and turned it into the charmingly eccentric Magique. Madame serves supper and drinks, Monsieur does his one-man show. Quite a few other French singer-songwriters perform here too. Come to the cabaret!

Open: Wed-Sun 8pm-2am; By the glass: beer (bottle) 23FF, wine 16FF; snacks (supper) available; French songs nightly; cash only

Rosebud 11 Ibis, rue Delambre, Paris 14e, Montparnasse ☎ 01 43 35 38 54
Métro: Edgar Quinet, Vavin (Map: 14 B6)

Rosebud is one of the only places that still remembers the Montparnos, painters and writers who frequented Montparnasse during the neighbourhood's golden years (1918-1930). The setting is quiet (polished wood and aged leather) but elegant in a devilishly sexy way. The waiters are highly cultivated and will concoct you a cocktail to die for: champagne cocktail, whisky sour, bloody Mary ... The conversation continues, discreet, witty and seductive.

Open: daily 7pm-2am; By the glass: beer 33FF, champagne 58FF; coffee10FF; meals and snacks available; credit cards accepted

Zango 58, rue Daguerre, Paris 14e, Denfert Rochereau ☎ 01 43 20 21 59
Métro: Denfert Rochereau (Map: 14 D6)

This theme bistrot offers ethnic décor, exotic cocktails and fusion food, as well as the chance to meet other travellers, swap notes about faraway adventures and plan your next escapade. A small library in the back room has travel magazines, maps, a computer with free Internet access and, in a special corner, all the Lonely Planet guides.

Open: restaurant: daily noon-2pm, 7.30pm-11pm; bar: Mon-Thurs noon-1am, Fri & Sat noon-2am, Sun noon-5pm; By the glass: beer 15FF-18FF, champagne 35FF; coffee 6FF-10FF; meals and snacks (tapas) available; web-bar; exhibitions of photography and travelogues, occasional concerts; AE CB EC MC V; €

Map: 14 B6

Métro: Edgar Quinet,
Montparnasse Bienvenüe

Smoking throughout

Pavement tables

L'Opportun
French (Burgundy/Lyon)

☎ 01 43 20 26 89
62-4, blvd Edgar-Quinet,
Montparnasse

This 'beaujolais-therapy centre' at the foot of the Montparnasse tower has everything you could want from a good wine bar: a (rather small) counter where you can enjoy a good glass of beaujolais or Loire valley wine (they also have fancier bourgogne and bordeaux vintages), and marble-topped tables, where you can relish authentic bistrot cuisine influenced by the traditions of Burgundy and Lyon. The starters, such as œufs en meurette (poached eggs with a wine sauce) or poêlées de champignons (pan-fried mushrooms), are generous. The mains reflect what's good at the market – maybe foie de veau (calf's liver) or a thick, tender cut of pork or beef served with (you guessed it) potatoes. Try out the specialities too, such as rognons entiers grillés au sel (whole grilled and salted kidneys) or salade de peaux de canard (duck skin salad). All dishes are sure to please those who know their meat.

starter: 45FF-105FF
main: 75FF-175FF
dessert: 40FF-65FF
Plat du jour: 80FF-95FF

AE CB V

Open: Mon-Sat noon-4pm, 7pm-midnight; reservations advisable

Map: 14 G5

Métro: Alésia

Smoking throughout

La Régalade
French

☎ 01 45 45 68 58
49, ave Jean-Moulin,
Alésia

For the French, the name of this restaurant conjures up images of feasting, which is entirely appropriate. Having established a very solid reputation, the chef has decided to let everyone, not just the rich, appreciate his talent. The set menu, offering a choice of starters, mains and desserts for a fixed price, can include a remarkable crémeux de mascarpone au céleri rave et pied de veau truffé (mascarpone with celeriac and truffled calf's foot) or poêlée de calamars et son risotto à l'encre de seiche (pan-fried calamari and risotto with cuttlefish ink). In the sweets department, there is a delicate pralinette croquante au chocolat accompagné d'un sorbet lait menthe (crunchy chocolate praline with mint sorbet). Everything is good here. At midnight on a week night, the place is still full and turning people away. Proof that this bistrot knows how to give sturdy regional dishes a touch of class.

Set menu: 195FF

CB EC MC V

Open: Tues-Fri noon-2pm, Tues-Sat 7pm-midnight; reservations essential

15ᵉ Arrondissement

La Motte-Picquet

Commerce

Vaugirard

Convention

15^e Arrondissement

After World War II, entire battalions of steel-workers were drawn into the orbit of the fifteenth arrondissement, clocking on every morning at the Citroën factory or one of the neighbourhood's numerous aeronautical companies. Over the years, the area has become more gentrified and residential. Ave de la Motte-Picquet, blvd Pasteur and ave Félix-Faure are peaceful places – too peaceful for some. But for Unesco, the the area seemed just right. Not far away, the Republic's future officers and gentlemen converge on the majestic École militaire. But the fifteenth arrondissement offers much more than its bourgeois homes and institutions. Parisians flock to the shops and restaurants that line rue de la Convention, rue de Vaugirard, rue Saint-Charles and rue du Commerce. On the quays, the tours de Beau-grenelle have long since abandoned their monopoly on futurism to the stylish, functional buildings occupied by television stations Canal Plus and France Télévision. The abattoirs at the porte Brancion have been ousted by a book market in the square Georges-Brassens and Parisians with their heart in the country can enjoy the parc André-Citroën, one of the capital's most beautiful open spaces.

L'Antre amis
French

☎ 01 45 67 15 65
9, rue Bouchut,
École Militaire

Map: 15 D8
Métro: Sèvres Lecourbe,
  Ségur

 Smoking throughout

 Pavement tables

Stéphane Pion started his career in the hospitality industry at the age of 13. In spring 2000, he finally fulfilled his dream of owning his own restaurant. L'Antre amis is both chic and convivial, a kind of luxury bistrot where carefully designed décor creates a quiet, warm atmosphere – a bold venture in this maze of dead streets. But the well-heeled locals don't need an invitation to savour the stylish, creative cuisine. The raviolis de foie gras et champignons au jus de volaille à la sauge (foie gras ravioli and mushrooms with a roast poultry and sage sauce) is stunning. The chef brings an expert touch to both fish and meat, the filets de rouget à l'encre de seiche (fillets of mullet with cuttlefish ink) and the croustillant d'agneau aux épices thaïes (crispy lamb with Thai spices) are cooked to perfection. Don't forget to order the warm caramel soufflé, so you can finish the evening in style.

starter: 55FF
main: 95FF
dessert: 45FF
Set menu: 180FF
Plat du jour: 95FF

AE CB EC MC V; €

Open: Mon-Fri noon-2.30pm, 7.30pm-10.30pm; reservations advisable

Aux Artistes
French

☎ 01 43 22 05 39
63, rue Falguière,
Pasteur

Map: 15 E9
Métro: Pasteur

 Smoking throughout

Don't hesitate to try out this little bistrot, near the new Montparnasse-Vaugirard station, with red walls, frescoes on the ceiling, curious objects scattered all around and jostling tables. The atmosphere is congenial and the service informal. You are provided with pencil and paper to write down your order. The food is simple, with a broad range of starters such as œuf mayonnaise, pommes à l'huile (potatoes with olive oil) or the very good taboulé maison (home-made tabouli). The mains, including the bavette (skirt steak), steak haché (minced steak) and the entrecôte (rib steak), are served a number of different ways. You can also have a good old bœuf bourguignon or a delicious truite meunière (floured trout fried in butter). After a little dessert, a coffee, and a chat with the people from the next table on the way out, you may consider joining the crowd and making this pleasant restaurant a regular spot.

Set menu:
  lunch 58FF (2 courses);
  dinner 80FF (3 courses)

cash only

Open: Mon-Fri noon-2pm, Mon-Sat 7pm-12.30am; reservations not accepted

15ᵉ arrondi

Banani

Indian

☎ 01 48 28 73 92,
01 48 18 68 72
**148, rue de la Croix-Nivert,
Boucicaut**

Map: 15 E5

Métro: Félix Faure,
Boucicaut

Smoking throughout

A warm welcome, cosy atmosphere, stylish cuisine (the recipient of a *fourchette d'or* for Indian cuisine) and attentive service give this restaurant enormous appeal. Majestic panelling adorns the façade, while sumptuous, finely sculpted wooden divinities rule over the more discreet charms of the interior décor. Open the imposing door and let the staff take care of you. The menu is impressive and it's difficult to know what to choose. In addition to classic tandooris and biryanis, the chef offers regional specialities from Bengal and Kashmir to Goa. For starters, the mutton tikka, a generous roast kebab of lamb and herbs, is delightfully tender. The poisson à la coriandre (fish with coriander) is an equally delicious surprise. Big eaters won't be disappointed here as the set evening menu (served with delectable cheese naan) is a feast in itself. The exotic desserts include a scrumptious saffron cake or a 'glace populaire indienne' (scoops of vanilla ice cream with mango coulis).

starter: 36FF-65FF
main: 46FF-89FF
dessert: 36FF
Set menu: 59FF (lunch),
140FF (dinner)
AE CB DC EC JCB MC V

Open: Mon-Sat 12.30pm-2.30pm, 7pm-11pm, Sun 7.30pm-11pm; reservations advisable (essential towards end of week)

Le Beau Violet

French/Corsican

☎ 01 45 78 93 44
**92, rue des Entrepreneurs,
Commerce**

Map: 15 E5

Métro: Commerce

Entertainment: Occasional
Corsican singing

Smoking throughout

When it's a grilled sardine day at this fisherman's restaurant, they leave the door open so the smoke can get out. Everything is done in the one room: the owner is ensconced behind the bar, cooking and keeping an eye on the grill. There's no menu, the waiter will tell you what the three plats du jour are, or you can telephone ahead to find out. On the day of our visit, there was cassolette corse (a tasty mix of rice, shellfish and calamari). It's tempting, but only comes in double serves. The salade de broccio aux herbes du maquis (broccio salad with wild herbs) is a nice and refreshing starter. Broccio is a kind of fromage frais, also used in the œufs brouillés (scrambled eggs) and the fadione, a cake that tastes as good as it looks.

starter: 38FF
main: 78FF
dessert: 30FF
Plat du jour: 50FF (lunch)
CB V

Open: Mon-Sat noon-2.30pm, 8pm-11pm; reservations advisable

15e rrond

Le Bistrot d'André

French

☎ **01 45 57 89 14**
232, rue Saint-Charles, Balard

Map: 15 F3

Métro: Félix Faure

Nonsmoking tables available

Pavement tables

Le Bistrot d'André proves the point that you don't have to be in the middle of the Dordogne to enjoy a salade de gésiers confits (salad with preserved gizzards) or a confit de canard pommes sautées (confit of duck with sautéed potatoes). Paintings, photos and models of various Citroëns adorn the walls of this staunchly Parisian bistrot, not far from the famous automobile company's former factory site. The owner's friendliness and cuisine will keep you coming back for more. Simplicity, generosity, a genuinely warm atmosphere and great value for money – the Bistrot d'André is a great find.

Open: Mon-Sat noon-2.30pm, 7.45pm-10.30pm; reservations advisable (for more than 5 people)

starter: 18FF-58FF
main: 64FF-84FF
dessert: 26FF-36FF
Set menu: 65FF (weekday lunch)
Plat du jour: 74FF

MC V

Le Dandrelin

French

☎ **01 45 58 16 00**
83, rue Leblanc, Balard

Map: 15 F3

Métro: Balard

Smoking throughout

The Dandrelin is a bit like a secret room in a lovely, simple house, a place where you meet up with friends almost as a matter of course. The close-set tables and soft lighting make it easy to talk, and the owner clearly takes great pleasure in making customers feel at home. But the real secret of this small restaurant is in the kitchen. Meat lovers will be in seventh heaven with the highlight of the menu being Charolais beef, served with béarnaise sauce (also served in a generous cut for two). Equally delectable is the charlotte d'agneau aux aubergines à la menthe et à la coriandre (lamb charlotte with eggplant, mint and coriander). An unforgettable spot.

Open: Mon-Fri noon-2.30pm, Mon-Sat 7.30pm-10.30pm; reservations advisable (especially towards end of week)

starter: 40FF-48FF
main: 62FF-140FF
dessert: 25FF-30FF
Plat du jour: 68FF

CB MC V

La Datcha Lydie
Russian

☎ 01 45 66 67 77
**7, rue Dupleix,
La Motte-Picquet**

Map: 15 C6

Métro: Dupleix, La Motte Picquet Grenelle

Smoking throughout

You really have to hunt down this *datcha* (Russian country house). Set back slightly from the Motte Picquet, just behind the Village Suisse, it's not much to look at. The interior is spacious (perhaps too much so?), peaceful and plain. There's nothing to indicate (apart from a few discreet posters) that you're entering Russian gourmet territory. However, this restaurant has its aficionados, and you can see why when you taste the chef's delicious golubsi (stuffed cabbage leaves) or the buf Pojarski (meat balls with herbs), served with flavoured kacha (small buckwheat pancakes). The borsch and the vatrouchka (Russian cheesecake) are also first-rate. This unpretentious restaurant, run by Lydie and Daniel (the latter trained at Dominique, a famous Russian restaurant in Montparnasse), proves that you can enjoy Russian cuisine in Paris without spending a fortune.

starter: 30FF-90FF
main: 70FF-90FF
dessert: 30FF
Set menu: 80FF (lunch),
135FF (dinner)

AE CB V

Open: Thurs-Tues noon-2pm, 7pm-10pm; reservations advisable (evenings)

Dix Vins
French

☎ 01 43 20 91 77
**57, rue Falguiére,
Pasteur**

Map: 15 E9

Métro: Pasteur

Smoking throughout

This tiny restaurant, hidden away on the far side of Montparnasse, is a huge success. Even if you've booked, you may have to wait a while at the bar. However, this is not such a bad thing in a temple dedicated to Bacchus: you'll be able to sample one of the carefully chosen wines, which the owner will decant into a carafe. Then there's the appetising menu to contemplate on the wall, and the stylish interior. The set menu will bring you face to face with a merlan frit en colère sauce tartare ('angry' fried whiting with tartare sauce) – very agreeable despite its name – or a tempting boudin noir (black pudding), followed by an excellent canette rôtie sauce au poivre (roast duckling with pepper sauce) or an old-style blanquette de veau (veal stew in white sauce). A clementine salad or a pear with chocolate sauce brings the restorative feast to a close.

Set menu: 100FF

€

Open: Tues-Sat noon-2.30pm, Mon-Sat 8pm-11pm; reservations advisable

El Fares
Lebanese

☎ 01 47 83 54 38
**166, blvd de Grenelle,
Cambronne**

Map: 15 D7

Métro: Cambronne

 Smoking throughout

This restaurant was set up in the early 1990s by the inhabitants of a small Lebanese village situated between Saïda and Beirut. The décor is banal, but customers get a lovely taste of eastern cuisine. There are cheap set menus, although it might be more enjoyable to share an assortment of meze. The tabouli, mtabal (eggplant purée with cream of sesame and lemon) and labni (fresh cow's milk cream cheese) make delicious cold hors d'œuvre, while scrumptious felafels, chicken wings and cheese pastries are served warm. Big eaters will go for the chiche taouk (kebab of marinated chicken fillets) or the traditional kefta (mince-meat kebab with onions and parsley). Baklava or ousmalié provide the final eastern touch to a superb meal.

starter: 25FF-35FF
main: 53FF-85FF
dessert: 25FF-38FF
Set menu: 58FF, 65FF,
125FF

CB MC V

Open: daily noon-3pm, 7.30pm-11pm; reservations not accepted

La Gitane
French

☎ 01 47 34 62 92
**53 bis, ave de la Motte Picquet,
La Motte Picquet**

Map: 15 C6

Métro: La Motte Picquet
Grenelle

 Nonsmoking tables
available

 Pavement tables

Since François Mouchet took over the Gitane more than 15 years ago, this restaurant has established itself as an ideal spot to have lunch *en tête à tête* or to take business guests. Although not exceptional, everything here bears the mark of good taste and high quality. The freshness of the ingredients, whether they come from the provinces or the sea, makes for lovely eating. The carpaccio de saumon frais à l'aneth (carpaccio of fresh salmon with dill) and the terrine de Saint-Jacques à la sauce ai-grelette (scallop terrine with a vinegary sauce) are nice starters. In winter, lovers of rich food will enjoy the cassoulet avec ses haricots tarbais (cassoulet with Tarbes beans), while the poêlée de rognons d'agneaux à la fleur de thym (pan-fried lambs' kidneys with thyme blossom) and the magret de canard au citron (fillet of duck breast with lemon) are among the deli-cious mains available all year round.

starter: 30FF-95FF
main: 65FF-110FF
dessert: 35FF-50FF
Plat du jour: 70FF-80FF

AE CB MC V

Open: Mon-Sat noon-2.30pm, 7pm-11pm; reservations advisable (especially lunch)

15ᵉ arrondi

Je Thé... me
French

☎ 01 48 42 48 30
4, rue d'Alleray, Vaugirard

Map: 15 F7
Métro: Vaugirard

Smoking throughout

Je Thé... me was once a late 19th century delicatessen, and the décor has been tastefully maintained. Now it's a secret alcove for lovers of fine food, hidden away in red velvet like a jewel. The shelves are backed with the original mercury mirrors, and stacked with liqueurs, teapots and coffee grinders – a reminder that this place has been dedicated to gastronomic pleasure for over a century. The tradition continues with an open fire and stylish cooking made from the best fresh market produce. You can't order à la carte, but you can choose poêlée d'écrevisses (pan-fried prawns) or saumon rôti aux herbes (roasted salmon with herbs) – among other dishes – from the set menu on the blackboard. The owner is so generous and the cuisine so assured, you'll be happy to let them surprise you with a dessert.

Set menu: 180FF

AE V

Open: Tues-Sat noon-2pm, 7.30pm-midnight; reservations advisable (towards the end of the week)

Kim Anh
Vietnamese

☎ 01 45 79 40 96
49, ave Émile Zola, Émile Zola

Map: 15 D4
Métro: Charles Michels

Smoking throughout

If there's such a thing as gourmet Vietnamese cuisine, this is it. Forget about kitsch and canteen-style eating, Kim Anh greets its customers (often regulars) with wall tapestries, white tablecloths and fresh flowers. The émincé de bœuf à la citronnelle (thinly sliced beef with lemongrass) is a skilful combination of flavours and the éventail de brochettes au bœuf, poulet et porc (assortment of beef, chicken and pork satays) offers a variety of tastes. Your mouth won't stop watering with the arrival of the caramelised langoustine or the crabe farci au four (oven-cooked stuffed crab). Crème de maïs (cream of corn) or ananas flambé (pineapple flambé) round off a first-class meal. The freshness of the food, elaborate presentation and quality of service make eating here a pleasure. Kim Anh maintains its high standards by opening at night-time only.

starter: 60FF-90FF
main: 100FF-150FF
dessert: 40FF-60FF
Set menu: 220FF

AE CB EC MC V

Open: daily 7.30pm-11.15pm; reservations advisable

Fusion cuisine

With globalisation upon us, appetites have become nomads and tourists, eager for bold new combinations of flavours. Sautéed squid with ginger. Sushi and salsa. Roast beef marinated in sake. Pasta with snails. Pot au feu with Asian vegetables. Fusion food first emerged from the melting-pot of the United States in the 1970s, casting off and setting sail for ethnic cuisines all over the globe. Japanese chefs trained in France and running the kitchens of top restaurants in New York, Tokyo and Paris began flirting with various mélanges. Then, in 1981, Austrian Wolfgang Puck, having already brought together chefs from faraway cultures, brought together a stunning array of ingredients. From Asia, the Far East and South America, ginger, sake, coriander, curry, lemongrass, chilli and miso turned culinary standards on their head in Puck's famous Californian restaurants.

This culinary intermixing has transformed menus – which now feature tortillas alongside raw fish – and the food on customers' plates. The contemporary concern with healthy eating has led chefs to make abundant use of Asian produce, which is low in animal fat. While creativity is encouraged, experts say that successful combinations must respect the texture and bring out the full flavour of each ingredient. This has always been the guiding principle of French gastronomy. In Paris itself, exemplary intermarriages are to be found at Sud, where South-West France and Latin America have given birth to an extraordinary foie gras with sweet potatoes, and at Fusion, where the fillet of duck breast with plum sauce and beautiful baby vegetables embodies the new Chinese cuisine.

Fusion cuisine might be hip, but is it revolutionary? Every culinary tradition has incorporated outside influences, and gastronomy has always seemed to be both a conservatory of tradition and a privileged site of cultural exchange. The emblematic dish of South-West France, cassoulet, is based on beans that originally come from the American contintent. As for *salé-sucré*, rebaptised 'sweet and sour' and often considered to be an Asian influence, how many people know that it was a feature of Roman cuisine, itself highly cosmopolitan?

Map: 15 D5
Métro: Charles Michels
Entertainment: Indian video clips from 9.30pm

Smoking throughout

starter: 39FF-120FF
dessert: 29FF-39FF
Set menu: 59FF (weekday lunch), 79FF (weekday lunch), 129FF,
CB EC MC V

Lal Quila
Indian

☎ 01 45 75 6
88, ave Émile
Comm

As soon as you're past the red, fortress-like façade, you're projected onto the big scree Indian gastronomy. A huge model of the Taj Mahal, a stucco colonnade and multicoloure mirrors make this restaurant feel like a Bon cinema studio. Kitsch and chic maybe, but certainly not trashy. While the main roles ar played by classics such as fish curry or chic biryani, there are also guest appearances fr dishes such as chicken shami kebab, not w known in France but extremely popular in nc ern India. The special audience prize goes t the shahi korma lamb, served with cream of cashew flavoured with cardamom and cinna mon. You'll realise when you taste this dish that the real stars at Lal Quila are on your plate.

Open: daily noon-2.30pm, 7.30pm-11.30pm; reservatio advisable

---

Map: 15 G8
Métro: Convention, Plaisance

Nonsmoking tables available

Set menu: 158FF
CB MC V

L'Oie cendrée
French (South-West)

☎ 01 45 31 9
51, rue Labrou
Conven

The room is simple yet elegant, with original exposed rafters and curtains, tablecloths an plates in matching colours with English flora patterns – all softly lit by little cut-glass lam The chef prepares generous serves of salad de gésiers (gizzard salad) with bilberry jam c brouillade d'œufs aux champignons (scramb eggs with mushrooms). Mains include rogno de veau à la crème d'ail (kidneys with garlic cream) and foie gras de canard landais mi-c au monbazillac (semi-cooked duck foie gras with sweet montbazillac wine). Seasoned wi subtle blends of herbs and spices, the duck the South-West yield magret à la graine de moutarde (duck breast with mustard seeds) confit á la purée d'oseille (duck confit with sorrel purée) and cassoulet. The delicious ta paysanne aux mirabelles (plum tart) brings t meal to a harmonious close.

Open: Mon-Fri noon-2pm, Mon-Sat 7.30pm-10pm; reser tions advisable

Le Quinson
French

☎ **01 45 32 48 54**
5, place Étienne Pernet,
Commerce

Map: 15 E5
Métro: Félix Faure,
  Commerce

 Nonsmoking tables
available

This Parisian institution was established in 1945 by Monsieur Quinson (from the Var) and has been attracting lovers of bouillabaisse with its own recipe of the renowned dish ever since. The new chef, who trained chez Jacques Cagna at the Maison du Danemark, has increased the variety of fish on the menu. Everything here is fresh and prepared on the premises. The slightly old-fashioned seaside ambience is livened up by the faultless service of a friendly young woman. The friture d'éperlans (deep-fried smelt) with tartare sauce or the langoustine ravioli are simple and light starters that leave plenty of room for the famous bouillabaisse. We recommend the version with rockfish fillets, which is easier to eat. The Cassis white is a particularly fine vintage – dry, well balanced and fruity – and complements the bouillabaisse perfectly.

starter: 35FF-55FF
main: 85FF-169FF
dessert: 32FF-38FF
Set menu: 70FF (children, 2
  courses + drink),
  108FF (lunch)
Plat du jour: 81FF

CB EC MC V; €

Open: Tues-Sat noon-2.30pm, 7pm-10.30pm; reservations advisable

---

Restaurant de la Tour
French

☎ **01 43 06 04 24**
6, rue Desaix,
La Motte Picquet

Map: 15 B6

Métro: Dupleix

 Smoking throughout

 Pavement tables

This prestigious restaurant has just changed hands. The new chef learnt his trade chez Jacques Cagna and at luxury hotels in England. The welcome is friendly and the warm tones and soft lighting of the southern-style décor have softened the dining room. A glance at the lavish menu will put old regulars at ease. This is seasonal cuisine with a touch of creativity. Try foie gras chaud de canard et son pain d'épices (warm duck foie gras with gingerbread), mesclun aux herbes et jus de truffes (mixed green salad with herbs and truffle sauce) or the saumon sur tagliatelles de concombres (salmon with cucumber tagliatelle). Even more extravagant is the pavé de chevreuil sauce aux airelles et poire au vin (thick-cut venison steak with bilberry sauce and pears stewed in wine) or filet de bœuf à la moelle crème au raifort (fillet of beef with bone marrow and cream of horseradish sauce). The desserts and wines are in keeping with this sumptuous menu.

starter: 50FF-140FF
main: 95FF-145FF
dessert: 55FF
Set menu: 135FF, 168FF
  (lunch), 198FF (dinner)

AE CB EC MC V

Open: Tues-Sat noon-2.30pm, 7pm-10.30pm; reservations advisable

Map: 15 D4

Métro: Charles Michels

Nonsmoking tables available

starter: 36FF-48FF
dessert: 22FF-25FF
Set menu: 79FF (lunch),
125FF, 155FF, 165FF
AE CB EC MC V

Sawadee
Thai

☎ 01 45 77 68 90
**53, ave Émile-Zola,
Beaugrenelle**

For 20 years this well-known restaurant, a short walk from the banks of the Seine, has been bidding *sawadee* (welcome) to lovers of Thai food. Don't be put off by the décor, which is rather cold and impersonal – the sophisticated cuisine more than makes up for it. Whether you order à la carte or choose one of the special gastronomic menus, you'll be able to enjoy the classic dishes of the ancient kingdom of Siam, such as prawn or chicken soup flavoured with lemongrass; spicy beef salad (a real treat); satay sticks (chicken, beef, lamb and pork) with peanut sauce; or fish dishes with coconut milk. There may not be many surprises, but this delicious traditional fare, rich in flavours and scents, evokes another world.

Open: Mon-Sat noon-2.30pm, 7pm-10.30pm; reservations advisable

Le Tire-Bouchon
French

☎ 01 40 59 09 27
62, rue des Entrepreneurs, Émile Zola

Map: 15 D5

Métro: Charles Michels

 Smoking throughout

Located in a busy street without charm, the Tire-Bouchon isn't much to look at. But ignore the surroundings, open the door and take a quick glance at the menu – you'll soon realise that this small restaurant, with its quiet, elegant atmosphere, has taken up the bold challenge of providing customers with haute cuisine for under 200FF. The service is discreet and refined, but it's the subtle, meticulously prepared food that wins our vote. From the starters to the perfectly matured cheeses and the desserts, the standard never drops. Gourmets will savour the delicious duo de foie gras et daïkon à la vinaigrette de figues (foie gras and daikon with a fig vinaigrette) and, for dessert, the fondant au chocolat with poached figs. A truly great restaurant with affordable prices.

starter: 45FF-90FF
main: 70FF-105FF
dessert: 35FF-45FF
Set menu: 115FF, 185FF
 (degustation)

CB EC MC V

Open: Mon-Fri noon-2pm, Mon-Sat 7.45pm-10pm; reservations advisable (weekends)

Le Triporteur
French

☎ 01 45 32 82 40
4, rue de Dantzig, Vaugirard

Map: 15 G7

Métro: Convention

 Smoking throughout

This restaurant is haunted by Fernandel, the 1930s comedian from Marseilles. There are numerous allusions to his films, including the tricycle (triporteur) at the restaurant's entrance. You may feel Fernandel watching you as you choose from the painting that serves as a menu. The food, however, has nothing nostalgic or stodgy about it: the croustillant d'andouille (smoked pork sausage) is a good old regional dish, but the aile de raie à la crème de vermouth (skate's fin with cream and vermouth sauce) should awaken your curiosity. The tajine d'agneau (lamb tajine) brings a touch of sunshine to the menu. If you're ready to throw caution to the wind, grab the rare chance to enjoy the marvellous tartare de canard au pistou et aux pignons de pin (duck tartare with pesto and pine nuts). Everything is beautifully presented, in the nouvelle cuisine style, and the service is friendly.

starter: 42FF-52FF
main: 82FF-110FF
dessert: 40FF

CB MC V

Open: Mon-Fri noon-2pm, 8pm-11pm; reservations essential

Map: 15 D7
Métro: Sèvres Lecourbe

Smoking throughout

Pavement tables

Le Troquet
French

☎ 01 45 66 89 00
21, rue François Bonvin,
Sèvres Lecourbe

A restaurant that changes its menu every day according to what's on offer at the market is rare enough to warrant a special mention. Indeed, the Troquet is already well known in the area, so it's best to book both for lunch and dinner if you want to savour the delectable food, lovingly prepared and served by the owners with lilting southern accents. It would be a shame to miss the fondant du risotto aux courgettes (risotto with zucchini), the aiguillettes de canard poêlées (pan-fried aiguillettes of duck), the finesse of the carrelet cuit à l'étouffée de basquaise relevée au piment d'espelette (plaice steamed Basque-style and seasoned with Espelette chilli) or the sweetness of the compote de pommes reinettes (stewed reinette apples) served with home-made coffee ice cream. If you *do* miss out, there's always the excitement of discovering the following day's menu. The décor is nothing special, but top-flight service brightens things up.

Set menu: 140FF (lunch, 3 courses), 155FF (4 courses), 170FF (dinner, 4 courses), 185FF (5 courses)

CB EC MC V

Open: Tues-Sat noon-2.15pm, 7pm-11pm; reservations essential for dinner, advisable for lunch

---

Map: 15 C5
Métro: Dupleix

Smoking throughout

Le Volant
French

☎ 01 45 75 27 67
13, rue Beatrix-Dussane,
La Motte Picquet

Le Volant ('The Steering Wheel') isn't just a restaurant, it's also a place of worship. The walls are covered with autographed photos of champion Formula One and rally drivers. Get behind the wheel yourself, and start the race with a fricassée de champignons (mushroom fricassée), a terrine de queue de bœuf (oxtail terrine) or poireaux vinaigrette (leeks with vinaigrette). Then you're in for some controlled skidding with the classic but enjoyable bœuf bourguignon and brandade de morue (creamed salt cod), or the delicious côtes d'agneau (lamb chops) with potato cakes. On the home straight, veer towards the mousse au chocolat or crème brûlée. By the time you cross the finishing line you'll have filled up with tasty, unpretentious French food, in an unusual and welcoming restaurant with all the buzz of a trackside stand.

starter: 40FF-58FF
main: 78FF-110FF
dessert: 38FF-48FF
Set menu: 138FF

AE CB V

Open: Mon-Fri noon-2.15pm, Mon-Sat 7.45pm-11pm; reservations essential

15ᵉ arrondi

16ᵉ Arrondissement

Étoile

Trocadéro

Passy

Porte de Saint-Cloud

16e Arrondissement

Squeezed in between the bois de Boulogne and the town hall, this arrondissement – the capital's biggest – attracts sarcastic remarks because of its peaceful, civilised appearance. Auteil, Passy and Victor-Hugo are in fact among the city's most highly rated neighbourhoods. The wide avenues radiating out from the place du Trocadéro are lined with sober, elegant buildings from the Haussmann era. Luxury boutiques abound, frequented by posh customers who desert the area come nightfall. It's here, on the banks of the Seine, that the architectural curiosity known as the 'Maison ronde' (Maison de la Radio) was constructed. Just below, nestling in a bosky bower, the maison de Balzac keeps alive the memory of the illustrious author of *Le Père Goriot*. Further north, the ultra-bourgeois ave Foch thumbs its nose at the restless ave de la Grande-Armée, teeming with motorbike fanatics. The sixteenth arrondissement also hosts football pow wows at the Parc des Princes and, as summer approaches, the thud of tennis balls on asphalt can be heard at Roland-Garros. There are some fabulous cultural institutions, including the Musée d'Art Moderne, the Musée de la Marine, the Musée de l'Homme and the beautiful Musée Guimet (devoted to Asian art).

Le Bistrot des Vignes

French

☎ **01 45 27 76 64**
1, rue Jean Bologne,
Passy

Map: 16 F5

Métro: La Muette, RER:
  Boulainvilliers

 Nonsmoking tables
available

Some dishes seem to have the knack for tantalising those tastebuds, and ravioles de canard et de foie gras aux figues, sauce au Madiran (duck and foie gras ravioli with figs and a Madiran sauce) is surely one of them. Le Bistrot des Vignes may be a smooth talker, but while it knows how to seduce gourmets, this small, quiet restaurant is also true to its word. Whether you choose the piquillos du Pays basque farcis à la brandade de morue (Basque piquillos stuffed with cod brandade) or the cassolette de champignons sauvages et d'escargots à la bourguignonne (cassolette of wild mushrooms and snails à la bourguignonne), you won't be let down. Elegantly presented desserts add a refined touch to this concert of flavours. You'll be back in no time for another helping, especially as Le Bistrot des Vignes updates its simple, inspired menu every month.

starter: 45FF-75FF
main: 95FF-120FF
dessert: 45FF
Set menu: 95FF
  (2 courses), 135FF
  (3 courses)
Plat du jour: 95FF

AE CB EC MC V

Open: daily noon-2.30pm, 7pm-10.30pm; reservations not accepted

La Cantine russe

Russian

☎ **01 47 20 65 17**
26, ave de New York,
Alma Marceau

Map: 16 D7

Métro: Alma Marceau

Entertainment: Private
  bookings with Russian
  and Gypsy musicians

 Smoking throughout

The Conservatoire Rachmaninov was founded in 1923. The statutes of this venerable institution guaranteed the students' sustenance and hence the right to a canteen. In the early days, there was a whole community of White Russians living in Paris, and princes turned taxi drivers or musicians would get together here over a glass of vodka. Ah, the Slavonic soul ... Today, the canteen still exists, taken over two years ago by a father-son team of Russian origin. You can savour tarama or herrings served with blinis, eggplant caviar, pojarski (poultry meatballs with dill), beef stroganov, chachliks (marinated lamb kebabs) and, to finish, vatrouchka (cream-cheese cake) or kissel (fruit jelly). Everything is delicious here, and the atmosphere is utterly charming.

starter: 40FF-65FF
main: 60FF-80FF
dessert: 30FF-40FF
Set menu: 110FF
Plat du jour: 45FF

CB EC MC V

Open: Mon-Sat noon-2pm, 8pm-10pm; reservations advisable

16ᵉ ARRONDISSEMENT

Map: 16 C7

Métro: Charles de Gaulle-Étoile, Kléber

Smoking throughout

Pavement tables

starter: 18FF-89FF
main: 68FF-192FF
dessert: 28FF-48FF
Set menu: 89FF (lunch),
110FF (tapas menu)
Plat du jour: 89FF

AE CB EC MC V

Casa Tina

Spanish

☎ 01 40 67 19 24
18, rue Lauriston, Étoile

What do you do if you feel like something Spanish but you happen to be in the vicinity of the Arc de Triomphe? Try out Casa Tina, a friendly place that looks exactly like a Madrid tapas bar. Gypsy music, walls covered with bullfighting posters and authentic azulejos (blue tiles), bright red bench seats and a big wooden bar with hams, bunches of garlic and peppers hanging over it ... The party atmosphere is contagious. The food is not exceptional, but you certainly won't go hungry. You can munch on a variety of tapas (fried calamari, grilled sardines, marinated vegetables and serrano ham), and wash it all down with a glass of sangria. Hearty eaters can choose a Valencia-style paella or gambas à la plancha (grilled king prawns) and finish with marinated dates and figs.

Open: daily noon-2.30pm, 7pm-11.30pm; reservations advisable

Map: 16 K3

Métro: Porte de St-Cloud

Smoking throughout

starter: 25FF
main: 60FF-65FF
dessert: 25FF
Plat du jour: 60FF-65FF

cash only

Les Caves angevines

French

☎ 01 42 88 88 93
2, place Léon-Beutel, Porte de St-Cloud

A short distance from Place de la Porte de St-Cloud, Les Caves angevines has long enjoyed a great reputation and incarnates the small neighbourhood bistrot that the French love so much. A real find in an area like this ... The atmosphere is casual and unfussy, and customers sit on small rustic stools while savouring charcuterie and cheeses brought back from the Auvergne by the owner himself, a native of the Cantal area. The meat dishes (rib of beef, skirt and rib steaks), andouillette from Guéméné and daily specials – all served with potatoes sautéed in garlic – will satisfy the most voracious of appetites. The chef's desserts – tarte, crème caramel, mousse au chocolat – are the perfect conclusion to a simple meal, which you can wash down with a nice drop of bourgueil or a *vin de pays* from the South-West.

Open: Mon-Wed & Fri 8am-8pm, Thurs 8am-11pm; reservations advisable

La Chaumière de Chine
Chinese

☎ 01 47 20 85 56

26, ave Pierre
1er de Serbie,
Étoile

Map: 16 D8

Métro: Alma Marceau

 Smoking throughout

You'd have to be crazy to travel from one end of Paris to the other for such a conventional Chinese restaurant, at least that's what we thought at first ... La Chaumière de Chine is packed with Chinese customers who come here to savour the same specialities as back home. The crabes mous en friture (soft crab fritters) are a particular favourite, not only because they're so delicious but also because this rare crustacean is only fished in the waters of Vietnam and Madagascar. Other offerings include canard farci (stuffed duck), abalones, fermented tofu and a whole range of typical dishes not listed on the menu but available upon request. There's also grilled wo tip (large dumplings), salade citronnée aux trois fruits de mer (lemon-flavoured salad with three varieties of seafood) or fish and meat served on hot iron platters. The Chinese embassy next door has annexed the restaurant!

Open: Mon-Sat noon-2pm, 8pm-10.30pm; reservations advisable

starter: 38FF-105FF
main: 55FF-480FF
dessert: 31FF-90FF
Set menu: 69FF (lunch),
  85FF, 99FF (dinner)

AE CB EC MC V

Chez Géraud
French

☎ 01 45 20 33 00

31, rue Vital,
Passy

Map: 16 E5

Métro: La Muette

Nonsmoking tables available

Géraud Rongier was once chef at La Cloche des Halles. Now he caters to a rather distinguished clientele in this somewhat straight-laced dining room, brightened up by a profusion of Longwy china. The delicious saucisson chaud (hot sausage), the œufs brouillés aux truffes (scrambled eggs with truffles) and the jeunes poireaux aux copeaux de foie gras (young leeks with shavings of foie gras) prove that the chef knows how to choose his produce. The côtelettes de marcassin (wild boar cutlets) and the foie de veau de lait poêlée (pan-fried calf's liver) are wonderfully tender. Savour them with wine bottled on the premises. For dessert, a good solid Paris-Brest au café will round off the feast. If you order à la carte the bill is a bit steep, but the quality of the food and service put this place firmly on the list of the neighbourhood's best restaurants.

Open: daily 12.30pm-2.30pm, Mon-Fri 7.30pm-10.30pm; reservations advisable

starter: 50FF-170FF
main: 150FF-200FF
dessert: 50FF
Set menu: 160FF

AE CB V

Map: 16 D6

Métro: Rue de la Pompe,
Victor Hugo

Smoking throughout

Pavement tables

starter: 28FF-35FF
main: 70FF-75FF
dessert: 25FF-30FF
Set menu: 85FF, 99FF
(lunch), 120FF (dinner)
Plat du jour: 72FF (lunch),
75FF (dinner)

AE CB MC V

Le 'G.R.5'
French (Savoie)

☎ 01 47 27 09 84
19, rue Gustave Courbet,
Victor Hugo

You barely notice this small, timeless neighbourhood bistrot with its mountain chalet ambience. Just as well for regulars and other customers, because it's always full. Old wooden skis and 1920s posters promoting the pleasures of hiking ('G.R.5' stands for Grande Randonnée 5 – Hiking Trail 5) and of Chamonix-Mont-Blanc set the tone. The owner-chef comes from Savoie, hence the abundance of regional specialities such as charcuterie, raclettes, tartiflettes (gratins of potato and cheese), fondues and local wines. Other dishes such as salade landaise au magret fumé (Landes-style salad with smoked fillet of duck breast), mozzarella aux figues fraîches marinée à l'huile d'olive (mozzarella marinated in olive oil and served with fresh figs) and brochette de gigot (lamb kebab) are simple, delicious and, along with the chef's tarts, contribute to this restaurant's popularity.

Open: daily noon-3pm, 7pm-11pm; reservations advisable

Map: 16 D6

Métro: Rue de la Pompe,
Trocadéro

Smoking throughout

Pavement tables

starter: 45FF-95FF
main: 60FF-115FF
dessert: 35FF-45FF
Plat du jour: 85FF

CB EC MC V

Le Paris Seize
Italian

☎ 01 47 04 56 33
18, rue des Belles-Feuilles,
Trocadéro

In this pleasant little Franco-Italian restaurant near Place de Mexico, the regulars probably don't even notice the appealing 1930s décor any more. Against a background of dark wood panelling, frescoes and painted mirrors depict sportsmen in full flight. Customers keep coming back for more of the simple and reliably tasty dishes, which include marvellous antipasti, homemade ravioli and gnocchi, San Daniele ham, escalopes de veau (crumbed Valdostène veal with melted mozzarella and Parma ham – a pure delight), spaghetti, penne and other kinds of pasta, all cooked to perfection. In short, good family trattoria cuisine, which makes the most of fresh produce. The service and regularly revised list of Italian wines both deserve an honourable mention.

Open: Mon-Sat noon-2.30pm, 8pm-10.30pm; reservations advisable

Le Scheffer
French

☎ **01 47 27 81 11**
22, rue Scheffer, Trocadéro

Map: 16 E6

Métro: Trocadéro

  Smoking throughout

In the heart of the chic 16th arrondissement, just near the Trocadéro, this classic restaurant has the plain, simple appearance of an old-style brasserie with the authentic décor and warm welcome that will never go out of fashion. Superlative cuisine is served without gimmicks. There is no set menu, just the best of French home cooking, including harengs pommes à l'huile (herrings with oil and potatoes), salads, grilled andouillette, the chef's confit de canard (confit of duck), magret de canard au poivre rose (fillet of duck breast with pink pepper), rognon de veau à la moutarde (veal kidneys with mustard), salmon tartare ... Everything is faultless, from the desserts (classic fondant au chocolat or crème caramel) to the wine list (which offers great vintages at moderate prices).

starter: 35FF-72FF
main: 75FF-98FF
dessert: 28FF-42FF
Plat du jour: 88FF

AE CB V

Open: Mon-Sat noon-2.30pm, 7.30pm-10.30pm; reservations advisable

---

Tampopo
Japanese

☎ **01 47 27 74 52**
66, rue Lauriston, Victor-Hugo

Map: 16 C7

Métro: Victor Hugo, Boissière

 Nonsmoking tables available

Soft lighting and subdued pale wood décor welcome customers to this oasis of Japanese serenity. The atmosphere is quiet despite the restaurant's small size – it seems nobody dares raise their voice. The set lunch menus, served with miso soup, a bowl of rice and fresh fruit salad, satisfy the most voracious of appetites. You can choose between tempura (vegetable and king prawn fritters in delicate, crispy batter) served in a wicker basket, or classic sashimi (raw fish). Just the presentation of this last dish will make your mouth water. At dinner, an extended menu includes Japanese fondues, meat and fish grills, and assorted sushi and sashimi presented on a boat. Lovers of Japanese culture will want to reserve one of the three traditional tables, where you sit down to eat only after taking off your shoes.

starter: 30FF-75FF
main: 80FF-210FF
dessert: 35FF-40FF
Set menu: 90FF, 95FF, 120FF (lunch), 145FF (lunch & dinner)
Plat du jour: 90FF-110FF

CB MC V

Open: Mon-Fri noon-2.30pm, Mon-Sat 7pm-10.30pm; reservations advisable

Map: 16 C8
Métro: Boissière
Dress code applies

Smoking throughout

Terrace & balcony
tables

La Terrasse
French/German

☎ 01 47 20 51 51
**30, rue Galilée,
Étoile**

Don't know what it means to indulge yourself?
Then head straight for La Terrasse. This bright,
airy restaurant is on the top floor of an opulent
building occupied by the Maison de la Sarre
(House of Saarland). Customers are treated to
sublime, panoramic views of the capital (Arc de
Triomphe, Eiffel Tower, Sacré Cœur, depending
on the table) and Franco-German specialities,
while soft music plays in the background. For
starters, go for the terrine de chevreuil (venison
terrine) or the fresh, beautifully presented
salade de Saint-Jacques aux aubergines (salad
with scallops and eggplant). For mains, the
bourride de lotte à la provençale (fillet of monkfish with creamed langoustines and a mouthwatering assortment of seafood) will win you over
immediately. The flavours are somehow just
right and surprising at the same time. For
dessert, big eaters will have no trouble polishing off the framboises poêlées à la glace
vanille (pan-fried raspberries with vanilla ice
cream). Expect friendly, unfussy service.

starter: 52FF-80FF
main: 82FF-180FF
dessert: 45FF-58FF
Plat du jour: 150FF

AE CB MC V

Open: Mon-Fri 9am-3.30pm, Tues-Sat 6.30pm-midnight;
reservations advisable (evenings & towards end of week)

Map: 16 D6
Métro: Trocadéro

Nonsmoking tables
available

Terrace tables

Le Totem
French

☎ 01 47 27 28 29
**17, place du Trocadéro,
Trocadéro**

Many born-and-bred Parisians would be surprised to learn that the Palais de Chaillot contains a restaurant. The first thing that strikes
you is the 15m-high ceiling, then you notice
how the imported timber gives the room
warmth. The solid menu of family-style dishes
should satisfy all palates. The chef is not one
to go in for experiments, and offers tried and
tested combinations such as carpaccio de
tomates au basilic (tomato carpaccio with basil)
or croustillant de foie gras aux figues (figs) for
starters and dorade créole et ses bananes
plantain (red sea bream) as a main. Enjoy
feuilletine au chocolat, coulis de chocolat as a
dessert. It's not so much the cuisine you'll
remember as the fabulous view from the Trocadéro. Given the volume of tourist traffic in the
area, this place is best avoided on weekends.

starter: 55FF-105FF
main: 95FF-145FF
dessert: 45FF-55FF
Set menu: 134FF (lunch)
Plat du jour: 120FF

AE CB D MC V

Open: restaurant: daily noon-2.30pm, 7.30pm-11.30pm; bar
& salon de thé noon-2am; reservations advisable in winter,
not accepted in summer

17ᵉ Arrondissement

Porte Maillot

Place des Ternes

Square des Batignolles

Monceau

17^e Arrondissement

The seventeenth arrondissement suffers from acute schizophrenia. Its southern neighbourhoods – with their beautiful, Haussmann-era buildings – seem like an extension of the eighth and sixteenth arrondissements, while its northern neighbourhoods assert their working-class, anarchistic identity. The wide avenues de Wagram, des Ternes and de Villiers have both a residential and commercial vocation and boast some of the capital's most famous shops and restaurants. The pedestrian rue de Lévis has its larger-than-life market. This part of the seventeenth arrondissement is dotted with elegant squares (cars have strict right of way!), such as the lush place du Général-Catroux, the place des Ternes with its flower stalls and the quieter place Wagram. Two of the capital's most emblematic squares butt up against the neighbourhood's western edge: place de la Porte-Maillot, dominated by the imposing palais des Congrès, and place de l'Étoile. Head north though, and you'll discover another country. Squashed up against this invisible border, the église Sainte-Marie des Batignolles and adjacent square are one of those magic spots that only exist in Paris. A maze of small streets with a pronounced working-class character stretches out around the avenue de Clichy, a pocket of old Paris that has survived without becoming ossified.

Au Petit Paris
Croatian

☎ 01 46 22 62 42
**32, rue Rennequin,
Place des Ternes**

Map: 17 G4

Métro: Ternes, Péreire

  Smoking throughout

For all (ex-)Yugoslavs, Paris is a mythological city. But Tony, the Dalmatian (Croatian) owner, has a personal vision of the capital which is endearing and rather tasty. His petit Paris is rustic and family-oriented, with wedding photos proudly on view. Meat dishes are cooked on a griddle in the middle of the room. Veal, beef and pork are prepared as meatballs, kebabs or fillets, and are served with sautéed potatoes and cabbage. This is heaven for meat lovers, although fish – a Dalmatian specialty – also gets a look in. Savour the cevapcici (skinless beef sausages) or the delectable pljeskavica (minced beef, lamb and veal with onion), along with one of the Croatian wines, which improve on acquaintance. After your meal, with a bit of luck, you may even get to chat to the larger-than-life cook, who's seemingly straight out of a madcap Kusturica comedy.

Open: Mon-Fri noon-2.30pm, 7.30pm-10.30pm, Sat 7.30pm-11.30pm; reservations advisable

starter: 35FF-60FF
main: 69FF-120FF
dessert: 25FF-35FF
Set menu: 59FF (lunch)

CB V

Bistro des Dames
French

☎ 01 45 22 13 42
**18, rue des Dames,
Place de Clichy**

Map: 17 F9

Métro: Place de Clichy

 Smoking throughout

 Terrace & courtyard tables

Why complicate matters? The Bistro des Dames will appeal to lovers of simple, authentic pleasures. The dining room, which looks out onto the street, is lovely, but during those humid Parisian summers it's the coolness and tranquillity of the small back garden that pulls in the customers. The terrace offers a great alternative on rainy days. An unembellished but faultless menu includes hearty salads, tortillas (Spanish omelettes with potatoes) and daily specials. The charcuterie platters deserve a special mention, in particular the gorgeous pâté de campagne, the authentic Guéméné andouille sausage and the paper-thin Serrano ham. The wine list does justice to this lovely fare. Simplicity has a lot going for it. Everything, in fact.

Open: Mon-Sat noon-3pm, 6.30pm-2am, Sun noon-2am; reservations not accepted

starter: 38FF-45FF
main: 40FF-78FF
dessert: 30FF-32FF
Plat du jour: 58FF

CB

Le Bistrot de Théo
French (South-West)

☎ 01 43 87 08 08
**90, rue des Dames,
Square des Batignolles**

Map: 17 F8
Métro: Rome, Villiers

Nonsmoking tables available

In the evening, rue des Dames is deserted apart from the nearby Théâtre Hébertot and this stylish, softly-lit bistrot. Enjoy a complimentary appetiser and an aperitif of Champagne-style soup while you drool over the description of dishes that have a distinct south-western influence. Delectable foie gras – the chef's specialty – served cold or warm exemplifies an authentic menu highlighting the simplicity and flavour of good provincial produce. The delicious aiguillettes de canard au miel et pommes fruits (duck breast with honey and apple) and the exquisitely creamy bouchon au chocolat (or any *dessert du jour*) will inspire you to come back to Le Bistrot de Théo, where customers are treated like guests.

starter: 48FF-85FF
main: 75FF-110FF
dessert: 40FF
Set menu: 75FF (lunch, except Saturdays), 135FF, 170FF
Plat du jour: 75FF
AE CB EC MC V

Open: Mon-Sat noon-2.30pm, 7.30pm-11.30pm; reservations advisable

Le Café d'Angel
French

☎ 01 47 54 03 33
**16, rue Brey,
Étoile**

Map: 17 H4
Métro: Charles de Gaulle-Étoile

Smoking throughout

While angels might not have a gender, they certainly have an appetite. Le Café d'Angel, a lovely spot just near the Étoile, is all the proof you'll need. Warm and elegant bistrot-style décor (comfortable banquettes, small white tiles and slate wall menus) heralds stylish but unpretentious cuisine. For starters, a refreshing tartare d'avocats et crevettes (avocado and shrimp tartare) competes for your attention with the soupe veloutée de lentilles et croûtons (creamy lentil soup with croutons, seasoned with a touch of tarragon). With the meal so deliciously under way, you can move on to veau sauce romarin (veal with rosemary sauce), served with mashed carrots or quenelles fondantes dans leur sauce aux moules, sur lit de poireaux (melting quenelles with mussel sauce served on a bed of leeks). At these prices, gluttony simply can't be a sin.

starter: 50FF-60FF
main: 90FF-105FF
dessert: 50FF
Set menu: 110FF (lunch), 180FF (dinner)
CB EC DC MC V

Open: Mon-Fri noon-2.30pm, 7.30pm-10pm; reservations advisable for lunch, essential for dinner

Caves Petrissans

French

☎ 01 42 27 52 03
**30 bis, ave Niel,
Place des Ternes**

Map: 17 G4

Métro: Ternes, Péreire

 Smoking throughout

This family restaurant has been looking after a lunch crowd of business people and a dinner crowd of regulars and passing gourmets since 1895. The décor leaves no doubt that this is *the* temple of fine wine. Indeed, it's difficult to know whether customers come primarily for the hearty regional cuisine or the extensive wine list – both are of such high quality. To kick things off, the caviar d'aubergine, rolled in a thin slice of cucumber, is beautifully presented. Most restaurants fail the andouillette sausage test, but Caves Petrissans excels with its grilled andouillette 'de Philippe Ravel à Riom' served with roast potatoes – this dish has character, flavour and melts in your mouth. The crème brûlée à la cassonade (soft brown sugar) is a stunning dessert. Needless to say, there's a wide range of vintages from all over France.

Open: Mon-Fri noon-2.30pm, 8pm-10.30pm; reservations advisable

starter: 45FF-90FF
main: 110FF-160FF
dessert: 48FF
Set menu: 175FF
Plat du jour: 110FF

AE CB DC MC V

Chez Léon

French

☎ 01 42 27 06 82
**32, rue Legendre,
Square des Batignolles**

Map: 17 F7

Métro: Villiers

 Nonsmoking tables available

Chez Léon is straight out of a Simenon novel – there's even a plaque honouring the late, great crime novelist. There is no place for the whimsical here: what you see is what you get. Salmon crêpes and terrine de raie (skate terrine) make great starters, followed by a thick rump steak or magret de canard aux pêches (fillet of duck breast with peaches). Big eaters can linger over the hefty cheese platter before demolishing the marquise au chocolat with arabica sauce. Wine buffs will enjoy ferreting out the interesting vintages on offer. Chez Léon has been around for about 30 years and some regulars seem to have been coming here since the early days. And why not? This place offers great service, generous food, well-maintained décor and, above all, respect for tradition.

Open: Mon-Fri noon-2.30pm, 7.30pm-10.30pm; reservations advisable (especially lunch)

starter: 48FF-100FF
main: 98FF-165FF
dessert: 50FF
Set menu: 170FF (wine included)
Plat du jour: 100FF-140FF

AE CB DC MC V

Map: 17 G8
Métro: Rome, Villiers

Smoking throughout

El Picador
Spanish

☎ 01 43 87 28 87
80 blvd des Batignolles,
Square des Batignolles

The walls are covered with the predictable trappings of Spanish folklore – guitars, shawls, fans and banderillas – but the small white tablecloths and wood panelling are a far cry from the noisy, festive ambience of the *ramblas*. In any case, it's the food on your plate – served in generous portions – that counts at El Picador. Gorgeous mezcla de tapas include capsicum, anchovies, serrano ham and olives. If you want to further your knowledge of His-panic charcuterie, the assiette du toréador (toreador's platter) is a must. The ternera à la catalana (veal with tomatoes and capsicum) and the bacalao à la vizcaina (fresh cod with garlic and tomatoes) are alternatives to the paellas – the real flagship of Spanish culinary delights. You'll just have time to wolf down a turon before the play starts next door at the Théâtre Hébertot.

starter: 49FF-118FF
main: 95FF-150FF
dessert: 40FF-55FF
Set menu: 95FF,
125FF, 160FF
AE CB DC EC MC V

Open: Wed-Sun noon-2pm, Tues-Sat 7pm-10.30pm; reservations advisable

---

Map: 17 F9
Métro: Place de Clichy

Smoking throughout

La Fourchette des Anges
French

☎ 01 44 69 07 69
17, rue Biot,
Square des Batignolles

La Fourchette des Anges: such a patronymic will immediately discourage poor sinners in search of a (culinary) god. May they rest as-sured. A few metres from the colourful Place Clichy, this charming little restaurant, baptised barely four years ago, is a gourmet haven for working-class and hip locals alike. Under the auspices of Cupid, the setting is chic without being intimidating, adorned with crimson hues and beaming cherubs. The delightful menu in the form of a papyrus encourages (unforbidden) sensual pleasures. Hot or cold starters, meat or fish: the host can turn his hand to anything. Unleash your tastebuds on the millefeuille with vegetables and mozzarella, before letting them tackle the heavenly poire pochée au caramel épicé (poached pear with caramel and spices). With such value for money, La Fourchette des Anges is surely a gift from the gods.

starter: 49FF-58FF
main: 82FF-93FF
dessert: 41FF-53FF
Set menu:
115FF (2 courses),
145FF (3 courses)
CB MC V; €

Open: Mon-Sat 7pm-11.15pm; reservations advisable

La Gaieté Cosaque

Russian

☎ 01 44 70 06 07
**6, rue Truffaut,
Square des Batignolles**

Map: 17 F9

Métro: Place de Clichy,
Rome

 Nonsmoking tables
available

Formerly a bistrot in rue des Dames, La Gaieté Cosaque is now a restaurant in rue Truffaut, but the spirit of the place hasn't changed. While the woman of the house does the cooking, her other half explains the finer details of the menu. Delicious zakuski include salades de choux blancs aux baies roses (salads with white cabbage and red berries), herrings sous manteau and eggplant caviar. There's also a hearty chachlik (lamb kebab à la caucasienne) and koulibiaca (a pie traditionally filled with fish, rice, vegetables and hard-boiled eggs). All dishes are served with potatoes, vegetables and the amazing buckwheat kacha. Don't pass over the homemade desserts, which include limonnik (lemon pie) and napoléons (*millefeuilles*). The set menus are uncharacteristically cheap for a Russian restaurant. Despite the absence of vin du pays, gaiety is guaranteed.

Open: Tues-Sat noon-3pm, Mon-Sat 7.30pm-11.45pm; reservations advisable (evenings)

starter: 20FF-199FF
main: 72FF-94FF
dessert: 30FF-37FF
Set menu: 69FF (lunch),
95FF, 135FF

CB V

La Gazelle

African

☎ 01 42 67 64 18
**9, rue Rennequin,
Place des Ternes**

Map: 17 G4

Métro: Péreire, Ternes

 Nonsmoking tables
available

Endless mirrors reflect a handful of rare masks at this upmarket restaurant, which embraces the traditional elements of African culture. The menu offers a vast array of dishes from the Ivory Coast, Senegal and, above all, Cameroon, such as calmar sauce didi (squid with didi sauce), crabe farci (stuffed crab), kedjenou, beignets de manioc (manioc fritters), nana au poivre (nana with a pepper sauce). Nostalgic customers are sure to find that special dish from their African sojourn. The ngondo sauce ivoire (shrimp and pistachio pâté), followed by doumba (goat in a parcel, served with plantain bananas and pilaf rice) makes for an interesting option. Many of the dishes are exquisite, the service is friendly, and the owner doesn't need too much prompting to talk about his past in Africa. Luxury comes at a cost, but the 160FF set menu makes it a little more accessible.

Open: Mon-Fri noon-2pm, 7pm-11pm, Sat 7pm-11pm; reservations advisable (towards end of the week)

starter: 38FF-120FF
main: 90FF-165FF
dessert: 40FF-60FF
Set menu: 140FF, 160FF

AE CB DC EC MC V

Map: 17 H3

Métro: Charles de
Gaulle-Étoile

Dress code applies

Smoking throughout

Graindorge
Flemish

☎ 01 47 64 33 47
**11, rue de l'Arc de Triomphe,
Étoile**

Soft-lighting, burgundy chairs and banquettes, efficient, discreet service – this must be the Graindorge. The name of this stylish restaurant means 'barley grain' and is a tribute to the breweries of Flanders (check out the drinks list). The décor is a bit lacklustre but the cuisine is truly inspired: just wait until you savour the delights of the house specialty, potjevleesch (four different kinds of meat slowly cooked together and served in aspic). But the chef here has more than one hat. For starters, the salmon tartare is so fresh you'd think it had jumped straight out of Norwegian waters onto your plate. Then the tender entrecôte (rib steak) will transport you to Argentina, unless you'd prefer the filets de rouget dorés sur le lit d'endives (fillets of golden mullet on a bed of endives). There must be a pilot in the kitchen.

starter: 58FF-98FF
main: 105FF-130FF
dessert: 50FF-60FF
Set menu: 168FF (lunch),
198FF (dinner)

AE CB V

Open: Mon-Fri noon-2.30pm, 7.30pm-11pm, Sat 7.30-11pm;
reservations advisable

Map: 17 H3

Métro: Argentine, Ternes,
Charles de Gaulle-Étoile

Smoking throughout

Il Grappolo
Italian

☎ 01 44 09 77 70
**11, rue d'Armaillé,
Place des Ternes**

At first glance, Carlo and Vincenzo appear to have nothing in common. One is from Naples, the other from Rome ... However, friendship knows no borders, and the two partners opened this restaurant together at the start of 2000. Delighted local inhabitants have quickly become regulars, even though there's only room for 22 settings. Italian conversation and smiling faces are the order of the day, and not a pizza in sight! The chef offers an alternative vision of his country with an impeccable menu including poire en feuillet avec jambon et sauce gorgonzola (thin layers of pear with ham and gorgonzola sauce), garganelli (small cigarette-shaped pasta) with mussels and broccoli, gnocchi with bacon, tomato and cheese. The tiramisù and café ristretto are obligatory stopovers on this transalpine voyage.

starter: 49FF
main: 69FF-89FF
dessert: 32FF

CB EC MC V

Open: Mon-Fri noon-2.30pm, Mon-Sat 7pm-10.30pm; reservations essential (evenings), advisable (lunch)

L'Impatient
French

☎ **01 43 87 28 10**
14, passage Geffroy-Didelot
Square des Batignolles

Map: 17 G8
Métro: Villiers

 Nonsmoking tables available

Homemade foie gras with the compliments of the chef, small perfume samples in the toilets, impeccable, friendly service – everything here speaks of elegance and conviviality. Lovers of fine food will be in their element as they savour dishes which are both copious and refined. Every item on the menu, from the ravioles de langoustines à la crème mousseuse au basilic (langoutine ravioli with a creamy basil sauce) and the pavé de saumon et son risotto d'olives (thick salmon steak with olive risotto) to the pommes rôties à la vanille (baked apples with vanilla) tastes like it must be the chef's specialty. Reservations are advisable, but if you've forgotten, L'Impatient's elegance extends to providing a lovely little room where customers can peruse the fabulous wine list while waiting *patiently* for a table.

starter: 52FF-90FF
main: 100FF-130FF
dessert: 45FF-50FF
Set menu: 130FF (dinner)
Plat du jour: 95FF

MC V

Open: Mon-Fri noon-2.30pm, Tues-Sat 7.45pm-10.30pm; reservations advisable

Kirane's
Indian

☎ **01 45 74 40 21**
85, ave des Ternes,
Porte Maillot

Map: 17 G3
Métro: Porte Maillot

 Smoking throughout

Kirane's unique specialities were handed down by her grandmother. Dishes which are fragrant rather than hot come to life in this elegant setting, where bronze and wooden gods nestled in alcoves watch carefully over the proceedings. During her six years as a chef, Kirane has perfected numerous recipes, including bharta masala (a fresh, creamy starter of crudités and eggplant) and mutton dhania korma (tender diced lamb marinated in a mixture of spices and cooked over a low flame). These dishes will gently awaken your tastebuds, while the Grover's red, a vintage from Bangalore, will bring out their full flavours. The desserts are also a delicious surprise: the gajar halwa (a type of confectionery served at the court of the Great Moguls) is just begging to be devoured.

starter: 39FF-95FF
main: 75FF-130FF
dessert: 35FF-49FF
Set menu: 79FF, 99FF
 (lunch), 165FF, 199FF
Plat du jour: 75FF, 85FF

AE CB DC EC MC V

Open: Mon-Sat noon-2.30pm, 7pm-11.30pm; reservations advisable (Thurs-Sat)

Macis & Muscade

French

☎ 01 42 26 62 26
110, rue Legendre,
Square des Batignolles

Map: 17 E9
Métro: La Fourche

Smoking throughout

The owner tells customers that he aims to excite their 'olfactory and gustatory emotions with harmonious combinations of different ingredients and natural, unrefined products'. A former creator of perfumes, he fulfils his purpose admirably, using his talents to create a new type of cuisine based on essential oils. The feuilleté de maroilles et sa salade à l'essence de ciste (*feuilleté* of Maroilles cheese accompanied by a salad with essence of rock rose), the carré d'agneau à l'infusion de thym (loin of lamb with an infusion of thyme) and the marquise au chocolat with cardamom are a winning trifecta, but it seems that however you place your bets, your tastebuds are the sure winner. The menu travels from one end of France to the other – each herb or essential oil evokes a particular landscape or region. The atmosphere is friendly, the service attentive and the value for money surprisingly good.

starter: 37FF-44FF
main: 70FF-98FF
dessert: 35FF-44FF
Set menu: 75FF Tues-Fri
(lunch), 130FF
Plat du jour: 65FF

AE CB EC MC V; €

Open: Tues-Fri & Sun noon-2pm, Tues-Thurs & Sun 8pm-10.30pm, Fri & Sat 8pm-11pm; reservations advisable (evenings)

Le Morosophe

French

☎ 01 53 06 82 82
83, rue Legendre,
Square des Batignolles

Map: 17 E8
Métro: Brochant

Smoking throughout

Le Morosophe? Please explain! 'The folly of wisdom', according to Dutch humanist Erasmus. Located in the elegant Batignolles neighbourhood, this chic, sophisticated but unostentatious restaurant, tastefully decorated with African statuettes and red banquettes, offers a serene atmosphere and fine food. Have an original appetiser, then get down to business: veal lovers will be in seventh heaven after polishing off the melting carré aux figues (rib of veal with figs), while the most audacious eaters will be transported by the andouillette de Chablis aux escargots (Chablis andouillette sausage with snails), which lovingly caresses the palate. The profiteroles aux chocolats live up to expectations and are a fitting conclusion to the meal. Wine can be ordered by the glass or the measure, perfect for single punters out on the town. The larger-than-life owner-philosopher, always ready with a *bon mot* or two, provides impeccable service.

starter: 45FF-90FF
main: 65FF-105FF
dessert: 40FF-55FF
Set menu: 150FF
Plat du jour: 75FF (lunch)

AE CB DC EC MC V; €

Open: Tues-Sat noon-2.30pm, Mon-Sat 8pm-10.45pm; reservations advisable

P'tit Bouchon gourmand
French

☎ 01 40 55 03 26
5, rue Troyon, Étoile

Map: 17 J4

Métro: Charles de Gaulle-Étoile

 Nonsmoking tables available

After having been an institution for almost a quarter of a century in the seaside town of La Baule (where the original P'tit Bouchon is still operating), Christian and Christian have set up near Place de l'Étoile. The theatrical red and black décor makes the establishment look a bit like Alcatraz, which the owners are the first to admit. Start off with crisp poireaux au vinaigre balsamique (leeks with balsamic vinegar) or a voluptuous camembert rôti sur son lit de salade (baked camembert with salad). For mains try a delectable Parmentier au veau with olives or something less familiar such as millefeuille de boudin noir aux pommes (black pudding millefeuille with apples). Since it opened last autumn, this p'tit bouchon ('li'l sweetie') has built up a faithful following. The friendliness of the two Christians must have something to do with its success.

Open: Mon-Fri noon-2pm, 7pm-11pm; reservations advisable (lunch), essential (dinner)

starter: 65FF-110FF
main: 75FF-140FF
dessert: 15FF-45FF
Set menu: 125FF
Plat du jour: 120FF

AE CB JCB V; €

La P'tite Lili
French

☎ 01 45 22 54 22
8, rue des Batignolles, Square des Batignolles

Map: 17 F9

Métro: Rome, Place Clichy

 Smoking throughout

 Pavement tables

This convivial wine bar, squashed in at the beginning of rue des Batignolles and not far from the Place de Clichy, is no place for snobbery. The owner, who prepares *and* serves the food, is a former theatre props woman and passionate antique-hunter – hence the décor, which gives this place an authentic feel. The menu features traditional cuisine with a strong influence from Lyons: tablier de sapeur (crumbed tripe), cervelle de canut (a herbed cheese) and saucisson de Lyon pistaché (garlic-flavoured sausage). Other regional cheeses include the flavoursome Pithiviers au foin (made from cow's milk and ripened under a layer of hay) and the Cotentin camembert, which is served with a knowing smile. La P'tite Lili sticks to the same formula for lunch and dinner. 'Everyone's welcome', says Lili, 'but remember – there are only 27 seats'.

Open: Mon-Fri noon-2.30pm, 7.30pm-midnight (orders taken until 9.30pm); reservations advisable

starter: 38FF-44FF
main: 60FF-64FF
dessert: 26FF-36FF
Plat du jour: 60FF-64FF

CB V

17ᵉ ARRONDISSEMENT

Map: 17 E4
Métro: Péreire

Smoking throughout

Pavement tables

Le Petit Gervex
French (seafood)

☎ 01 43 80 53 63
**2, rue Gervex,
Péreire**

This oasis of tranquillity is sheltered from the nearby bustle of the city by trees. In a chic setting, classic fish and seafood dishes are served without fuss. Delicious friture d'éperlans et sa sauce tartare (deep-fried smelt with tartare sauce) or sardines grillées au sel de Guérande et aux huiles pimentées (grilled sardines with Guérande sea salt and seasoned oils) caress the palate. The pavé de saumon á l'unilatéral (salmon steak) holds no surprises, but sesame seeds team up perfectly with a delicious carpaccio de thon (tuna carpaccio). Pain perdu sauce caramel (French toast with caramel sauce) heralds an enjoyable transition to sweetness. The 150FF set menu offers all these pleasures as well as cheese. Notwithstanding its modest name, the waters of Le Petit Gervex hold a great catch.

starter: 45FF-85FF
main: 85FF-120FF
dessert: 40FF-50FF
Set menu: 115FF, 150FF

AE CB EC MC V

Open: Mon-Sun noon-2pm, Mon-Fri 7.30pm-10pm; reservations advisable

---

Map: 17 G3
Métro: Porte Maillot

Smoking throughout

Rech
French

☎ 01 45 72 29 47,
01 45 72 28 91
**62, Ave des Ternes,
Porte Maillot**

Don't be put off by the unwelcoming façade or the name of this restaurant, which, in *verlan* (backwards slang), might concern budget eaters ('cher' means 'expensive'). Leave behind the hustle of the Porte Maillot and treat yourself to the soothing, old-fashioned décorum of Rech. The woodwork, softly lit by orange lamps, is redolent of the Belle Époque. Even the thoughtful waiters seemingly belong to the turn of the century. The house specialties – oysters, shellfish and fish – live up to their reputation. The filet de bar au beurre nantais et aux échalotes (fillet of bass with white wine, butter and shallots), served with preserved potatoes, will convert the staunchest of red meat fanatics. Rech also offers a wide range of camemberts, as well as baba au rhum piqué de zestes d'orange (rum baba flecked with orange peel). You can't put a price on such old-world pleasures!

starter: 38FF-130FF
main: 88FF-320FF
dessert: 39FF-60FF
Set menu: 165FF (lunch)
Plat du jour: 120FF

AE CB DC EC V

Open: Mon-Sat noon-2.30pm, 7pm-11pm; reservations advisable

Le Sud

French (Provence)

☎ **01 45 74 02 77**
91, blvd Gouvion Saint-Cyr,
Porte Maillot

Map: 17 G2

Métro: Porte Maillot

Dress code applies

 Smoking throughout

 Garden courtyard tables

Le Sud recreates the dazzling colours of Provence with great panache. Tiles and earthenware pots in ochre tones are a perfect match for the yellows and blues of the furniture. An intimate atmosphere belies the enormous dimensions of this restaurant, and olive trees in a central, inner courtyard add an extra touch of local colour. The cuisine exalts the riches of the Mediterranean, transformed by Provençal tradition into bourride (fish soup), bouillabaisse de Toulon and filets de rougets au coulis de langoustine et romarin (fillets of mullet with langoustine and rosemary coulis). The meat dishes are also outstanding – the 'confit d'agneau de ma grand-mère' ('grandmother's confit of lamb'), served with fresh pasta, simply melts in your mouth. The service is attentive and the clientele quiet. While the bill is a bit steep, this sun-drenched setting at the foot of the Palais des Congrès is an unforgettable treat.

starter: 62FF-68FF
main: 138FF-168FF
dessert: 54FF-62FF

AE CV DC EC MC V; €

Open: Mon-Sat noon-2pm, 7pm-11pm; reservations essential

Teeru Bi

Afircan/Senegalese

☎ **01 53 31 00 05**
35, rue Jonquière,
Guy Môquet

Map: 17 C9

Métro: Guy Môquet

 Smoking throughout

Pay no attention to the outside, there really *is* a Senegalese restaurant here – it's right at the end of the hallway. In a plain setting, with white walls, floor and ceiling friezes, a few paintings are all that remind you that you've come for a taste of Africa. Like the décor, the food is simple and unsophisticated, making few concessions to European cuisine. Tuck into acras de morue (small fried balls of spicy cod purée), fatayas (meat fritters), pastel (grouper fritters), tiebou diene, mafé and millet couscous. You can add chilli to the dishes if they aren't flavoursome enough for your taste and, if you go overboard, the tiacri (a dessert based on curdled milk) is a perfect palate soother. The service is invariably friendly, but then 'Teeru Bi' *does* mean 'welcome' in Wolof.

starter: 27FF-40FF
main: 60FF-129FF
dessert: 20FF-30FF
Set menu: 65FF (lunch),
 90FF, 120FF

CB V (minimum 150FF); €

Open: Mon-Sat 11.45am-3pm, 7.30pm-11pm (until midnight on Fri & Sat); reservations not accepted

Map: 17 E9

Métro: La Fourche

Smoking throughout

Pavement tables

La Tête de Goinfre/La Cave du Cochon
French

☎ 01 42 29 89 80
16, rue Jacquemont,
Batignolles

The collection of pigs which grateful customers have given the owner of La Tête de Goinfre ('Greedy Pig') may betray a taste for risqué humour, but food remains a serious matter at this friendly bistrot. Picnic on the popular co-chonaille (charcuterie) while you're waiting for a table, and once seated, launch into salade de magret (duck fillet salad), filet de harengs (fillets of herring) or poireaux vinaigrette (leeks vinaigrette) for starters. Then try bavette à l'échalote (skirt steak with shallots), boudin noir (black pudding) or saumon poché (poached salmon) as a main. Jean-Pierre goes to market every day and changes his menu accordingly. The wines live up to this respectable bistrot fare (especially the house bordeaux and the côte-du-rhône 'Parallèle'), as do the desserts (cheese platter, tarte du jour, mousse au chocolat). Along with the adjoining La Cave du Cochon ('Pig's Cellar'), La Tête de Goinfre is a place to pig out in style.

starter: 29FF-52FF
main: 69FF-89FF
dessert: 29FF-35FF
Plat du jour: 79FF-89FF

CB EC MC V

Open: Mon-Sat noon-2.30pm, 8pm-11pm; reservations advisable

Map: 17 J4

Métro: Charles de Gaulle-Étoile

Smoking throughout

Le Troyon
French

☎ 01 40 68 99 40
4, rue Troyon,
Étoile

The setting is rustic and escapist, with an eclectic array of reproductions by Magritte, Hopper and Velázquez adorning the Burgundy-stone walls, an apt allusion to the chef's creative cuisine. Bringing a contemporary flourish to traditional recipes, every day presents a challenge in the form of five or six new starters, mains and desserts. You may have loved the fondant de cailles jus au vieux porto (quail with aged-port gravy) or the rascasse rôtie nage d'orange à la badiane (roast scorpion fish in orange and star anise sauce), but don't expect to find it on the following day's menu. The only constant is the invincible moelleux au chocolat rio guayaras, a magnificent 70% cocoa. Delicious sweetmeats are served from an antique biscuit tin with coffee – don't let your mobile phone interrupt this melting moment!

Set menu: 198FF

AE CB V

Open: Mon-Fri noon-2pm, 7.30pm-10pm; reservations advisable

18ᵉ Arrondissement

Montmartre

Jules Joffrin

Porte de Clignancourt

Barbès

BEST

■ **Au bon coin**
Neighbourhood restaurant you'll want to take home

■ **Taka**
Zen dining in Japanese bower

■ **Thu Thu**
Try the speciality – Vietnamese crêpes

L'Oriental (p 262)

18ᵉ Arrondissement

The eighteenth arrondissement thrives on crowds and a strong sense of community. Its old-fashioned, village atmosphere is lovingly preserved without being dolled up. When you've got Montmartre and Sacré Coeur, what more do you need? Cascading steps, streets with old cobblestones, small houses with wooden shutters in narrow, quiet lanes ... the charm of the Butte is eternal. Seen from above, Paris is a distant dream veiled in greys and blues. Rue Caulaincourt and rue Junot flaunt their bourgeois credentials, while the streets around the square Willette, place des Abbesses, rue Lepic and marché Saint-Pierre become steeper and narrower, the inhabitants younger and hipper (but not too much so). The lights of the Moulin Rouge dominate blvd de Clichy. Another picture-postcard scene superimposes itself. Flanked by the red or blue neon signs of peepshows, Pigalle runs its sad, lifeless course. A different village emerges in rue de Clignancourt, opening up into the world of la Goutte-d'Or. Eastern colours and rhythms brighten the walls of blvd Barbès, blvd de la Chapelle and rue Marx Dormoy. Market stalls and shops overflow with merchandise while people shout out to each other across the narrow, crowded footpaths.

Au bon coin

French

☎ 01 46 06 91 36
**49, rue des Cloÿs,
Mairie du 18e**

Map: 18 D3

Métro: Jules Joffrin

Entertainment: Live jazz on sunny days

 Smoking throughout

 Pavement tables

This corner restaurant-bar has been in the family for three generations. The décor is unremarkable, but the owner's cheerful, unpretentious manner will win you over instantly. Au bon coin operates as a neighbourhood bar throughout the day, while at meal times Jean-Louis Bras gives free reign to his passion – wine. Let him recommend just the right drop: you won't regret it. The lunch menu offers simple dishes made with fresh market produce. The more elaborate dinner menu includes the chef's light spinach ravioli and a hearty salade périgourdine (Périgord-style salad) for starters, followed by the traditional but sumptuous saucisson de Lyon à la beaujolaise or, for starving appetites, ratiflette (like a tartiflette, but served with raclette-style melted cheese rather than Reblochon). This is a place where you immediately feel at home. We'll be back tomorrow…

starter: 15FF (lunch), 28FF-38FF (dinner)
main: 42FF (lunch), 72FF-78FF (dinner)
dessert: 15FF-20FF (lunch), 25FF-35FF (dinner)
Plat du jour: 42FF

cash only; €

Open: restaurant: Mon-Sat noon-3pm, Mon-Fri 7pm-9.30pm; bar: Mon-Fri 7am-10pm, Sat 8am-3pm; reservations not accepted

Au Petit Budapest

Hungarian

☎ 01 46 06 10 34
**96, rue des Martyrs,
Abbesses**

Map: 18 G4

Métro: Abbesses

Entertainment: Live music Fri & Sat after 8pm

 Smoking throughout

It's not often you get to sample the Slavonic flavours of Hungarian cuisine in Paris. Andreas rectified this when he opened Au Petit Budapest two years ago. With old etchings and Gypsy music, this former artist has recreated the atmosphere of a late-19th-century tavern. From the paprikash au bœuf épicé (paprikache with spicy beef) to the gâteau au fromage blanc (cream cheese cake), his menu offers a refined version of popular Hungarian cuisine. The crêpe à la Hortobagy (crêpe filled with meat and crème fraîche) is deliciously melting and surprising light. If you get lost in this new culinary territory, ask for directions – the owner will be more than happy to explain the background of each dish. An ideal spot to pinch a few recipe ideas.

starter: 45FF-75FF
main: 65FF-85FF
dessert: 35FF-55FF
Set menu: 95FF, 125FF (lunch & dinner)

CB V

Open: Tues-Sun 11.30am-3pm, 8pm-midnight; reservations not accepted

Map: 18 G3
Métro: Pigalle, Abbesses

Smoking throughout

Ayutthaya
Thai

☎ 01 42 64 19 53
**5, rue Houdon,
Pigalle**

For 20 years, this small restaurant near Place Pigalle has been exalting the flavours of Siam. Named after the former kingdom's capital city, Ayutthaya is decorated with sepia photos – including one of the king and his wife – that evoke those glory days. An altar and Buddha figurines make a refreshing change from the usual kitsch. The dishes are extremely delicate and flavoursome if not particularly copious. Poisson en morceaux à la vapeur et au jus de coco (steamed pieces of fish with coconut juice, served in a banana leaf), salade de bœuf à la menthe (beef salad with mint, served cold) and seiches sautées au basilic (sautéed cuttle-fish with basil) will entrance lovers of Thai cuisine and convert newcomers.

starter: 45FF-50FF
main: 50FF-60FF
dessert: 20FF-25FF
Set menu: 90FF

cash only

Open: Tues-Sun noon-3pm, 7.30pm-11.30pm; reservations advisable (especially evenings)

Map: 18 G3
Métro: Abbesses

Smoking throughout

Chez Toinette
French

☎ 01 42 54 44 36
**20, rue Germain Pilon,
Montmartre**

The convivial atmosphere of this aptly named restaurant is rivalled only by its fine cuisine. In the heart of one the capital's most touristy neighbourhoods, Chez Toinette has kept alive the tradition of old Montmartre with its simplic-ity and culinary expertise. Game lovers won't be disappointed, as regulars already know. Per-dreau (partridge), biche (hind), chevreuil (roe-buck) and the famous filet de canard à la sauge et au miel (fillet of duck with sage and honey) are the house specialities and go well with a glass of bordeaux. Don't miss this small, inexpensive restaurant as you wander the narrow, paved streets of the 'Butte'.

starter: 30FF-35FF
main: 60FF-90FF
dessert: 25FF-35FF
Plat du jour: 42FF

cash only; €

Open: Tues-Sat 8pm-11pm; reservations advisable

Le Dépôt des Photographes
French

☎ 01 46 27 24 24
44, rue Joseph de Maistre, Montmartre

Customers are greeted warmly at this small wine bar next to the Montmartre cemetery, a welcome retreat from the bustle of rue des Abbesses. Quick snacks include hot or cold tartines made with Poilâne bread and served with a small salad. Platters of farmhouse cheese and charcuterie, bursting with flavour, are the perfect foil to a judicious selection of wines. In addition, Le Dépôt des Photographes sells bread, charcuterie and a few types of pastries, all of which are scrumptious. As the name suggests, it also organises exhibitions of fine photography as well as live performances of jazz and *chanson française*. You'll soon be a regular at this simple, lively and original spot.

Open: Mon-Sat noon-2am; reservations not accepted

Map: 18 E2

Métro: Place de Clichy, Abbesses

Entertainment: Live jazz, *chanson française* and rock Wed-Sat 9pm

 Smoking throughout

 Pavement tables

main: 25FF-90FF
dessert: 25FF-30FF
Set menu: 120FF
Plat du jour: 45FF-60FF

CB MC V

L'Étrier Bistrot
French

☎ 01 42 29 14 01
154, rue Lamarck, Montmartre

From the outside, there's nothing remarkable about this bistrot, located in a quiet corner of Montmartre at the bottom of the rue Lamarck, a short walk from ave de Saint Ouen. You might hesitate to go in, but once seated, you'll be glad you did. The mouthwatering smells of the 'cuisine du marché' – only the best fresh produce – waft around the intimate room, accompanied by discreet classical music. The owner explains that the menu changes constantly, and takes the liberty of recommending the specialities of the house, including gâteau de foie de volaille (chicken liver loaf), rognons de veau (veal kidneys) and tatin d'endives (tarte tatin made with chicory!). You can be sure your taste buds are in for a treat. If anyone still had reservations after the main, the tasty, elaborate cheese platter would surely win them over. The price of the set menu for lunch is almost absurdly low.

Open: Mon-Sat noon-2.30pm, 7.30pm-10.30pm; reservations essential

Map: 18 D2

Métro: Guy Môquet

 Smoking throughout

starter: 75FF
main: 117FF
dessert: 55FF
Set menu: 140FF (lunch), 180FF

CB MC V

Map: 18 F3

Métro: Blanche, Abbesses

Smoking throughout

Gang Seng
Tibetan

☎ 01 46 06 71 91
**40, rue Lepic,
Montmartre**

This tiny restaurant is quiet at lunchtime, but livens up in the evening with the arrival of an exuberant clientele of Tibetans and admirers of the 'Roof of the World'. After a simple, charming welcome, you climb a steep staircase to the upstairs room, decorated with wall hangings and banners in the bright colours of Tibet. Along with delicious bread hot from the oven and tea served with milk and spices, Gang Seng offers dishes from the eastern part of the country. The flavours of tchasha (chicken soup with bamboo shoots, coconut milk and coriander) and the finely sliced grilled beef and lamb with coriander and turmeric are reminiscent of southern Chinese and Thai cooking. Don't miss a refreshing dessert of yüldrog (fromage blanc with chestnut cream and dried fruit) or lassi (yoghurt mixed with honey).

starter: 22FF-30FF
main: 50FF-69FF
dessert: 15FF-35FF
Set menu: 65FF (lunch),
89FF, 109FF

CB MC V

Open: Wed-Sun noon-2pm, Tues-Sun 7pm-11pm; reservations advisable (especially for dinner)

Map: 18 G4

Métro: Abbesses

Smoking throughout

Pavement tables

L'Homme tranquille
Modern French

☎ 01 42 54 56 28
**81, rue des Martyrs,
Montmartre**

The first thing you notice as you enter this small restaurant (with only 30 seats) is that John Wayne looks more resolute than ever ... The original poster of John Ford's *l'Homme tranquille* (The Quiet Man) leaps out from the post-70s paraphernalia of this instantly likeable spot. An unpretentious menu varies each day and offers real home-made food, such as terrines or a salade au saint-marcellin chaud (warm saint-marcellin salad), followed by gigot d'agneau en tajine (tajine of lamb), poulet au miel et coriandre (chicken with honey and coriander) or fish. For dessert, the texture of the chocolate mousse will leave connoisseurs speechless. The warm welcome isn't the least of this restaurant's charms. The friendly, discreet hosts have combined all the necessary ingredients for a convivial, casual night out.

starter: 38FF
main: 64FF-88FF
dessert: 28FF-38FF
Set menu: 128FF
Plat du jour: 65FF-86FF

CB

Open: Tues-Sat 7.30pm-11.30pm; reservations advisable

Kismet
Indian

☎ 01 44 92 05 21
2, rue Eugène Carrière, Montmartre

Map: 18 E2

Métro: Guy Môquet

   Smoking throughout

Pavement tables

Kismet looks out over the leafy foliage of the Montmartre cemetery. This charming Indian restaurant boasts a bright setting, thick carpet and well-trained staff. The chef is from Kashmir, so customers are treated to the specialities of that beautiful mountainous region. Settle in to Srinagar and Jammu pace with a thé au lait et à la cardamome (white tea with cardamom). To begin the meal you'll be torn between cailles (quails) and beignets de crevettes (shrimp fritters), served with a scrumptious chapati. The tikka massala chicken, cooked in a tandoori oven, is the restaurant's most popular dish, but we also recommend you try the exceptional flavours of the curry du Cachemire (Kashmir curry) with chicken, lamb or shrimps. To finish, the Goa-style ice cream is a delicious surprise. A great neighbourhood restaurant with light food at affordable prices.

starter: 28FF-99FF
main: 45FF-99FF
dessert: 25FF-35FF

MC V; €

Open: Sun-Fri noon-2.30pm, 7pm-11pm, Sat 7pm-11pm; reservations advisable on weekends

La Mascotte
French (seafood)

☎ 01 46 06 28 15
52, rue des Abbesses, Abbesses

Map: 18 F3

Métro: Abbesses, Blanche

 Smoking throughout

 Pavement tables

La Mascotte is a small, unassuming restaurant that could be easily missed among the hordes of competitors in this touristy area. That would be a great pity. This friendly spot is frequented by regulars devoted to its fish, seafood and regional cuisine. In winter, don't hesitate to sample the variety of huîtres (oysters) or the palourdes (medium-sized clams), moules (mussels), bulots (whelks), tourteaux (large crabs) and homards (Atlantic lobsters). Sit at the terrace in summer while you savour the delicious fricassée de pétoncles (fricassee of queen scallops) or the distinctive, well-matched flavours of the salmon and haddock tartare. Meat lovers won't be disappointed by the Corrèze pork, Aubrac beef and various regional delicacies such as Auvergne sausage and Troyes andouillette. The wide range of estate wines is a big plus for inquisitive customers at this lovely, inexpensive restaurant.

starter: 24FF-58FF
main: 65FF-96FF
dessert: 23FF-45FF
Set menu: 75FF, 88FF, 155FF
Plat du jour: 65FF, 72FF

CB V

Open: Tues-Sun 7am-1am; reservations advisable

18e ARRONDISSEMENT

L'Oriental
Moroccan

☎ 01 42 64 39 80
76, rue des Martyrs, Montmartre

Map: 18 G4
Métro: Pigalle

Smoking throughout

The Pigalle neighbourhood is awash with restaurants, and you get the impression that they're all much the same. But there are good reasons to choose L'Oriental. The décor is appropriately atmospheric, with little grill-work balconies, wall hangings and mirrors. The pastilla (puff pastry tart) makes a beautifully sweet introduction to the meal, while tchakchouka (a sort of ratatouille with eggplant, peppers and an egg), served very hot in a stoneware dish, is an excellent concoction. You can continue with tagine des Rois, made with chicken or lamb, figs, dates, almonds and apricots, or with a somewhat undistinguished couscous. The desserts were mixed: the farandole de spécialités orientales ('dance' of Oriental specialities), which sounds voluptuous, turned out to be scrawny, but the blackcurrant sorbet kaci was nicely garnished and full of flavour. The service is efficient and attentive.

starter: 36FF-60FF
main: 85FF-120FF
dessert: 30FF-40FF
Set menu: 89FF (weekdays)
AE CB EC MC V

Open: Mon-Sat noon-2.30pm, 7pm-11pm; reservations advisable (towards the end of the week)

Osteria Ascoloni
Italian

☎ 01 42 62 43 94
98, rue des Martyrs, Abbesses

Map: 18 G4
Métro: Abbesses, Pigalle

Smoking throughout
Pavement tables

Imagine a house perched on the rooftops of Paris, with unaffected décor, genuine atmosphere and the somewhat old-fashioned charm of simple restaurants where food is the only thing that matters. The set menu at Osteria Ascoloni is both original and generous. Four antipasti are served in succession: beignet de brousse (brousse fritters); tartine de poivrons rouges et de marscapone (bread with capsicum and mascarpone); gratin de cœurs d'artichaut (artichoke hearts au gratin); and tranche de cochon de lait avec sa tomate sèche (slice of sucking pig with sun-dried tomato). But where would this Italian restaurant be without a worthy main course? The pâtes au pistou (pasta with pesto sauce) is cooked al dente and served piping hot. The plot thickens for dessert with a difficult choice between pana cotta aux fruits rouges (pana cotta with red berries) and tiramisù. This central Italian cuisine is authentic, homey and – needless to say – oozing with style.

Set menu: 125FF (3 courses)
cash only

Open: Mon-Sat 7pm-2am; reservations advisable

Piccola Strada

Italian

☎ **01 42 54 83 39**
6, rue Yvonne-le-Tac,
Montmartre

Map: 18 G4

Métro: Abbesses, Pigalle

  Smoking throughout

It's a real pleasure to dine in this little red and ochre chocolate box with its tranquil atmosphere and friendly service. The lighting is soft, as is the velvet on the bench seats. The quality cuisine attracts numerous regulars and a few travellers. The menu offers a broad choice of simple or sophisticated Italian dishes. The salade chaude de trévise et panchetta (warm radicchio and pancetta salad) is tangy, slightly crunchy and full of flavour. There's no place for pizza in this establishment, where the linguine, penne, fusili and other pasta dishes are all highly tempting. The tagliatelles au blanc et à l'encre de seiche (tagliatelli with cuttlefish and ink) is worth a special mention. It's a masterpiece of aesthetic and culinary radicalism: snow-white strips of cuttlefish nestling in jet-black pasta – and that's it. Definitely a dish for minimalists!

Open: daily noon-2.30pm, 7pm-11.45pm; reservations advisable (evenings)

starter: 50FF-80FF
main: 50FF-85FF
dessert: 38FF-49FF
Set menu: 79FF (weekdays)

CB DC EC MC V; €

Le Relais Gascon

French (South-West)

☎ **01 45 58 58 22**
6, rue des Abbesses,
Montmartre

Map: 18 G4

Métro: Abbesses, Pigalle

 Smoking throughout

 Pavement tables

Between Pigalle and Montmartre, a short stroll from Place des Abbesses, this bistrot-style restaurant offers a relaxed atmosphere and authentic regional cuisine. Regular customers and passing tourists are treated to unsophisticated but healthy and copious dishes from the south-west of France. The famous salade géante (giant salad – the house speciality), salmon 'détente', goat's cheese 'béarnaise' and the 'sud-ouest' confit will satisfy big eaters, while the piperade (omelette with tomatoes and peppers), tartiflette (a gratin of potatoes and cheese) and magret (fillet of duck breast) are equally scrumptious. If you're *still* hungry, fill up on traditional gâteau basque or the classic crème brûée. Le Relais Gascon is a homey place: you'll leave feeling well fed and watered, looking forward to the next get-together.

Open: daily 10am-2am (lunch from noon, dinner until midnight); reservations advisable (weekends)

starter: 32FF-69FF
main: 52FF-78FF
dessert: 25FF-35FF
Set menu: 69FF, 109FF
Plat du jour: 45FF (lunch weekdays)

cash only

Map: 18 F3
Métro: Blanche

Smoking throughout

Le Restaurant
French

☎ 01 42 23 06 22
**32, rue Véron,
Montmartre**

You're no longer in Pigalle but haven't quite reached Montmartre – welcome to Le Restaurant's stamping ground for the last decade. Hotchpotch décor, a noisy atmosphere, friendly if occasionally underwhelming service, and rich and generous cuisine. The moules à l'ail au poivre et à l'huile d'olive (mussels with garlic, pepper and olive oil) will delight even those who generally steer clear of seafood. The melting fondant d'agneau en tajine (tajine of lamb) will also tickle your tastebuds. Some customers come here just for the canette rôti au miel (roast duckling with honey), embellished with coriander and figs. The huge dessert platter includes every sweet on the menu, although you may be too full to partake by this stage. Le Restaurant may not be the be-all and end-all in terms of cuisine, but this is a fine restaurant in an area with plenty of competition.

starter: 50FF
main: 90FF
dessert: 40FF-50FF
Set menu: 120FF
(2 courses)
AE CB DC EC JCB MC V

Open: Mon-Thurs 7.30pm-11.30pm; Fri & Sat 7.30pm-midnight; reservations advisable

---

Map: 18 F2
Métro: Abbesses, Blanche

Smoking throughout

Terrace tables

La Rughetta
Italian

☎ 01 42 23 41 70
**41, rue Lepic,
Montmartre, Abbesses**

Located between Pigalle and Montmartre, where rue Lepic begins winding up the 'Butte', this Italian restaurant attracts both posh and bohemian crowds of locals. The décor is warm and a bit kitsch (Venetian masks and ochre walls), and a small terrace is set up for those long summer nights. But it's for a real taste of Italy that customers 'climb' this far: sumptuous beef carpaccio served with capers, parmesan, basil and crushed olives; melting ravioli with cream and basil; and, a godsend for those who can't make up their mind, the 'Rughetta', a double pizza, one side calzone and the other side of your choice. Finally, the ultimate test – the tiramisù is succulent. This place is a huge hit and now has several sittings.

starter: 55FF-95FF
main: 60FF-105FF
dessert: 42FF-70FF
Set menu: 89FF (weekday
lunch)
cash only

Open: daily 12.30pm-2.30pm, 7.30pm-11.30pm; reservations advisable

18e ARRONDISSEMENT

Le Soleil Gourmand
French (Mediterranean)

☎ 01 42 51 00 50
**10, rue Ravignan,
Montmartre, Abbesses**

Map: 18 F3

Métro: Abbesses

 Smoking throughout

Open the door of the Soleil Gourmand and take in the warm atmosphere of the Mediterranean south. Yellow and ochre walls, wrought-iron furniture embellished with suns (imported from Morocco, the whole lot is for sale) and, most of all, twin sisters Élisa and Christine, who opened this small pocket of paradise where 'mobile phones are frowned upon'. Don't study the menu too hard – Élisa will explain in her warm voice the choice of salads, savoury tarts and oven-baked bricks (stuffed fritters), which change in keeping with seasonal market produce and the mood of the moment. Treat yourself to the tarte aux oignons, poivrons, raisins et pignons grillés (tart with onion, capsicum, grapes and grilled pine nuts), the assiette du Sud (southern platter) and, for dessert, home-made ginger, almond milk, tiramisù or wild peach ice cream. The fondant is unforgettable and will leave chocoholics walking on sunshine.

Open: Mon-Sat 12.30pm-2.30pm, 8.30pm-11pm; reservations advisable

starter: 55FF-80FF
main: 55FF-80FF
dessert: 30FF-44FF
Plat du jour: 70FF

CB EC MC V

Map: 18 G3
Métro: Abbesses, Pigalle

Smoking throughout

Taka
Japanese

☎ 01 42 23 74 16
1, rue Véron,
Abbesses

On the corner of two deserted streets between the red-light district of Pigalle and the hip Place des Abbesses, this beautiful Japanese bower comes as quite a surprise. Ultra-fresh tempura, sushi and sashimi feature alongside lesser-known family dishes that you cook yourself at the table. The kamo nabe (long, thin slices of duck and vegetables cooked in miso sauce) or the shabu shabu (slices of beef and vegetables cooked in seaweed stock with a hot sauce made from soy and vinegar) are a real feast. Finish in style with terre gelée ('frozen earth' – the chef's cake) or green tea sorbet.

starter: 35FF-40FF
main: 90FF-110FF
dessert: 15FF
Set menu: 120FF

CB V

Open: Mon-Sat 7.30pm-10pm; reservations essential

Map: 18 D5
Métro: Jules Joffrin

Nonsmoking tables
available

Thu Thu
Vietnamese

☎ 01 42 54 70 30
51 bis, rue Hermel,
Mairie du 18e

Thu Thu ('autumn, autumn') is without doubt one of the best Vietnamese restaurants in Paris. The little room is humble in appearance, sparsely decorated with a few plastic flowers and pot plants bathing in the glow of pink neon. Treasures, however, are waiting in the kitchen. The bœuf aux sept plats (seven beef dishes) is especially good, but it's best to order it when you make your booking, otherwise the wait is rather long. But it's worth it for the Vietnamese fondue, and the pleasure of making your own spring rolls with helpful tips from the waiter, who is the cook's son. A multitude of flavours – ginger, mint, coriander and many others. And that's just the first of the seven dishes! The others are equally stylish. The unusual and renowned Vietnamese crêpes are a speciality here and are made according to a top-secret recipe.

starter: 40FF-65FF
main: 55FF-110FF
dessert: 25FF-45FF
Set menu: 160FF
Plat du jour: 49FF

CB EC MC V

Open: Tues-Sun noon-2pm, 7pm-10.30pm; reservations advisable

La Tour de Pise
Italian

☎ 01 42 57 33 74
16, rue Letort,
Mairie du 18e

Map: 18 C4

Métro: Simplon, Jules Joffrin, Porte de Clignancourt

 Nonsmoking tables available

 Pavement tables

If you're in the area, don't miss La Tour de Pise. You'll immediately feel at home in this friendly family restaurant, which is always busy, even on weekends. Generous, authentic fare contributes to the typically Italian spirit of conviviality. The classic menu offers a panorama of Italian flavours. Pizzas, pasta and meat or fish dishes should delight even those who are normally left cold by Italian food. There's even a special children's menu. Customers are looked after by warm, unpretentious staff and receive a complimentary aperitif from the owner by way of welcome. A genuine, top-notch neighbourhood restaurant.

starter: 41FF-83FF
main: 48FF-89FF
dessert: 17FF-46FF
Set menu: 74FF (lunch), 130FF (dinner)

CB MC V; €

Open: Tues-Sun noon-3pm, 7pm-11pm; reservations advisable (weekends)

Le Village Kabyle
Berber/North African

☎ 01 42 55 03 34
4, rue Aimé Lavy,
Jules Joffrin

Map: 18 D5

Métro: Jules Joffrin

 Smoking throughout

The décor is warm and well tended, with ceiling rugs and eastern trinkets ... Wally, the chatty owner, was born in the Algerian Sahara, but has embraced Kabylia and its cuisine. The house speciality, oignons confits (preserved onions), are combined with tomatoes as a delicious appetiser. Mains include panse de brebis farcie (stuffed ewe's belly), ragoût d'agneau avec olives et citrons (lamb ragout with olives and lemon), various couscous dishes and excellent tripes de bœuf en sauce (ox tripe in sauce). The meat is meltingly tender, the semolina light as a feather. Wines from around Kabylia are the perfect accompaniment to this cuisine. For dessert, the gâteau aux fruits secs avec son coulis d'orange (cake with dried fruit and an orange coulis) is a fittingly sweet conclusion to this delectable desert crossing.

starter: 38FF-45FF
main: 75FF-94FF
dessert: 40FF
Set menu: 160FF

CB V

Open: Tues-Sat noon-2pm, Mon-Sat 7.30pm-10.30pm; reservations advisable

Bars & Cafes – 8, 16, 17 & 18e

Au 24 24, rue Biot, Paris 17e, Clichy/Batignolles ☎ 01 42 94 29 65 Métro: Place de Clichy (Map: 17 F9)

Four small coffee tables and a few bench seats with cushions along the wall – welcome to Au 24! The hostess warmly invites customers to take a seat, have a chat and order something to drink or nibble on. There's wine, beer, punch and charcuterie, cheese and soup (which changes daily) on offer.

Open: Mon-Thurs noon-3pm, 7pm-midnight, Fri & Sat noon-3pm, 7pm-2am; By the glass: beer 12FF; coffee 8FF; snacks available; credit cards accepted

La Buvette tropicale 40, rue des Dames, Paris 17e, Clichy/Batignolles ☎ 01 45 22 06 92, Métro: Place de Clichy, Rome (Map: 17 F9)

Coffee or chocolate punch, vanilla coffee, cinnamon coffee, ginger juice ... Still need convincing? This colourful bar moves to the warm rhythms of the Indian Ocean – a corner of Zanzibar in Batignolles and May's smile and kind nature will lift your spirits. Try the boudin créole, poulet colombo or one of the salads.

Open: 7pm-2am, beer 20FF-24FF (bottle), champagne 290FF (bottle); coffee 10FF; meals available; credit cards accepted

Cafétéria du musée d'art naïf 2, rue Ronsard, Paris 18e, Montmartre ☎ 01 42 58 72 89 Métro: Anvers (Map: 18 F5)

At the foot of Montmartre, the steel and glass edifice of the Halle Saint-Pierre, formerly a covered market, now houses a gallery of naive art, workshop activities for children, a bookshop and a cafeteria. Daily newspapers and the staff's antics head a list of attractions which make this an ideal spot for brunch or afternoon tea (the Katmandu tea and the carrot cake are absolutely scrumptious).

Open: daily 10am-6pm; By the glass: beer 20FF; coffee 7FF; snacks available; credit cards accepted

Cave des Abbesses 43, rue des Abbesses, Paris 18e, Montmartre ☎ 01 42 52 81 54 Métro: Abbesses (Map: 18 F3)

In a small, welcoming room at the back of this wine shop (well known locally for its affordable fine wines), you can savour goat's cheese from Berry with a glass of Saint-Véran '98, before moving on to rosette du Morvan (dried pork sausage from the Morvan) accompanied by an Irancy '97. What a great way to start the evening!

Open: Tues-Fri 5pm-9.30pm, Sat & Sun noon-9.30pm; coffee 8FF; snacks available; cash only

The Cricketer Pub 41, rue des Mathurins, Paris 8e, Madeleine ☎ 01 40 07 01 45 Métro: Madeleine (Map: 8 F8)

Chips with salt and vinegar, the *Sun*, darts championships and a large range of alcoholic drinks from the UK ... you've crossed the Channel without even realising it! But at 9pm on Tuesdays, when quiz night starts at The Cricketer Pub, customers forget their legendary British reserve.

Open: Mon-Fri 11am-2am, Sat & Sun 4pm-2am; By the glass: beer 20FF, champagne 40FF; coffee 10FF; meals available; Tues quiz nights, big British sporting events shown on TV; credit cards accepted

Le Cyrano 3, rue Biot, Paris 17e, Clichy ☎ 01 45 22 53 34 Métro: Place de Clichy (Map: 17 F10)

This former theatre cafe is decorated with magnificent mosaics, scenes from Cyrano de Bergerac and pennants of the big football teams (the owner's passion). The Cyrano officially closes at 8pm, but friends and conversations linger.

Open: daily 8.30am-8pm; By the glass: beer 14FF; coffee 8FF; snacks available; cash only

La Fourmi 74, rue des Martyrs, Paris 18e, Pigalle ☎ 01 42 64 70 35 Métro: Pigalle (Map: 18 G4)

Halfway between the Cigale and the Divan du Monde, La Fourmi makes a great stopover before or after a concert. People flock here for the ultra-hip décor – zinc, patina, mirrors and a superb 'hedgehog' centre light – as well as the atmosphere, music and unbridled conversation. Fleeting and fashionable perhaps, but so lively!

Open: Mon-Fri 8am-2am, Sat & Sun 10am-2am; By the glass: beer 14FF; coffee 8FF; snacks available; credit cards accepted

Jungle Montmartre 32, rue Gabrielle, Paris 18e, Montmartre ☎ 01 46 06 75 69 Métro: Abbesses (Map: 18 F4)

A corner of West Africa on an outcrop of the Butte Montmartre (thanks to Raf, the man with the plaits!). We'd walk a million miles for the ginger punch, which soon gets you chatting and dancing. The atmosphere is hyper-festive thanks to nonstop DJ Duboïd Mix Muzic and a kora player nearly every night. If you're feeling peckish, maffé or chicken yassa are available for a song.

Open: daily 11am-2am; By the glass: beer 18FF-25FF, ginger punch 20FF; coffee 10FF; meals and snacks available; DJ and kora players, dancing; credit cards accepted

Les Noctambules 24, blvd de Clichy, Paris 18e, Pigalle ☎ 01 46 06 16 38 Métro: Pigalle (Map: 18 G3)

This bar in the Place Pigalle stays open late and is a perfect spot if you're in the mood for a nightcap but don't feel like going to a club. The band creates a mercurial atmosphere with a disconcerting variety of covers, from Dalida and Jo Dassin to Claude François. You can dance the night away though, without feeling the slightest bit self-conscious. Roger, the barman, has been working here for more than 20 years, and really looks after the customers.

Open: daily 10am-4.30am; By the glass: beer 25FF, champagne 50FF; coffee 15FF; snacks available; cash only

Olympic Café 20, rue Léon, Paris 18e Goutte d'or ☎ 01 42 52 29 93 Métro: Château Rouge (Map: 18 F7)

This community bar in the Goutte d'or neighbourhood is full of surprises. From plays and film screenings to concerts in the basement, this is a breeding ground for young, creative people bursting with original ideas. The monthly program available at the bar also includes events at the Lavoir Moderne Parisien, another springboard for young talent, just down the road at number 35.

Open: daily 6pm-2am; Beer (by the glass) 15FF, champagne 350FF (bottle); coffee 10FF; entertainment program available; cash only

Sir Winston 5, rue de Presbourg, Paris 16e, Étoile ☎ 01 40 67 17 37 Métro: Kléber (Map: 16 B7)

Sir Winston is made for lovers of classy, British ambience. The large lounge rooms hide alcoves suffused with soft music, which create a cosy setting. People from posh neighbourhoods meet after work for a beer at the bar or to sip cocktails in deep leather easychairs. A perfect spot to smoke a cigar là la Churchill, in good company.

Open: daily 9am-4am; By the glass: beer 26FF, champagne 55FF; coffee 14FF; snacks available; DJ Wed-Sat nights, gospel and jazz Sun afternoons; dress code applies; credit cards accepted

Wassana

Thai

☎ 01 44 70 08 54
10, rue Ganneron,
Place de Clichy

Map: 18 F1
Métro: Place de Clichy,
La Fourche

Smoking throughout

The décor and background music are unexceptional but the smiling service and delicious food are absolute winners. Red curry, white coconut milk and green Thai herbs accompany many of the dishes, from chicken and pork to king prawns and other seafood. The colours of this cuisine blend together perfectly, as do its sweet, savoury and spicy flavours. A feast for the eyes as well as the tastebuds ... The Wassana isn't one of those restaurants where you dispatch your meal with a quick coffee straight after the main course. In this oasis of tranquillity, not far from the hectic blvd de Clichy, it's nice to linger over desserts such as the flan thaï (Thai-style tart) or the riz noir au tapioca (black rice with tapioca). A variety of enticing set menus is also on offer at lunchtime.

starter: 35FF-55FF
main: 48FF-80FF
dessert: 25FF-28FF
Set menu: 65FF, 85FF,
135FF (lunch)
Plat du jour: 45FF (lunch)
AE CB

Open: Mon-Fri noon-2.30pm, Mon-Sat 7pm-11.30pm; reservations advisable

Zozak

Greek/Kurdish

☎ 01 42 59 95 44
42, rue Véron,
Abbesses

Map: 18 F3
Métro: Abbesses

Smoking throughout

There are some lovely places to eat in rue Véron, which runs parallel to the hectic rue des Abbesses. If you like Mediterranean cuisine, don't miss Zozak's. The menu offers a combination of Greek and Kurdish dishes, including assorted meze, koya kebab (with Kurdish sausage), brochette de poulet mariné au citron (chicken kebab marinated in lemon juice) and halva and honey pastries. Each meal is served with bulgur wheat, crudités and oven-baked potatoes. For drinks, start with a traditional ouzo before moving on to retsina or bouzbag. This friendly spot is run by a Kurd who remains deeply attached to his homeland (pay him the courtesy of ordering 'eastern-style' coffee, *café à l'oriental*, rather than 'Turkish', *turc*, at the end of your meal). If you come again, you'll be treated like a regular customer and friend.

starter: 26FF-48FF
main: 48FF-65FF
dessert: 20FF-28FF
Set menu: 62FF (lunch),
72FF (dinner)
CB MC V

Open: Mon-Sat noon-2pm, 7pm-11.30pm; reservations advisable

19^e Arrondissement

Buttes-Chaumont

La Villette

Stalingrad

Belleville

19^e Arrondissement

The Buttes Chaumont, the canal de l'Ourcq and the Parc de la Villette are the nineteenth arrondissement's winning trifecta. Combining the traditional with the innovative, the old-fashioned with the highly contemporary, this area makes a virtue of its contradictions. It may not have the intrinsic beauty of central Paris but is nonetheless full of delightful surprises. Narrow streets lined with small houses (around rue de Mouzaïa or above ave Mathurin-Moreau) await the aimless stroller. The parc des Buttes-Chaumont, with its strange rocky promontory, attracts local inhabitants at the first light of dawn. The quays along the canal de l'Ourcq have been transformed over the past few years and are now one of the area's main attractions. Along with the parc de la Villette, of course, whose abattoirs – immortalised by Boris Vian – have made way for a cultural centre (cité de la Musique, exhibitions, open-air cinema, games for children, the Zénith concert hall) and a burgeoning cité des Sciences et de l'Industrie.

L'Iliade
Greek/Turkish

☎ 01 42 01 19 22
59, rue de Belleville, Belleville

Map: 19 K4

Métro: Belleville

 Smoking throughout

For 11 years Monsieur Emmungil, L'Iliade's Levantine owner, has been serving classic family food with a strong Turkish influence. While you're waiting for a table, enjoy the succulent Kalamata olives with a glass of retsina. There's an assortment of meze, including kanarya and haydari (fresh cheese with zucchini, eggplant, capsicum, mint and garlic), a scrumptious börek with sesame (cheese fritter) and smpouk (eggplant, artichoke heart, olive oil and basil). If you only try one thing on the menu, make sure it's the islim kebab, a leg of lamb with tomato and eggplant, cooked for five hours over a flame and then in the oven. Regulars do battle over this unforgettable dish! Rôti de pommes au miel (roast apples with honey) or home-made baklava – a rare treat – make lovely desserts, followed by eastern-style coffee with Egyptian mocca. Tastes like nectar or ambrosia ... an immortal drink, to be sure.

starter: 40FF-95FF
main: 60FF-95FF
dessert: 30FF-45FF
Set menu: 58FF-129FF

V; €

Open: Mon-Fri 11.30am-3pm, 7.30pm-midnight; reservations advisable (towards the end of the week)

Lao Siam
Thai

☎ 01 40 40 09 68, 01 42 39 33 59
49, rue de Belleville, Belleville

Map: 19 K4

Métro: Belleville

 Nonsmoking tables available

With its garish neon lights and kitsch décor, Lao Siam looks just like all the other Asian restaurants in this neigbourhood. But the setting quickly fades into insignificance when you set eyes on the menu, which features more than 120 exquisite Thai specialities. Everything is mouthwatering, from the classic beef and duck with coconut milk and bamboo to the more unusual salads – méduse à la citronnelle (jellyfish with lemongrass), couenne de porc (pork rind), pattes de poulet (chicken's feet) – and mysterious dishes such as poisson du temple de l'aurore (fish from the temple of dawn) or abalone salad. You can also indulge in bo bun or poisson cuit dans les feuilles de bananier (fish cooked in banana leaves). Don't hesitate to ask one of the numerous regulars (which includes a large Thai contingent) to recommend a dish.

starter: 20FF-128FF
main: 32FF-135FF
dessert: 18FF-40FF

CB EC MC V

Open: daily 11.30am-3pm, 7pm-11.30pm; reservations advisable

Organic markets triumph

Sunday morning, blvd Raspail. It's only 9am, but already a mass of people are filling up their shopping bags at the stalls. The regular customers of the capital's most famous organic market are instantly recognisable. There's a mother and kids, an elderly person telling his life story to the cheese seller... Everyone has a reason for buying organic produce: to rediscover the taste of the fruit and vegetables of one's childhood, to protect the environment, to eat healthily. The organic market at Raspail first started in October 1989. At the time, its customers were considered to be a fringe group. But since the advent of genetically-modified food, mad cow disease and the subsequent soul-searching about our dietary practices, the Raspail market has been packed, as have similar markets at Batignolles (17e arrondissement) and place Constantin-Brancusi (14e arrondissement) on Saturdays and at place Saint-Charles (15e arrondissement) on Fridays. An increasing number of organic stalls are also appearing at traditional markets, such as Bastille, Monge, Maubert and Nation.

Map: 19 J4

Métro: Buttes Chaumont, Pyrénées

Nonsmoking dining room (smoking salon)

Pavement tables

starter: 29FF-39FF
main: 40FF-70FF
dessert: 25FF
Plat du jour: 58FF, 62FF
cash only

Mon Oncle le Vigneron
Senegalese/French

☎ 01 42 00 43 30
2, rue Pradier,
Buttes Chaumont

In the light, spacious dining room at Mon Oncle le Vigneron, everyone sits together at a large wooden table. Customers are greeted by the Senegalese hostess and her French husband, who take it in turns to prepare a *plat du jour* based on the market produce and mood of the moment. We started with a highly spiced pâté (with Espelette chilli), before moving on to the soupe de mouton à la sénégalaise (mutton soup) and potatoes ingeniously seasoned with ginger. The menu offers equally tempting dishes with preserved ingredients, such as piperade (a Basque dish of scrambled eggs with green and red peppers, garlic, tomatoes and ham), poulet basquaise (Basque-style chicken cooked with tomatoes, sweet peppers, garlic and ham) and confit de canard (duck). A drop of *vin de pays* goes well with this simple farmhouse fare. If you're a smoker, coffee in the smoking salon is a nice way to end an informal, convivial meal.

Open: Fri-Wed 11am-2.30pm, 6pm-10pm (later on weekends); reservations advisable (evenings)

Pavillon Puebla
French (Catalonia)

☎ 01 42 08 92 62
**Parc des Buttes Chaumont,
Buttes Chaumont**

Map: 19 H4

Métro: Buttes Chaumont

Dress code applies

Entertainment: Piano (that customers can play)

 Smoking throughout

 Covered terrace tables

In the heart of Parc des Buttes Chaumont, an opulent Second Empire building houses this oasis of serenity. Pavillon Puebla's plush, stylish interior is decorated with light, warm tones and numerous tapestries, centre lights and candelabras. There is a private terrace for sunny days. In terms of culinary pleasure, we went straight for the Catalonian menu, the restaurant's undisputed centrepiece. Its Mediterranean accents are a feast for the eyes as well as the taste buds. For starters, we loved the coca aux escargots et à la ventrêche (well-kneaded, perfectly crunchy puff pastry filled with snails and bacon). For mains, the hostess recommended the pinyata des pêcheurs d'Ouille, a delicious, subtle mixture of braised fish served in a casserole. The desserts – figues rôties au vin de Banyuls (baked figs) and bras de gitan ('Gypsy's arm') – live up to expectations. The well-trained staff offer sound advice.

starter: 116FF-170FF
main: 136FF-220FF
dessert: 70FF-110FF
Set menu: 190FF, 260FF

AE CB EC MC V

Open: Tues-Sat noon-2.30pm; 7.30pm-10.30pm; reservations not accepted

La Pièce de Bœuf
French

☎ 01 40 05 95 95
**7, ave Corentin Cariou,
La Villette**

Map: 19 C4

Métro: Corentin Cariou

 Nonsmoking tables available

Well known for more than 30 years, La Pièce de Bœuf's current owner, a former butcher, has been at the helm for the past 12 years. Everything here is highly traditional, from the waiters' livery to the silent butler who appears before dessert to the choice of cigars offered after coffee. A classic menu features gésiers de canard confits (ducks' gizzards), pied de porc grillé (pig's trotters), rognon de veau aux trois moutardes (veal kidneys with three types of mustard), filets de harengs (herring fillets), sole … all of which are usually served with endive and gratin dauphinois (oven-baked potatoes with cheese). The meat dishes are prepared with great care. The entrecôte poêlée et sa sauce à la moelle (pan-fried rib steak with bone marrow sauce) deserves a special mention. A well-endowed wine list allows customers to choose just the right drop. This is conservative cuisine for businesspeople undaunted by the sometimes steep bill.

starter: 50FF-120FF
main: 85FF-145FF
dessert: 50FF
Set menu: 185FF
Plat du jour: 85FF-145FF

AE CB EC MC V

Open: restaurant: Mon-Fri 11.45am-3pm, 7pm-10.30pm; bar: Mon-Fri 9am-midnight; reservations not accepted

Map: 19 J4

Métro: Belleville, Pyrénées

Entertainment: Music, songs or stories Wed nights (at least once a month)

Smoking throughout

starter: 34FF-38FF
main: 58FF-98FF
dessert: 24FF-32FF
Set menu: 55FF
(3 courses), 62FF (lunch)

CB EC MC V

Valentin
Argentine

☎ 01 42 08 12 34
**64, rue Rebeval,
Belleville**

New customers are greeted with a warm handshake and treated like regulars at this small, friendly restaurant. But a word of warning: vegetarians, enter at your peril! People come here to tuck into a nice slab of Argentine red meat and to enjoy the live music of Riton la manivelle, king of the barrel organ. If you want to make an Argentine night of it, start with the Correntina (grilled capsicum with coriander, garlic, tomatoes and a thick, sweet purée of fresh fruit) and finish up with the banane à la confiture de lait. If you are wondering why the owner doesn't look the slightest bit Argentine, it's because he comes from Auvergne. Hence the strange intrusion on the menu of tripoux (bundles of sheeps' offal and feet), which, just between us, give the Latino beef a run for its money.

Open: Tues-Sat noon-2pm, 8pm-11pm; reservations advisable

20ᵉ Arrondissement

Père-Lachaise

Ménilmonant

Gambetta

Maraîchers

20e Arrondissement

The twentieth arrondissement has retained its sentimental, working-class character. Its buildings might not be much to look at, but venture inside and you'll be surrounded by the hubbub of spirited conversation. The city centre is far away, the Eiffel Tower a beacon on the horizon. This Paris is rough and rebellious, friendly and alive, a veritable village. The multicultural tone of rue de Belleville and rue de Ménilmontant is amplified by blvds de Belleville, de Ménilmontant and de Charonne. The air is filled with the aroma of coriander, saffron and cumin, and the exotic sounds of languages from faraway lands. A colourful, abundant market spills out over the footpaths of blvd de Belleville. The hustle and bustle is intense. A barrel organ grinds out a tune as the greyness and concrete disappear. In the narrow streets, squares, courtyards and blind alleys of the twentieth arrondissement, in its dilapdated, restored or modern houses and buildings, a myriad of tiny details merge into a harmonious whole. People here lead unpretentious lives. The long, undulating rue des Pyrénées weaves its way through neighbourhoods that reveal surprising angles and vistas.

Les Allobroges
French

☎ 01 43 73 40 00
**71, rue des Grands-Champs,
Maraîchers**

Map: 20 G9

Métro: Maraîchers,
RER: Nation

Dress code applies

Nonsmoking tables
available

In this soulless neighbourhood, there's a chic enclave where inspired cuisine prevails. The tasteful décor, staunchly loyal clientele and impeccable service at Les Allobroges allow nothing to distract from Olivier Pateyron's brilliant, elegant creations, whose mouthwatering names adorn the menu. The tomates confites dans leur purée d'olives or fresh salmon with bacon offer an enticing prelude. The concert of flavours continues in full symphony with the souris d'agneau braisée, son ail confit et sa huppe de laurier (knuckle-joint of braised lamb with preserved garlic and a crest of bay leaves) or, in a more minor key, brandade de haddock au basilic (brandade of haddock with basil). The rich, pure marquise au chocolat is a fitting finale. Stylish details, such as soupe de potiron (pumpkin soup), served at the table, or the chef's delicious petits pains (bread rolls), confirm Les Allobroges as a first-rate, affordably priced restaurant.

Open: Tues-Sat noon-2pm, 8pm-10pm; reservations essential

main: 72FF-125FF
dessert: 60FF
Set menu: 98FF, 148FF
   (vegetarian menu), 181FF
Plat du jour: 95FF

AE CB EC MC V

Au Casque d'Or
French (Auvergne)

☎ 01 43 58 44 55
**51, rue des Cascades,
Pyrénées**

Map: 20 E3

Métro: Jourdain

Nonsmoking table
available

Gourmets, movie buffs and the nostalgic, get yourselves to Au Casque d'Or. This small restaurant, which pays tribute to Jacques Becker's classic film (of which several scenes were shot in rue des Cascades) has added the stars of Auvergnat cuisine to the credits since being taken over in 1998. The menu features – alongside stills from the film – charcuterie 'direct from the Auvergne', a soup called 'Simone' and a leek-vinaigrette terrine. The mains are the Auvergne's superstars, with pounti aux pruneaux (bacon, onion and Swiss chard hash with prunes), typical tripoux (small bundles of highly seasoned sheep's or calf's tripe), famous truffade (thick potato and cheese pancake) and charismatic cochon de lait à la fleur de miel (suckling pig with honey). Well-cast desserts include regional cheeses, crème caramel, the chef's tart and a delicious pain perdu des princesses. The proceedings are directed by a cheerful, attentive team.

Open: Mon-Fri 10.30am-3pm, daily 7pm-1am; reservations advisable (weekends)

starter: 30FF-45FF
main: 60FF-105FF
dessert: 20FF-35FF
Set menu: 60FF (2 courses
   and coffee; lunch only)

EC V

Map: 20 E3
Métro: Pyrénées

Nonsmoking tables available

Pavement tables

Aux Deux Rives
Berber/North African

☎ 01 46 36 01 30
288, rue des Pyrénées, Pyrénées

This Berber restaurant looks enticing from the outside and brings together a diverse crowd at the top end of Ménilmontant. It's also the hang-out of Benjamin Malaussène, the hero of Daniel Pennac's Belleville saga. Amid the joyful clamour of voices, you can savour copious tajines and hearty couscous, or other main courses such as the pavé maître d'hôtel (maître d'hôtel steak) and the méchoui (spit-roast lamb), all served with vegetables. But start with a crispy brick au thon et aux œufs (fritter of tuna and egg) or a chakchouka merguez (a highly sea-soned potato and onion ragout cooked with an egg and garnished with merguez sausage). A selection of elaborate, mellifluous pastries are a fabulous touch of sweetness at the end of the meal. Slightly intoxicated by the Médéa wine, surrounded by red and gold fabrics and wall hangings, you soon start to feel like a pasha.

starter: 22FF-36FF
main: 52FF-78FF
dessert: 18FF-35FF
Set menu: 68FF (lunch)

V

Open: daily noon-2.30pm, 7pm-11.30pm; reservations advisable

Map: 20 C2
Métro: Belleville, Pyrénées

Smoking throughout

Le Baratin
French

☎ 01 43 49 39 70
3, rue Jouye-Rouve, Belleville

A superb panoramic view of Paris and the buzz of Belleville are just a short walk from this wine bar. It is often full, what with the regulars and people dropping in to check the place out. Conversations are lively, especially after a few glasses of wine. The menu changes every day: soupe de potiron (pumpkin soup) or beignets de fleur de courgettes (zucchini flower fritters); veau de lait aux crosnes et pommes de terre, sauce au vin (milk-fed veal in a wine sauce with chinese artichokes), or lapin au romarin et son tian de légumes (rabbit with rosemary and baked vegetables); and to finish, little regional cheeses. Herbs and accompaniments play an important role in this simple, country cooking. Wine is served by the glass at the counter or in attractive carafes (the art of decanting is not dead!). You can trust the owner to choose you something good.

starter: 35FF-45FF
main: 68FF-85FF
dessert: 30FF-45FF
Set menu: 73FF (lunch during the week)
CB EC MC V

Open: restaurant: Tues-Fri & Sun 11am-3pm, Tues-Sun 6pm-11.30pm; bar: Tues-Sun 11am-1pm; reservations essential

Bistrot de Chez Nous
French

☎ **01 43 70 77 93**
**81, rue de Bagnolet,
Alexandre Dumas**

Map: 20 F7

Métro: Alexandre Dumas

Nonsmoking tables available

'Martine vous accueille' ('your host is Martine') says the menu and, sure enough, there she is, working on her own, warm and larger than life. You feel at home and at the same time miles from Paris in this country tavern. The décor is tacky and joyful: gleaming yellows, greens, and the red of the roses on the tables complement the chromos. A stuffed rooster hovers feebly above the customers. The dishes combine simplicity, freshness and tradition. Starters include crudités, escargots (snails) and delicious coquilles Saint-Jacques à la provençale (scallops), while no-nonsense mains range from fondue savoyarde or bourguignonne to classic tête de veau ravigote (calf's head with ravigote sauce) and confit de canard aux pommes de terres sarladaises (duck). On Fridays, there's seafood, freshly delivered. Home-made desserts, wine from the barrel and selected vintages make everything at the Bistrot de Chez Nous great!

Open: Mon-Sat noon-4pm, Mon-Fri 7.30pm-11.30pm; reservations not accepted

Set menu: 92FF
Plat du jour: 45FF, 92FF

cash only

Vintage vegetables make a comeback

Their association with the war years and the Occupation condemned Jerusalem and Chinese artichokes, swedes and salsifies to long, dark years of exile, but these former staples seem to be making something of a comeback. About time: too many Parisian menus are sorely lacking in vegetable matter. The problem is that fresh vegetables are labour-intensive: gone are the days when waiters spent the morning preparing beans in a far corner of the dining room. Swedes and salsifies require effort (ie, money) to cook properly. So, let's welcome back these survivors from the past. Their increasing availability is to be applauded, although everything ultimately depends on the variety of vegetables and the way in which they're prepared.

Map: 20 G6

Métro: Alexandre Dumas, Gambetta

Smoking throughout

Pavement tables in mall

Le Café Noir
Modern French

☎ 01 40 09 75 80
15, rue Saint Blaise, Saint Blaise

Restored buildings and hip bars have breathed new life into the 20th arrondissement. This large, brasserie-style dining room offers cuisine with 'new flavours' and attracts a loyal clientele from all walks of life. The Café Noir is so popular that even if you've booked a table, you may still be asked to wait at the bar ... The menu offers ingenious combinations such as taboulé de blé aux écrevisses (tabouli with crayfish), brouillade d'escargots aux cèpes (scrambled snails with cep mushrooms), magret de canard au gingembre et cannelle (duck breast with ginger and cinnamon) and filet de bœuf au foie gras et pain d'épices (fillet of beef with foie gras and gingerbread). Full though you may be, you won't be able to resist the mousse au café et aux noix (coffee and walnut mousse) or the tourtière de Gascogne aux poires. The smiling, friendly service makes up for the preliminary wait, while everything else confirms this restaurant's excellent reputation.

starter: 42FF-125FF
main: 75FF-130FF
dessert: 32FF-45FF

CB EC MC V

Open: Mon-Sat 7pm-midnight, Sun noon-midnight; reservations advisable (evenings)

Le Café Noir

Chez Jean

French

☎ 01 47 97 44 58

38, rue Boyer, Ménilmontant

Map: 20 E4

Métro: Pyrénées, Ménilmontant

Entertainment: Live jazz and singing (Fri & Sat after 9pm)

  Smoking throughout

It's a steep climb up to Chez Jean, on a quiet street in the heart of Ménilmontant. With its wooden bar, soft lighting and walls covered with interesting paintings and photos, this is a local bistrot with a real personality. The proprietor is a perfect host. You can start with a little Parmentier de raie à l'ail (skate with potatoes and garlic) or a soupe de légumes aux épices douces (mildly spicy vegetable soup), before succumbing to the timbale de porc aux champignons à l'indienne (pork marinated in lemon and spices, fresh ginger, and mint) or the chiquetaille de lapin chasseur et purée maison (wild rabbit). All of the dishes are prepared with great care and served in generous portions. This is unpretentious, quality cuisine, with imaginative touches that bring out the flavours. Naturally, the desserts are homemade, and the prices are very reasonable.

starter: 35FF
main: 75FF
dessert: 30FF
Set menu: 49FF & 66FF (lunch), 98FF (dinner)
Plat du jour: 39FF (lunch), 75FF (dinner)

CB V

Open: Mon-Fri noon-2pm, Mon-Sat 8pm-11pm; reservations advisable

Chez Ramona

Spanish

☎ 01 46 36 83 55

17, rue Ramponneau, Belleville

Map: 20 B3

Métro: Belleville

 Smoking throughout

Tucked away in an anonymous street of Belleville, this family restaurant is known only to the initiated. From the outside, *Chez Ramona* looks just like a small neighbourhood grocery store, but inside, at the top of a spiral staircase, customers enter a dining room with checked tablecloths, garlands, plates on the wall and statuettes of the Virgin Mary. Enjoy the background flamenco as you savour a real paella, made with fresh ingredients. The owner-chef, Ramona, has a strong personality, and you can see her busily working as you arrive. The menu isn't huge, but the chorizo sausage, anchois frais avec tomates, calamars à la planche (grilled squid) and the excellent gambas à l'ail (king prawns with garlic) will delight the fussiest of eaters. By the end of the evening, you'll feel right at home. A word of advice – Chez Ramona operates on Spanish time, so it's better after 10pm.

starter: 20FF-50FF
main: 40FF-70FF
dessert: 20FF

CB EC MC V

Open: Tues-Sun 8pm-midnight; reservations advisable

Map: 20 C3
Métro: Belleville

Smoking throughout

Krung Thep
Thai

☎ 01 43 66 83 74
**93, rue Julien-Lacroix,
Belleville**

Well away from rue de Belleville, it's Christmas every day at this Thai restaurant, where garlands and thoroughly, if unintentionally, kitsch décor (fake flowers, bricks and gilt) abound. A low table is set up on a platform, which you step over before sliding your legs into a central pit so you're sitting comfortably and at just the right height (not for those wearing tight skirts or suffering from lumbago!). The raviolis de crevette à la vapeur (steamed shrimp ravioli) and the crab have an agreeable taste, the salade de fleur de bananier (banana blossom salad) fills the air with a lovely fragrance, while the poulet enrobé d'une feuille de bananier melts in your mouth. Staunch regulars don't mind the long wait for a table or the smoke-filled dining room.

starter: 30FF-60FF
main: 45FF-300FF
dessert: 12FF-75FF

cash only; €

Open: daily 6pm-midnight; reservations advisable

Map: 20 C5
Métro: Père Lachaise

Smoking throughout

Pavement tables

Les Lucioles
French

☎ 01 40 33 10 24
**102, blvd de Ménilmontant,
Père Lachaise**

This small neighbourhood bar, recently transformed into a hip, Oberkampf-style bistrot complete with country furniture, retro tinware and an enormous, glittering, metal praying mantis on the ceiling, has a peaceful, harmonious atmosphere. A varying menu invariably stimulates customers' curiosity and appetite, with pride of place reserved for fish and mushroom dishes. Escargots and ravioli with cèpes (mushrooms) or Royans (sardines) make excellent starters, followed by sumptuous mains such as magret aux foie gras et trompettes (duck breast with foie gras and 'trumpet of death' mushrooms), rognons de veau (veal kidneys) or, in a more original vein, the melting, brilliantly matched saumon frais et compote de choux. There's a variety of scrumptious desserts, including a huge red-berry crumble. If you're dining on a restricted budget, try the intriguing tarte au boudin noir (black pudding) or one of the other savoury tarts on offer. This might not be haute cuisine, but it's a clear cut above standard bistrot fare.

starter: 42FF-48FF
main: 72FF-125FF
dessert: 28FF-35FF

CB EC MC V

Open: Mon-Fri 8am-2am, Sat & Sun 10am-2am; reservations not accepted

Merivan
Kurdish

☎ 01 43 49 08 03
**19, rue Ménilmontant,
Ménilmontant**

Map: 20 C4

Métro: Ménilmontant

 Nonsmoking tables
available

This authentic Kurdish restaurant is run by the same team who set up the Dilan in the village Montorgueil. In a spacious room with cob walls, customers are initiated into the culinary specialities of Kurdish nomads and Anatolian shepherds, as well as delicacies from the banks of the Bosphorus. See if you can smell the mountain air of Kurdistan as you sample the soupe aux lentilles rouges (red lentil soup), the feuilles de blette au fromage battu (chard leaves with beaten cheese), the poulet aux noix et à l'ail à la georgienne, the beignets de courgettes (zucchini fritters) or the spicy assortment from Bostane, the owner's native town. You may even discover the shepherd within when you taste the qeli, a rudimentary dish with mutton and onions. Or hear the street music of Gaziantep while indulging in the mirani, lamb on a bed of eggplant.

starter: 30FF-40FF
main: 55FF-75FF
dessert: 30FF-35FF
Set menu: 59FF (lunch)

MC V

Open: Mon-Sat noon-3pm, daily 7.30pm-11.30pm; reservations advisable (evenings)

Le Mistral
French

☎ 01 46 36 98 20
**401, rue des Pyrénées,
Pyrénées**

Map: 20 C2

Métro: Pyrénées

 Smoking throughout

 Courtyard tables

This brasserie has been run since 1954 by the same family, originally from Laguiole and Espalion (Aveyron). The father was a *bougnat* (a coal merchant who also runs a small café), and used to store the coal in what is now the dining room. His two sons look after the business today. For lunch, a set menu offers great value for money with a charcuterie platter, followed by a pavé de bœuf served with traditional aligot (mashed potato, garlic and melted cheese). A range of extremely affordable set menus is also available in the evening. This is traditional fare, not highly embellished gourmet cuisine. If you're in a hurry, try the cantal or the roquefort with a drop of marcillac. As easy as pie and absolutely scrumptious.

starter: 22FF-28FF
main: 54FF-72FF
dessert: 17FF-22FF
Set menu: 59FF (except
    Sun), 72FF, 82FF, 88FF,
    98FF

CB EC MC V

Open: restaurant: daily noon-3pm, 7pm-10.30pm, bar: daily 6am-midnight; reservations not accepted

20e arrondi

Bars & Cafes – 19e & 20e

Abracadabar 123, ave Jean Jaurès, Paris 19e, La Villette, Stalingrad
☎ 01 42 03 18 04 Métro: Laumière (Map: 19 F4)

Abracadabra! In the middle of nowhere, neither in the 'burbs nor in Paris proper, the success of this unusual venue has been something of an adventure, a conjuring trick. The energy here is unbelievable! And there's real magic – beyond illusion – in the form of eclectic concerts, paintings, cinema, slam (urban poetry) and all manner of happenings that thrill a mixed crowd of hip, arty types and locals. Incredible but true!

Open: Tues-Sat 5.30pm-2am; By the glass: beer 15FF, champagne 40FF; coffee 12FF; snacks available until 1am; plays, Turbulences Energetiks (happenings), live music and DJ; credit cards accepted

Aux Folies 8, rue de Belleville, Paris 20e, Belleville ☎ 01 46 36 65 98 Métro: Belleville (Map: 20 B3)

A place to experience the quintessential spirit of Belleville, Aux Folies has a gorgeous terrace for sunny days, which doubles as a stage for local buskers. Along with the Zorba, a bit further down the hill, this bar is a favourite among those who, at six in the morning, still can't bear the thought of going home.

Open: daily 6.30am-midnight; snacks available; cash only

Bar de la Réunion 52, rue de Bagnolet, Paris 20e, Père Lachaise
☎ 01 43 73 43 79 Métro: Alexandre Dumas (Map: 20 F7)

Not far from the rue Éponyme, this bar is aptly named. Photos of famous and unknown performers; poems about immigration; concert posters and unusual objects are an eloquent and nostalgic testimony to a happy mix of cultures. Billiard fans, chess players and regulars mingle in a friendly atmosphere. The owner, Rabah, who is Parisian by adoption, has given real soul to this authentic place.

Open: Mon-Sat 9am-2am; By the glass: beer 13FF; coffee 7FF; snacks available; film screening & discussion with director on the last Sat of each month, chess games on Thurs, occasional concerts; cash only

Dar Zap 84, blvd de Ménilmontant Père Lachaise, Paris 20e, Ménilmontant
☎ 01 43 49 10 64 Métro: Père Lachaise, Ménilmontant (Map: 20 C5)

A place to zap the greyness of Paris ... from the foot of the stairs, the décor, incense, soft lighting and, above all, a smoking room straight out of *The Arabian Nights*, transport you to another world. Customers recline on shimmering cushions while sipping Ti Maroc, cinnamon coffee or peppermint tea. In summer, the serious lounging extends to the neighbouring cul-de-sac.

Open: daily noon-2am; By the glass: coffee 10FF; meals available; Eastern percussion band occasionally; cash only

Euro-Bar 6, rue Victor-Letalle, Paris 20e, Ménilmontant ☎ 01 46 36 30 35
Métro: Ménilmontant (Map: 20 C4)

This neighbourhood bar in the Ménilmontant strip has DJs and bands from Wednesday nights onwards. The sounds of reggae, ragamuffin, afro-jazz, rock and sound system (that is, a DJ and singer) will blast you away. The atmosphere is often more than lively (and can be quite off-putting), depending on the night, the crowd and the weather. The coconut punch is delicious. A 30FF entry charge sometimes applies.

Open: Mon-Sat 5pm-2am, Sun 8pm-2am; By the glass: beer 15FF; coffee 11FF; snacks available; live bands & DJs; credit cards accepted

La Flèche d'Or 102 bis, rue de Bagnolet, Paris 20e, Pére Lachaise ☎ 01 43 72 04 23 Métro: Alexandre Dumas, Porte de Bagnolet (Map: 20 G6)

In the industrial décor of this former railway station on the outer edge of central Paris, you can listen to DJs almost every night. With a solid reputation for promoting young talent, the Flèche d'Or has become a hip place for Parisians to start a night on the town. For further details, pick up a monthly program at the door, or consult the bar's Web site at www.flechedor.com.

Open: daily 10am-2am; By the glass: beer 10FF, champagne 40FF; coffee 6FF (10FF after 9pm); snacks available; DJs, open stage Tues nights (a springboard for young performers), poetry Sun mornings; credit cards accepted

La Fontaine d'Henry IV 42 bis, rue des Cascades, Paris 20e, Belleville ☎ 01 46 36 06 52 Métro: Jourdain, Pyrénées (Map: 20 E3)

A curious fountain flows in the rue des Cascades – a watering place that keeps unpredictable hours, a tiny bar from another time decorated with bits of this and that, where the villagers of Belleville sit around three rickety tables and chew the fat. This priceless establishment is run by Zoubir, who always wears a tie, holds himself stiff as a poker, mumbles words of welcome, and, with a shaky hand, pours out an avalanche of peanuts for the new arrivals.

Open: daily 3pm-11pm; beer (by the bottle) 12FF, champagne (glass) 25FF; coffee 6FF; cash only

Glazart 7-15, ave de la Porte de la Villette, Paris 19e, La Villette ☎ 01 40 36 55 65 Métro: Porte de la Villette (Map: 19 B5)

With trophies salvaged during various expeditions – worksite materials, SNCF lights, furniture from friends and even the old Euroline station – Glazart resembles one of the first San Franciscan artist's lofts. This spare, warehouse-style venue is devoted to artistic discovery and cross-fertilisation. The multidisciplinary happenings, unfettered by any constraints of genre, will energise and surprise you.

Open: Thurs & Fri 8.30pm-2am, Sat 10pm-5am, opening hours on other days according to program; By the glass: beer 20FF, champagne 40FF; exhibitions, theme nights; dress code applies on theme nights; credit cards accepted

Le Gobe-Lune 14, rue de Bagnolet, Paris 20e, Pére Lachaise ☎ 01 40 24 00 99 Métro: Alexandre Dumas (Map: 20 E7)

The owner, Jack, is a colourful presence in this neighbourhood bistrot. The conversation is laid-back during the day, more animated around aperitif time. There's live entertainment on Friday nights – accordéon-musette (old-fashioned accordion music) or French rock – and plenty of atmosphere on other nights of the week as well. Jack likes to describe his establishment as 'anything but trendy'.

Open: daily 8am-2am, July-August 11am-2am; By the glass: beer 11FF; coffee 6FF; live music Fri nights, photo exhibitions, bawdy songs, theatre troupe; cash only

Local Rock 206, ave Jean-Jaurès, Paris 19e, Parc de la Villette ☎ 01 42 08 06 65, Métro: Porte de Pantin (Map: 19 E6)

Wine barrels converted into tables and stools, rhythm and blues, portraits of rock stars above the bar: the Local Rock is aptly named. Every night, Marco, a larger-than-life character with a Buffalo Bill look and the gift of the gab, serves customers with a level of energy that would make the most drug-enhanced racing cyclist turn green with envy.

Open: daily (Mar-Oct/Nov) 9am-2am; By the glass: beer 12FF, champagne 35FF; coffee 6FF-10FF; occasional concerts; credit cards accepted

La Maroquinerie 23, rue Boyer, Paris 20e, Gambetta ☎ 01 40 33 30 60, Métro: Gambetta (Map: 20 E4)

The Maroquinerie is located in a factory courtyard formerly occupied by maroquineries (tanneries) and since converted into a concert venue with a terrace. The simplified, open plan has a friendly atmosphere. An original calendar of events, including debates, plays and concerts, makes this a favourite meeting spot among inquisitive Parisians. There's a small selection of meals, or you can just have a drink.

Open: Mon-Sat 11am-1am; beer (by the glass) 15FF, champagne (bottle) 350FF; coffee 10FF; meals and snacks available; concerts, readings, poetry, plays, debates and dinner dances; credit cards accepted

La Mère Lachaise 78, blvd de Ménilmontant, Paris 20e, Père Lachaise ☎ 01 47 97 18 64 Métro: Père Lachaise (Map: 20 C5)

This lovely, spacious cafe really belongs in the hip neighbourhood of Oberkampf, and stands apart from the Kabyle bars and grocery stores that line the blvd de Ménilmontant. The terrace is an ideal spot for an afternoon Sunday brunch and children can play safely on the wide pavement. Be sure to check out the permanent exhibition of works by famous Japanese photographer, Araki, in the new section of the cafe.

Open: daily 11am-2am; By the glass: beer 12FF-14FF, champagne 35FF; coffee 6FF-9FF; snacks and meals (brunch 11am-5pm) available; dance floor; credit cards accepted

Lou Pascalou 14, rue des Panoyaux, Paris 20e, Ménilmontant ☎ 01 46 36 78 10 Métro: Ménilmontant (Map: 20 D4)

A lovely, big room with ochre walls adorned with paintings; easy conversation at a huge bar; unforgettable cocktails (try the caïpirinha for a real taste of Brazil) and the standard draught beers, wines and pastis. This is Lou Pascalou, a friendly place that is popular with locals as well as with those from further afield (notably young bohemian intellectuals). Perfect for a summer rendezvous, when the terrace is always busy.

Open: daily 9am-2am; By the glass: beer 14FF (16FF after 10pm); coffee 11FF (13FF after 10pm); snacks available; TV Bocal on the first Wed of each month; credit cards accepted

Le Pataquès 8, rue Jouye-Rouve, Paris 20e, Belleville ☎ 01 40 33 27 47 Métro: Belleville (Map: 20 C2)

Le Pataquès shares a long, proud history with its neighbourhood, Belleville, and is steeped in libertarian ideals. This community bar promotes artists and organises photo exhibitions, readings, debates and performances of old Parisian street songs – it offers a slice of life with capital 'L'. Customers come here for a drink (just the one!) and end up staying for hours, caught up in one of the many conversations taking place at the bar.

Open: Tues-Fri 5pm-midnight, Sat & Sun 10am-1am; By the glass: beer 11.50FF; coffee 6FF; snacks available; street songs, jazz, accordion and musette (tiny room), photo exhibitions, debates (citizens, libertarians), theatre; cash only

Le Piston Pélican 15, rue de Bagnolet, Paris 20e, Père Lachaise ☎ 01 43 70 35 00 Métro: Alexandre Dumas (Map: 20 E7)

With its mouldings and vats, which are relics of a bygone era when wine was sold by the litre, the former headquarters of the 20th arrondissement brass band has preserved its late-19th-century charm. In the morning, fresh newspapers are left on the bar, while in the evening, the multicultural, working-class and bohemian clientele solve the world's problems over a pint. The cosy atmosphere warms up on the weekend to the strains of the stereo or live music.

Open: Mon-Fri 8am-2am, Sat & Sun 10am-2am; By the glass: beer 15FF, champagne 38FF; coffee 11FF; meals available; occasional live music; credit cards accepted

Le Soleil 136, blvd de Ménilmontant, Paris 20e, Ménilmontant ☎ 01 46 36 47 44 Métro: Ménilmontant (Map: 20 C4)

This bar in Ménilmontant has a vast sunny terrace. The perfect spot to spend an afternoon reading or chatting over a beer, or to enjoy a late pre-dinner drink in summertime. Given the location on the boulevard and right next door to the Montagnard (another bar), it's a bit of a target for musicians, fire-eaters and other busking acts.

Open: daily 9am-2am; By the glass: beer 15FF; coffee 10FF; cash only

Les Trois Arts 21, rue des Rigoles, Paris 20e, Pyrénées ☎ 01 43 49 36 27, 01 43 49 63 95 Métro: Jourdain (Map: 20 E2)

The Trois Arts is an old-style bistrot that knows how to look after its clientele of friends, regulars and locals. The Orchestre International des Trois Arts play live jazz on Sunday, as does Bouillon Cube on Tuesday from about 6pm or 7pm. You might also catch the occasional theatre act here. Home-made food is available (65FF set menu in the evening or couscous towards the end of the week).

Open: daily 8am-2am; By the glass: beer 12FF; coffee 7FF; meals available; live jazz & theatre; credit cards accepted

Smoking throughout

Pavement tables in summer

Samsara
Indian

☎ 01 43 66 02 65
3, rue du Jourdain, Belleville

Nan, chappati, paratha, pakora, samosa, tikka, sahi shorma, tandoori ... the possibilities are endless, but don't worry, it's all explained in the menu. Chicken, fish and lamb dishes are served with your choice of rice or vegetables, often generously drizzled with sauce. The poulet (chicken) tandoori and the agneau (lamb) sahi korma aux noix de cajou, amandes et pistaches are both meltingly tender. Beware of the cloves in some dishes! In the evening, regulars and first-timers in search of new flavours appreciate the efficient service in this rather Bollywoodian setting, while others come for the quick set menus on offer at lunchtime. In Sanskrit, 'Samsara' means the transmigration of beings. This restaurant might not transport you to India, but it certainly has good karma.

starter: 20FF-120FF
main: 52FF-70FF
dessert: 22FF-30FF
Set menu: 42FF, 48FF
(lunch), 99FF
Plat du jour: 42FF
CB EC MC V; €

Open: daily noon-2.30pm, 7pm-11.30pm; reservations advisable

Smoking throughout

Les Trois Marmites
French

☎ 01 40 33 05 65
8, rue Julien-Lacroix, Ménilmontant

On the window it says 'cuisine familiale': family cooking. That's appropriate if you consider the warmth and intimacy of the neat green and ochre room, the generosity of the serves and the cheerful service. But it doesn't do justice to the creative and carefully prepared dishes on the set menu, which is excellent value and changes from day to day. There are three choices for the starter, the main and the dessert. For example, you might have a clafoutis de poireaux au chèvre (leek pancake with goat's cheese), followed by pavé de saumon à l'oseille (salmon steak with sorrel) and an ample tarte aux poires et au chocolat (pear and chocolate tart) for a sweet finish. Wash all this down with a fine wine at a good price, and you'll be convinced they've got the menu just right.

Set menu: 83FF
CB EC MC V

Open: Tues-Sun 8.30pm-2am (meals served up until closing time); reservations advisable

Le Village de Paris
Algerian

☎ 01 43 56 88 43
**24, rue Sainte Blaise,
Alexandre Dumas**

Map: 20 G6

Métro: Alexandre Dumas

 Smoking throughout

 Pavement tables

Since opening in the early 1980s, this restaurant has stuck to the same format. Instead of a menu, customers are presented with an array of self-serve aperitifs. The table is then cleared of bottles to make room for a sumptuous banquet: egg and cheese bricks (fritters), followed by a procession of tajines and couscous with four different types of semolina (barley, with grapes, plain and with 28 herbs). The owner asks customers to make a wish with their first mouthful ... After an elegant sufficiency, waiters bring fruit with ice, eastern pastries with caramelised pistachios, Turkish delight and, to finish, peppermint tea. An out-of-the-ordinary meal.

Open: daily 7pm-1am; reservations advisable (especially weekends)

Set menu: 160FF

credit cards accepted

Zéphyr
French

☎ 01 46 36 65 81
**1, rue Jourdain,
Jourdain**

Map: 20 D2

Métro: Jourdain

 Smoking throughout

 Pavement tables in summer

If you need proof that life exists beyond the Buttes Chaumont, visit this elegant 1930s bistrot. Discreet service, geometrical wood panelling and stylish cuisine have made Zéphyr a huge hit among local residents. The set lunch menu is extremely affordable while the enticing *carte* changes every three months. If you're lucky, you'll get to savour the petits choux de blé noir aux huîtres et poireaux (buckwheat petits choux with oysters and leeks) or the côtes de sanglier sautées à la compote de coings et au potiron (sautéed wild boar chops with quince compote and pumpkin). The desserts are simple and delicious: fondant de noix et grany smith (walnut and apple fondant) or crème brûlée au café et à la cardamome. End with a stroll in the nearby park.

Open: Mon-Fri noon-2.30pm, Mon-Sat 8pm-11pm; reservations advisable for lunch and essential for dinner

starter: 40FF-68FF
main: 85FF-130FF
dessert: 40FF-45FF
Set menu: 75FF (lunch),
168FF (lunch & dinner)

AE CB EC MC V

Lonely Planet Offices

Australia
90 Maribyrnong St, Footscray
Locked Bag 1, Footscray VIC 3011
☎ 03 8379 8000 fax 03 8379 8111
email: out2eat@lonelyplanet.com.au
talk2us@lonelyplanet.com.au

USA
150 Linden St, Oakland, CA 94607
☎ 510 893 8555 TOLL FREE: 800 275 8555
fax 510 893 8572 email: info@lonelyplanet.com

UK
10a Spring Place, London NW5 3BH
☎ 020 7428 4800 fax 020 7428 4828
email: go@lonelyplanet.co.uk

France
1 rue du Dahomey, 75011 Paris
☎ 01 55 25 33 00 fax 01 55 25 33 01
email: bip@lonelyplanet.fr

Web
www.lonelyplanet.com or AOL keyword: lp

Lonely Planet Images
lpi@lonelyplanet.com.au

Lonely Planet Products

Food Guides

Lonely Planet's **Out to Eat** series takes its food seriously but offers a fresh approach with independent, unstuffy opinion on hundreds of hand-picked restaurants, bars and cafes in each city. These gourmet companions are arranged by neighbourhood, packed with dependable maps, garnished with scene-setting photos and served with quirky features.

For people who live to eat, drink, and travel, the **World Food** series explores the culinary culture of various countries. Entertaining and adventurous, each guide is packed with detail on staples and specialities, regional cuisine and local markets, as well as sumptuous recipes, comprehensive culinary dictionaries and lavish photos good enough to eat.

City Products

City Guides offer an in-depth view of over 50 cities around the globe. Featuring the top restaurants, bars and clubs as well as information on accommodation and transport, these guides are suited to long-term and business travellers and anyone who wants to get the most out of a city. They come with reliable, easy-to-use maps, cultural and historical facts and a run-down on attractions, old and new.

For the discerning short-term visitor, **Condensed** guides highlight the best a destination offers in a full-colour pocket-sized format designed for quick access. From top sights and walking tours to opinionated reviews of where to eat, stay, shop and have fun.

CitySync lets travellers use their Palm™ or Visor™ hand-held computers to discover a city's highlights, with tips on transport, history, cultural life, major sights, and shopping and entertainment options. It can also quickly search and sort hundreds of reviews of hotels, restaurants, and attractions and pinpoint the place on scrollable street maps. Go to www.citysync.com for downloads.

Lonely Planet Online

Lonely Planet's award-winning Web site has insider information on hundreds of destinations, complete with interactive maps and relevant links. There's also the latest travel news, 'on the road' reports, guidebook upgrades, travel links, online book sales, and a lively traveller's chat area. Go to www.lonelyplanet.com or AOL keyword: lp.

Acknowledgements

Thanks to all the restaurants and cafes who kindly allowed us to take photographs for this edition:

Astier, l'Aubergeade, Le Café Noir, Chez Albert, Clown Bar, L'Épicerie, L'Homme Bleu, Joe Allen, L'Oriental, Viaduc Café

INDEX

INDEX

RESTAURANT NAME	PAGE NUMBER	Late night	Outdoors	Private room	Serves children	Wheelchair access	Business
Boteco, 11e ☎ 01 43 57 15 47	156	●	●				
Boucholeurs (Les), 1er ☎ 01 42 96 06 86	17						
Bûcheron (Le), 4e ☎ 01 48 87 71 31	56						
Café Barge, 12e ☎ 01 40 02 09 09	185	●	●	●	●		
Café Cannelle, 11e ☎ 01 43 70 48 25	157						
Café d'Angel (Le), 17e ☎ 01 47 54 03 33	244						●
Café de la Nouvelle Mairie (Le) 5e ☎ 01 44 07 04 41	72		●				
Café de la Poste, 4e ☎ 01 42 72 95 35	56						
Café d'Enfer, 14e ☎ 01 43 22 23 75	213		●		●		
Café Noir (Le), 20e ☎ 01 40 09 75 80	282		●				
Cafetière (La), 6e ☎ 01 46 33 76 90	87			●			●
Cailloux (Les), 13e ☎ 01 45 80 15 08	200						
Cale aux Huîtres (La), 11e ☎ 01 48 06 02 47	158	●			●		
Cambodge (Le), 10e ☎ 01 44 84 37 70	137		●				
Cambodian, 1er ☎ 01 42 60 59 46	137						
Caméléon (Le), 6e ☎ 01 43 20 63 43	88						
C'amelot (Le), 11e ☎ 01 43 55 54 04	157						
Cantine russe (La), 16e ☎ 01 47 20 65 17	235					●	
Cartet, 11e ☎ 01 48 05 17 65	158						●
Casa Olympe, 9e ☎ 01 42 85 26 01	123						●
Casa Tina, 16e ☎ 01 40 67 19 24	236		●				
Caspienne (La), 6e ☎ 01 45 48 11 39	88						
Caves angevines (Les), 16e ☎ 01 42 88 88 93	236						
Caves de Solignac (Les), 14e ☎ 01 45 45 58 59	214						
Caves Petrissans, 17e ☎ 01 42 27 52 03	245						●
Chant des Voyelles (Le), 4e ☎ 01 42 77 77 07	57		●				●
Chardenoux, 11e ☎ 01 43 71 49 52	159						●

INDEX

INDEX

RESTAURANT NAME	PAGE NUMBER	Late night	Outdoors	Private room	Serves children	Wheelchair access	Business
Gaieté Cosaque (La), 17e ☎ 01 44 70 06 07	247						●
Galerie 88, 4e ☎ 01 42 72 17 58	61	●	●				
Galopin (Le), 10e ☎ 01 53 19 19 55	141						
Galopins (Les), 11e ☎ 01 47 00 45 35	165		●				
Gang Seng, 18e ☎ 01 46 06 71 91	260				●		
Gazelle (La), 17e ☎ 01 42 67 64 18	247						●
Gitane (La), 15e ☎ 01 47 34 62 92	225		●				●
Gli Angeli, 4e ☎ 01 42 71 05 80	43		●				
Gourmands (Les), 14e ☎ 01 45 41 40 70	215				●		●
'G.R.5' (Le), 16e ☎ 01 47 27 09 84	238		●				●
Graindorge, 17e ☎ 01 47 64 33 47	248					●	●
Grand Appétit, 4e ☎ 01 40 27 04 95	61						
Granterroirs, 8e ☎ 01 40 27 04 95	116						
Grapillon (Le), 2e ☎ 01 40 28 96 04	31						
Haïku, 11e ☎ 01 56 98 11 67	166						
Hangar (Le), 3e ☎ 01 42 74 55 44	43		●			●	●
Hélices et Délices, 5e ☎ 01 43 54 59 47	76			●			
Homme Bleu (L'), 11e ☎ 01 48 07 05 63	167	●	●				
Homme tranquille (L'), 18e ☎ 01 42 54 56 28	260		●		●		
Huitième Sud (Le), 8e ☎ 01 47 20 81 18	117		●	●			
I Golosi, 5e ☎ 01 43 54 59 47	127						
Il 34, 7e ☎ 01 45 55 80 75	107		●				●
Il Buco, 2e ☎ 01 45 08 50 10	32		●				
Il Grappolo, 17e ☎ 01 44 09 77 70	248						●
Iliade (L'), 19e ☎ 01 42 01 19 22	273						
Il Sardo, 9e ☎ 01 48 78 25 38	128						●
Impatient (L'), 19e ☎ 01 43 87 28 10	249			●			●

INDEX

INDEX

RESTAURANT NAME	PAGE NUMBER	Late night	Outdoors	Private room	Serves children	Wheelchair access	Business
Lô Sushi, 8e ☎ 01 45 62 01 00	117	●					
Loup Blanc (Le), 2e ☎ 01 40 13 08 35	34					●	
Lozère (La), 6e ☎ 01 43 54 26 64	93						
Lucioles (Les), 20e ☎ 01 40 33 10 24	284	●	●				
Mâchon d'Henri (Le), 6e ☎ 01 43 29 08 70	94						
Macis & Muscade, 17e ☎ 01 42 26 62 26	250		●				●
Main d'Or (La), 11e ☎ 01 44 68 04 68	171		●				●
Maison de l'Aubrac (La), 8e ☎ 01 43 59 05 14	118	●					
Marais-Cage (Le), 3e ☎ 01 48 87 31 20, 01 48 87 44 51	45			●	●		●
Mascotte (La), 18e ☎ 01 46 06 28 15	261	●	●				●
Mavrommatis, 5e ☎ 01 43 31 17 17	77		●	●			●
Menabe l'Île Rouge, 13e ☎ 01 45 65 04 11	204						
Menekse, 11e ☎ 01 40 21 84 81	171						
Menthe et Basilic, 9e ☎ 01 48 78 12 20	129						●
Merivan, 20e ☎ 01 43 49 08 03	285			●			●
Milonga (La), 6e ☎ 01 43 29 52 18	94			●			
Mirama, 5e ☎ 01 43 29 66 58/01 43 54 71 77	77						
Mi Ranchito, 9e ☎ 01 48 78 45 94	129				●		
Mistral (Le), 20e ☎ 01 46 36 98 20	285		●				
Mon Oncle le Vigneron, 19e ☎ 01 42 00 43 30	274		●				
Morosophe (Le), 17e ☎ 01 53 06 82 82	250				●	●	●
Mousson (La), 1er ☎ 01 42 60 59 46	25						
New Balal (Le), 9e ☎ 01 42 46 53 62	130						●
O à la Bouche (L'), 14e ☎ 01 56 54 01 55	215		●	●	●		●
Oie cendrée (L'), 15e ☎ 01 45 31 91 91	228			●			●
Opportun (L'), 14e ☎ 01 43 20 26 89	218		●				●
Opus lounge, 3e ☎ 01 40 29 44 04	45	●		●			●

INDEX

RESTAURANT NAME	PAGE NUMBER	Late night	Outdoors	Private room	Serves children	Wheelchair access	
Orestias, 6e ☎ 01 43 54 62 01	95						
Oriental (L'), 18e ☎ 01 42 64 39 80	262			●			
Osteria Ascoloni, 18e ☎ 01 42 62 43 94	262	●	●				
Oulette (L'), 12e ☎ 01 40 02 02 12	189		●				●
Paquebot (en la botela) (Le), 1er ☎ 01 42 21 19 00	25						●
Paris Seize (Le), 16e ☎ 01 47 04 56 33	238		●				●
Parmentier (Le), 10e ☎ 01 42 40 74 75	141						
Partie de campagne, 12e ☎ 01 43 40 44 00	190		●		●		
Pataquès, 12e ☎ 01 40 33 27 47	190	●					
Pattaya, 1er ☎ 01 42 33 98 09	27		●				
Pavillon Puebla, 19e ☎ 01 42 08 92 62	275		●	●			●
Pet de lapin (Le), 13e ☎ 01 45 86 58 21	205		●			●	●
Petit Gervex (Le), 17e ☎ 01 43 80 53 63	252		●				●
Petit Saint-Benoit (Le), 6e ☎ 01 42 60 27 92	95	●	●				
Petit Vatel (Le) 6e ☎ 01 43 54 28 49	96		●				
Phénix Café, 10e ☎ 01 47 70 35 40	142		●				
Pho 14, 13e ☎ 01 45 83 61 15	205		●				
Piano dans la cuisine (Le), 4e ☎ 01 42 72 23 81	63						
Piano Fou (Le), 11e ☎ 01 40 38 40 03	172						
Piccola Strada, 18e ☎ 01 42 54 83 39	263						
Pièce de Bœuf (La), 19e ☎ 01 40 05 95 95	275						
Pooja, 10e ☎ 01 48 24 00 83	143						
P'tit Bouchon gourmand, 17e ☎ 01 40 55 03 26	251			●		●	●
P'tite Lili (La), 17e ☎ 01 45 22 54 22	251		●				
Quatre et Une Saveurs (Les), 5e ☎ 01 43 26 88 80	78		●				
Quincampe (Le), 3e ☎ 01 40 27 01 45	46						●
Quinson (Le), 15e ☎ 01 45 32 48 54	229			●	●		●

INDEX

RESTAURANT NAME	PAGE NUMBER	Late night	Outdoors	Private room	Serves children	Wheelchair access	Business
Terrasse (La), 16e ☎ 01 47 20 51 51	240		●				●
Tertulia (La), 4e ☎ 01 42 71 32 55	67						
Tête de Goinfre (La)/Cave du Cochon (La), 17e ☎ 01 42 29 89 80	254		●				●
Thu Thu, 18e ☎ 01 42 54 70 30	266						
Tire-Bouchon (Le), 15e ☎ 01 42 72 08 63	231						
Tire-bouchon (Le), 2e ☎ 01 42 21 95 51	36						
Toccata (La), 11e ☎ 01 40 21 04 59	175		●				
Totem (Le), 16e (musée de l'Homme) ☎ 01 47 27 28 29	240	●	●		●		●
Tour de Pise (La), 18e ☎ 01 42 57 33 74	267		●		●		
Tournebride (Le), 5e ☎ 01 43 31 42 98	83	●	●				
Triporteur (Le), 15e ☎ 01 45 32 82 40	231						
Trois Marmites (Les), 20e ☎ 01 40 33 05 65	290						
Troquet (Le), 15e ☎ 01 45 66 89 00	232		●				●
Troyon (Le), 17e ☎ 01 40 68 99 40	254						●
Valentin, 19e ☎ 01 42 08 12 34	276						
Veggie, 7e ☎ 01 42 61 28 61	110						
Velly, 9e ☎ 01 48 78 60 05	132						●
Viaduc Café, 12e ☎ 01 44 74 70 70	193	●	●	●			●
Village de Paris (Le), 20e ☎ 01 43 56 88 43	291	●	●				
Village Kabyle (Le), 18e ☎ 01 42 55 03 34	267						●
Villaret (Le), 11e ☎ 01 43 57 75 56	175	●					
Vins des Pyrénées, 4e ☎ 01 42 72 64 94	68	●					●
Vivario (Le), 5e ☎ 01 43 25 08 19	84						
Volant (Le), 15e ☎ 01 45 75 27 67	232						
Voyageurs du Monde, 2e ☎ 01 42 86 17 17	36						●
Vy Da, 13e ☎ 01 47 07 37 75	208						
Waly Fay, 11e ☎ 01 40 24 17 79	180					●	

INDEX

INDEX

INDEX

INDEX

INDEX

INDEX

INDEX

Notes

Notes

Notes

Notes

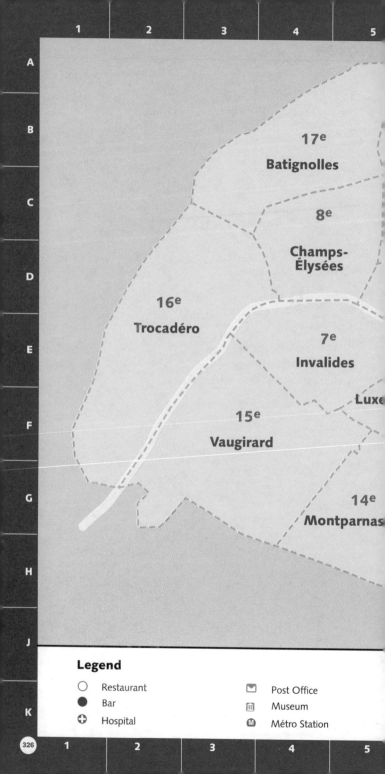

Legend

○ Restaurant ✉ Post Office
● Bar 🏛 Museum
✚ Hospital Ⓜ Métro Station

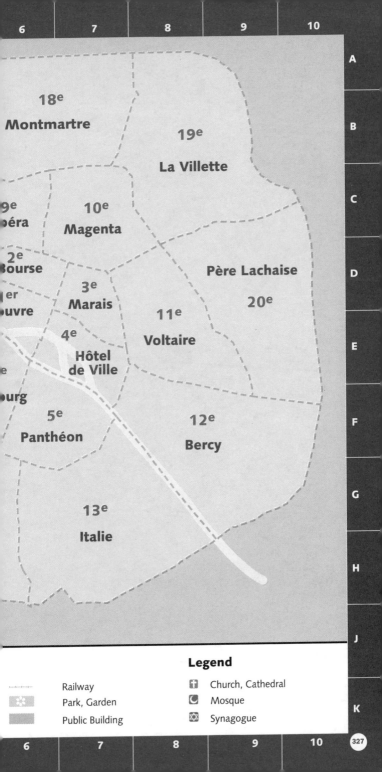

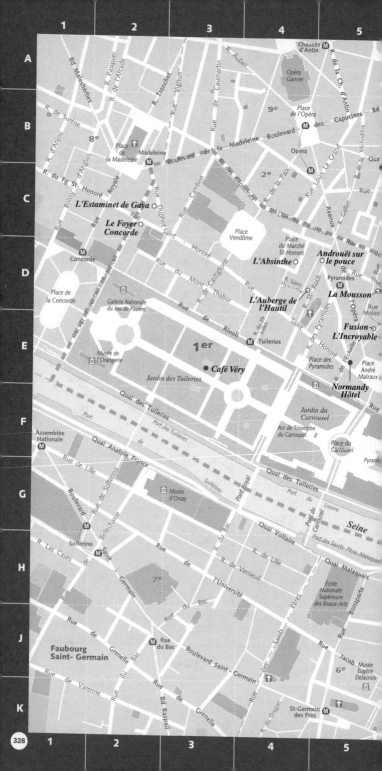

PARIS 1er

A

Bd Haussmann Richelieu R. Bergère
Italiens M Bd Montmartre Drouot Musée Grévin
Passage des Princes Grands Boulevards R. du Faubourg
Passage Jouffroy
Bd Poissonnière

B

R. de Gramont
R. de Richelieu
R. St-Marc
Bonne Nouvelle M Bd de Bonne Nouvelle
otembre
du Quatre Septembre R. de la Lune
Augustin
R. des Jeûneurs Sentier

C

Vivienne
Montmartre
Bourse M 2e
R. Notre-Dame des Victoires
R. Réaumur R. des Petits Carreaux
de Cléry R. d'Aboukir R. du Caire
Bibliothèque Nationale Sentier M
R. de la Banque

D

Restaurant du Palais-Royal
Petits R. du Mail R. d'Aboukir R. L. Bellan
R. St-Sauveur R. St-Denis R. de Palestro
Les Boucholeurs
Champs Place des Victoires R. Montmartre Montorgueil R. Greneta Bd de Sébastopol

E

La Bettola
Banque de France Rue Hérold Rue Étienne Marcel Rue Tiquetonne
Rue J.-J. Rousseau Pattaya ○
Palais Royal Entre Ciel et Terre Coquillère L'Épicerie ○ Étienne Marcel M R. de Turbigo
Aux Caves Sélections Joe Allen ○ 3e
R. St-Martin

F

Palais Royal Musée du Louvre Drluant Galerie Véro-Dodat Papou Lounge Les Halles M La Fresque ○
Rivoli R. Berger Comptoir Paris-Marrakech R. Pierre Lescot R. Rambuteau
Jardin l'Oratoire Louvre Le Paquebot R. Saint-Honoré 1er R. St-Denis

G

Musée du Louvre Cour Carrée Louvre Rivoli M de Rivoli R. Berger Bd de Sébastopol
Jardin de l'Infante Place du Louvre Rue du Pont Neuf Châtelet R. des Halles M de Rivoli R. St-Martin 4e R. du Renard

H

Quai du Louvre R. de l'Amiral de Coligny R. de l'Arbre sec Rue Pont Neuf M Le Relais chablisien R. Bertin Poirée
Pont des Arts Quai de la Mégisserie Place du Châtelet M Châtelet Avenue Victoria M Place de l'Hôtel de Ville
Quai de Conti Place du Pont Neuf Pont Neuf Quai de l'Horloge Pont au Change Pont Q. de Gesvres d'Arcole

J

Rue Place Dauphine Conciergerie Palais de Justice Quai des Orfèvres Palais Cité M Q. de la Corse Pont Notre-Dame Hôtel Dieu
Dauphine 6e Quai des Grands Augustins Île de la Cité

K

Seine Mazarine Buci Rue St-André des Arts St-Michel M

0 m | 200 | 400
0 yd | 200 | 400

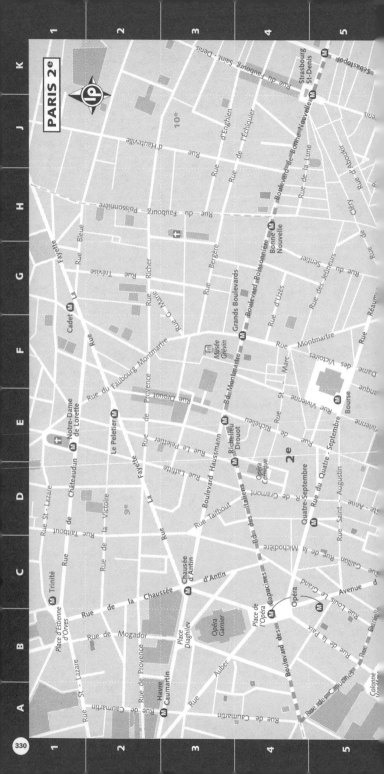

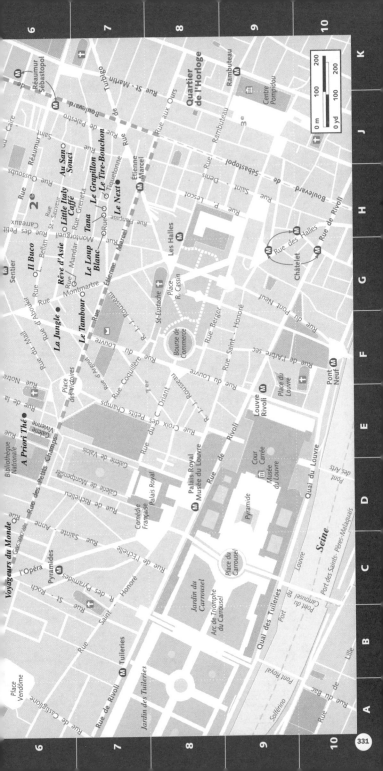

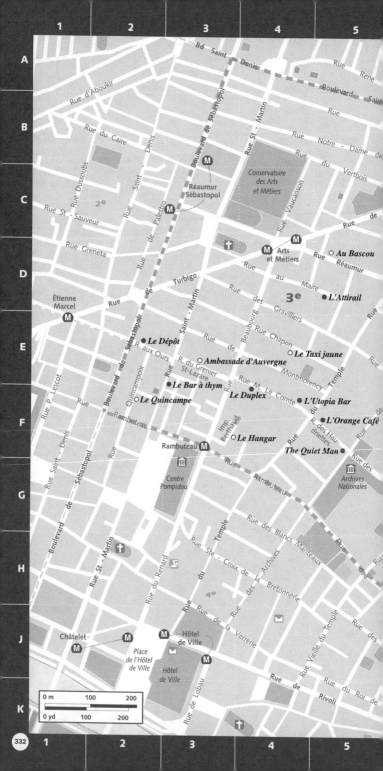

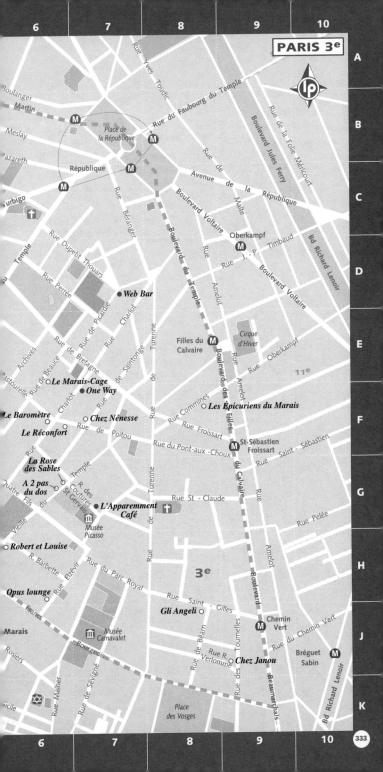

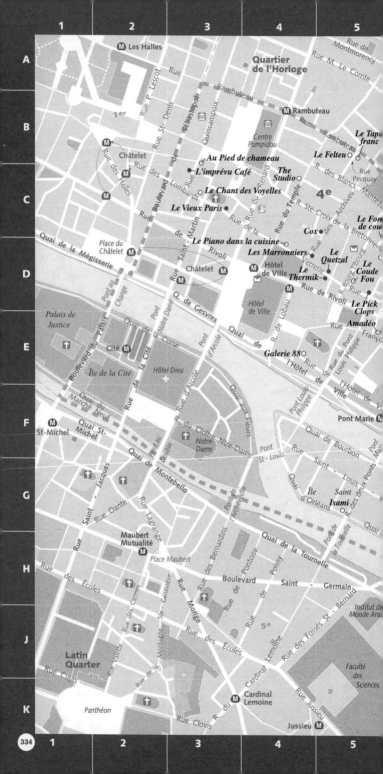

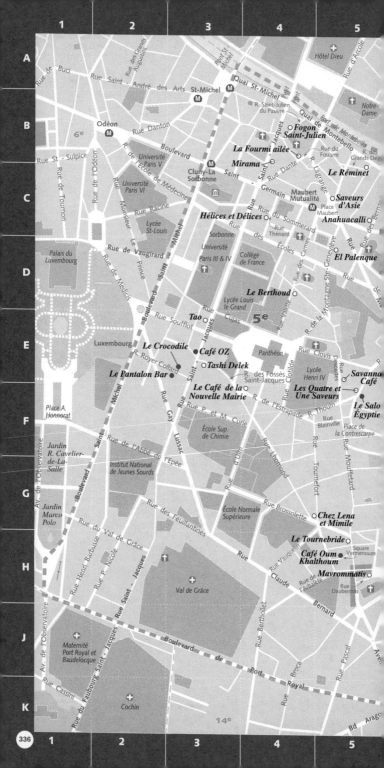

A

B

C

D

E

F

G

H

J

K

6 7 8 9 10

Quai de l'Hôtel de Ville
Rue Charlemagne
Pont Louis-Philippe
Pont Marie Ⓜ
Quai de Bourbon
Rue Saint-Paul
4ᵉ
Quai des Célestins
Voie Georges Pompidou
Pont St-Louis
Pont Marie
Rue Saint-
Louis en l'île
Quai d'Anjou
Boulevard Henri IV
R. des Deux Ponts
Île
Quai d'Orléans
Île
Saint - Louis
Ⓜ Sully Morland
Pont de la Tournelle
Quai de Béthune
Boulevard Henri IV
Rue de Sully
R. de l'Arsenal
Boulevard
Vivario
Quai de la Tournelle
Pont de la Tournelle
Pont de Sully
Pont de Sully
Boulevard
Pont Henri IV
Rue Mornay
Hôtel Cochin Poissy
Rue Crillon
Saint -
Germain
Quai Henri IV
Morland
Maison de la Vanille
Rue des Fossés St-Bernard
Café littéraire de l'Institut du monde arabe
Rue du Cardinal Lemoine
Lemoine
Institut du Monde Arabe
Pont Saint-Bernard
Quai de la Rapée
Comptoir Méditerranée
Faculté des Sciences
Quai Saint - Bernard
Ⓜ Quai de la Rapée
Cardinal Lemoine
Rue
Jussieu Ⓜ
Jussieu
Cuvier
Ménagerie
Pont d'Austerlitz
Arènes de Lutèce
Rue Linné
Rue
○**Amore Mio**
Lacépède
Jardin des Plantes
Rue Monge
Rue de la Clef
Rue Geoffroy
Serres Tropicales
Muséum National d'Histoire Naturelle
Rue Buffon
Gare d'Austerlitz
Ⓜ
Le Foyer du Vietnam
Mosquée de Paris
Rue
Cour d'Arrivée
La Mosquée de Paris ●
Rue Daubenton
Saint - Hilaire
Boulevard de l'Hôpital
Gare d'Austerlitz
Censier Daubenton
Rue
Censier
Rue Poliveau
Université Paris III.
5ᵉ
Rue de l'Essai
Le Coco de Mer ○ Marcel
Rue du Fer à Moulin
Saint -
Ⓜ St-Marcel
La Pitié-Salpêtrière
Le Refuge du passé
Boulevard
13ᵉ
Rue Dumeril
Université Paris VI C.H.U.

0 m	200	400
0 yd	200	400

Seine
Quai du Louvre
Port des Saints-Pères-Malaquais
Quai Malaquais
Pont des Arts
Pont Neuf
1er
Quai de l'Horloge
Île de la Cité
Conciergerie
Palais de Justice
École Nationale Supérieure des Beaux-Arts
Rue Bonaparte
Rue de Seine
Rue Mazarine
Quai de Conti
Rue Dauphine
Quai des Orfèvres
Quai des Grands Augustins
Boulevard du Palais
Rue Jacob
Le Douze
6e
Au 29
Rue des Grands Augustins
Musée Eugène Delacroix
La Cafetière
Chez Albert
La Soummam
Rue St-André des Arts
St-Michel
Quai St-Michel
Le Petit Saint-Benoît
Rue Saint-Benoît
Le Restaurant des Beaux-Arts
Les Étages Saint-Germain
Germain
Korean Barbecue
St-Germain des Prés
Rue de Buci
Orestias
Rue de Seine
A la cour de Rohan
Rue de l'Ancienne Comédie
La Lozère
B. Palissy
Mabillon
Rue du Four
Boulevard
Rue Grégoire de Tours
Odéon
Rue St-André
Rue Danton
Le Mâchon d'Henri
Coolin's
R. Clément
Rue Guisarde
Rue Mabillon
Rue Lobineau
Rue des Canettes
Germain
Rue de l'École de Médecine
Cluny-La Sorbonne
La Milonga
Le Petit Vatel
Rue St-Sulpice
Odéon
Boulevard St-Michel
Colombier
St-Sulpice
Rue de Seine
Le 10
Rue de l'Odéon
Rue Monsieur le Prince
Rue Racine
Rue des Écoles
Mézières
Rue Madame
Rue Bonaparte
Rue Férou
Rue Servandoni
Rue Garancière
Rue de Tournon
Rue Corneille
La Paillote
Indonesia
Chez Diane
Le Chipiron
Rue de Vaugirard
Vaugirard
Rue de Médicis
Boulevard
Rue Cujas
Rue Soufflot
Jardin du Luxembourg
Panthéon
6e
Saint-Jacques
5e
R. de l'Estrapade
Rue Vavin
Rue
Auguste
Comte
Lycée Montaigne
Université Paris V
Rue Michelet
Rue de l'Abbé de l'Épée
Rue Gay
Lussac
Rue d'Ulm
Rue Lhomond
Av. de l'Observatoire
Boulevard
Saint
Michel
Rue Pierre et M. Curie
Le Caméléon
Rue des Feuillantines
Rue du Val de Grâce
Boulevard du Montparnasse
Rue Henri Barbusse
Rue P. Nicole

0 m	200	400
0 yd	200	400

Au Sauvignon

La Cigale

Banga de Mayotte

7e

Café du
musée Rodin

Aux délices
du Shezuen

Clementine

341

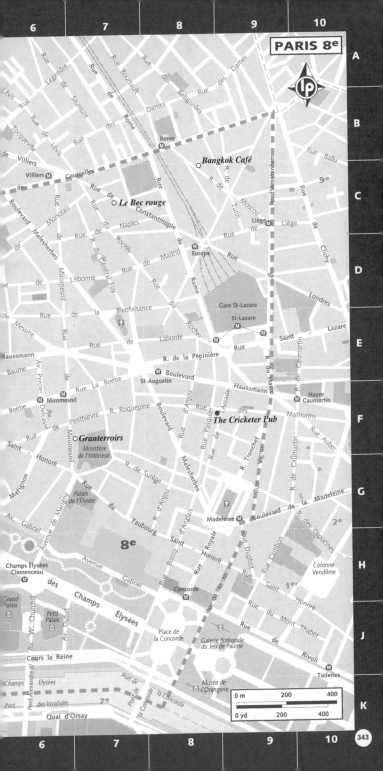

Bangkok Café

Le Bec rouge

Granterrors

The Cricketer Pub

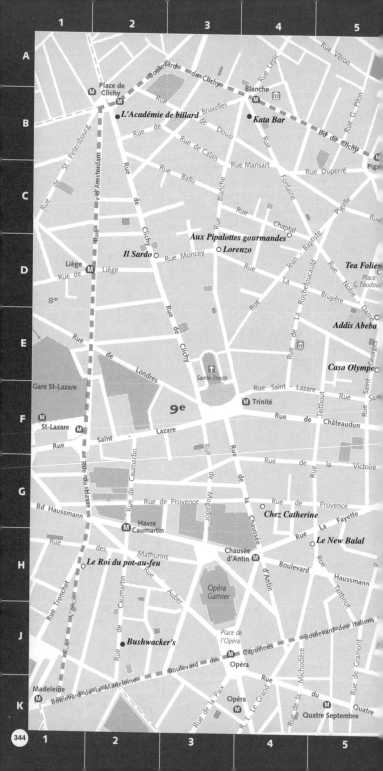

A

B

C

D

E

F

G

H

J

K

Ⓜ Abbesses
✉ Rue Y. Le Tac

Rue Houdon

Rue Martyrs

18ᵉ

Ⓜ Pigalle

Rue P. Picard

Rue d'Orsel

Rue de Steinkerque

Rue Séveste

Rue d'Orsel

Rue d'Orsel

Rochechouart

Boulevard de

Anvers Ⓜ Rochechouart

Place D'Anvers

Rue Gérando

Rue de Rochechouart

Rue du faubourg Poissonnière

Avenue Trudaine

Rue de Dunkerque

○ **L'Auberge du Clou**

Victor Massé

● **Salsa Loco**

Rue

Rue Condorcet

Rue Rodier

Rue Turgot

Rue

Rue Pétrelle

Rue de la Tour d'Auvergne

Rue Milton

9ᵉ

Rue de Maubeuge

Rue de Rochechouart

Rue de Bellefond

Rt-Georges

Rue des Martyrs

Lorette

○ **Chez Jean**

Lazare

Ⓜ Poissonnière

○ **Velly** **Menthe et Basilic** ○

R. Lamartine

Rue de Maubeuge

Rue Lamartine

Rue Buffault

Rue Lamartine

Rue de Rochechouart

Rue de

Fayette

Montholon

Mi Ranchito ●

10ᵉ

✝ Notre-Dame de Lorette

Ⓜ

Rue de Châteaudun

Cadet Ⓜ

Rue Fayette

Rue Bleue

Rue de Trévise

Rue du Faubourg

Rue Saulnier

Le Peletier Ⓜ

○ **Les Diamantaires**

R. Cadet

○ **Le Bistro de Gala**

La Fermette d'Olivier ○

El Mauresque ○

Rue Montmartre

Aux Berges du Sud ●

Rue Richer

Rue des Petites Écuries

Lafitte

Rue de Provence

Rue G. Marie

Rue le Peletier

Rue Chauchat

Rue Drouot

Passage Verdeau

○ **I Golosi**

Rue de la Grange-Batelière

Rue du Faubourg

Rue d'Hauteville

Passage Jouffroy

m Musée Grévin

Rue Bergère

Rue d'Enghien

Richelieu Drouot Ⓜ

Ⓜ

Ⓜ Bd Montmartre

Rue de l'Échiquier

Rue Richelieu

Rue Vivienne

Passage des Panoramas

Ⓜ Grands Boulevards

Bd Poissonnière

Rue du Faubourg

Rue de

2ᵉ

Rue Saint - Marc

Rue Montmartre

Ⓜ Bonne Nouvelle

Bd de Bonne Nouvelle

Septembre

Bourse

0 m	100	200
0 yd	100	200

Ⓜ Bourse

6 7 8 9 10

A

B

C

D

E

F

G

H

J

K

6   **7**   **8**   **9**   **10**

Rue Piat

Rue des Envierges

Rue des Couronnes

Rue de l'Ermitage

Rue de des Pyrénées

Rue Prévécourt

Parc de
Belleville

Rue des Couronnes

Rue de la Mare

Rue des Cascades

Rue de Ménilmontant

Rue Pelleport

Rue de Savies

N-D de
la Croix

Pelleport Ⓜ

Rue de Ménilmontant

Rue Boyer

Rue des Pyrénées

Rue Orfila

Orfila

Ménilmontant Ⓜ

Le Robinet Mélangeur ●

Rue des Panoyaux

Rue Sorbier

Rue de la Bidassoa

Rue Villiers de l'Isle Adam

Avenue Gambetta

Rue Pelleport

Tenon ✚

Boulevard de Ménilmontant

Rue de Tlemcen

Rue des Amandiers

R. des partants

Gambetta Ⓜ Gambetta

Gambetta Ⓜ

Gambetta Ⓜ

Lycée
Voltaire

Avenue

Gambetta

Rue des Rondeaux

R. de la Cour des Noues

la République

Avenue

Rue des Pyrénées

Chemin Vert

Père Lachaise Ⓜ

20ᵉ

Rue Stendhal

Rue Duranti

Rue de la Folie Regnault

Rue Servan

Boulevard de Ménilmontant

Cimetière
du
Père Lachaise

**A la Bonne
Franquette** ○

Rue de la Roquette

Philippe
Auguste Ⓜ

Bd. de Charonne

Bagnolet

Voltaire

Rue Léon

Avenue de Charonne

Alexandre
Dumas

Rue

de

Rue de Vitruve

Léopard Café ●

Rue de Charonne

Philippe

Alexandre Ⓜ
Dumas

Boulevard de Charonne

Rue Alexandre Dumas

Vignoles

Réunion

L'Armagnac ●

Charonne Ⓜ

Boulevard Voltaire

Alexandre

Dumas

Rue Planchat

Rue Planchat

Rue des Haies

Le Sot-l'y-laisse ○

Chardenoux ○

**L'Écailler
du Bistrot** ○

Chanzy

Rue

Boulets
Montreuil Ⓜ

Auguste

11ᵉ

Buzenval Ⓜ

Rue de Buzenval

Avron

Les Funambules ●

Rue de Montreuil

Boulevard

Rue des

La Folie Milon ●

Avron Ⓜ

Rue
Montreuil

Rue de Buzenval

Faidherbe
Chaligny Ⓜ

Le Serpent qui danse ○

Rue de Montreuil

Rue du Faubourg-Saint-Antoine

de

Voltaire

Rue

Bd de Taillebourg

Bd. de Charonne

Khun Akorn ●

✚
Antoine

Rue Chaligny

Rue de Reuilly

Chez Ramulaud ○

Rue Claude Tillier

12ᵉ

La Dame brune ○

Extra Old Café ○

Av. de Bouvines

Av. de Taillebourg

Rue de Lagny

Reuilly Diderot Ⓜ

Boulevard Diderot

Nation Ⓜ

Diderot

Reuilly Diderot Ⓜ

0 m	200	400
0 yd	200	400

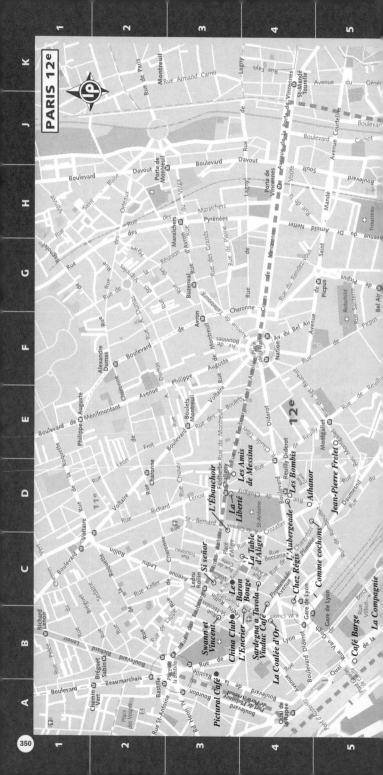

PARIS 12e

350

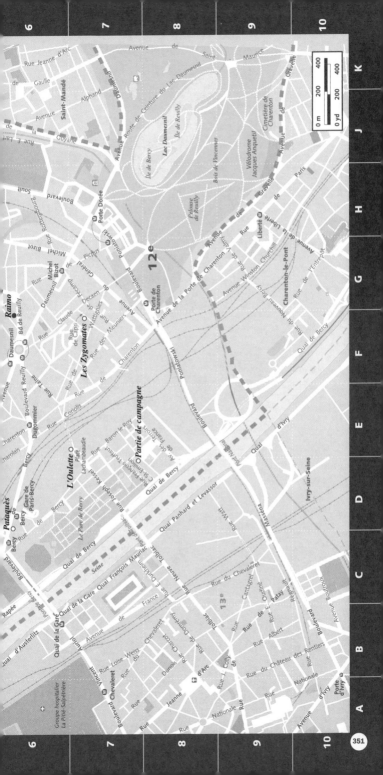

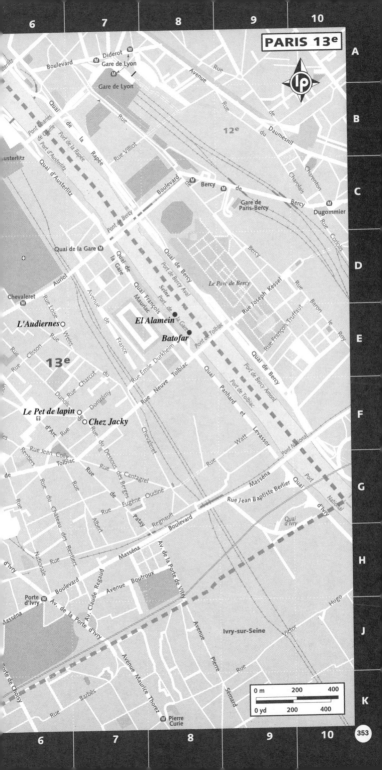

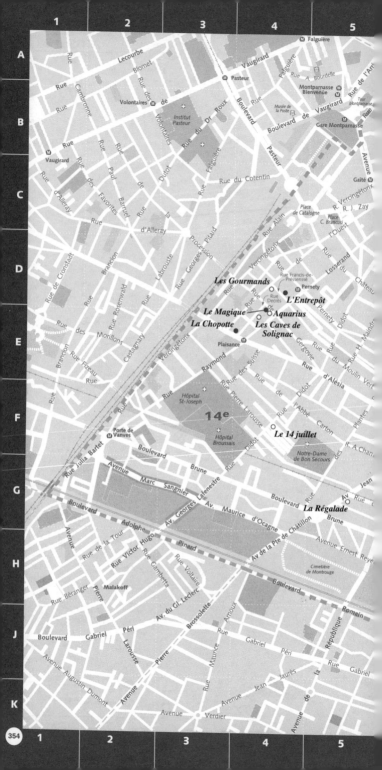

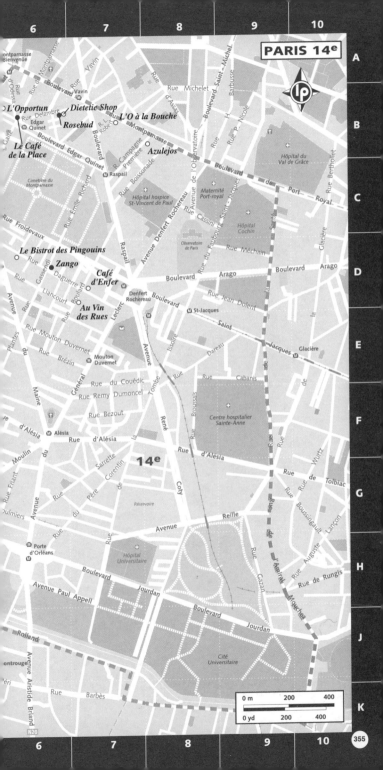

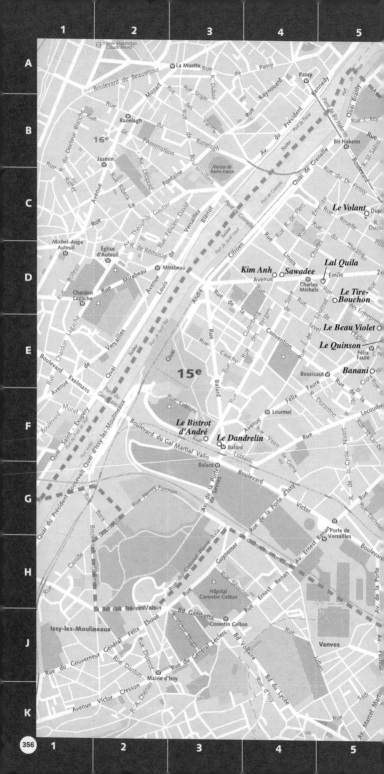

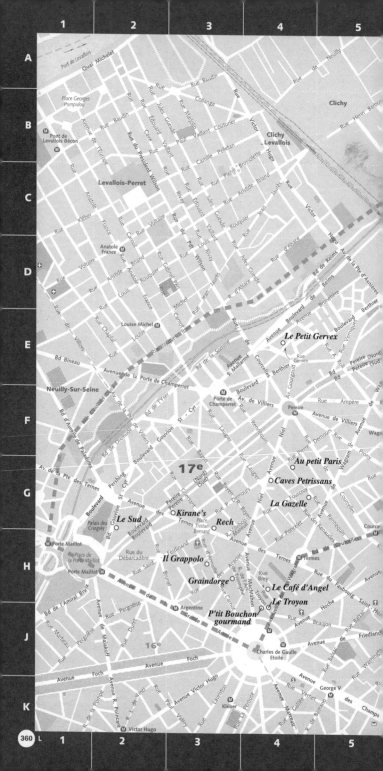

A
B
C
D
E
F
G
H
J
K
L

1 2 3 4 5

Port de Levallois
Quai Michelet
Place Georges Pompidou
Pont de Levallois Bécon
Levallois-Perret
Avenue de l'Europe
Rue Baudin
Rue Baudin
Rue Jules Guesde
Rue Marjolin
Collange
Rue du Président Wilson
Rue Édouard Vaillant
Cave
Paul Vaillant-Couturier
Rue Camille Pelletan
Rue Pierre Brossolette
Rue Aristide Briand
Rue Carnot
Rue Anatole
Rue Kléber
Rue Voltaire
Rue Jean Jaurès
Rue Rivay
Rue du Président Wilson
Rue Louis Rivay
Anatole France
Rue Louis
Rue Aristide Briand
Rue Chaptal
Louise Michel
Michel
Rue Jean Jaurès
Clichy
Rue Henri Barbu
Clichy Levallois
Rue Victor Hugo
Rue Anatole France
Rue Rouquier
Rue Jean Jaurès
Rue Victor Hugo
Rue d'Alsace
Bd de Reims
Av de la Pte d'Asnières
Reims
Brunemont
Boulevard
Berthier
Boulevard
Avenue de la Porte de Champerret
Bd Bineau
Neuilly-Sur-Seine
Bd d'Aurelle de Paladines
Av. de la Pte des Ternes
Pershing
Boulevard
St. Cyr
Bd de Douamont
Boulevard Gouvion
St. Cyr
Avenue
Boulevard
Avenue de la Somme
Avenue S. Mallarmé
Courcelles
Porte de Champerret
Av. de Villiers
Boulevard
Pereire
Rue Gervex
○ Le Petit Gervex
Rue A. Roll
Pereire (Nord)
Pereire (Sud)
Rue Ampère
Avenue de Villiers
Bd
Rue Berthier
Av Gourgaud
Rue Pierre Demours
Niel
Wag
Prony
17e
Pereire (Nord/Sud)
Rue Bayen
Rue Laugier
Rue Laugier
Rue Rennequin
Au petit Paris ○
○ Caves Petrissans
Fourcroy
La Gazelle ○
Rue des Renaudes
Cource
Palais des Congrès
○ Le Sud
Kirane's ○
Place Tristan Bernard
Rech ○
Rue Poncelet
Rue des Acacias
Rue Brey
Ternes
Termes
Rue du Faubourg Saint-Ho
Porte Maillot
Place de la Porte Maillot
Porte Maillot
Rue du Débarcadère
Rue Saint-
Il Grappolo ○
Rue Brunel
Graindorge ○
Rue de Montenotte
Av de Wagram
Le Café d'Angel ○
Le Troyon ○
Hoche
Beaujon
Bd de l'Amiral Bruix
Avenue de
Rue Duret
Argentine
Grande
Armée
P'tit Bouchon gourmand ○
Avenue Carnot
Avenue de
Friedland
16e
Foch
Avenue Foch
Charles de Gaulle Étoile
Avenue de
George V
Rue Washington
R. L. L. Rue
Rue de la Pompe
Rue Victor Hugo
Avenue Foch
Avenue Victor Hugo
Kléber
Rue de Bassano
Champs
L Victor Hugo

Teeru Bi

17e

18e

Macis & Muscade

Le Morosophe

La Tête de Goinfre

Bistro des Dames

La Gaieté Cosaque

Au 24

La Fourchette des Anges

La Buvette tropicale

La P'tite Lili

Chez Léon

Le Bistrot de Théo

Le Cyrano

L'Impatient

9e

El Picador

Parc Monceau

Gare St-Lazare

St-Lazare

0 m   200   400
0 yd   200   400

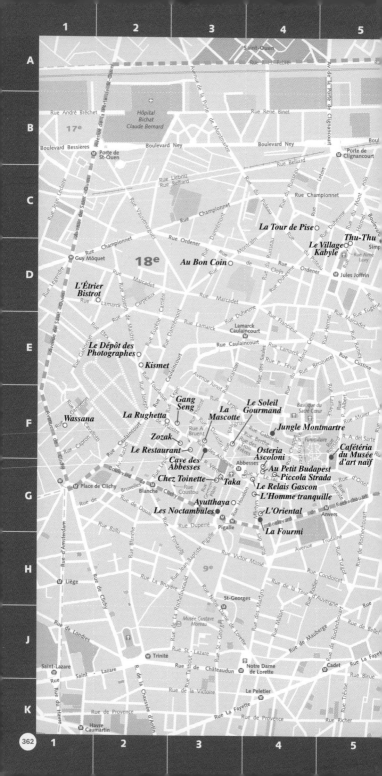

6 7 8 9 10

A
B
C
D
E
F
G
H
J
K

18ᵉ

19ᵉ

10ᵉ

Boulevard Ney
Boulevard Ney

Porte de la Chapelle

Rue de l'Evangile

Rue Boucry

Rue Cugnot

Rue Pajol

Rue Marc Séguin

Rue de la Chapelle

Rue de Torcy

Marx Dormoy

Rue Riquet

Rue Riquet

Marcadet
Poissonniers

Rue Ordener

Rue Marcadet

Rue Ordener

Rue Boinod

Championnet

Simplon

Rue des Poissonniers

Bellard

Boulevard de la Porte des Poissonniers

Av. de la Porte de la Chapelle

Boulevard Aubervilliers

Boulevard Ornano

Rue de la Chapelle

Rue Marc Dormoy

Rue philippe de Girard

Rue Pajol

Rue du Département

Doudeauville

Rue Léon

Rue des Poissonniers

Rue Labat

Boulevard Barbès

● *Olympic Café*

Chateau
Rouge

Rue Myrha

Rue Stephenson

Rue Poulenceau

Rue de la Goutte d'or

Rue du Maroc

Rue de Tanger

Rue de l'Aubervilliers

Boulevard de la Villette

Barbès
Rochechouart

Boulevard de la Chapelle

La Chapelle

Boulevard de la Chapelle

Stalingrad

Boulevard

Jaurès

Rue du Fbg Poissonnière

Boulevard de Magenta

Hôpital
Lariboisière

Rue de Maubeuge

Gare du Nord

Gare du Nord

Rue La Fayette

Rue du Faubourg Saint-Denis

Rue Louis Blanc

Rue du Château Landon

Rue de l'Aqueduc

St-Martin

Rue La Fayette

Rue du Faubourg St-Martin

Rue Louis Blanc

Quai de Valmy

Quai de Jemmapes

Louis Blanc

Château
Landon

Rue E. Varlin

Colonel Fabien

Poissonnière

Rue de Chabrol

Rue La Fayette

Rue d'Alsace

Boulevard de Magenta

Rue du Fbg St-Denis

Rue du Fbg St-Martin

Quai de Valmy

Quai de Jemmapes

Canal Saint-Martin

Gare de l'Est

Gare de l'Est

Rue du 8
Mai 1945

Rue d'Hauteville

Rue de Paradis

des Petites Écuries

10e

| 0 m | 200 | 400 |
| 0 yd | 200 | 400 |

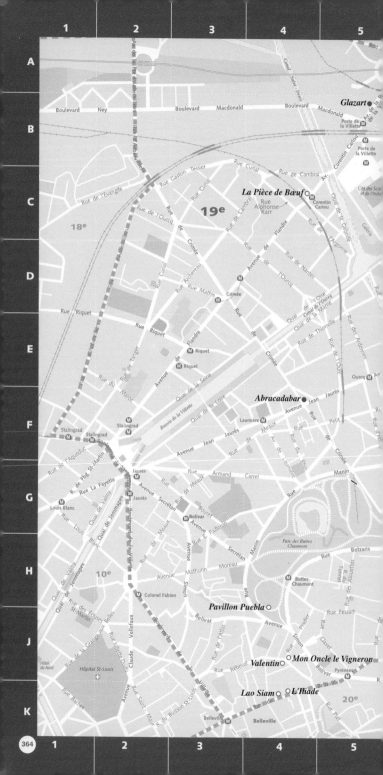